POLITICS, HISTORY, AND CULTURE

A series from the International Institute at the University of Michigan

SERIES EDITORS: George Steinmetz and Julia Adams

Series Editorial Advisory Board

Fernando Coronil
Mamadou Diouf
Michael Dutton
Geoff Eley
Fatma Müge Göcek
Nancy Rose Hunt
Andreas Kalyvas
Webb Keane

David Laitin
Lydia Liu
Julie Skurski
Margaret Somers
Ann Laura Stoler
Katherine Verdery
Elizabeth Wingrove

Sponsored by the International Institute at the University of Michigan and published by Duke University Press, this series is centered around cultural and historical studies of power, politics, and the state — a field that cuts across the disciplines of history, sociology, anthropology, political science, and cultural studies. The focus on the relationship between state and culture refers both to a methodological approach — the study of politics and the state using culturalist methods — and a substantive one that treats signifying practices as an essential dimension of politics. The dialectic of politics, culture, and history figures prominently in all the books selected for the series.

Salt in the Sand

MEMORY, VIOLENCE, AND THE NATION-STATE

IN CHILE, 1890 TO THE PRESENT

Salt in the Sand

LESSIE JO FRAZIER

Duke University Press   Durham & London   2007

© 2007 Duke University Press

All rights reserved

Printed in the United States of America

on acid-free paper ∞

Designed by C. H. Westmoreland

Typeset in Carter & Cone Galliard

by Keystone Typesetting, Inc.

Library of Congress Cataloging-in-

Publication Data and republication

acknowledgments appear on the last

printed page of this book.

Pat, Piner, Lynn — my foundation
Phil, Jhenefer, Jhony, Maiara, MacIntyre
— my future

Contents

Illustrations

Acknowledgments

There is something decidedly cathartic in the fact that within the space of a week or so last December I finished reviewing the copyedited manuscript of this book, delivered a baby, and learned of General Pinochet's death — all just days shy of the 99th anniversary of the Escuela Santa María Massacre. This was the finale of a seventeen-year project that has accrued many debts, both joyful and bittersweet.

First and foremost, I thank the people — scholars, activists, and others — with whom I have worked in Chile. In Santiago: thanks to Ercilla Mellín, RAICES, Marco Ruíz, Gabriel Cea, and Fanor Larraín of the Fulbright Commission. My 1990 coursework with Manuel Antonio Garretón provided an initial orientation to Chilean social movements. Members of the Sebastián Acevedo Movement Against Torture provided a hands-on education by incorporating me into the movement in 1990–91. Numerous scholars generously offered insights: Elisa Fernandez, Luis Castro, Julio Pinto, Enrique Reyes Navarro, Sonia Montecino, Germán Palacios, Angélica Gimpel Smith,

Mario Garcés, Carlos Maldonado, Sergio Grez T., Claudio Teitelboim, and Eduardo Devés. The late Elena Cafferena opened the MEMCH archive to me. The staff of PRAIS along with Ministry of Heath officials, SERNAM, and the Reconciliation and Reparations Commission, as well as the Association of PRAIS Beneficiaries, provided key insights into their work. I appreciate assistance from the staff of the Biblioteca Nacional, Archivo Nacional, Biblioteca Central of the Universidad de Chile, and Ministries of Education and Foreign Relations. Over the years, my trips to Chile fruitfully intersected with other visiting researchers, particularly Kjungin Cho, Janet Finn, Joel Stillerman, Lisa Baldez Carey, and Joe Scarpaci.

Iquique, of course, is at the core of this study. There I thank, among the many, many people who contributed to this study: Jorge Reyes, María Inéz Cándida Perez, Cecilia Castillo, Miriam Salinas, Patricio Rivero O., Nelson Calderon, Marcos Ugarte, Flavio Rossi, Bernardo Guerrero for initial institutional affiliation, and Sergio González Miranda for access to the regional government papers archive. The staff of the Municipal Library, Casa de Cultura, and Obispado de Iquique further facilitated local archival work. Exchanges with people in the state sector were critical, especially the Ministry of Education, municipal and regional government offices, SERCOTEC (economic projects), and PRAIS. Staff of the Regional Museum and the Naval Museum offered their perspectives on their collections. My fieldwork has been enriched through interaction with a number of civic associations, among them the Chilean Human Rights Commission–Iquique chapter, Hijos de Salitre, Association of Business and Professional Women, Association Against Violence Against Women, Association of Tour Guides, the Municipal Choir, Academia de Idiomas del Norte, the Teachers' Union, various neighborhood associations, the Catholic Grandmothers' Club, and the Association of Northern Writers, as well as with political parties, including the Socialist, PPD, Radical, Christian Democratic, and Communist Parties. The Taller de Historia Popular that I co-facilitated with Guillermo Ross-Murray was sponsored by the Obispado, CREAR, and TER. My primary focus was working with the Association of Ex-Political Prisoners of Pisagua, now the Pisagua Foundation.

Outside of Chile, I thank the staff of the Institute for Social History in Amsterdam (especially Mieke Ijzermans for her hospitality), the Foreign Records Office in London, the film museum and archive in Berlin, Lutz Götze, Walter Heynowski, and the Ministries of Foreign Relations of Bolivia and Peru.

The shape of this book was worked out initially at the University of Michigan in lively dialogues and writing exchanges with Beth Notar, Kate Zirbel, Bridget Hayden, Michelle Gamburd, Tom Williamson, Melissa Johnson, Deb Jackson, Coralynn Davis, Abdollah Dashti, Steven Pierce, Lisa Lindsey, Leila Hudson, Mike Schroeder, Jennifer Jenkins, Karen Robert, John Stiles, Julie Hastings, Rebecca Scott, Roger Rouse, Ann Stoler, Sally Humphreys, Ruth Behar, and Julie Skurski. In South Carolina, I thank Ann Kingslover, Mike Scardaville, Elaine Lacey, Tom Lekan, Karl Gerth, Kasey Grier, Kay Edwards, Nicola Ristic, and Meili Steele. I owe special thanks to Andrew Cousins, Kate Brown, and Susan Vanderborg.

I presented pieces of this book at numerous colloquia, workshops, and conferences where the project benefited from engaged feedback. An especially formative professional experience — especially in terms of honing my ideas about memory — was the Dartmouth Humanities Institute's "Acts of Memory," convened by Leo Spitzer, Mieke Bal, and Jonathan Crewe. I thank them and the other institute participants, especially Marita Sturken. At the University of Missouri, St. Louis, Mark Burkholder, Susan Brownell, Kathy Gentile, and Karen Lucas graciously offered an institutional home at a critical juncture in my career. This project found its final home at Indiana University with encouragement from Suzanna Walters, Jeanne Peterson, and my other colleagues in the Gender Studies Department, along with fellow Latin Americanists Daniel James, Jeffrey Gould, Peter Guardino, and Arlene Diaz.

I am fortunate to have had vital professional support from Fernando Coronil, Bruce Mannheim, Alice Kasakoff, John French, Peter Winn, Steve Stern, Leo Spitzer, Ana Alonso, Marisol de la Cadena, Kay Warren, Francisco Zapata, Florencia Mallon, María Luisa Tarres, Mary Kay Vaughan, and the late Ken Cmiel, who encouraged me to stick with my "end of history" critique.

The Politics, Culture, and History Series editors Julia Adams and George Steinmetz carefully commented on the entire revised dissertation and the series editorial board met with me in a formal seminar to discuss the project; the comments generated by this process were very helpful in the first round of revisions as I prepared the manuscript for press review. My Duke University Press editor Rafael Allen then enthusiastically contributed his own insights and supervised the first round of external readers' reports while Valerie Millholland skillfully shepherded the next three rounds. Julia Adams provided patient, generous, and supportive counsel throughout this important process. I also thank Duke staffers Miriam Angress, Katie Courtland, Erin Hathaway, and especially Pam Morrison and Tricia Mickelberry. John French and four other readers for the press all impacted this project by providing careful and extensive comments.

For technical support, I appreciate research assistance from Jodi Barnes, Rebecca Shrum, and Kathy Mancuso; help with maps from Tamara Wilson and Natalie Hartman; help with editing from Louisa Castner, Jeanne Barker-Nunn, and Michel Lafantano; help with the index from Diana Witt; and help with Spanish-language issues from Carmen García-Prieto, Lluis Rivera, and, rather heroically, Michael Ugarte.

A project involving years of field, archival, and interview time and travel across three continents requires substantial funding. Crucial support came from the following institutions: the University of Michigan (Rackham Graduate School, Anthropology and History Program, Latin American Studies), the University of South Carolina (College of Liberal Arts, Office of the Vice-Provost for Research, Women's Studies), Indiana University, the National Science Foundation, the Fulbright Scholar Program, the Wenner-Gren Foundation for Anthropological Research, the American Historical Association (Albert J. Beveridge Grant), the Conference on Latin American History (Lewis Hanke Award), and the Dartmouth College Humanities Institute Fellowship.

I have counted on personal support and inspiration from Lynn Hotchkiss, Pat and Piner Stevens, Pati Ruíz, Marisol Figueroa, Kim Scaliatine, Kirsten Dow, Diane Soles, Laura Ahearn, Mary Ann Mahoney, and John, Peggy, and Gene Somoza. I look with great optimism toward the future with my splendid family: Phil, Lluisa Jhenefer, Bernardo Jhon-Paolo, Maiara Kathryn, and MacIntyre Loden Lennon.

Lastly, this book owes its most profound debts to Guillermo Ross-Murray, Baldramina Flores Urqueta de Lizardi, Luis Morales Marino, and Mark Somoza. Generous comments on the manuscript in its advanced stages came from Laura Westhoff, Rosario Montoya, Margaret Power, Janise Hurtig, Ed Murphy, and Jodi Pavilack. Deborah Cohen shared a chunk of her own tenacity in seeing me through each stage over the years. Her intellectual smarts, writerly eye, friendship, and loyalty over the long haul have not only productively shaped this analysis but, ultimately, ensured that I have been able to complete this book.

Introduction

ETHNOGRAPHY, HISTORY, AND MEMORY

Chile is internationally regarded as a model nation-state in both economic and political terms, making it an ideal place to research questions of nation-state formation. Indeed, even in the early nineteenth century, Chile was seen as an exceptionally stable republic relative to the other newly independent countries of the Americas. The historians Gabriel Salazar and Julio Pinto argue that in Chile the state consolidated well before the nation. The Chilean state has remained coherent and maintained its integrity despite numerous periods of intense conflict with heavy doses of state violence. In the wake of such violent conjunctures the state's ability to recover a wide social consensus regarding its legitimacy has enabled policymakers to engage in creative economic and political experimentation.

In economic-policy circles Chile is considered a model for neoliberal, market-driven reforms in areas such as public health, education, and social security, even for the United States. In terms of political policy Chile is looked to as a model for democratization and the resolution of past political conflicts, given its return to democratic governance after nearly twenty years of military rule. It pioneered the rubric of reconciliation picked up by African and Eastern European countries at the beginning of the twenty-first century.[1] In fact, Chile has long influenced the political economy imaginings of broader international communities. In the 1940s Chile orchestrated arguably the world's most effective popular-front governing alliance against fascism. In the 1960s and early 1970s Chile's attempt to forge a democratic path to socialism (through elections and legislation) in spite of the Cold War polarization of politics was relatively successful; the crushing of that democratic project was therefore felt acutely by people around the world who had looked to Chile as representative of new political possibilities.

According to the current triumphalist, technocratic view, Chile is the darling of neoliberal economic theorists, but when I began my research on Chilean nation-state formation, in 1990, many scholars from around the world emphasized to me the affective place that Chile held for many people outside of its borders. A South Asian scholar explained to me how in 1973 he and his colleagues had sadly watched Chile's experimental democracy fall to a military coup. One U.S. historian explained that participating in the Chile solidarity movement of the 1970s marked a formative period of her professional and political life as she worked on behalf of exiled Chilean fellow students and scholars. An Indonesian scholar reminisced about a friend of his who, unable for political reasons to speak about the collapse of Indonesia's transformative political vision for the nation-state and the subsequent violence, had instead written a dissertation on Chile. The affective ties that people around the world have felt for Chile since the 1970s exemplify sympathetic memory: "I offer solidarity for your suffering" or "Your plight is like and thus can represent mine." In sympathetic memory there is a clear demarcation of "your" history and "mine," and the kind of emotional ties and subsequent political actions they elicit are supportive and not usually proactive.

For many scholars and activists committed to social justice, Chile — especially in the 1970s and 1980s — became a site of mourning for lost radical projects. Chile had become a model for socialist state building and many saw their own hopes in it; its story is one of the appropriation of memories of violence to express identification with particular political projects. Though these reminiscences reference a violent rupture, Chile became an important site not because it was marked by political violence, but rather because its achievements in developing a sophisticated and dynamic participatory political system made its collapse into military rule all the more devastating. State violence casts into relief questions of nation-state formation (e.g., was a particular instance of the state's use of violence legitimate and, if so, in whose interests?). The influence of this dynamic was increasingly evident as I examined whether the 1973 coup was just a blip in an otherwise democratic political history and found a much more complicated story: deployments and contestations of memories of state violence were about mobilizing affective ties integral to the forging of political projects in struggles for power centered, especially in Chile, around nation-state formation.[2]

When I lived on the Chilean frontier — near the country's northern border with Peru and Bolivia — I myself experienced how memories of violence can elicit the various connections that people feel across state borders. One of the first places I got to know was a maritime union hall where the main wall was a mural commemorating the 1886 Chicago Haymarket Massacre, the history of which had been faithfully detailed in May Day commemorations in Chile until the 1973 coup. Similarly, Chile's annual public commemorations of International Women's Day (March 8th) included a detailed accounting of the 1911 New York Triangle Factory Fire, which took the lives of scores of working women. It is striking that both stories, largely silenced in much of the United States (even in Chicago and New York), have been so meaningful to so many Chileans. Whose history are they, then? Such connections serve as cathartic memory, a deeply felt sense that "this history is *our* history," based on strong affective ties and passionate emotions, and often drawn on to inspire direct actions like unionization or demands for women's rights. These allegiances often are grounded not in national identity but in other affiliations, particularly class and politics.

With regard to the question of who owns any given historical episode, I take an off-center look onto the nation-state from the frontier — a place only partially incorporated into the nation — aiming to denationalize History as the automatic purview of the nation-state.[3] I challenge the idea of a unified national memory by attending to the fact that nation-state formation is not a single project, to the nuances of local stories, and to the integrity of the hopes and desires of those who came before us. Though this volume has the nation-state as its object of analysis, the idea of the nation-state must first be denaturalized and the cost of its enforcement remembered.

The story of nation-state formation is about the nationalizing of historical memory through the process of either cutting it off from "me" or making it "mine" in the prioritizing of national affiliation over other connections, such as those of class or other imaginings of collectivities. As the rich scholarship on memory and the nation shows, the nation is an idea narratively grounded in an authenticating past combined with a future-oriented idea of progress. Therefore, political projects centered around the nation-state must engage in the work of memory. As the nature of those competing projects changes over time, it would seem that the shape of the memory-work required to bring supporters on board might likewise change. However, in the academy, memory has remained a surprisingly static category. Building on current scholarship, I trace how over the course of more than a hundred years "memory" itself has changed in relation to changing broad sensibilities (*mentalité*, doxa, culture) — not just the content of what gets remembered, nor even the preferred formats or containers (e.g., monuments, songs, official histories), but the very shape of memory: how it produces emotion to bring people on board with particular political projects in particular ways.

This book is, in part, a response to the call of thinkers such as Amitav Ghosh and Derek Walcott for a more cosmopolitan framing of history in the hope that a cross-cultural approach can continue the work of — in the historian Prasenjit Duara's words — "rescuing history from the nation" by making explicit the ways in which the nation-state is constructed from the stories told about it and the ability of the state to enforce those narratives at the cost of other vectors of connection.[4] Even as I analyze the particular dimensions of nation-state formation for countries such as Chile, I question the nation-state as the automatic analytic terrain of history and national citizenship as a basis for authorizing or deauthorizing renditions of history and possibilities for connections between peoples across times.

At its core, *Salt in the Sand* marks my effort to apply a dual historical and anthropological perspective in order to forge a historical ethnography of nation-state formation and cultural transformations in

Chile. By nation-state formation, I refer to an ongoing process of delimiting political arenas for imagining and defining subjectivities (collective and otherwise), institution-building, and demarcating relations between the state and other vectors of social relations.[5] The state is an arena of struggle involving multiple actors, institutions, and practices of governance, all of which are involved in creating and policing the notion of the state as a singular entity in relation to other, supposedly different realms, like society, the market, the family, and so on.[6] Prevailing works on nation-state formation tend to depict it as emerging from one foundational moment, from moments of regime change, or from the unfolding over time of one kind of state. In contrast, I posit that the nation-state is always in formation, a process that persists regardless of whether or not there are changes in state forms; however, the state generates its own linear narrative of progress, one that obscures the more entangled story of its making.

Just as one understands the state to be, to some degree, defined by its legitimated use of violence, also critical to the modern state project is the hegemonic process of defining the nation, with the limits of the nation-state set and defended at the frontier. Centering the frontier, I study the intertwining of the state's use of violence with memories of that violence, a dynamic and conflictive process involving multiple collectivities. Official state memory — created, propagated, and forcefully imposed to the exclusion alternative visions of the past — constitutes a vital component in crafting the nation *and* generates the affective ties suturing the nation together. Affective ties can be defined in terms of the kinds and degrees (strengths) of identification or connection with political projects that are fostered at particular moments. Since political projects require emotional drive in order to garner support and participation, the creation of particular emotions helps generate attendant kinds of political action (e.g., pity brings in donations for famine relief, whereas outrage over a bombing inspires support for invasive security measures and even war). Memory is not the only way of producing such interactions; however, the nation-state's grounding in foundationalist rationales — that the nation-state is autochthonous to or springs naturally from a given territory — requires the forging of particular kinds of memory.

In building on an established literature that posits nation-states as always in formation, I also interrogate the broad shape of memory as changing over time in relation to particular political projects.

Nation-state formation is not a moment but an ongoing process in which time has no necessarily discrete boundaries: the past is not necessarily the past. Thus, the changing manner — or memory-work — by which temporal demarcation is effected within a historical narrative to ground the idea of the nation-state as a processually emerging, autochthonous, and coherent entity is a crucial component of nation-state formation. Tracing the history of memory — the shifts in memory's contents, forms, contexts, and practices — elucidates processes of nation-state formation, the spaces in which these processes occur, and the histories of those peoples and conflicts that have exceeded the bounds of nationalist, state-oriented projects.

The title *Salt in the Sand* refers to the sodium-nitrate mining at the end of the nineteenth century in the desert region of Tarapacá along Chile's northern frontier, an area also known as the birthplace of the Chilean labor movement. The word *salt* stands for more than the story of the extraction of mineral wealth; it represents the sweat, blood, and tears of human beings that make that history meaningful. In Chilean history Tarapacá was a site of military glory dating from the period of national conquest, a site of labor strikes and massacres during the era of nitrate extraction, and a site of state detention and violence during World War II and the Cold War. More recently, during Chile's transition from military dictatorship to civilian rule, it became the site of the first excavation of a mass grave. Of greatest significance, however, is that the military has throughout the twentieth century centered this remote region in its version of official national memory. By anchoring its relationship to this specific site, the military casts itself as caretaker of the nation, which points to the central riddle of Chile's current situation: how has the military (a key entity in the Chilean state apparatus), despite more than a century of state violence, maintained its largely unassailable role as guardian of national memory?

The Chilean state, in stark contrast to many of its neighbors, has remained remarkably solid as an idea and a set of institutions in which various sectors have continued to invest, even in the context of shifting notions of who and what constitutes the nation and who will be empowered as citizens to make those determinations. Over the course of Chilean history, military sectors have asserted their position as loyal, apolitical arbiters of that process. However, an investigation of alternative visions of national history — especially those from labor movements, political agitators, artists of both "high" and popular culture, and human-rights movements—demonstrates how memories of political violence have informed the conjunctures between state policies and oppositional activism and have shaped subsequent conflicts between them. Some memories, in other words, were made national, included as part of the national emotional glue and in particular political projects, while others were subordinated in various ways.

Methodology: Where Disciplines Intersect, Where Disciplines Collide

To analyze the multiple memories of state violence and their impact, I have incorporated diverse source materials, including literary works; artifacts, texts, and performances of popular culture; commemorative architecture; oral interviews; and my own experiences as an observer-participant during years of field study in Chile. My approach and interpretations of these sources draw on a number of thinkers often referenced under the transdisciplinary rubrics of cultural studies, subaltern or postcolonial studies, feminist studies, and queer theory. While these sometimes disparate analytic sources and frameworks do not necessarily coalesce into a single model for thinking about memory and state violence in processes of nation-state formation, they do allow me to approach close-to-the-ground research materials from a number of directions. This constellation of theories and sources allows me to pursue praxis: an integration of theory and evidence as a "real"-world intervention.[7]

The book is a culmination of ethnographic and archival research spanning a decade and a half. Historians generally privilege documentary artifacts as primary sources of data, with the idea that by immersing themselves in a wide variety of documentary sources ("the archive"), they can begin to answer the elusive and never completely answerable question "What might it have been like to live back then?" My own research involved extensive archival work with local and national government records, personal papers and diaries, historiography, educational materials, popular literature and music, periodicals, political pamphlets, and consular papers, materials that together enabled an approximate reconstruction of constellations of social memories and their relationships to state policies and social movements, as well as of the historical context for and events surrounding specific moments of state violence.

In calling this an ethnography, I try, as an anthropologist, to answer the questions "What would it be like to be live in this other place or be from this other culture?" I have used primarily methods of participant-observation — long-term immersion in a particular social context ("the field") — taking a holistic approach to the intersecting facets of human life that modernist social science has divided up under rubrics of politics, economics, social hierarchies, and, of course, culture, that elusive set of meaningful practices that are complexly shared, exclusionary, and contested. In my extensive ethnographic work, I observed and interacted with various civic associations, political parties, women's and environmental groups, local schools, and government programs such as the Mental Health and Human Rights Project. During intensive periods of participant-observation, I focused on human-rights groups and civic associations representing long-dismantled nitrate-mining communities, and co-facilitated a local history workshop in Northern Chile. Attentive to public commemorations, I analyzed museums as forms of historical representation. I compiled detailed individual and family oral histories and conducted extensive informal interviews to situate local actors in the structures and events of regional and national histories. Drawing on my background in both history and anthropology, I took into consideration not only temporal depth and context but also the experiences and visions of the social actors.

Both in my analysis of memory and forgetting and in the narrative strategies of each chapter I hold history and ethnography in tension, as, through this book, I myself participate in the politics of memory practices. Bernard Cohn notes that History considers the Past its purview, while Anthropology views the thick Present as its disciplinary territory.[8] Though there are many issues that mutually interest the two disciplines, their points of departure and directions of analysis are in fact quite different. History moves forward from a definite moment in the past (congealed in the archive), ostensibly to answer a question about the past, with chronology providing the vital cause-and-effect narrative. Anthropology begins in the present (defined by the moment of fieldwork) and moves back (much as in drawing a kinship chart), looking for the antecedents of its own experience.

What historians and anthropologists do have in common, however, is a general interest in the cross-cultural endeavor of imagining what life would look like from a different context or point of view. Both value a perspective that is at once deeply engaged and yet somehow apart, different in time for one and in place for the other: the historians' rule-of-thumb being that one must let some years pass before beginning to think critically about "the past"; the anthropologists' sense being that the critical gaze of "the observer" can bring fresh questions to the naturalized parameters of a particular cultural context. Integrating History and Anthropology requires a multipronged research methodology based on long-term engagement with research subjects and a holistic approach that takes into account the multiple facets of human relations in the world.

This interdisciplinary methodology shapes each chapter distinctively. While chapter 3, on forgetting, looks like a narrative history because it must counter the erasure of two particular conjunctures, chapter 4, on remembering, resists straightforward narrative because it would replicate the reification of the event in question. An anthropologist, on reading a draft of this manuscript, remarked that despite the way every chapter weaves together contemporary and past issues, the reader could barely grasp the present, that it continually slipped away in my telling. A historian responding to the same draft commented on the challenge presented by an account organized not by an explicit chronology but rather by a dialectical analytic movement forward in time. Satisfying neither History nor Anthropology completely, the book calls into question both modes of analysis by refusing to see past, present, and future as already existing, discrete units. Instead, this volume dialectically reveals movements between these categories as they emerge at particular conjunctures.

Although parts of this text are located temporally and progress according to the traditional rules of narrative, other sections are anchored by place or by ethnography to reveal the stories behind the history. Historical ethnography offers a glimpse into the lives of the people who make — indeed, are — history. In doing so, it allows one to explore the interpolation of subjectivity, the contradictory and tangled formations of particular configurations of subjects, respecting the complexity and integrity of what some might call personal memory (e.g., a grieving parent whose child has been lost to a firing squad), while still trying to understand its relation to the more overtly public side of memory, that is, the particular experience of grief, emerging from and constituting cultural codes, and its political consequences for other people.[9] In this project I am concerned with the tensions between these memories as a site of struggles for political power or, in the critic Henry Krips's words, "the formation of antagonisms as sites of interpolation."[10] In exploring the politics of memory,

I have found that the alchemical mixture of history and ethnography can truly breathe life—struggle, conflict, passion—into the sometimes moribund body of facts and figures that cultures accrue.

Historical ethnography also enables an understanding of the past through analysis of how it is reflected in—not absent from—the present. The presence and use of historical memory in the lives of all classes of people in Chile speaks volumes not only about the current social and political organization but also about the political and social structures of the past hundred years. I attempt to make sense of this long, painful, and creative period in Chilean history and to show how it has influenced Chile's entrance into the twenty-first century.

The Shape of the Historical Ethnography

Salt in the Sand is broadly chronological in that the balance of each chapter moves the narrative further along in time. This volume is also shaped dialectically as a conjunctural history in that it looks at specific moments of state violence and how they are interrelated. Each chapter dialectically moves from a violent conjuncture to trace out how various sectors either silence or mobilize memories of that state violence and the impact of these memories on subsequent patterns of nation-state formation and concomitant political mobilizations and conflicts. This study does not serve as a comprehensive account of a century of Chilean history, but rather analyzes key conjunctures in order to deal with longer-range processes of memory as fundamental to nation-state building. Some scholars may be uncomfortable with a nonlinear narrative, but by being both nonlinear and broadly chronological, this book problematizes the role of chronology in historical analysis. It makes visible the fact that any attempt to tell the past is not a reflection of something that was already there but is itself an act of memory. Any effort to tell history—even a chronologically driven one—is itself an intervention in the politics of memory. *Salt in the Sand* thus brings to historical scholarship the contributions of anthropology and cultural studies, which posit that human experience is more messy than can be described by simple causal links and clear chronology. It uses instead a dialectically chronological narrative to impart a more truly human sense of the way in which events unfold.

Although I argue for the historical interrelatedness of the conjunctures of state violence and memory, I refuse to naturalize or prioritize the contextual narrative, but instead link them together.

Contextual narrative is complemented and challenged by comparative analysis of the morphology—shape or structure and form—that the struggle over memory takes. As Florike Egmond and Peter Mason proclaim, morphological analysis is not only a practical tool but also good theory: "We reverse the hegemony of history over morphology. In doing so, we open up a plurality of contexts that otherwise would be excluded *a priori* by the imposition of the protocols of historians." For Egmond and Mason, morphology enriches context by underlining "the fact that contexts, by virtue of their provisional nature, are not given but are themselves constituted within a field of contestation."[11]

I analyze the changing morphology of memory as intertwined with —and constitutive of—its historical contexts, especially in light of contemporary understandings of History as a memory-practice of continual negotiation between those in power and those who want power. Though the history of memory provides the narrative thread connecting the conjunctures I have chosen to explore, I treat these conjunctures comparatively, asking why and in what forms certain moments are remembered (chapter 4) when others cannot be recalled except through chronological litany (chapter 3).[12] The case of Chile demonstrates that foundational violence does not always have to be forgotten as the nation-state transforms and as notions of difference and belonging shift across time.[13] For example, during the Popular Unity period (1970–1973), the Escuela Santa María Massacre of 1907 could be told as a story of martyrdom and persistence, because martyrdom was an emphasis central to Popular Unity rhetoric.[14] The history of workers seizing mining camps in 1890 and 1925, on the other hand, did not conform as well to the demands of gradualist, cross-class projects, because the mine workers had used explicitly revolutionary rhetoric and violence. Yet the silencing of events fifty years after their occurrence does not mean that the news was repressed at the time. While the state specifically prohibited most newspapers from publishing accounts of the 1907 massacre, the 1925 massacre was reported in great detail by the pro-government press and used rhetorically in debates on national and international controversies. To address the question of why certain events gain currency over time while others are elided, an account based on both morphology and dialectical chronology provides a better answer to the comparative historical puzzles posed.[15]

In this volume I layer analyses of trends and transformations in

Tarapacá—and Chile more generally—over more than a century. I also look at specific cases in greater historical and ethnographic depth. Like memory, or déjà vu, this volume revisits historical conjunctures and issues in different places in different ways in order to challenge assumptions. Rather than presenting a catalog of memory types, I look at changes in the morphology of memory over time.

Part 1, "Templates," which comprises chapters 1 and 2, foregrounds the politics of memory in the postdictatorship era (1990–present), as Chile has moved from military dictatorship to civilian governance. By focusing on the Present, I introduce the predicaments I encountered in my fieldwork on the ambivalent relationships between various state and nonstate actors as they dealt with legacies of human-rights violations. The dilemmas of the Present generated questions that I pursued historically in archives and oral histories, looking for cultural lessons and tools that might offer political alternatives.

In chapter 1 I delineate three political periods of nation-state formation, offering a detailed overview that provides a historical and cultural context for the rest of the book. I then present a template (or model) for each period of nation-state formation, positing predominant forms of memory that emerged from the dynamics in the political culture of that time: (1) the oligarchic state period and rise of the labor movement (1890s–1930s), in which the predominant form of memory was catharsis; (2) the populist period of political party formation (1930s–1973), which was characterized by empathy; (3) the neoliberal period beginning with the military dictatorship and solidarity movements and shifting into a civilian regime (1973–2005), a period that entailed memory as sympathy that waned, leaving the dual modes of melancholy and nostalgia. While the first and last of these periods are of particular interest, the middle one illuminates the role of memory in the Left's hegemonic project: its bid for the state. Though this template posits as dominant for each period an affective mode through which mobilized sectors cohere with political projects, other modes may also be present, though not necessarily. Rather than being a rigid paradigm, this broad periodization of nation-state formation and memory provides a template for rethinking ruptures and continuities in Chilean political culture. Shifts in the forms and uses of memories of state violence across these three periods constitute the narrative backbone of this account.

Chapter 2 builds on my periodization to establish a structure for a history of memory in Chilean nation-state formation. Political projects generate and frame memory—in particular, memories of state violence—as a kind of emotional glue with which to connect and mobilize people in specific ways. Methodologically, this chapter benefits from the literary criticism technique of close reading along with ethnography, making a case for the change over time of broad predominant cultural sensibilities. This chapter explores in-depth the shifts in modes of memory over a long-range view of Chilean history. As with any historical account, the predominant sensibilities—in this case, modes of memory—of any given period may be present earlier and linger afterward with important effects. However, modeling the predominant mode of memory as a part of the larger political culture of mobilization provides a nuanced historical context for understanding the politics of memory over time. This is especially necessary for thinking about the contemporary period (the usual sole focus of scholarship on memory and national trauma) in order to understand the possibilities and constraints facing Chile today, as people there deal with the legacies of state violence and political activists struggle to find ways of encouraging people to reengage in the political system and reinvest confidence in the state as the guarantor of a common project.

With an analytic template for thinking about the intertwined history of nation-state formation and memory established, part 2, "Conjunctures," which comprises chapters 3–6, turns to selected crucial moments to consider in-depth transformations in political culture as expressed and enacted in processes of remembering and forgetting particular moments of state violence.

Chapter 3 constructs a regional history of the militarized frontier zone during two periods of mobilization and repression: one at the beginning of the nitrate era, with the first general strike of 1890 and an uprising of workers during the Civil War of 1891; the other in June 1925, with one of the last great labor mobilizations of the nitrate era. These aggressive strikes and repressions, which bookend the nitrate period, were subordinated in Chilean narratives in favor of other moments more exemplary of martyrdom. Even given the overwhelming emphasis on the nitrate era in the historiography, studies of these events have taken the form of one or two brief articles or small mentions in larger works. To date, no scholar has drawn them together, used a similar array of local and international sources, or considered the moments of state violence in relation to the memories of those events as expressed in modes of popular culture for which the nitrate era is famous, such as poetry, songs, journalism, and workers' theater. Doing this work reveals the vitality of non-elite cultures in the face of overwhelming state negligence and overwhelming state violence in defense of (national and international) elite interests in spite of ambivalence within the country. This ambivalence, combined with overwhelming external pressures, led to the military intervention at the end of the nitrate era. The military and its supporters explicitly used a rhetoric of reshaping national memory in an effort to dismantle oppositional (cathartic) cultures and to reimagine the nation to incorporate non-elite sectors.

Dealing with more exemplary martyrdom, chapter 4 discusses how the 1907 Escuela Santa María Massacre came to be a key organizing event in local and national historical memories of state violence. This chapter explores the shape of memory in the populist period from the 1930s until the military coup, a period that entailed—even under Rightist presidencies—the expansion of the political system based on coalition, cross-party projects and the concomitant expansion of participation and citizenship for non-elite sectors. Diverse sectors coalesced around a broader notion of the state as the expression of the nation which should be the purview of "the people," inclusive of non-elites, such that even the more conservative administrations had to engage with this framework. Since this volume looks at nation-state formation through moments of violence and memories of that violence, the populist period carries herein a different weight than the moments of most dramatic rupture; it is a crucial link in the broader argument about shifts in the shape of memory over the course of the century. Chapter 4 elucidates the challenges of a political culture that expanded the conception of the nation to a cross-class (empathetic) one by nurturing a vibrant political-party system that subsumed most prior forms of collective mobilization into a political system increasingly oriented around gaining access to the state as the locus of liberatory possibility.

Chapter 5 examines how moments forgotten and remembered interweave in the fragmented history of a single place, the small desert port of Pisagua, beginning with the profound impact of the excavation of a mass grave of executed prisoners had on the process of transition from dictatorship to formal democracy in 1990. It describes how the Association of Ex-political Prisoners of Pisagua attempted to construct and defend a counterhegemonic narrative that generated a different kind of tie among them, as survivors, and thus a claim to a special status for themselves and their vision in Chile's famous transition to democracy. Linking the Pisagua of 1973 to other moments in local history led to conflicts within the group, within the broader community, and within the state. Rather than simply focus on the violence of the 1973 military coup and the dictatorship, this chapter contextualizes these events within the long history of the state's use of Pisagua as a detention site. Pisagua represents the history of state violence and resistance in its capacity as a detention camp: for political prisoners in 1948, for homosexual men in the 1920s, for German and Japanese Axis nationals in 1943, for "communists" in 1956, for political prisoners in 1984, and for "common" criminals who were executed and buried along with "political" prisoners in 1973. The longer history forces one to question whether the 1973 coup marked an aberration in Chilean history—as political elites and the historiography have claimed—or whether the continuities and differences in the use of this single site offer important lessons about Chilean state-formation, a process grounded in the push-pull struggle to legitimate and delegitimate uses of state violence even as memories of state violence became incorporated into oppositional subjectivities (e.g., the human-rights movement during the dictatorship) as well as into appeals for alliances (sympathy)—within Chile and internationally—to roll back the dictatorship.

Chapter 6 engages with the positions of various social actors as they negotiate the politics of memory in contemporary Chile. This chapter explores models of memory in an attempt to offer an emancipatory politics capable of projecting a different future, especially in the context of a triumphalist late-twentieth-century modernity, which relegates the past to anachronism (melancholy) or superseded curiosity (nostalgia) and the future to the repetition of the present. As scholars like Elizabeth Jelin and Steve Stern have shown, memory-making as a form of sociopolitical action has been central to politics since military rule.[16] Administrations have tried to develop technologies of memory to manage problematic psyches and sites in relation to the demands of social actors with multiple subjectivities and political projects of their own.

While other scholars focus attention on how different versions of the past compete, I look at that competition in the context of the broad shape of memory as emergent from Chilean nation-state formation. In the most recent period this process entailed the consolidation of civilian rule with an already established economic model. This necessitated bringing together, in a renewed faith in the state, divergent sectors of the populace, from those who favored military rule and those who lost state monopoly to those who had been excluded violently from claims to the nation-state. Many conceptions of the past have been mobilized, but they share a common broad sensibility that includes a sense of dramatic rupture between the Present and the Past based on a largely shared periodization of the Past. By placing the current moment in the long-range view of nation-state formation and memory in Chile, this study goes beyond diagnosing or even inadvertently replicating the state's own narrative of itself in favor of a broader understanding of the deep predominant cultural structures and constraints Chileans face.

In the conclusion I turn once more to the problem of the transition to democracy, arguing that the history of memory can provide insights into the various ways in which past, present, and future can be connected in political projects in which memory serves as a call to action. Examining memories of Chilean state violence shows how nation-state formation, rather than being a narrative of increasing democratization marked by an odd setback (the 1973 coup), has entailed a push-and-pull tension between moments of exclusion and incorporation of non-elite sectors and of civic collectivities outside the state (and state-oriented political party) purview. Moments of radical exclusion were followed by state rhetoric that explicitly discussed negotiating national memory as a way of making the polity cohere. However, within those moments of exclusion one finds the creative demands of contestatory and per force semiautonomous voices (e.g., social movements under the dictatorship in the 1980s). Democracy in the nation (understood in its most inclusive sense) requires spaces for contestatory voices that remain in true dialogue with — but are never completely subsumed by — the state and political parties invested in the contest over that state. Ultimately, for small subordinate nation-states such as Chile, the constraints imposed by political economies of scale and the ongoing strength of antidemocratic sectors (e.g., pro-military coup fascists) leave few resources with which to sustain a semiautonomous contestatory civil society (including think-tanks and social movements independent of the political parties) and the alternative visions it can sustain.

The dynamic reconstitution of temporal boundaries — past, present, future — is especially evident in the historiography of Tarapacá, as the region simply disappears from the scholarship after 1930 as it lost centrality in national and global economies. It is also absent from the current politics of memory in Chile, in which the 1973 military coup marks a complete historical break. The insistence on 1973 as the radical moment shapes the spatial-temporal dynamics of memory such that all that passed before constitutes the distant past, the two decades of dictatorship the recent past, and the postdictatorship years after 1990 the present, with insufficient explanatory or political efforts to connect them in a politics for the future. This dynamic virtually forecloses the possibility of a longer historical narrative capable of rigorously analyzing processes of continuity and change. The state's narrative framework of regime transition instantiates and exacerbates this dynamic. The task of this book is to disrupt this temporal demarcation (periodization) by tackling the story of nation-state formation as constituting and being constituted through the interpellation of subjectivities affectively mobilized in political projects. Political memories shape collectivities' senses of connection to each other — including the state — by constituting relationships across space and time.

My goal is twofold: first, to understand how memory works to create political subjectivities which are emergent from the changing parameters of the relationship between the state and other actors; second, to denaturalize the Present, to unsettle one's sense of where one is as an onlooker and participant in the political questions of one's times and in how one makes connections with the struggles of other eras. I attempt the vexing task of "predicting the present," as Terry Eagleton wrote in his reading of Walter Benjamin, "of reading its unique 'astrological' configuration before it has slipped away — and of prognosticating the past, deciphering its images with vigilance before they sink back into the *mémoire involuntaire*."[17] Memory, "a question of 'routine' as well as of the illuminating flash," thus provides a helpful venue for such interdisciplinary explorations.[18] My intention is not to explain how the Past influences the Present, but rather to show that, especially for those in the hinterlands of postcolonial nation-states who inhabit a "geography of haunted places," the past is intertwined with the present and that the conditions of possibility for arrival in the (ethnographic) present constitute privilege.[19]

PART I *Templates*

Memory and
the *Camanchacas Calientes* of
Chilean Nation-State Formation

In May 1991, during my stay in Santiago, Chile had just entered the second year of a shift to formal democracy. This shift, officially termed "the transition," moved Chile from the military regime of General Augusto Pinochet, which had ruled since the 1973 coup, toward an elected coalition of political parties, despite the fact that the new civilian regime operated under the scrutiny of the former dictator and the military he still controlled. Political tensions had been exacerbated by the assassination of Jaime Guzmán, a major ideologue in the former military regime, a prominent senator, and a law professor; Guzmán had crafted both the terms of transition between regimes and the baroque constitution, which was designed to protect and institutionalize the prerogatives of those who had ruled earlier and to constrain the initiatives of those who sought to mold a new political system. Guzmán's murder had prompted the nervous new civilian government, eager to demonstrate its ability to maintain law and order, to permit police raids of shantytowns and mass detention of "suspects."[1] To the horror of those who had held great hope for the new government, the murder served as the government's justification for unleashing the state's repressive forces in all-too-familiar ways.

As I walked late one evening through a downtown pedestrian mall, a group of young folk musicians were performing for passersby and an audience of about fifty that had gathered around them. Dressed in alpaca ponchos and blue jeans, the folk musicians played several pieces of Andean music on panpipes, guitars, *charangos*, and drums. In the middle of their street-corner set, the musicians announced their next song by noting the ongoing police raids and stating: "Today our government is in crisis over the death of one rich man. Here is a song about the deaths of many." To audience applause, which grew even more enthusiastic as they recognized the first notes, the group performed the opening movement of *Santa María de Iquique: Cantata popular* (commonly known as "Cantata Santa María de Iquique") a familiar retelling of the government's 1907 massacre of striking nitrate workers in Tarapacá, two thousand kilometers away at the northern frontier.[2]

How do such memories of repression shape collective subjectivities? In this case, the street performers employed music instantly recognizable to many in their audience; this music, in turn, elicited an emotional response based on collective memories of the original incident and its linkage to new instances of repression and also on memories of prior performances of the memory-form itself, in other words, this particular music. The cantata had emerged from the New Song Movement of the 1960s, in which artists reinterpreted folk melodies and genres in order to create and validate the political category of "the people," bearers of an authentic national culture and thus legitimate claimants to state power and economic resources. After the military coup of 1973, many of the movement's artists were killed or exiled and their music banned. Nonetheless, those exiled artists performed their music worldwide, working to isolate the military regime internationally and to generate support for opposition groups within Chile. During the years of dictatorship (1973–1990), many in the opposition used the events and characters of the long-ago Tarapacá massacre portrayed in the cantata as an allegory for the more

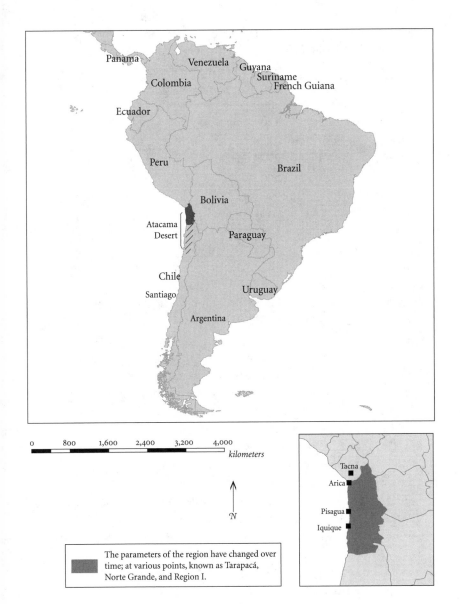

Map 1. Regional map of Tarapacá (Region I), Chile. Map by Tamara Wilson.

recent military overthrow of the Popular Unity government that had governed Chile in 1970–1973, an allegory that vindicated Popular Unity's attempts to enact a gradual socialist transformation of the state, despite its having been declared a failure by the military dictatorship and by many civilian politicians as well.

Thus it was that in the constricted and delicate political arena of transition from military to civilian rule, I witnessed street musicians calling on memories of state violence, connecting through analogy the Tarapacá strikers of 1907 and the residents of Santiago's poorer neighborhoods who in 1991 were being politically harassed. By playing the cantata, the musicians implicated the current civilian government as comparable to the repressive Chilean state that had existed more than eighty years earlier. This parallel is surprisingly absent in professional histories of Chile, which either deal with times before or after, but not during, the 1973 coup, thus reinforcing the notion that the post-1973 violence was an aberration in the nation's otherwise democratic history. Memory, for all its complexities, is a useful analytic category because it places the historical observations of professionals alongside those of street musicians and reveals both to be political interventions. Thus, one can take as a serious proposition the connection made by the street musicians and their audience between the two moments of state violence as being about the ways in which the state secures certain interests at the expense of others.

The musicians' critical analogy demonstrated the political vulnerability of the new civilian government. Although the government had won the electoral contest against the military regime by speaking a language of justice and had identified itself as advocating for a broader collective of citizens and a more just distribution of resources, the civilian officials were eager to avoid charges by the pro-military opposition that they were ineffective in maintaining "order" — the lack of which the new generation of politicians understood as having contributed to the demise of the Popular Unity government, since disorder had been a key charge in the anti-Popular Unity propaganda. In prioritizing "order" over civil liberties, however, the civilian leadership risked being seen as the latest players in the long history of state violence in Chilean history.

By evoking the cantata to accuse the new government of state violence, the street musicians also tapped into memories of decades of violence in the North, which had made the region famous as a site of violence. However, in addition to its legacy of colonial violence, military glories of national conquest, and suppression of striking workers, Chile's northernmost region, Tarapacá, was also the birthplace of the country's labor movement and major political parties. For Chileans, therefore, Tarapacá symbolized state violence and rebellious vitality, repression and transformation.

The seemingly simple incident of the street musicians raises questions about the ways in which political and social struggles for dominance (hegemony) can employ narratives, images, and sensations from the past to animate or resist specific projects. Furthermore, it shows how hegemonic processes operate both in spite of and in intimate linkage with histories of state violence by creating possibilities, significations, and constraints for that violence.[3] The idea and particular elements of "the past" get mobilized in multiple ways to generate specific kinds of support (affective ties) for political projects, while other aspects of the past must be erased to make those projects viable — in short, the cultural and political processes of remembering and forgetting.

The memories sustained in narratives — such as historiography, educational texts, or state documents coming from or intimately connected with the state — adopt, deny, or erase specific aspects of the histories of both repression and resistance, which in turn inform the tactical choices of political players on the deployment of violence. Social movements in Chile, such as the contemporary human-rights movements, emerge at particular conjunctures, constructing and sustaining memories through songs, poems, plays, folk tales, and the like in order to "recover" memories of state violence for their own political projects. In addition, groups such as the Chilean political parties represented in the state via congress or the presidency attempt to transform structures of power from within, as well as wider understandings of the past within the cultural frameworks available to them at any given point in time. These competing memories are a key component of hegemony, and by examining their deployment one can better understand the ways in which power and violence are intertwined.

Memory in Northern Chile's Tarapacá has persisted as a nebulous realm filled with the promise, but never the guarantee, of liberatory action. Although widely regarded as a positive component in political struggles, memory has also often played a role in domination. Even as activists, artists, and leaders have refashioned their own stories of struggle, their own and dominant visions of the past also have contributed to a history of deception and degradation. Throughout the twentieth century, state officials and allies have used forms of memory to occult state violence in Tarapacá. Both state officials and oppositional activists in Santiago—Chile's capital, located almost two thousand kilometers south—have summoned images of northern desert violence at critical political junctures in the contest over national memory.

Memories of state violence have played a key role both in the constitution of alternative collective projects (e.g., social movements) as well as in state formation, as an examination of their dynamics over time makes clear.[4] Although national memory is traditionally considered the purview of the upper middle classes and the intelligentsia and is articulated in schools, media, and professional history, there is, in fact, a dialectic between and among what come to be regarded as "national" and oppositional memories. On the one hand, the idea that a national memory exists is in part the work of architects who must be specified and defined at any given moment, since the ability to assert a national memory is the product of a struggle for hegemony: thus, the notion that the state makes memory is an effect of the state as an arena of contestation. Oppositional memories are also made by a cast of actors that changes depending on who has less access to the power of the state at any given moment and that includes members of the official opposition and members of sectors marginal even to the opposition. In Chile, different sectors, including those among elites and non-elites, were or were not included in either the national or oppositional fields according to the degree to which they were incorporated or expelled from the political arena, especially as that arena became increasingly organized around the nation-state over the course of the twentieth century.

As I began this research, I was stunned by the brutality of the military dictatorship and inspired by the courage of Chilean human-rights groups struggling for democracy. Yet I remained puzzled by the historical narrative that held sway among the coalition of democratic oppositional parties, a narrative that denied the significance of state violence in the longer course of Chilean history by defining it as an exception, rather than the norm. The opposition parties maintained that Chile was exceptional among Latin American countries for its hundred-and-fifty-year tradition of democracy, a tradition ruptured by the 1973 military coup, whose extreme violence against the Chilean people was depicted as completely unprecedented in degree and scale.[5] The parties of the postdictatorship coalition, the Concertación, talked about state-sponsored brutality, authoritarianism, and even military intervention as historical aberrations from which democratization would return Chile to its authentic, natural state. The violence of the coup was considered a blip in Chile's history.

However, even aberrations have to be accounted for in historical analysis. As I explored the antecedents to the 1973 coup, fellow historians of Chile questioned the logic of putting the coup and prior incidents of violence on the same analytic plane and also of looking at the Chilean state as the *same* state across regimes and even types of regimes. As I looked back in time, I began to see that the story of the state varied dramatically according to the storytellers' position. The scale and kinds of violence that followed the 1973 coup were indeed unprecedented for elite and some middle-class sectors, which had been relatively unscathed in earlier conflicts. But for non-elite sectors, especially in certain localities, did the state violence following the 1973 coup represent relative continuity or dramatic rupture? And could human rights — a set of discourses largely emerging in the post–World War II international political context and often used to frame the recent violence — be useful as an analytic category for thinking about Chile's earlier periods of violence, periods that could in turn enhance current understandings of the politics of human rights?[6]

To answer these questions, I looked to the Northern Chilean desert province of Tarapacá, a place whose state violence has a deep temporal resonance and where contemporary human-rights issues have been key. The many struggles of people from Tarapacá, known as the "cradle of Chilean politics," implicate violence as integral both to state formation and to memories of that formation, and suggest that violence enters into the making of Chilean politics precisely from this northern cradle. The cruel legacies of even colonial Tarapacá emerge in tales of indigenous slaves working the silver mines of Huantajaya; in the major religious dance festival of La Tirana (the female tyrant), the incarnation of the Virgin as a renegade Incan princess who taunted and warred against Europeans until her conversion and martyrdom; and in accounts of the brutal treatment of Chinese indentured labor in the nineteenth-century guano industry.[7] The Chilean military conquest of the nitrate riches of Tarapacá from Peru in the War of the Pacific (1879) cemented the centrality of violence on the frontier in Chilean state formation. But violence works in relation to political projects, not apart from them. While many studies of memory and the nation support the idea of the nation-state as constituted by a foundational moment of state violence, which must then be forgotten for the nation to cohere, I argue that nation-state formation instead entails an ongoing dynamic of violent conjunctures policing belonging and negotiated memories of that violence.

Political projects that blend coercion and consent to build viable claims to power (hegemony) require certain connections between their constituency and the project; and what is required to build claims changes over time depending on the political project. A long-range view pulls together periods and phenomena (e.g., labor history, political history, cultural history) not usually connected in the historiography and can reveal shifts in the affective ties mobilized in various projects of nation-state building. Even in Chile, where state building has been central to the overarching political culture, nation-state formation does not take a single form, nor is it a single project at any given moment. "The state" comprises multiple actors, organizational forms, agendas, and ideologies. In state formation those divergent aspects coalesce into an entity that exudes coherence, continuity, and agency — for example, in its ability to set and enforce policies, deliver services, and represent itself vis-à-vis other states and interests.

For any political project to work, citizens must care about and invest appropriately in that project: if fascism is at stake, citizens must be willing to militarize and die; if syndicalism is at stake, citizens must be willing to unionize and strike and even support the strikes of others. Scholars have pointed to the centrality of memory in nation-building, memory being the core of a unified imagining of the nation's story, with different memories representing the positions of competing actors.[8] For Chile, such analysis has been applied only to the post–1973 coup era.[9] Drawing on this work on memory and competing visions of the nation, I look over a longer period of time to map the changes in political culture by tracing out the predominant shared mode of memory for different periods.

Memory becomes the glue that binds diverse actors to political projects, and to be effective, the glue has to make sense not only ideologically for the project it serves but also in terms of much wider cultural logics (doxa, scripts, schema, mentalité, culture). Those cultural frameworks are themselves shaped not only by ideological interventions but even more so by cultural dynamics beyond the control of particular actors. For example, 1930s German fascism gained traction only because of the cultural sensibilities of the time, such as hyper-aesthetic images of the male body and of certain landscapes, which the fascists exploited and exaggerated.[10] Even when discredited in dominant politics, these ideologies and sensibilities were never totally eradicated but reemerged in new, albeit less empowered, forms at other conjunctures (e.g., skinheads in 1980s Britain). In terms of methodology, one must resist the temptation to employ memory as a transhistorical category in which only the content, format, or venues change.[11] Instead, one can best understand the way a particular form of memory works at any given moment by using a broader model in which memory is understood as part of the glue (the memory-work) that makes people care about and participate in political projects; this glue must change in relation to the changing forms of those projects, along with the terms of political contests and cultural sensibilities in general.[12]

Memory (a key way of generating affective ties) flows from particular kinds of political projects. I not only explore memory as content (what gets remembered) or containers (monuments, literature, holidays) of the past, but I also develop a template for examining how relationally delineated moments in time forge particular affective ties, that is, modes of relating one person or group to other persons or groups and degrees of identification with an other.[13] The very shape of memory varies across time because the kinds of affective ties change, as does the line separating past, present, and future (periodization). For example, the sense of proximity to the U.S. Civil War felt by a Southern Daughter of the Confederacy, who likely refers to the war as the "Late Unpleasantness," might contrast with that felt by a Midwesterner, who might or might not even know whether her great-great-grandfather fought.[14] Changes in the kinds of affective ties and sense of proximity to any given past moment happen both because of explicit ideological work and because of larger cultural shifts, the latter usually being more significant. The culturally specific emotional connections and drives that constitute memory thus have a history.

For political projects, memory is a powerful way of building the ties required to carry out projects of nation-state formation—how people come to identify with, support, and even sacrifice for any given project. The degree to which those ties that constitute social movements and political mobilizations or institutions (e.g., political parties, unions, human-rights groups) are horizontal (e.g., class solidarity) and/or vertical (e.g., nationalism) vary, as do the ways of imagining connections to projects of nation-state building. The use of memory in all of these projects is about shaping particular subjectivities, including those of polities, without which these projects would be unimaginable.

I present a model for looking at the broad context of moments of state violence, of moments of recuperation and mobilization, and of the connections and gaps between these events and historical narratives. Through a historical and ethnographic account of memory as social action, I elaborate the ways in which competing social memories enable, constrain, and inhibit action both in non-elite sectors and social institutions, and in exercises of state power.

Tarapacá in the *Camanchacas Calientes* (Hot Mists) of Chilean History

A study of Tarapacá, with its desert plains and ports, offers a unique vantage point for the study of memory, state terror, national dynamics, and subaltern cultures in twentieth-century Chile, a vantage point whose intriguing elusiveness perhaps stems from the interaction of its people with its physical geography. When I returned to Chile in 1998, I met again with Alfonso Reyes, a former political prisoner who had been held at the concentration camp at Pisagua and in other prisons. We met in his hometown, Iquique, a port city and the capital of Tarapacá. Alfonso directed my attention to the late afternoon sky filled with clouds that extended over the ocean. He explained to me that clouds moving inland were chilled by the waters of the Humboldt Current before stretching over the coastal mountain range, where they would transform into a dense fog and advance toward the Andes until they completely covered the *pampa*, the strip of land that forms the table of the Atacama Desert. This dramatic ascent covers a mere 150 kilometers.[15] This is the *camanchaca*, a fog that appears daily from autumn until spring, forming in evenings and disappearing each morning as the desert sun burns off the humidity. I recounted to Alfonso what I knew: that since the heyday of the nitrate-mining industry (1890–1930), northern folklore has associated the camanchaca with subversive and even nefarious actions. Under the cover of this fog, workers would meet to organize strikes. The fog also hid robbery, assassination, and betrayal. Elaborating on this dual association, Alfonso explained that las camanchacas were pre-Incan indigenous groups of fishers who, from time to time, would go to the Andes to pick food in the oasis orchards of other indigenous groups. He added that the phrase "to kill with the camanchaca" originated in the nitrate era, when Chileans would knife their (often Peruvian and Bolivian) rivals, crimes hidden by the fog. Alfonso said, "Things are *done* under the camanchaca."[16]

The camanchaca appeared often in conversations I had with *pampinos* (people of the desert) about the era of nitrate mining that spanned the late nineteenth century and the early twentieth. The pampinos liked to tell the joke about the nitrate miner who went to his British supervisor and reported that the camanchaca had set in and so all work had been halted. The ignorant but arrogant foreigner imperiously commanded, "Very well then, get a gun and go hunt this camanchaca down!" That the camanchaca eluded the voraciousness of the extractors of Chile's wealth, the precious salt that gilded their patrimony, delighted these pampinos.

The camanchaca's elusive, autonomous mobility appears in another common saying, used to describe a nitrate miner who, in search of better wages, conditions, or adventure, suddenly left one nitrate camp for another: "Se fue con la camanchaca" (He took off with the camanchaca). This saying is still used to describe sudden departures. The camanchaca thus offers an apt metaphor for thinking about memory in northern Chile: persistent, elusive, ironic, and both sheltering and obscuring possibilities for emancipatory politics. Today, the pampa is littered with the debris of extractive industry, and the inhabitants' sense of abandonment is palpable in the slag heaps and dynamited trenches of the old nitrate fields.

This abandonment is manifested in the historiography of the North, which stops abruptly in the 1930s with the collapse of the nitrate industry. In providing a narrative of Tarapacá that spans from the late nineteenth century to the present, I join historian Luis Castro's effort to, in his term, de-nitrate (*desalitrizar*) regional history.[17] Ironically, the fact that most historical accounts do not reach beyond one period of time makes Tarapacá an ideal place to challenge a central problem in the historiography of Chile: the tendency to place the 1973 coup, subsequent dictatorship, and transition to democracy in a longer historical explanatory framework that defines the coup as an isolated, singular moment of state violence. Furthermore, the fact that scholarly literature is laid out in topical divisions (e.g., labor versus political versus cultural topics) obscures broader shifts in the political cultures of nation-state formation, since each period has its own lens and preferred forms of subjectivity (e.g., "workers," "the people") and, hence, interpellations.[18]

To construct a long-range perspective on nation-state formation that places the memory-work of elites along side that of violently marginalized sectors, I elucidate the conjunctures of state violence where shifts in the affective ties that connect divergent actors to political projects — that is, the political cultures of nation-state formation — emerge most clearly. Although chapter 2 elaborates the analytic framework for tracing modes of memory shaping Chilean political culture over time, I offer here an overview of the broad processes of nation-state formation as lived on the frontier. Four themes regarding Chilean nation-state formation emerge from the intersection of national and regional history: (1) the sovereignty and very form of the nation-state as negotiated vis-à-vis imperialism; (2) the tensions generated as a tenacious elite dealt with the expanding claims of nonelite sectors, especially as these sectors gained, lost, and gained wider access to the political system; (3) the role of the military as a key state sector that came to see itself as an apolitical institution mediating competing political interests and thus anchoring the nation; and (4) the resiliency of the Chilean state as an entity in which actors across the political spectrum are able to invest — despite the variety of contending visions of the nation — and how that investment in state-oriented political culture often came with the damping down of contestatory voices and movements. The following overview presents the North as a place where the tensions of nation-state formation, true for Chile in general, come together most visibly as dramatic mobilizations and clashes. Moreover, this overview provides the reader with a general sense of the trajectory of Chilean history to support the conjunctures dealt with in each chapter.

The Oligarchic Parliamentary State and the "Heroic" Period of Nitrate Mining (1890–1930) * In 1879 Chile defeated Peru in the War of the Pacific and conquered the territory of Tarapacá and with it its "white gold," the world's largest geological supply of sodium nitrate.[19] Chilean interests and workers had been heavily involved in nitrate production since the industry's beginnings in the 1860s. Increasing government instability in the Andean republics — Peru and Bolivia — and the initiatives of those republics to exert more national direction over the nitrate industry finally encouraged Chile, with the support of

British interests, to declare an audacious war for which it was largely unprepared. Remarkably, the Peruvian-Bolivian alliance proved even more inept, and Chile won the nitrate fields. Both Peru and Bolivia were politically humiliated: Peru lost a key source of its wealth, the nitrate fields of Tarapacá, and Bolivia lost both its nitrate fields and its access to the ocean. The War of the Pacific, along with military conquest of southern indigenous lands, expanded Chile's territory and its fortune by providing export revenues sufficient to secure the leisure, wealth, and authority of the nation's oligarchy and the state it controlled.[20]

The Chilean oligarchy had built remarkable consensus since the early-nineteenth-century War of Independence from the Spanish, and because of this consensus Chile was an exceptionally stable republic among the newly independent Latin American countries. This stability happened under de facto authoritarian leadership and via the unity of the small oligarchical elite who determined the shape of the emerging political system — remarkable given that civil wars between elite liberal and conservative parties had torn up so many other countries. The oligarchy viewed the nation as their particular purview and their role vis-à-vis the rest of the populace as one of paternalist guardianship.

Thus, given that, according to the historians Gabriel Salazar and Julio Pinto, the state consolidated well before the nation in nineteenth-century Chile, international warfare presented a context in which Chile could bind the state to a more encompassing conception of the nation through militarized patriotism. Broader incorporation of the populace came as poor people were mobilized to fight for the nation on conquered soil.[21] The expansion and consolidation of the Chilean state in newly conquered territories of the North cast as the fundamental national protagonist the *roto chileno*, a racialized category of worker-soldier whose industry mined the nitrate fields of the North and whose mestizo fighting valor had enabled the territorial conquest.

In this way, the War of the Pacific not only wed the oligarchy and state to a reliance on an enclave export economy but also forged the centrality of the military as the guardian of national honor. The 1879 war made Tarapacá famous for its battle sites and its war heroes, and secured for the North an enduring place in Chilean military history.[22] For the Chilean military, order is honor; thus, to defend national honor on the frontier and ensure internal order, the Chilean military has occupied Tarapacá since the War of the Pacific. Yet, as noted by Pinto, shortly after conquering the territory, the Chilean state sought to win legitimacy in the region by restraining an overly enthusiastic military occupying force that had carried out frequent punitive and preemptive raids against local residents.[23] Thus began a complex dynamic between state administrative officials and the agents of state violence in crafting a ruling project. To mitigate the military raids, the Chilean government launched a project they called "Chileanization," the incorporation of the territory and its population into the Chilean nation-state through avenues such as primary and adult education and religion,[24] key vehicles for promulgating official memory.

However, building official national memory entailed the challenge of dealing with ongoing violence within the state and against the populace. By the end of the nineteenth century, nitrate was firmly in the hands of British interests and, to a lesser extent, other European business interests, all of whom insisted that the Chilean state maintain social order for the nitrate industries in Tarapacá by repressing strikes and other labor activities.[25] As the primary source of national revenue, the province of Tarapacá and its capital, Iquique, became the sites of internal state contests, most notably the military battles during the Chilean Civil War of 1891 between President José Manuel Balmaceda and the Congress over the role of foreign interests in the nitrate industry. President Balmaceda favored greater domestic control over key sectors of the nitrate industrial infrastructure, especially the British-owned railways that carried the nitrate from the desert plains to the ports, while Congress, defending the interests of an oligarchy that lived off of minimal nitrate rents, supported policies friendly to foreign investment in the export enclave. During the civil war, Iquique was even declared the national capital by the British-backed congressional forces that had sailed north to claim the customs house for their cause. Nitrate moved the nation-state north. Nitrate also kept the nation-state looking outward.

From 1890 to 1930, nitrate was exported to Europe for use in fertilizer and explosives until Europeans developed a cheaper synthetic (1916). As the nexus between foreign and national interests, Iquique, a port city and the administrative core of the booming mining industry, also became the center of the first major labor organizations and general strikes in Chilean history. The ability to launch strikes was remarkable in part because the nitrate industry drew labor not only from Southern Chile but also from Argentina, Peru, and

Bolivia (all Chilean state rivals), which meant that the labor movement had to surmount vast ethnic and national differences in this frontier zone.[26] Transnational migration, by virtue of the juxtapositions made in crossing frontiers, tends to make national subjects (with attendant prejudices) out of migrant laborers.[27] Yet, workers shared experiences entailed in wage labor and were further united by the particular nature of the desert nitrate industry, in which an acute concentration and number of workers had to rely completely on wage labor. Together, these conditions facilitated the growth of a vibrant labor movement. Labor organizations were but one facet of the workers' initiatives; they also created civic associations, including schools, adult-education programs, cultural centers, women's centers, and publications.[28]

As nitrate workers became better organized and launched repeated strikes for better conditions, the working-class communities of Tarapacá were confronted with a number of violent assaults by the Chilean military between 1890 and 1930. The most famous of these was the 1907 massacre (memorialized in "Cantata Santa María de Iquique" and many other works) in which striking workers and their supporters were slaughtered in the courtyard of a public school, the Escuela Santa María de Iquique.[29] Though this was but one of a number of violent repressions, the attack at the Escuela Santa María came to symbolize the struggles of the labor movement in Chile at that moment and for later generations.

With World War I, the boom-and-bust cycles of the international economy reached roller-coaster proportions. In Chile fluctuations in prices meant economic and political volatility, because the national economy, arguably more than any other in the world at that time, was driven by an enclave export sector (nitrate) and thus organically tied to the world economy.[30] This economic instability, exacerbated by ongoing pressures from labor (buttressed by the example and internationalist initiatives of the Russian Revolution and the flourishing of anarchist revolutionary movements), culminated in the armed forces' intervention against the stalemate of oligarchic parliamentary politics that had characterized the state from the 1890s to the mid-1920s. The military, under Carlos Ibáñez del Campo, pushed through legislation and fiscal reform, especially increased provisions for the armed forces and labor laws. Ultimately, the crisis led to a constitutional convention that generated the Constitution of 1925. This period of political crisis and authoritarian military intervention in the central state was marked in the already militarized North by an ongoing violent border dispute with Peru—not resolved until 1929—and by massive military campaigns against striking workers in 1924 and 1925 (including the La Coruña massacre).

This period of nation-state formation was marked by a consolidation of the idea of the Chilean nation through military conquest (primarily of the North) and the oligarchy's ongoing monopoly of access to the state—an oligarchy that rhetorically imagined the nation as a patriarchal family, lived off of a cut of the revenues from the enclave export economy of the North, and stalemated the political process with its death-grip on parliamentary politics and its extensive use of the military to suppress non-elite agitation, especially in the North. To a large degree, both elite and non-elite sectors recognized the incommensurability of their interests and mobilized the rubric of absolute class warfare (in which the Chilean elite's interests were also those of international elites). In the context of state and elite negligence, non-elite semiautonomous civic life flourished even as elite political culture stagnated. The stalemate in formal politics was broken by military intervention which reoriented nation-state formation (Constitution of 1925) according to an emerging vision of the nation-to-state nexus.

The Populist Period: Mass Expansion of the Political System (1930–1973)

* I term "populist" the period that occurred between the two major military interventions of the twentieth century, because of the ongoing dynamic in which political culture across the ideological spectrum became oriented around vibrant multiparty coalitions whose main aim was to access state power (primarily through the presidency), an aim justified by claims to the nation as incorporating wide swaths of the populace ("the people").

The military intervention of the 1920s broke down the oligarchy's monopoly on politics in the form of a gridlocked parliament. This military intervention together with the economic devastation of the Great Depression, the collapse of the nitrate industry, and the ongoing mobilizations of non-elite sectors forced a dramatic expansion of the entire political system. Multiple political parties encompassed an array of ideological positions and began to build thriving party cultures (with their own modes of organization, songs, traditions, etc.) that incorporated both party militants and their wider social networks. In terms of state formation, access to state power required coalition building between parties to compete for the increasingly powerful presidency. Furthermore, politics was based on a new premise about the nature of the state-nation nexus: that the polity for the nation-state was composed of "the people," writ large. Though different administrations handled these dynamics in varying ways, even the old parties of the elite adapted themselves to the new political formation, albeit ambivalently. This dynamic flourished until the 1973 military coup, when the military once again stepped in to reorient nation-state formation.

In using a broad brush-stroke to paint this period as populist, I note the historian Paul Drake's caution that populist ideologies undergirded a system of paternalistic state capitalism that in many ways exacerbated inequalities even as Chile made important gains in areas such as housing, health, and education.[31] Still, the exponential expansion of the political system in spite of the gap between ideology and practice is actually a testament to the hegemonic success of a national-popular project. A national-popular project is one in which "the people" (defined broadly to include non-elite sectors) is seen as the core of the nation which should be expressed by the state even as encompassing cross-class political projects compete for the state by anchoring their claims in nationalism.

Even though the definitive decline of nitrate mining after 1929 (following the crisis dating from World War I) rendered the North an economic backwater, Tarapacá continued to be a center of Chilean working-class mobilization and resistance, especially in the rise of multiparty national-populist politics. The little nitrate production that remained was reorganized as a joint venture between the Chilean state and U.S. investors. Though Tarapacá had lost almost its entire economic base, regional political and social connections and skills cultivated in the nitrate era remained.[32] The military intervention of the mid-1920s led to the Ibáñez del Campo dictatorship, a period marked by grave political persecution.[33] Ibáñez del Campo's authoritarian efforts to mitigate the economic decline of the 1920s drowned under the tide of the Great Depression. The collapse of Chile's export-driven economy created a space for more participatory politics and for the rise of multiple cross-class political parties that became direct players in the contest over the central state, initially in the form of short-lived socialist juntas and eventually stabilizing in the coalition governments of the Popular Front.[34] The Popular Front followed a political model promoted by the Soviet Union, via the

Chilean Communist Party, of creating governing alliances with the Socialist, Social Democrat, and Radical Parties to combat fascism around the world. Chile's Popular Front was arguably the most successful case of such experimental coalitions and, at least in the Chilean context, demonstrated the necessity and advantage of coalition governments in the emerging mid-twentieth-century political system.[35]

Specifically, Chilean politics took on a three-pronged form of parties self-defined as leftist (predominantly the Communist and various Socialist Parties), centrist (the Radical Party, the Social Democrat Party, and the Falange Party, which would become the Christian Democrat Party — these parties, especially the Christian Democrat, could swing ideologically depending on a number of factors from geopolitical to personal politics), and rightist (the Liberal Party, the Conservative Party of the landed oligarchy, and a number of fascist movements).[36] Thus, the relational categories of Left, Center, and Right mapped a multiparty, multiclass political system relying on alliances between sectors to establish government administrations. The continuities in the shape of this political culture as directed overwhelmingly toward competitive positions vis-à-vis the state mark the period between the military intervention of the 1920s and that of 1973, when the military once again stepped in as a purportedly apolitical force to reorient nation-state formation.

Although the populist period marked the end of Tarapacá's economic importance for the nation, Tarapacá nevertheless offers one of the best vantage points for tracing out the rise of vibrant populist political culture — a testament to the strength of the cultural and social fabric woven during the nitrate era, which continues to lend the region particular significance in the broader national imaginary. The most important parties of the Left and Center — namely, the Communist, Socialist, and Christian Democrat Parties — were born or at least nurtured in the North.[37] Thus, even after the decline of nitrate mining, the North played a vital role in national politics as the breeding ground for national political and labor leaders and as a stronghold for political parties of the Left. To this day, the office of senator from Tarapacá continues to be coveted across the political spectrum, as it indicates both political clout and greater political aspirations; it is often held by distinguished public figures (like Pablo Neruda) or by political-party presidents and national presidential hopefuls (like Arturo Allessandri Palma, who made his early political reputation as the "Lion of Tarapacá"). At the same time, due to its strategic importance as a frontier and its symbolic importance in militarist national history, the North has been the proving ground for military officials; of particular note, both Ibáñez del Campo and Pinochet served in the North just before intervening in national politics. Tarapacá's charged dual role in national-populist and militarist versions of nation-state history largely explains the acute violence of political conflict in the region, which reached its pinnacle in the Cold War era.

With the onset of the Cold War and the consolidation of the United States as the key foreign player in the Chilean political economy, which was by then dominated by copper mining, the state under Radical Party President Gonzalez Videla broke with the Popular Front alliance and banned the Chilean Communist Party, imprisoning Communist Party members and other political and labor activists.[38] The main prison camp—located in Pisagua, a nitrate port in the province of Tarapacá, which was almost completely deserted at the time—was used as a detention center again in 1956 and, more important, after the 1973 military coup.[39]

In 1973 the military intervened in politics to thwart the *vía chilena*, Chile's self-proclaimed "Road to Revolution/Socialism," meaning the redistribution of economic and political resources (much along the lines of Western European states) through democratic processes, specifically elections and legislation (in explicit contrast to Cuba's armed revolution). Led by President Salvador Allende, the Popular Unity coalition government—comprising the Communist, Socialist, and Social Democratic Parties, as well as radical elements of the Christian Democrat Party and the Christian Left—was narrowly elected to continue the profound economic reforms (meant to counteract the appeal of "communism") begun under the prior Christian Democratic administration of Eduardo Frei and funded by U.S. President John F. Kennedy's Alliance for Progress: namely, the break-up of large unproductive estates and the nationalization of the copper-mining industry. As a historic stronghold for the Left, Northern Chile played a key role in this democratic revolution, and it became the point of initiation for a number of the Allende government's policy initiatives, especially those dealing with the distribution of consumer goods.

The initial success of these transformations galvanized the Chilean Right, fascist sectors of the military (both active and retired, a number of the top ranks of which had been trained in 1930s Germany), and the United States (acting in the interests of the U.S. military's

Cold War strategists and of major U.S. corporations such as Anaconda Copper and International Telephone and Telegraph) in an alliance formed to derail the democratic revolution through a three-phase initiative: first, in what they called Track I, the alliance attempted to prevent Popular Unity's election by generously financing the opposition, through a publicity campaign designed to terrorize the population, and through military unrest; second, in Track II, having failed to impede Allende's election, it tried to prevent Allende from assuming office, most notably by the paramilitary assassination of the head of the armed forces, General René Schneider; and Track III, having failed to prevent Allende from taking office, it conspired to unseat the Popular Unity government through massive economic destabilization (undercutting the price of copper, withdrawing international financing, and creating shortages of consumer goods) along with violent political and military unrest (both within the armed forces and by paramilitary groups — unrest exacerbated by the paramilitary activities of leftist revolutionary groups).

In Northern Chile the effects of the destabilization were particularly acute, since much of the contraband for the black market (including a dynamic drug trade) entered through the North.[40] The smugglers bought cheap Chilean products — especially food — and sold them in Peru and Bolivia, creating *desabastecimiento*, grave shortages of food and basic goods like clothes, paper products, soap powder, and other household items. This was known as the *contrabando de hormigas* (ant smuggling): in effect, Chile was hemorrhaging vital consumer goods through its northern frontier, exacerbating the impact of merchants' hoarding and of the U.S. economic embargo designed to bring down the government. The lack of basic goods successfully undermined public support of the socialist state. Partially in response to illegal commerce, the North became the testing ground for state interventions geared toward the provisioning of the population through more rational and secure distribution of goods. The destabilization campaign was further magnified in the North because ongoing frontier tensions with Peru kept the military on constant alert there.[41] This third phase of destabilization propelled the extremely violent military coup of 11 September 1973, with the subsequent execution and disappearance of thousands and the exiling of nearly 10 percent of the population.[42] The North was particularly targeted for repression, given its high level of political mobilization and militarization. Right-wing paramilitary groups had even made advance preparations in Iquique to make it their stronghold should the military coup not progress as smoothly as planned, that is, in case of substantial armed resistance by defenders of Chile's democracy. Thus, Tarapacá was the site of especially widespread terror (along with the indigenous agricultural lands of the South) since the military needed to immediately ensure control over the region. In Iquique approximately 8 percent (about 1,000) of the young adult male population (twenty to forty years of age) was rounded up and taken mainly to the prison camp at Pisagua (along with at least five people over sixty years of age who had been prisoners there in 1948), where almost all of the region's top political leaders (of the parties participating in the overthrown government) were executed. Prisoners were also kept in the Telecommunications Regiment in Iquique. So-called wartime courts-martial (*consejos de guerra*) were held both in Iquique and Pisagua. Tarapacá was the last stop on the infamous Caravan of Death, an operation in which Pinochet appointed a death squad which traveled by helicopter up the length of the country to consolidate rule by ensuring that regional commanders quickly executed the Left's leadership. In Pisagua the Northern regional commander had already implemented military control so enthusiastically that the death squad merely stopped by to toast the military's success.

The populist period of nation-state formation entailed the dramatic expansion of the political system — due to intra-elite competition and pressure from below — to incorporate non-elite sectors of the population and a fundamental reorientation of political culture around a vision of the state as expressing the nexus between nation and the people (understood as broadly encompassing sectors across the populace). This resulted in a highly competitive multiparty political culture (born in the North) oriented around gaining access to the state through coalition politics. These coalitions required alliances based on mutual understanding across differing though partly compatible interests (what I call empathy). Chile remained an enclave export-oriented economy enmeshed in Cold War geopolitics (epitomized in the series of Pisagua prison camps). The image of Chile as a laboratory for ideological projects took hold in this period. The effort to use the state to redistribute power and wealth more equitably and with greater sovereignty vis-à-vis foreign business interests resulted in elite consolidation in consort with those foreign interests to back a military intervention aimed at redirecting the path of nation-state formation.

The Neoliberal State from Bureaucratic-Authoritarian Military Dictatorship and International Human-Rights Solidarity to Civilian Rule (1973–2006) * The military overthrow of the Popular Unity government resulted in General Pinochet's rise to power and the imposition of his military rule through what political scientists term the bureaucratic-authoritarian state. Such regimes usually have hyperformal structures of rule and procedure, even within states that rely on heavy doses of coercion, tightly limited access of nonmilitary sectors to the state apparatus, and an almost complete shutdown of civil society. That Chile's bureaucratic-authoritarian military regime and the subsequent civilian regime could be considered part of the same period of nation-state formation may be somewhat surprising. Yet, both regimes were encompassed by overarching processes of state formation: the building up to and implementation of the 1980 Constitution and the restructuring of the Chilean political economy around neoliberal principles of a free-market economy facilitated by a laissez-faire state.

The overtly fascist design of the 1973 prison camp at Pisagua in terms of the physical plant and organizational structure revealed the fascist underpinnings of the military regime — evidence of the continuities in institutional culture between pro-coup military sectors and the Prussian-trained army that emerged from the 1891 Civil War when it defeated the vestiges of the republican military forged in the Wars of Independence and the conquering military which had participated in indigenous suppression and the War of the Pacific. Authoritarian tendencies instilled by the Chilean army's early Prussian trainers were cemented through ongoing military connections, including the training of army officers in 1930s Germany; although in retirement by 1970, this officer corps played a key role in the anti-democratic agitation and logistical planning that made the coup possible. Fascist tendencies melded well with the Cold War ideologies of National Security Doctrine, which drew on counter-insurgency warfare tactics developed by France and the United States, including individual torture and generalized fear (state terror). Using the National Security Doctrine's rendition of the nation as a specific territory encompassing a culturally homogenous populace (which entailed the eradication of ideological difference), the military redrew the governing map of Chile, establishing numbered "regions" that were, in effect, military command zones (Tarapacá was Region I). A parallel command structure — one for the military per se and another for the state apparatus—further consolidated power in the hands of General Pinochet, who had wrested control of the coup junta. The remolded military asserted itself as the apolitical guardian of national honor and attempted to structurally and culturally reshape both the military and the nation. Thus, even while seizing the state to radically militarize the nation, Chile's bureaucratic-authoritarian state built on national and international continuities in military institutional culture and the broader political culture.[43]

Though never able to comfortably consolidate his control over Chile and thus having to rely on the ongoing terrorization of the population, Pinochet ruled by decrees expressed in exaggerated legalistic style but with no constitutional basis. For example, the civil codes were edited to suit the military and republished as though they expressed legal continuity. The military implemented neoliberal economic restructuring of the economy, selling off state properties and industries, cutting social services and opening up privatization (especially in healthcare and education), and facilitating foreign investment through monetarist regulation of the export-oriented economy. These economic initiatives built on two prior reforms: the break-up of unproductive large estates and the revenue-generating nationalization of copper. With these elements already in place, Chile could launch export-oriented agribusiness (apples, grapes, wine, etc.) and leverage its international-debt situation. State social services— especially healthcare, education, and utilities—that had been virtually eliminated in the name of anticommunism were now available for commodification. Seeking a more permanent institutional framework to legitimize the regime, Pinochet's government in 1980 ratified a pro-military constitution that provided for further institutionalization measures—namely, a referendum on military rule—at the end of that decade.[44]

Together with efforts to manufacture institutional legitimacy, state violence continued to be a defining feature of military rule. After the initial widespread executions and disappearances, which were designed to eliminate the civilian Center-Left leadership and pro-civilian military personnel and thus to consolidate military control, the most demographically significant manifestation of state repression was the military's use of internal exile (relegation) and external exile (nearly 10 percent of the population ended up abroad for some period of time), achieved both directly, by expelling people, and indirectly, by making it clear that certain people should flee for their lives. The exiles used their political and cultural skills to mobilize international support, which came to be called "solidarity," to pressure for Chile's return civilian rule. Exiled Chileans also showed support for anti-authoritarian causes in other parts of the world and thus became a model for subsequent solidarity movements, such as the anti-apartheid coalition on South Africa and the opposition to U.S. intervention in Central America.

The Chilean solidarity movement was aided by international outrage over the Chilean military's cooperation with other military regimes in the region (e.g., the infamous Operation Condor, whereby people exiled from one country to another were hunted down by joint security forces) and over assassinations of exiled Chileans in other countries (most important, U.S. government support of Pinochet chilled when a car bombing in Washington killed a former Popular Unity government official and his U.S. assistant).

Internal support of the military was eroded not only by growing international pressure to reform but also by Chile's ongoing vulnerability to fluctuations in the world economy in the recession of the early 1980s, and there was a concomitant flourishing of "new" social movements among the populace: human-rights organizing, largely a middle-class phenomenon; the seizure of settlement land for poor people; shantytown efforts to organize for basic needs (soup kitchens, collective purchasing of food and other necessities, alternative-education projects); the establishment of research institutes for the opposition; support services for activists, such as mental-health clinics; and the renewed use of cultural forms to mobilize the populace, such as music (including *peñas*, or folk-music events), crafts (including the famous *arpilleras*, or quilted depictions of state violence), theater, and religion (liberation-theology study groups). Many of these efforts benefited from international solidarity funds and especially from the Chilean Catholic Church and were supported by progressive Catholic international orders such as the Maryknolls. Thus flourished a contestatory — though semiclandestine — civic sphere of vibrant social movements that embodied multiple collectivities.

The military responded with a renewed campaign of generalized state terror — although especially in poor neighborhoods — including the torture, imprisonment (e.g., the Pisagua prison camp of 1984), and disappearance of activists. International branches of the exiled political party leadership encouraged armed resistance to military rule, which was met with similarly brutal repression and limited military success.[45] Nevertheless, the mobilizations did erode the military's claims to legitimate rule and forced it to keep to the terms of its own constitution, which provided for an up-or-down plebiscite on military rule under General Pinochet at the end of the 1980s.

From the earliest years of his military rule, General Pinochet considered development of the North to be his pet project, given that, prior to the coup, he had spent a number of years in the area as regional commander and often as acting governor. The military, too, had decided to reinforce the region, albeit for strategic reasons: they anticipated another Peruvian war in light of the hundredth anniversary of the War of the Pacific. In addition to strengthening its armed presence, the military regime initiated a series of public works in Iquique, such as paving roads, regularizing the water supply, restoring historic buildings, and fomenting economic development by expanding the existing free-trade zone (originally meant for importing affordable food supplies and, later, industrial equipment) to include large quantities of consumer luxury goods. At the same time, the North was one of the regions hardest hit by the dictatorship, in terms of percentage of the population affected by human-rights violations and the degree of military surveillance, as represented by the high ratio of military personnel and families to the civilian population. As in the nitrate era, the North was a place of key symbolic and material importance both for the military on the Right and for the mobilized non-elite sectors on the Left. As such, the North was a region of intense conflict.

Nation-state formation under military rule saw a reorientation, in the 1980 Constitution, around a conception of the nation grounded in a delineated territory and a homogeneous culture, with the military as the ultimate instantiation of the state's mandate to guard that national honor. Because of certain internal elite and international alliances, the military regime increasingly embraced a neoliberal conception of the laissez faire state whose primary mandate was the facilitation of market forces. In doing so, General Pinochet and his supporters developed close (sympathetic) friendships with the neoliberal vanguard in other nations, especially with Britain's Margaret Thatcher. Oppositional sectors mobilized against the military in "solidarity" movements that generated powerful appeals for sympathy within Chile (from less-politicized sectors) and internationally (from both governments and organizations).

Attempting to legitimize its rule by keeping to the terms of the 1980 Constitution, the regime held a plebiscite on military rule in 1988. The military lost. As stipulated in the constitution, the loss resulted in presidential and congressional elections, which led to the reestablishment of civilian rule in 1990. Governing through a coalition of Center-Left parties known as the Concertación, the three subsequent, civilian administrations (Aylwin, 1990–1994; Frei, 1994–2000; Lagos, 2000–2006) intensified the export-oriented neoliberal reforms begun under Pinochet's regime, though they significantly increased attention to issues of poverty. Yet they could not dismantle many of the legacies of military rule, including the everyday authoritarian structures of military privilege and institutional mechanisms designed both to insure overrepresentation of military-regime interests and to inhibit the ability of the civilian regime to make significant changes in the trajectory of nation-state formation. The 1980 Constitution imposed electoral limits that gave disproportional congressional representation to minority parties (at that time, the Right), packed the congress and the judiciary with pro-military senators and judges, limited civil rights, and emphasized centralized rule. Furthermore, the personnel and internal structures of the military, including Pinochet's role as commander-in-chief, persevered through the 1990s (due to generational turnover in leadership, this began to change by the time of the Lagos administration). Such legacies remained in place until the 2005 constitutional reforms, which modified the most overt authoritarian structures.

Most important, for the first decade after military rule, the civilian administrations were largely unable, despite the official rhetoric of reconciliation, to resolve the legacies of human-rights abuses—the fates of the disappeared; the locations of remains of the executed; the civil rights of ex-political prisoners; reparations for subjects of human-rights abuses; the pursuit of judicial trials for human-rights violators—nor address ongoing human-rights violations.

Since the return to civilian rule in 1990, Tarapacá, and specifically Pisagua, has become infamous for the mass grave of some of those killed in 1973. The grave was excavated by the civilian government's allies, who strategically uncovered the remains of this period of Chile's violent history in an effort to shame the military into compliance with the new civilian regime. To the Chilean human-rights movement, the ports of Pisagua and Iquique, and the region of Tarapacá more generally, became national symbols for the recuperation of both the dead and their stories. The excavation of the mass grave and the strength of the local human-rights movement prompted the then recently inaugurated democratic regime to treat Tarapacá as a pilot site for a mental-health and human-rights reparation project for former political prisoners and families of the disappeared. For the political leaders of the governing parties, the detention camps and the mass grave at Pisagua came to represent a pathological breakdown of the organic link between the Chilean state and civil society, a link that required suturing. For many human-rights activists, Pisagua encapsulated a Chilean history of state violence that spanned the twentieth century.[46]

Today Tarapacá is integral to Chile's internationally lauded "free-market miracle." Its primary industries are fishmeal (a Green Revolution project of the 1960s) and copper mining, which appeared more recently due to advances in technology. Pisagua, though still sparsely populated, is slated for development as a tourist destination, and Iquique is once again a thriving port city, with over 175,000 inhabitants and the second-fastest-growing economy in the country. On the other hand, the 1990s construction boom in high-rises can be attributed in part to drug-money laundering, and Tarapacá is home to a notorious arms plant owned by the international arms trafficker Carlos Cardoen.[47]

Iquique continues to be a major strategic and administrative center for the military and has also become a regional commercial and tourist center since a *zona franca* (duty-free zone) was established by the military in 1976.[48] In summer months, shoppers from Argentina, Peru, Bolivia, and southern Chile converge on Iquique's beaches and in its stores. Most recently, Iquique once again registered on the global map when the international press reported that Al Quaeda monies had been traced through that city. Iquique's tendency to focus its economy internationally has remained in place since the era of the nitrate-enclave economy, but even with such vigorous economic activity, Iquique retains the aura of a dusty frontier town in a highly centralized nation-state. Despite its apparent provincialism, Iquique is marked by profound historical changes in the constitution of the nation-state, and study of the region reveals the century-long struggle between international capital, the Chilean state, and local interests.

The postdictatorship era of neoliberal state formation foregrounded the ideal of a civilian, representative regime while preserving as the only imaginable option the market-oriented mandate for state practices of governance. Political parties that had survived in exile reasserted themselves in social movements and nongovernmental organizations as the appropriate locus of activism oriented toward access to the state. The state-driven model of national reconciliation attempted to forge a broader vision of the nation that could bridge the deep divisions between the sector of the population (some 30 to 40 percent) that consistently supported the military regime and those sectors alienated by human-rights abuses and/or economic policies. In the name of national sovereignty, the civilian regime pushed back against international efforts to resolve human-rights activists' claims for justice. The authenticating story of the nation still necessary for any nation-state has increasingly relied on nostalgic evocations — across the political spectrum — of significant moments in Chilean history. Any social or ideologically defined sector that has questioned that framework or tried to reassert demands from prior eras — whether that sector be the remnants of the Communist Party or even General Pinochet himself — has been deemed an anachronism.

Conjunctures of History and Memory in Chile

Within this largely conventional periodization of Chilean politics as defined broadly by the formal structures of governmental regimes — the oligarchic period (1890s–1930s), the populist period (1930s–1973), and the military dictatorship (1973–1990) and postdictatorship (1990–present) period of the market state — particular forms of memory (an explicitly subjective way of connecting past, present, and future) that predominated throughout those periods help specify the nature of change and continuity in political culture.

Political culture comprises particular worldviews and practices through which political sectors are constituted and struggle for power. Nation-state formation has an affective component through which competing political sectors vie for allegiance, loyalty, and solidarity, sectors themselves constituted through these very affective ties. In examining historical shifts within and between these periods of state formation, one cannot presume (as the historiography tends to) that any of these structural changes are necessarily either emancipatory or oppressive, but rather that their often contradictory, ambiguous, and multifaceted characters must be specified for each historical conjuncture.[49]

Prior moments of mobilization and violence inform subsequent conjunctures through deployments of social memory.[50] The re-entrenchment of the state in the wake of violence often works not through simple models of forgetting or silencing, but by narratively subsuming opposition into "stories of national origins, myths of founding fathers, genealogies of heroes. . . . [I]nvestigating the nation is here complicit with the nation's own story."[51] State coercion, in particular, violently obviates forms of emplotment other than its own. Rather than reinforce this obligatory nation-state story, I avoid a narrative-based account by linking the conjunctures that shape my account not chronologically but with a discussion of how the state became the prime object of political desire for actors across the political spectrum during the twentieth century. Central among these processes has been the struggle over memory, from the crafted "forgetting" that inhibited the potential of cathartic memory during the nitrate era, often referred to by labor historians of Chile as the heroic period (1890–1930), to the equally crafted "remembering" that cultivated empathetic memory during the populist period (1930–1973).

The historical contexts for these forms of memory have shaped the constitution of solidarities and political forms, and thus subjectivities. In Chile the expanding political system was negotiated in struggles between and among elite and non-elite sectors, which opened up political participation by shifting historical subjectivities from primarily class-based to populist categories. Even though populist-era political rhetoric still used heavy doses of class language, the expansion of politics to incorporate non-elite sectors, combined with intra-elite competition, necessitated building cross-class coalitions: Popular Unity linked the working classes, middle-class sectors, and some elite youth through ideologies of socialism; the pro-coup sector bound the middle and working classes to elites through ideologies of patronage, nationalism, and consumer discontent.[52] Historical subjectivities shifted from ones forged around class conflict to those ordered by the populist political system and created in the dynamics of regime transitions from socialist democracy to dictatorship to free-market liberal democracy.[53]

The three periods of nation-state formation (with concomitant oppositional sector growth) can be characterized by the forms of memory predominant in Chilean political culture at the time:

(1) memory in the oligarchic-state and labor-movement era was cathartic; (2) memory in the populist-state period was empathetic; (3) memory in the neoliberal-state period was sympathetic during the military dictatorship and oppositional solidarity movements, but came to be dually marked by melancholy and nostalgia during the period of civilian governance. Thus the play of memory in political culture has a history: it changes over time, as political sectors incorporate modes, themes, and images of the past into ideology in different ways at different moments in time. Enforcing History, in this sense, is integral to nation-state formation. Thinking about History as a form of memory enforced, repudiated, and recrafted according to the conjuncture in question reveals how processes of nation-state formation play out as control over definitions of the past and how such definitions have played into struggles for present and future power.

Structures of Memory in Nation-State Formation

The play of memory in politics reflects the larger question of the relationship between ideology and culture. Ideologies as explicit political projects to shape people's understandings of the world are only viable to the degree to which they make sense within larger cultural logics (themselves a moving target, because they change in relation to shifting sensibilities and conditions of possibility) and thus the degree to which people can imagine themselves (their subjectivity which is not prior to but made in the act of recognition) in those projects. This is a dialectical process, since the specific purpose of ideology is to change popular notions of common sense.[54] Thus, the meanings people give to histories of state violence are not constant, but rather are transformed as they are rehabilitated and redeployed through multiple genres or containers of memory, such as songs, poetry, novels, testimonies, theater, state documents, textbooks, historiography, biography, and other cultural texts such as museums and monuments.

Within larger cultural logics, memories of state violence and popular opposition can then be used by political actors to either constrain or facilitate social action at particular historical conjunctures.[55] At certain times, they may be coopted by more dominant sectors, leaving alternative perspectives to be maintained and transmitted principally in the quiet corners of frontiers, while in other periods they can act as oppositional memories, sparking further collective action aimed at creating a more just society. In the words of an old song of the nitrate era,

Huérfanos gime el pueblo	Orphans, cry the people
bajo cadena	under chains
pero tiene en el pecho	but they hold in their breast
una promesa	a promise
Una promesa, sí,	A promise, yes,
que llegará,	that will be fulfilled,
vendrá como un flor	will come like a flower
la libertad	liberty[56]

The unknown writer of this song turned to poetry to document the memories of labor and state violence in his region, showing that memory as a form of social action is not merely a recitation of facts, but springs from and creates historically specific structures of feeling.[57] Memory's history in twentieth-century Chile thus reveals how different emotional or affective stimuli have served to link forms of memory with forms of sociopolitical organization within political projects. In using memory as a call to action, political activists map relations between the past and present, and link both with visions of the future.[58]

Structures of feeling provide a particularly apt model for thinking about the history of memory, especially those forms of memory that contest dominant discourses about the past, the present, and even the future. Raymond Williams argues that structures of feeling work as a methodological tool for exploring the history of cultural politics within which given generations or periods take on "characteristic elements of impulse, restraint, and tone."[59] For instance, what one generation understands about a previous era reveals what they see as distinct about their own moment.[60] This sensibility works as their own "particular sense of life," which leads to ethical postulates about the best or most proper solutions to persistent human concerns, such as the distribution of power or the sharing of resources. Memory is a genealogy or family tree, in the sense that it is the collective understanding of previous generations' ways of life, which shapes the feeling each generation has about itself, which, in turn, configured into semantic formations such as songs and slogans, propels social relations and change.[61] Mapping a periodization of social history onto structures of feeling can thus offer a "hypothesis of a mode of social formation, explicit and recognizable" in particular forms of memory.[62]

To the extent to which any given use of memory for political ends makes sense within the available structures of feeling, memory-projects mobilize political actors through appeals for action that generate various forms and depths of attraction and repulsion. Thinking of memory as also a part of explicit political work resonates with Louis Althusser's conception of ideology as key for the interpellation of subjectivity; like a police officer summoning someone on the street, the invocation of ideology acts as a hailing, in part coercive, that compels response.[63] The evocation of memory, however, can also work like the African American call-and-response ritual between a collective and its leaders, wherein the response serves to validate the integrity of the call.[64]

In Chile memory has been used as a call to action in both of these modes. Memories of state violence are multiple both in content and in the variety of contending interests who may attempt to mobilize them. Thus, these varying uses of memory can have multiple effects. Memories of state violence have been taken up in ways that have promoted discipline, including discipline within the state and within political organizations and social movements; yet memories of repression have also led to mutual recognition of suffering and struggle, which have promoted critical and creative collective action.

Memories cannot be dismissed as mere sentimentality. As part of subjectivity, memory works through the creation of affective ties, ties on which political alliances depend. Various periods of nation-state formation in Chile are marked by different predominant forms of emotional glue: cathartic, empathetic, sympathetic, and melancholic-nostalgic. One form of political memory may be most characteristic of a given period, but it can overlap with others, and a form predominant in one period may be foreshadowed earlier and linger afterward.

In the oligarchic period, oppositional sectors, most notably labor movements, employed memory in a call for cathartic transformation. By linking past repression to then present conditions, non-elite sectors were able to mobilize their rage and passion, creating working-class civic associations, cultural productions, mutual aid societies, and labor brotherhoods as they struggled for more just relations with their employers and the state.[65] With its emphasis on direct labor action, early-twentieth-century, nitrate-era politics thus demanded individual identification with communal emotion: "this history is mine." It foregrounded (collective) heroes engaged in praxis. During the populist period, new political movements mobilized memory in the form of empathy to unite various sectors of society in political alliances working together for the expansion of participation in the political system. Midcentury populist alliances thus strove to incorporate non-elite sectors into the formal political system in cross-class alliances: "your history is a part of mine." They emphasized (individual and collective) martyrs striving for utopia. During the dictatorship that followed, memory was used by human-rights activists to elicit sympathy in the hope of mobilizing Chileans around issues of daily survival and with the purpose of building international solidarity against the military regime: "I understand *your* history and will support your cause." Sympathetic memory privileged grassroots victims and issues of political voice. Meanwhile, the Right and the dictatorship sought to legitimize authoritarianism through sympathetic international appeals first to the Cold War National Security Doctrine and later to neoliberalism. Finally, in the transition to civilian governance that began in 1990, various attempts to connect past and present to a vision of the political future largely degenerated into appeals to melancholy (mostly for the Left) and nostalgia (mostly for the Right and de-politicized sectors).

Memory as a form of social action implicitly, and sometimes explicitly, emanates from and constitutes historically specific structures of feeling. Configurations of memory entail political modes and strategies that emerge from and are characteristic of particular historical conjunctures; however, these conjunctures are in no way limited to the predominant (hegemonic) political modes and strategies, but are also linked to counterhegemonic structures of feeling and are differentiated by complex relations between social sectors. Thus, these strategies also may exist in earlier, related forms (though not necessarily) and may persist in other moments as critical counterpoints to predominant structures of feeling. The latter forms of memory (especially cathartic memory) can disrupt one's sense of the present and may at times offer a pathway to alternative futures.

The way memory as an affective call to political action makes possible through a larger cultural logic certain subjectivities (e.g., "human-rights" activist as a post-1948 category), while others become anachronisms (e.g., "communist" after 1990) is particularly poignant in the North. The North itself, for example, dropped out of the historiography as a relevant region after nitrate collapsed. Still, the North continued to be written into the national imaginary by poets such as Andres Sabella, Mario Bahamonde, and Pablo Neruda, and novelists like Nicomedes Guzmán and Volodia Teitelboim. Teitelboim's fictionalized account of the 1948 Pisagua prison camp, *The Seed in the Sand*, claimed that moment of state violence as generative of oppositional consciousness for Chilean Leftists.

In these creative works, political actors who earlier in the century were defined primarily by class position and cast as heroes were subsumed in midcentury populist constructions of "the people," in which actors were defined primarily by their political party and the privileged actor was the martyr. Popular Unity's "democratic road to socialism" had attempted to capture the state by forging a nexus between people-nation-state, a continuation of efforts by Popular Front governments of the 1930s and 1940s to reshape conceptions of the relationships between inhabitants of the nation-state from those between patrons and clients in an oligarchic state to those between equal claimants to participation in the socialist state. What was it like to inhabit a region known as the cradle of the Chilean labor movement and of political parties committed to the working class when late-twentieth-century politics declared these collective characters obsolete? When even scholars announce "The End of Class as a Historical Subject"?[66] In dismissing or interpellating subjectivities by eliciting affective ties to particular political projects, the politics of memory and memory as politics can also reshape political geographies within the nation, accruing power to some regions and rendering others hinterlands.

Memory determines who becomes included and excluded under the rubric of the nation, and consequently to whom the state responds. It also determines the place of particular nation-states in regional and global arenas. Chile's attempt to enact an anti-imperial, democratic socialism made it a site of possibility for people in many places around the world. Therefore, this is not a book about memories: it is a historical ethnography of nation-state formation. The nation-state — the ostensible unit of analysis — is not a given, but a process under investigation. To get at nation-state formation, one needs to attend to the particular creation of places as points of access both in political practices and in scholarly analysis (as a politically implicated phenomenon).

While this study explores memory and violence in a particular region of a particular nation, it nevertheless suggests the ways in which place shifts as the setting for historical action at particular moments.[67] If one accepts Doreen Massey's definition of social space as "the articulation of social relations which necessarily have a spatial form in their interactions," then place entails webs of relations that "may remain in the place or stretch beyond it, linking specific places to one another."[68] This elasticity is especially pertinent to frontier territories marked by invasion, migration, and desertion, because officially sanctioned history is, as Johannes Fabian observes, "event-centered; places, rather than space, serve to localize memory."[69] The contingency of this place-event nexus problematizes the localization of memory, thus avoiding a comfortable nostalgia or claim to authenticity.[70]

At the same time, especially for non-elite groups, the twentieth century has witnessed ever more localized state discipline. In Chile the localization of state control informed the military regime's efforts to regionalize state authority by redrawing Chile's political map, replacing provinces with regions that corresponded to a strategic command chain. Localization of state coercion and the region's ongoing insertion into global economies meant that almost any assertion of identity based on place had to be wedged against the predominant tide.[71]

An ethnography of a frontier zone such as Tarapacá demonstrates that place does not merely anchor memory but is also transformed *through* memory. The mutual constitution of place and politics is especially potent for frontiers, which constantly index nation-state formation. The scholars Silvio R. Duncan Baretta and John Markoff suggest that in Latin American history the frontier functions as a place where "the capacity for violence is structured in social life" in the quotidian defense of the frontiersman's personal honor and in the military defense of national honor.[72] This conception of place "approaches the nation via its edges" so as to look at processes of exclusion as well as inclusion, as the very term *frontier* implies, processes of conflict and differentiation that the nation-state must constantly promote and defend.[73] The frontier as national edge is, according to Ana Alonso, "viewed as lying at the margins of state power, between the laws of society and the freedoms of nature, between the imperatives of obedience and the refusals of defiance."[74] This localization of obedience exposes the necessary contradictions in nation-state formation.

For the highly centralized Chilean nation-state, the North has served as a frontier zone of military danger and honor, adventure and opportunity. Although in military and economic terms the North is synonymous with the nation's past, since the mid-twentieth century state policy has promoted the region as embodying a potential future, by predicting a war with Peru and a resurgence in exports. For the Chilean state, the North both has propelled Chile into modernity and threatens to hold Chile back among the metaphorical ruins of extractive industry made public in a regionalized territorial dispute.

The state's strategic concern with its frontier contrasts starkly with views from the North. Two years after my encounter with the street musicians in Santiago, I visited the desert plains of Tarapacá, where I was reminded again of the pampinos' profound sense of abandonment and persistence. While regional stories about the camanchaca — whether mocking the arrogance of a British nitrate supervisor or suggesting the absence of those who move about in search of a better life — underlined autonomy and mobility, they described movement only within a demarcated terrain. The occupants of Tarapacá thus reinforced their tenacious presence in this forbidding landscape.

Moving across the Pampa Tamarugal during my first visit, I was struck by the persistence of the indigenous vegetation for which this part of the region was named. Inhabiting this place where virtually nothing else grows was the *tamarugo*, a large, leguminous tree with an extraordinarily long root capable of reaching through the desert's crust to drink from subterranean rivers. The trees were part of a state reforestation project, for although they had once almost completely covered the desert plains, the nitrate industry had used them to fuel cauldrons for boiling salted sand down into nitrate.

Hungry for more desert lore, as well as relief from the sun, I sought shade on a porch belonging to an elderly inhabitant of one of the ghost towns. For over two hours, this woman recounted stories of the town's heyday as a commercial and entertainment center for the surrounding nitrate camps and its later decline and abandonment.[75] The daughter of a prosperous shopkeeper who had lost everything but the family home when the industry collapsed, she had refused to leave even as the town depopulated and decayed; her large wooden house now sheltered only her and dozens of cats. At the end of her story, she pointed a gnarled finger toward the tree across the road and declared, "See, I'm like that tamarugo that nobody waters. No one cares for me, but I persist."

Just as this woman embodies human persistence in a foreboding region, this book pushes against accounts of Chilean history in which certain episodes of state violence and certain groups of people have been obscured, obscured, in part, through a refusal to tell a bigger history and to interrogate its meaning. Conjunctures of state violence — especially those before and after the 1973 coup — are seldom connected in a longer historical view. Tarapacá is the ideal place to do such work precisely because the North drops out of official histories after the nitrate era even as it is especially marked as a repeated site of state violence in national memory across the political spectrum. Memories of abandonment and persistence are essential to the history of this landscape of violence and regeneration.

Twenty years, a hundred years, nitrate absorbed the pampino's spirit.

And now, at the end of so much history, of so much wounded dawn

that they tell me of, come and see my land, come and see the

broken iron, the dead camps, the abandoned land.

Come and listen to the silence in the cold cemeteries of the pampa. . . .

My land is a repentant landscape in the middle of a heroic history.

—MARIO BAHAMONDE, "Les vengo a contar"

Structures of Memory, Shapes of Feeling

CHRONOLOGIES OF REMINISCENCE AND REPRESSION

IN TARAPACÁ (1890–PRESENT)

Mario Bahamonde, a Chilean poet and scholar, lamented what he called the repentant history of his region, the northern Chilean desert. The North had been the center of nitrate mining at the end of the nineteenth century, when nitrate, as a source of fertilizer and explosives, was perhaps the single most critical commodity in industrial and imperial expansion. Political activism spawned by labor movements during this time caused the region to become known as the cradle of Chilean politics. However, the world wars, the 1929 crash that culminated industry declines from World War I, and the development of synthetic nitrates in 1916 resulted in economic abandonment of the North and made the Chilean nitrate-mining industry an anachronism. Yet the fervor of political contests continued. From the 1973 coup to the 1990 transition to civilian rule, Chile's military subjugated the remote region with particular brutality. In the context of such political and economic degradation, people of the North have struggled to mobilize the past for their emancipatory projects, for different visions of the future.

Bridging the disciplines of anthropology, history, and literary studies to understand how these Chileans manage to sustain an ongoing spirit of struggle in a setting of abandonment and anachronism, I further elaborate my template for thinking about the history of memories of state violence: the shifts between memory mobilized in political projects as catharsis, empathy, and sympathy. These forms differ according to the degree of intensity of the sentiments they invoke and the degree of connection to or separation from (i.e., identification with) political projects they cultivate as they call on members to engage in various actions. In nation-state formation, states silence certain memories in order to build other ties (emotions) among the polity vis-à-vis the state. In fact, the nation-state requires particular modes of affective connection, especially in subordinate countries with fewer resources and options in geopolitical terms. This predicament is especially visible in the "repentant landscapes" of national frontiers, given the constraints on sovereignty imposed by neo-colonialism and imperialism.

Patricio Rivera, my fellow researcher, and I perched on stools in a one-room, termite-gnawed house as the desert seeped through the wallboards. Gales shrieked outside, and we were quite happy not to still be wandering outside in the dust storm, scavenging for oral histories. The far wall of the house was incongruously dominated by an enormous, ornately gilt-framed portrait of Czar Nicholas of Russia and his family—most likely an imperial relic imported by some late-nineteenth-century European nitrate baron and abandoned after the crash of 1929. (So suddenly had foreign administrators departed one mining camp that workers' children had found the evening tea—china cups, saucers, and all—still laid out on the fine oak dining tables of the managers' club.) Such sumptuous vestiges of capitalist occupation were often sold in Iquique's antique shops or displayed in regional museums dedicated to the nitrate era. The house in which we took refuge sat on an unpaved street in one of the towns of the northern Chilean pampa, exhaling the stale scent of dust, sweat, and cigarettes. Inside, we debated early-twentieth-century labor history with the middle-aged, working-class man whose grudging hospitality we temporarily enjoyed.[1]

Our host waved at us manuscript pages from his own 1,500-page historical novel and an accompanying set of 500 poems covering the early nitrate era to the present. His sources included local lore he had learned from his miner father, the Chilean history he had studied in Santiago on a scholarship during the country's pre-1973 experiment with socialism, papers uncovered in his excavations of garbage pits, and old newsprint that papered the interior walls of the town's abandoned houses, brothels, and shops. With neither favoritism nor prejudice, he wove each scrap of information into his masterwork. The only reason he would bother talking about local history with us, he explained, was that he wanted to know more about an organization called the Federation that, according to numerous references in the bits of newspaper and local lore, had played an important role in nitrate-era politics. When our answer — that we thought that it had been one of the first major labor unions in Chile — was not in sync with his painstakingly researched understanding, he declared us charlatans for pretending to be historians of the nitrate era.

Despite his belligerence, the passion of his challenge forced us to consider the politics of nostalgia and History in this landscape marked by the downfall of both extractive industry and socialist projects. In the course of my research, I listened to many commentaries on how this region of abandoned nitrate fields could once again prosper for anyone wise enough and with means enough to either pursue desert agriculture (using the vast subterranean rivers that purportedly swelled below) or resume nitrate production (capturing the current market's supposed preference for natural rather than synthetic products). Clearly, according to the people I interviewed, there was plenty of nitrate left in the ground.[2]

At first, I labeled this insistence — that that which is now worthless is in fact potentially priceless — an unproductive, reactionary mode of nostalgia. Nevertheless, those who had remained in the orphaned, nearly abandoned working-class towns of the North, with their severe boom-and-bust cycles, did have reason to suspect that the present desolation of the desert might be due to a temporary ruse. After the 1929 market collapse, the state filled much of this wasteland with military bases and target ranges — an assertion of its strategic value to the state — while the rest was bought up by Chilean businessmen, who dismantled the old camps and sold their materials for scrap but quietly held on to the "empty" lands — an assertion of their potential value in speculative markets.

My encounters with a historical perspective on the region that was not based on either state strategic values or capitalist values raised the question of whether I could so easily dismiss nostalgia as a reactionary political position. Could working-class memories of bonanza and abandonment instead rally the past in ways that provided a historical context of persistence and that complemented the struggles of human-rights activists to mobilize memory despite attempts by those in power to render obsolete their lament? I began to think more carefully about memory as a historically and culturally specific phenomenon, one for which characteristics and conditions of possibility must be specified and explained for any given moment. I have drawn on a transdisciplinary toolkit to develop analytic tools for a much richer differentiation of modes of memory as implicated in nation-state formation and political projects that may exceed the bounds of that political process at any given moment.

Modes of memory across the periods of nation-state formation differ in three key ways: (1) the kind and degree of emotional drive, (2) the political and cultural positioning of similarity and divergence between groups, and (3) the demarcation of the past-present relationship. The history of memory in Chile is not a narrative of increasing social justice, as the architects of regime transition as "democratization" would suggest, but of a decline in the emotional drive and kind of affective connection to the nation-state needed to produce it. This trajectory has been amplified on the frontiers of the postcolonial nation-state where the path of disjuncture and decay has rendered the coherent telling of local history nearly impossible. Still, some in Tarapacá, like the ghost-town historian-poet, persist in writing their histories even in the face of upheaval and abandonment. A range of emotions are condensed into my model of memory's morphologies (catharsis, empathy, and sympathy). As these morphologies shift across periods of nation-state formation, what emerges are the dialectical relationships between state and non-state actors and their creative uses of memory, which range from imposition, deployment, rejection, and contestation.

Shapes of Feeling: Catharsis, Empathy, and Sympathy

Cathartic Memory in "Heroic" Contestations of Oligarchic State Formation (1890–1930) ∗ Cathartic memory, as in the Aristotelian sense, is not simply purgative but in fact radically transformative.[3] Antonio Gramsci conceives of a synthetic historical moment, the attainment of the consciousness which would enable people to transform their history, and describes this soaring of imagination as "catharsis": "the passage from 'objective to subjective' and from 'necessity to freedom.' Structure ceases to be an external force which crushes . . . and is transformed into a means of freedom, an instrument to create a new ethico-political form and a source of new initiatives."[4] He continues, "To establish the 'cathartic' moment becomes . . . the starting-point for all the philosophy of praxis," as well as the basis for affective alliances for transformative projects.[5] Cathartic memory resembles Walter Benjamin's revolutionary remembrance, a "perpetually combative 'presence of mind' bred in the shocks of class struggle" that, together with more unconscious images and emotions, is "constantly nurtured and evoked to nourish the present."[6] The Chilean historian Gabriel Salazar distinguishes between forms of memory that attempt to "sterilize" the past and "memory for action," which he understands as the historical memory of power that "advances in longitude and latitude toward processes that construct the future reality."[7] Similarly, cathartic memory is a call for direct, militant, and transformative action that claims past suffering in the anticipation of future struggle.

Chilean labor historians have characterized the era of dramatic nitrate prosperity (roughly 1890–1930) as the heroic period of Chilean labor history, a period when working-class politicocultural mobilization attained epic proportions based on an articulated class consciousness. Thus, politics in that era revolved around a highly specified language of class conflict in which the predominant structure of feeling entailed catharsis.[8] For example, celebrations of May Day in the North, which were coordinated by the labor movement and press, taught the particulars of the Chicago Haymarket Massacre in great detail, complete with biographies and sketches of the martyrs who had fought for the eight-hour workday. The labor press did this not out of sympathetic solidarity ("I understand your history"), but rather as a cathartic expression of their own history ("this history is my history").[9]

Elias Lafertte, a nitrate miner who became head of the Chilean

Communist Party, recounted how as a young man he, along with small groups of miners from various nitrate camps, came down from the pampa to Iquique to attend the 1912 May Day commemoration announced in *El Despertar de los Trabajadores*, the main working-class newspaper. Lafertte went directly to the press, and there, at a preparatory session for the following day's events, he learned the origins of the occasion from Luis Emilio Recabarren, a key leader of the Chilean Left: "Recabarren did not relate the events of Chicago as a simple episode isolated in history, as a battle whose heroism is valued and then forgotten. No, he told of the Chicago martyrs' sacrifice as part of the worldwide and permanent struggle of workers, that it was a step forward in the path of workers' conquests. But there remained for the future many other conquests, among them that of Power, to finish with humanity's greatest defect: the exploitation of man by man."[10] Through cathartic memory, Recabarren fused the struggles of workers in late-nineteenth-century Chicago with the struggles of laborers in twentieth-century Tarapacá, and he did so in order to inspire an ongoing fight, a "permanent and worldwide struggle," against structures of exploitation. The history of Chicago workers became *his* history. In place of an episodic and heroic account of repression, which he aptly labeled a form of forgetting, Recabarren recalled the Haymarket massacre as one conjuncture in a history of struggle, a future of many other conquests. Lafertte, listening intently, recognized his own story in this history and began telling others gathered in the newspaper room of his own experiences as miner and typesetter. So great was the pull of that affective connection that he stayed in Iquique, the provincial capital and primary nitrate port, to work in the newspaper and labor organizations.

That those same organizations promoted the fame and widespread performance of "El canto a la pampa" (Song to the Pampa), written by Francisco Pezoa, a working-class anarchist and journalist for *El Despertar*, further underlines the force of cathartic memory in the nitrate era.[11] A denunciation of the 1907 Escuela Santa María massacre, the lyrics begin,

> I sing to the pampa, the sad land
> condemned land of damnation
> where greenery is never seen
> not even in the most lovely season.
>
> . . .

> Sublime victims that went
> from the pampa full of faith
> found
> only the ruinous shrapnel.[12]

The song depicts the exploitation of the nitrate worker, "the pariah of capital."

> Until one day like a lament
> out of the deepest recesses of the heart
> through the alleys of the encampment
> rang a tone of rebellion:
> groans from many chests,
> of much ire was the clamor
> trumpeting of the rights
> of the poor working people.
> . . .
> I demand vengeance for the valiant
> pulverized by the shrapnel
> I demand vengeance for the orphan
> sad and mourning remained.
> I demand vengeance for those who came
> Of the workers who bared their chests
> I demand vengeance for the pampino
> who, there in Iquique, learned to die.[13]

Rebellion accents lament and lament is always already within rebellion. The workers are not disparate, but rather dialectically related and emergent. The orphan remains, and thus destruction is not complete. There is a generational continuity in the affective connection between the adults who have been destroyed and the orphan who remains and whose subjectivity is created by that act of defiance and the resulting destruction. However, state violence is not generative; rather, it is worker rebellion that is productive of ongoing, oppositional subjectivities. Furthermore, the dead are not passive victims, but rather agents active in determining their own destiny: they "came," they "bared their chests," they "learned to die." This last predicate is especially intriguing, suggesting as it does that death is not a cessation; it presupposes an ongoing process and implies that the lesson will be repeated. The song also undergoes a powerful shift in voice, from the third person to the first, which underscores the affective impulse of the music and demands that the singer take on the fight for justice. The lament rising from working people in the earlier verse becomes the singer's own in a mobilization of cathartic memory.

Writing about Chilean popular song in the early 1930s, Acevedo Hernández pointed to Pezoa's song as paradigmatic of revolutionary poetry, noting that its words of "hate, desecration and vengeance" had been sung by literally thousands of workers: "The poet feels the pain in his proletarian soul, his cry interprets that of the masses, it is a type of proletariat 'Marseillaise.'"[14] For Acevedo, Pezoa's "El canto a la pampa," with its demand for workers' rights, "accent of rebellion," and "vengeance for the mourning orphan," represented a moment of cathartic transformation in working-class consciousness. "When the people learned to sing their pain they comprehended that they were on their way. . . . Now they do not cry, they protest! Lost was the picturesque sense, it erased authority . . . and in doing so, unchained the singing slave — as the poet says — 'to the rhythm of his own chains.'"[15] During the nitrate era, political meetings and events in Tarapacá always began with the singing of "The International" along with the "Song to the Pampa," which enacted a doubled, and at the time seemingly uncontradictory, allegiance that bridged local and transnational loyalties.[16]

Cathartic memory confronted and directed rage against injustice toward the militant pursuit of change. After 1929, catharsis no longer formed memory's primary affective mode as populist political parties rechanneled the oppositional energies of non-elite sectors toward a successful bid for the state.

Empathetic Memory and "the People" (1930s–1973) * By the 1930s, the so-called heroic period of Chilean labor history had given way to populist politics infused with the rhetoric of collective martyrdom and utopia. Espoused by political parties, this rhetoric subsumed a language of class to promote the interests of the non-elite, broadly conceived of as "the people," as in this typical example of populist poetry, taken from "Message to the Pampa of the Future," by Luis Polanco, a barber of peasant origins.

Hay terror en tu pasado,	There is terror in your past,
pero eso ha de terminar,	but this will end,
habrás de ser germinal	you must be germinal

de un Edén nunca soñado;	of an Eden never dreamed of;
veras trigales dorados	you will see golden wheat fields
meciéndose en tus arenas,	cradling like a baby in your sands,
lo que hoy son tus calicheras	what are today your nitrate deposits
las veras hechas jardín,	you will see them made into a garden,
oirás el agua bullir	you will hear the water boil
en tus ardientes laderas.	on your ardent slopes.
. . .	. . .
Pampa triste y dolorida,	Pained and sad pampa,
no reniegues del dolor,	do not give up in pain,
habrá florecer de amor	there will be a flowering of love
en tu roja entraña herida;	in your red wounded core;
vas a vivir otra vida	you will live another life
con alegres alboradas.	with joyful sunrises.[17]

This poem relegates suffering firmly to the past and portrays a utopia of the desert in bloom as romantic and uneventful — a Garden of Eden — or rather, the return of daily rhythms of another time. The Edenic references to an innocent yet self-caused expulsion reveal not an image of the future, but a restoration of past order. The poem envisions another originary moment (ostensibly some unspecified "future") in a millenarian spirit, an upheaval leading to the restoration of an idyllic past. The poem is addressed to "you," the pampa: the landscape is personified to such an extent that it becomes the suffering figure, takes on the emotions of its residents. In this sense, martyrs, who are neither the subject nor object of the poem, can only pertain to the past and never achieve the status of heroic figures for the future because their history serves as an authorization for others' actions.

Polanco's poem appeared in a popular poetry collection edited by Diego Muñoz, who promoted non-elite writing by organizing events such as the 1954 National Congress of Popular Poets and Singers (through the Universidad de Chile) and by publishing the work of more than two hundred non-elite poets. Enthusiasm for folk poetry, song, and history flourished until the 1973 coup, when the military labeled these subversive and squashed publication, recording, and research. Leftist political activists had drawn on popular culture as a source of political inspiration that they could encourage, edit, and shape into a transformative national political project. They were convinced that Chilean society could be transformed organically by fusing non-elite culture with that of the nation-state, a fusing through which a socialist state and society would gradually emerge. Yet, just as Polanco's poem cautions against a vengeful or despondent stance in favor of an ostensibly more productive one, the Left's vision for the future also had a cautionary undertone of unease, an awareness that workers' growing rage against injustice might not respect the official Left's gradualist model of change.[18]

The achievements and limits of empathetic memory emerged in Chile's long, phenomenally successful populist period, from the Popular Front governments of the 1930s and 1940s through the 1970–1973 Popular Unity government.[19] Populist politics mobilized memory to create empathetic alliances in which, leftist-political-party leaders believed, carefully crafted memories of prior suffering and struggle would mark an arena of shared experience.[20] Representatives of popular sectors would thus be able to assert "the people" to be the authentic bearers of the nation in their attempts to transform the state.[21] According to political party leaders, this model of political and social transformation would suture together collectivities whose relative political and cultural autonomy in earlier eras had "unproductively" emphasized mobilization around conflicts of class interests and were thus implicated in the violence of the past.

In contrast to the prior cathartic mode of memory, empathetic memory ("your history is a part of mine") encompasses the experiences of past struggles (regarded as more temporally distant) as building up to the present and softens the degree of radical difference between present-day sectors in order to make possible cross-sector alliances. Populist empathy is about the incorporation of non-elite sectors into the nation-state political process; as such, it takes on the narrative logic of the nation-state predicated on an expansionist view of history as progress that subsumes the past into a greater present.

Sympathetic Memory Challenging Authoritarian Exclusions in Neoliberal State Formation (1973–Present) * With the collapse of Chile's populist political system after the 1973 coup, the military consolidated a "protected democracy" and instituted a drastic reorientation of state and economy around the neoliberal free-market model. Political activists who survived both within Chile and in exile were forced to redirect their organizational activities to an international audience. The military brutally closed down internal civil society, at first forbidding and later severely constraining almost all forms of associative life, and anti-authoritarian activists had to forge alliances internationally to fight against the dictatorship. Anti-authoritarian sectors mobilized past incidents of state violence to generate sympathy for the Chilean people, the quintessential example being the 1907 Escuela Santa María massacre. For the resistance, such events served as allegories for the devastation and horror of the present.

Opponents of the military regime prolifically scripted historical allegories (in the form of poetry, plays, historical studies, and novels) to depict their own struggles. For example, in what would turn out to be the waning years of the military regime, one of the most productive independent-research institutes in the North published the following poem — "Los aparecidos de la Santa María" (The Santa María Specters), by "Pigmalión" — as one of the winning entries in a regional literary competition.

La noche . . . la noche inmensa	The night . . . the immense night
De anhelo devastado	Of devastated longing
De silencio embravecido de pulsos . . .	Of emboldened silence . . .
Dicen que venían de la vida	It is said that they came back from life
Con el corazón manchado de nostalgias	With nostalgia-stained hearts
Y que pedían copos de horas	And that they asked for daily prayers
Recién caídos en el árbol del latido	Newly fallen on the howling tree
Que le crecieron telarañas a sus nombres	Cobwebs grew from their names
Y que vagaban en la escuela	And that they wandered the school
Pintando sentencias en la pared del destino.	Painting sentences on destiny's wall.
Dicen que eran fantasmas	It is said that they were ghosts
Que cultivaban hongos en sus heridas	growing mushrooms in their wounds
Y en los papiros de la vigilia	And on the vigil papyrus
Escribían los nombres del verdugo . . .	They wrote the executioner's names . . .
La noche . . . la noche inmensa	The night . . . the immense night
De estrellas desclavadas,	Of stars unfastened,
De paraíso derretido	Of paradise melted
En la fragua del temor,	In the forge of fear,
De recuerdos plantados	Of recollections planted

En el páramo del olvido	In the high bleak plain of forgetting
los aparecidos . . .	the specters . . .
los aparecidos . . .	the specters . . .
los aparecidos . . .	the specters . . .[22]

In the poem, most likely composed at some point in the 1980s, the military dictatorship—then well into its second decade and aspiring to long-term rule—constitutes an "immense night" of silences and devastation. The word chosen for those killed in the 1907 Escuela Santa María massacre, *aparecidos*, indexes the word *desaparecidos*, the missing victims of the post-1973 military regime. The poet explicitly deploys a language of memory to describe the predicament of those who came before: with their own recollections "planted in the plain of oblivion" and thus lost in their own right, memory now points to the struggles of the present as the specters become witnesses of new atrocities. Significantly, though their own names are enshrouded by cobwebs, these specters keep vigil and document the identities of the executioners, which implies a reckoning to come. (The prioritizing of writing as resistance echoes lyrics sung, in reference to human-rights victims, during demonstrations by the Sebastián Acevedo Movement against Torture in the 1980s and early 1990s: "I write your name on my city's walls.") Central to "Los aparecidos de la Santa María" is the loss of direct memories of the 1907 events— "devastated longing" obscured by cobwebs and fungus—which cuts the specters loose as vehicles of meaning who can reference the suffering of those in the present. The specters, in an allegorical effect, offer a sort of solidarity.

Sympathetic memory thus differs from empathetic memory in its lesser degree of connection between past and present and in its more detached call to political action.[23] Whereas empathetic memory has been deployed to both mobilize and discipline populist political movements, sympathetic memory has served as a call to discursive witnessing and to the solicitation of solidarity based not on common struggle, but rather on human concern as a simile ("your situation is like mine"). Often sympathetic memory engages allegory in using the subordinate story to talk about the dominant.[24] As in "Los aparecidos de la Santa María," the "stain" of nostalgia marks a definitive break between past and present and sharply constrains the accessibility of that past. The rupture between past and present implied in sympathetic memory is what comes to definitively characterize the neoliberal period as one of nostalgia-melancholy during the latter years of the dictatorship and at least the first decade of the post-dictatorship period.

The sympathetic memory apparent in "Los aparecidos de la Santa María" further serves as a point of entry into the neoliberal-era politics of memory in that the institute that sponsored the literary competition and published the winning entries, Taller de Estudios Regionales (Regional Studies Workshop), was itself an example of the very successful politics of international solidarity. During the 1980s, Chilean oppositional activists both within the country and abroad galvanized international financial support to pour funds into independent Chilean institutes and thus enable the research of intellectuals who had been excluded from the universities by the military regime and its promotion of neoliberal epistemologies. In a continuation of populist initiatives, many of the institutes incorporated aspects of popular education and cultural outreach into their work, with a number even specializing in this area. Much influenced by Gramscian understandings of culture as a long-term terrain of political struggle, many organizers of institutes and other oppositional groups recognized the need to battle the neoliberal regime's efforts to dismantle Chile's political culture, which was based on an ethics of collective solidarity, and to inculcate instead one of individual consumer interest. In organizing opposition to the military regime, non-elite literary competitions served a didactic formative purpose: to instill a capacity for sympathy as part of the human-rights sensibility that had become current in national and international politics.

Sympathy — like catharsis and empathy — was not a tactic confined to Chilean political culture; rather, it was part of broader dynamics of political culture in the middle to late period of the Cold War. In 1973 a clandestine documentary made by East Germans posing as right-wing (West German) military sympathizers exposed Europeans to the conditions of the prison camp at Pisagua, which had been reopened after the military coup, and galvanized the international pressure that shut it down, at least for that moment.[25] The film's international shock value derived from the historical connections the filmmakers made between then contemporary Pisagua and Northern Chile's history of labor repression, the self-identification of prisoners in the film with political movements of the Left (this was especially powerful for East Germans who identified with Communist Party militants), and the Chilean military's explicit imitation of Nazi Germany's repressive techniques (coinciding with the beginnings of Europe's official grappling with the legacies of the Holocaust).[26] The German documentary not only contributed to sparking the international solidarity movement that constrained the military regime but also, in subsequent years, affirmed the released political prisoners' own sense of what they had been through, in the form of videos and published stills smuggled back into Chile. This affirmation was crucial because former prisoners' perceptions of themselves as historical agents had been eroded as, decade after decade, the dictatorship explicitly and even the human-rights movement implicitly assigned the prisoners culpability for their own economic, social, and political losses: the dictatorship repeatedly justified its actions as the only viable political possibility, and the human-rights movement privileged the experience and needs of the families of those who did not survive, again isolating the former prisoners.

Under the dictatorship, Chilean human-rights groups learned to elicit sympathy from international organizations eager to support their fight against military rule; during the transition to civilian rule, they hoped that this solidarity would continue, since some recognized the long-term challenge of eradicating the dispositions, emotional habits, and ways of relating to one another instantiated under the authoritarian system. Yet, in spite of the continuities in state formation (represented by the 1980 Constitution) and the intensification of the neoliberal model, Chile was now internationally recognized as having a democratic regime, which suggested that its citizens should no longer be in need of solidarity, least of all in sectors outside of the state and the arena of formal politics. Therefore, in the waning days of sympathetic memory, as international solidarity became more scarce and was formally channeled through the state, there emerged a new model of the politics of affinity with regard to where oppositional political culture belonged. Efforts to evoke continued solidarity through sympathetic memory often resulted in little more than pity, due to the withering away of the basis for mobilizing sympathetic memory to generate alliances.

For example, in 1993 the Association of Ex-Political Prisoners of Pisagua designed a series of holiday greeting cards that represented aspects of the ex-political prisoners' history and their future projects. These aspects included their primary goals, such as building a mausoleum for themselves (future place); key points of collective reference, such as the excavated mass grave and the English clock tower in

Pisagua (past places); and key symbols, such as the dove emerging from a cupped pair of unchained hands (emotive place). Each image was accompanied by text that extended the association's season's greetings. Before I returned to the United States from Chile that year, the association's steering committee asked me to take the cards and send them to organizations that might be interested in funding the work of the association. It also requested that I renew contact with a U.S. psychologist who had visited Iquique and had proposed working with the association to promote human-rights projects in northern Chile. When I delivered a set of cards to the psychologist, however, he told me that the (rather unorthodox) holiday greetings were symptomatic of "pathetic" unprocessed collective trauma; the association's attempt to evoke political solidarity, which entailed building a sympathetic relation similar to the kinds of alliances human-rights groups' cultivated during the dictatorship, was now understood instead as a pathology requiring professional help.

Thus, while the greeting cards indeed elicited a reaction, it was not the one the ex-political prisoners intended. This response could be due to greeting cards' more general limitations as a genre of political action and to the limitations of the sympathy they hoped to evoke as a form of alliance. Greeting cards carry a connotation of mass-produced and sanitized sentiments, of intimate yet mass-marketed messages. The greeting card is a fetish — of even the most intimate of social relations — and thus sympathy becomes a commodity. In this sense, greeting cards were a fitting choice as a genre of expression in Chile, where the neoliberal model put in place by the military and deepened under civilian rule called for the redefinition of citizenship through consumption and the prioritization of market relations over former political cultures.[27] Hence, there was a certain irony, implicit or explicit, in pouring a political message into such a typically commercial and often trite form. Moreover, the ex-political prisoners' failed attempt to elicit an alliance through the greeting-card genre demonstrated sympathy's frequent inability to cut across human experience or to act as a translator for decoding the ways that human-rights groups represented their experiences.

The psychologist's conclusion corresponded with both the limits of sympathetic memory as a political mode and the emerging politics of memory promoted by Chile's new civilian regime. Hoping to channel the energy of the social movements emerging in the aftermath of the 1973 coup, the government promoted the notion of reconciliation, which they understood as recovery through forgiving and moving on from the past.[28] Human-rights movements were trapped in a psychological model of the revindication of victimhood through healing and reincorporation into "normal" civil society. The call for solidarity, internationally and within Chile, resulted in a relatively calm transition from the military regime to civilian rule in 1990 — but there was a price. Political parties appropriated social movements in their attempts to recreate a political system in which all alliances would strive toward power within the state apparatus, which chipped away at the basis for sympathetic memory and thus caused a general waning of sympathetic memory in favor of the increasingly predominant dyad of melancholy-nostalgia. In the polarized struggles that occurred during military rule, alliances were more clear-cut as either for or against military rule, and sympathetic memory was particularly effective because it provided a basis for (an ultimately hegemonic) coalition that connected divergent sectors into an oppositional force. Sympathetic memory waned during the civilian regimes as the political spectrum opened up and became more complex, with the basis for alliances shifting back toward class-based consensus around the neoliberal model. Thus, political affect generated through sympathy was largely diffused into melancholy and nostalgia.

Still, despite these dominant trends, earlier forms of allegiance have reemerged, marked by the stubborn resilience of human-rights activists on the distant frontiers of national politics.

The Persistence of Cathartic Memory in the Neoliberal State Formation's Shift to Melancholy-Nostalgia

The scholar David Eng argues that melancholia at the end of the twentieth century "has come largely to define how we think about our subjectivities." Eng concludes expansively, "Melancholia and its generalized connection with depression in the popular imagination have come to describe numerous subjectivities inhabiting multiple areas of the globe."[29] To the extent that Chile has come to be the paradigm of the nation-state in late capitalism, Eng's insight applies in that country perhaps more than anywhere else in world, with Chilean social scientists reporting astronomical levels of depression in the general populace. The postdictatorship era has indeed been marked by the decline of sympathy and the increase of nostalgia and melancholy. But some voices push back against the predominant mode of memory by drawing on the vestiges of prior modes to generate critical stances that begin to imagine a way out of the current state of affairs.

At the end of the twentieth century, the transition from military to civilian rule proved disheartening for those who had fought the military dictatorship. Through a multitude of social movements, the 1973 coup's political orphans strove to survive and defeat the military's project that had attempted to revamp Chilean society by engorging the military-nationalist components of political culture. In 1989 Chileans succeeded in ousting the military government by, remarkably, voting the overconfident dictator out of office. However, transition to a representative system revealed the underlying legitimacy of authoritarian rule: in subsequent plebiscites the military's faction consistently received 40 percent of the vote. As this reality became increasingly apparent, political-party coalitions made compromises that weighed heavily on those involved in human rights, in shantytown movements, and in a multitude of other social movements; recently, for example, the Chilean state employed nationalist rhetoric to oppose Spain's attempt to bring General Pinochet to trial for human-rights crimes.

Some activists, politically orphaned, have attempted to write, think, and rebuild networks in an effort to work through their despair. Their efforts are not — as defined by the now governing coalition of democratic parties — the "work of mourning": a contained and state-guided process, temporally circumscribed as "the transition to democracy." The Chilean political elite's model of transition entails historical reflection and forgiveness intended to move Chile away from its painful past and toward the pragmatic prosperity and peace of a neoliberal state and economy. Rather than engage in politics as mourning, the orphans of regime transition refuse to relinquish the past; they grope toward a politics which might bind their own memories to a political vision for the future by, in de Certeau's terms, "reemploying" catharsis. Like the catharsis exemplified by Pezoa's much earlier cry for justice, "The Song to the Pampa," activists mobilize forms of memory whose passion might pull them away from the prevailing, state-endorsed modes of nostalgia and melancholy.

The poet Guillermo Ross-Murray Lay-Kim is one such orphan. His name embodies the jumbled history of Tarapacá: his forebears came from divergent places to make their fortune in the nitrate industry. A university student during the Popular Unity years, he participated in a revolutionary organization, though, by his own admission, he wasn't particularly skilled at fighting or running. His compatriots foresaw repression and asked him — as a poet, dramaturgist, and historian — to become the group's archivist, their caretaker of memory. Due to the group's policy of refusing exile, few survived the dictatorship. Ross-Murray Lay-Kim himself evaded capture by going into self-imposed internal exile, moving about the North and relying on bonds of childhood friendship to shelter him during the first decade of the military regime. In the early 1980s he resurfaced to participate in the growing social movements challenging the military regime. He helped found a Catholic laypeople's organization inspired by liberation theology, which encouraged people to interpret the Bible based on their own lives and use it as a tool for political change. In addition, he helped found the Association of Friends and Families of the Disappeared and Executed in Northern Chile.

Complying with his vow to preserve the group's papers, memories, and vision, Ross-Murray Lay-Kim kept a diary from the day of the coup, 11 September 1973, to the day on which the civilian regime was inaugurated in 1990. A diary composed in documentary or testimonial mode would have suited neither his poetic disposition nor the pragmatics of life under military rule, namely, the need for secrecy and discretion to avoid arrest. His journal includes hundreds of images, poems, parables, allegories, and many more devices and forms, all encoded records of events and political commentary, complete with complementary files of news clippings and documents.

After the coup, the military government shut down most institutions in civil society and thus denied the conditions of possibility for collective memory. In its place, the dictatorship portrayed Chile to be in a civil war with the forces of global communism, forces that had threatened to destroy the nation until the military stepped in to save the country by eradicating the cancer of subversion. The military used this story to legitimize its own place as the guardian of the Chilean state's integrity and honor. Given the shutdown of civil society, for nearly two decades Ross-Murray Lay-Kim devoted himself to creating what he called the "subversion of memory."

In times of penury,

some (if not

the majority) hang from another's heart, cover their ears and go about placidly,

falsely.

Others—the

minority—forget their lives to confront Darkness.

I (now, too

tired for love; unsuited for war!) have opted for this SUBVERSION OF MEMORY.

Perhaps, a stubborn form also of survival. And, why not? moreover, of a secret battle, solitary and tragic.[30]

While exhaustion made forgetting a tempting solution, Ross-Murray Lay-Kim instead survived by pursuing this subversion of the military state's and its supporters' memory and storing in his secret archive and personal diary the obstinate components of a recuperative and potentially radically transformative, cathartic countermemory. The literary critic Sergio Gaytan called this "day by day annotation of quotidian events" under military rule a "national intra-history" that "will acquire unsuspected dimensions either by its transcendence or futility." The quotations of public figures along with press clippings of advertisements, spectacles, economic indicators, and curious statistics cryptically document a rhetorical field particularly disconcerting given "the profound abyss between the promised word and the real happenings." In other words, the military's explanation of events and conditions diverged drastically from people's daily experiences of life under military rule.[31]

In Ross-Murray Lay-Kim's project, the poetic form itself is resistant: it does political work. The political strategy of this poetic form is to conceal itself, to make itself difficult, and to enact the difficulty of remembering under military rule. The difficulty and opaqueness of the poetic diary contrasts with the readily consumable, mass-marketed, yet supposedly intimate generic images associated with greeting cards. Greeting cards were actually a fitting genre for the period of authoritarian rule, when the military and its economic technocrats restructured the Chilean economy around neoliberal, free-market principles; this reorganization, along with privatization, opened up the Chilean economy to foreign investment and many sectors of social life to "the market." In this context greeting-card memories were part of the emerging consumer culture fostered under military rule, which the ex-political prisoners picked up on and sought to use to elicit sympathy in the form of international solidarity. Ross-Murray Lay-Kim's persistent opacity in an economy of mass-produced intimacy formed the core of his attempted subversion of memory.

Since the shift from military to civilian rule, Ross-Murray Lay-Kim has persisted in writing poetry that engages rage and betrayal. The precarious conditions of regime transition in which the military personnel and organization remained intact through the 1990s did not allow for legal redress of the dictatorship's crimes, except in the most prominent cases. Fearing military reprisals and holding together tenuous political coalitions, the civilian regime promoted reconciliation instead of justice. The pragmatic model of transition as reconciliation entailed a demand for forgiveness without a complete revelation of the past and acknowledgment of wrongdoing—in other words, without broad access to justice. Ross-Murray Lay-Kim expressed the sense of rage and betrayal of those frustrated by the constraints of transition.

Los que saben y vieron	Those who know and saw
Los que olvidan y saben	Those who forget and know
Los que saben y niegan:	Those who know and deny:
¡Malditos sean!	Damn them!
Los que emergen—¡ahora!—	Those who emerge—now!—
Los que lloran y hablan	Those who cry and speak
como el reptil y el loro:	like the reptile and the parrot
¡Malditos sean!	Damn them!
Los que fueron y ríen	Those who lived and laughed
Los que fueron y callan	Those who lived and shut up
Los que mienten y fueron:	Those who lie and lived:
¡Malditos sean!	Damn them![32]

This poem undefines: it forces the reader to ask why the poet is so very abstract. Why not specify the who and the what? The object is implicit. Everyone knows the object, so the poet does not have to articulate it, and the listener is thus forced into complicity: "you all know this, they may be among you." By insisting from the beginning on interrogating "those who forget and know," the poet signals that the object has never really been lost. The poem begins with those who know and saw—the witnesses—then points to those who forgot (an active, though possibly private, process) and know. In other words, in the impossible combination of knowing and forgetting lies their complicity: they don't really forget. The poem then indicts those who deny, which, unlike forgetting, is a public act. Ross-Murray Lay-Kim thus raises issues of how memory and forgetting are articulated and how the remembered and the unremembered circulate. In the poem's second stanza, actors make public enunciations, but their speech does not make them human: the reptile cannot speak in the sense of producing sound, and the parrot just repeats.

Denouncing betrayal through forgetting and damning the opportunists of regime transition, Ross-Murray Lay-Kim printed his poem alongside a small map of South America on which he starred Tarapacá's capital, mnemonically specifying the location of anguish and anger. The poem is an inscription — a kind of map in itself — and the poem and the place become interchangeable. The map and the poem become mutual keys as, in the substitution of place and event, the object is specified by location. Ross-Murray Lay-Kim sent copies to his friends in commemoration of the twentieth anniversary of the coup and read his poem at public forums on numerous occasions. The poem shocked its various audiences, even those generally sympathetic to his position, in its complete contrast with and refusal of post-transition, neoliberal linguistic etiquette.[33] Transition vocabulary relied on words like *compromise*, *opportunity*, *advantage*, and *reconciliation*, and shunned words like *fight*, *right*, *liberty*, and, most definitely, *vengeance* and *damnation*. Ross-Murray Lay-Kim used the words of his poem to attack the official lexical fields, a subversion of memory.

Ross-Murray Lay-Kim also read the poem at a 1993 conference of northern writers sponsored, in part, by the regional office of the Ministry of Culture and Education.[34] The conference embodied the battle over memory between those who had gained a tenuous hold on the state and those who remained on the political frontiers, who persistently challenged this hold and demanded that the civilian regime confront the legacies of the past. Like Ross-Murray Lay-Kim, most of the writers at the conference paid special attention to issues of the relationship between language and politics. Moreover, the incident that ended the conference made clear that the new civilian government also recognized the importance of language. The planners even scheduled a panel session on culture and politics in which Ross-Murray Lay-Kim presented a paper on state policy and the role of the artist.[35] He argued that, in fact, the current government had no cultural policy but relied on a random aggregation of projects and bureaucratic initiatives locked into a vertical, centralized structure, which did not allow for the kind of critical dialogue from which an adequate cultural policy could emerge. One ill-conceived project to which Ross-Murray Lay-Kim referred was a huge geoglyph, located in the middle of a desert plain just south of Tarapacá, that spelled out the phrase "Ni pena ni miedo" (neither sorrow nor fear). This piece was designed by the Santiago poet Raúl Zurita and financed at great expense by private contributions from Santiago and by funds from Tarapacá's Ministry of Public Works. Ross-Murray Lay-Kim spoke at length about the peculiarity of a public-works office in the North sponsoring a cultural project initiated in the capital and spending precious funds on a work visible only to the privileged few who could fly over it. At a time when the human-rights movement struggled to submit the military to judicial process and to extract information regarding the fate of those who disappeared or were killed, the ambiguity of the poet's message resounded in a particularly disturbing way for many activists.

A vigorous discussion ensued, with the regional vice minister of culture (who had passed out complimentary copies of his own writings published by his office) reminding the conference participants to be more grateful to and less critical of the state, which had provided a great deal of support for the conference.[36] The vice minister of culture then canceled the wrap-up discussion that was scheduled to take place the next morning and handed to the moderator what he called "conference conclusions," which were to be read as closing remarks — clearly an attempt to impose narrative closure to the event and thus enforce the postdictatorship civilian regime's official politics of memory. The conference participants adjourned to their own unofficial wrap-up debate, amazed that the final episode had embodied so crudely the issues of culture and power that they had come together to explore.

State policies of reconciliation — framed as national mourning operating within the memory dynamics of melancholy and nostalgia, and expressed in a language of neoliberal opportunity — have thus at times been confronted by activists using alternative modes of memory that decry betrayal and refuse obsolescence.

Chronology and Memory's Orphans

In 1983, with the dictatorship firmly ensconced, the Catholic Church and human-rights activists carved out a space for organized opposition to the military. A group of pro-democracy scholars and educators formed Santiago's New History Workshop and edited a series of textbooks, *Popular History Notebooks: History of the Workers' Movement Series.* Initiated at the request of broad-based movements opposing military rule and sponsored by funds from international organizations, this popular-education project (and others like it) began from the premise that a historical understanding of political and economic circumstances could offer non-elite sectors a basis for political organization.[37] The resulting popular-history notebooks periodized Chilean post-independence labor history as follows: 1820–1880, formation; 1880–1920, exclusion; 1920–1970, integration; 1970–1973, participation; and 1973–present, new exclusion. The content of the notebooks implies that this periodization is one of relative inclusion or exclusion vis-à-vis the nation-state; this scheme thus highlighted the possibilities for the rise of a national-popular political project in Chile.

Chile's twentieth-century oppositional movements, dominated by unions and political parties with broad constituencies, steadfastly organized political alliances to more profoundly link Chilean state formation with the formation of "the people."[38] David Forgacs explains Gramsci's concept of the national-popular as a part of a war of position that entails the ever-present danger that the bourgeoisie could reappropriate hegemonic gains; in other words, there is always a threat of a process of class de-formation or loss of oppositional subjectivity.[39] This "treacherous" populist utopianism, in Terry Eagleton's reading of Walter Benjamin, betrays the working class, forcing them into a future that "will never be realized because it exists to repress the past, robbing the class of its hatred by substituting dreams of liberated grandchildren for memories of enslaved ancestors."[40] This dynamic emerged in Chile in the dismantling of cathartic memory and the rise of midcentury populist projects (using empathetic memory) and in the rebirth of social movements as political parties after the 1990s shift to civilian rule (expressing memory as melancholy-nostalgia). Projects mobilizing a national-popular memory have had only relative autonomy from dominant sectors; they have been constrained by the contradictions inherent in structures of feeling that have remained intertwined with military-state affective forms.[41] In other words, political coalitions promoting the interests of non-elite sectors rely on nationalist sentiment in a bid for the state, even as they have yet to question the military's claim to being the core of the nation-state.

In 1990 dominant Left parties gained a new foothold on the

history-generating capacity of the state when they participated in the triumphant coalition of antimilitary parties. In light of these victories, the New History Workshop would most likely update their chronology of labor history: 1990–present, new inclusion. Of course, this would be an optimistic gesture given the neoliberal state's ongoing privileging of exclusionary technocratic knowledge. Regardless, in the logic of the New History Workshop's chronology, non-elite politics remains oriented toward the nation-state, so the story of popular struggles must conform to that of the nation-state in a "dynamic of inclusion and exclusion."

This periodization, however, epitomizes the kind of history writing — historical narratives recounting continuity over time and the singularity of human experience as it fed into a single, collective project — that Foucault opposed with countermemory.[42] To Foucault, such conventional plots replicated bourgeois psychology's account of an individual's memory of his or her life as the development of a single identity, while countermemory constituted through a genealogical methodology drew out aspects of rupture, discontinuity, and incommensurability in a life-story.

The capacity to connect, to insist on a complete history, may be the privilege of the inhabitants of only a few places, a privilege even less likely to be claimed on the nation-state's frontiers. The poet Mario Bahamonde characterizing the North as a "repentant landscape in the middle of a heroic history"; the working-class local historian who was compelled to extract the complete epic of twentieth-century Tarapacá from traces of paper on the walls of ghost-towns; and Guillermo Ross-Murray Lay-Kim, the poet-diarist who, to subvert state-sanctioned memory, chronicled daily life in Northern Chile under the dictatorship—all pay the penance of solitude for daring to construct a story of continuity on an abandoned frontier.[43] These northern writers, in their stubborn acts of survival and fidelity, have insisted on the subversion of memory, an insistence not based on a celebration of rupture, but instead embraced as a strategic move, given that the only memory of state violence permitted in postdictatorship Chile (melancholy-nostalgia) subordinates the suffering of the past to a homogenizing project of national reconciliation. This state project equates those who remained and died, those who remained and lived, and those who left and returned as ghosts with those who profited from this history. Celebrations of countermemory as a liberatory practice must be tempered with attempts to mobilize memory at the hinterlands; political actors in postcolonial states have only a precarious hold on the power to organically connect "state" and "society," and thereby to forge a national memory.

An old nitrate-era song begins: "Orphans, cry the people / under chains / but they hold in their breast a promise." The Antillian poet Derek Walcott movingly describes the limitations of historical denunciation for postcolonial people born from the "monumental groaning and soldering of two worlds."[44] Genealogically the progeny of both the oppressors and the oppressed, these postcolonial children protest: "I say to the ancestor who sold me, and to the ancestor who bought me, I have no father, I want no such father, although I can understand you, black ghost, white ghost, when you both whisper 'history.'"[45] Yet these children are not simply heirs to this legacy; rather, as with the people of Tarapacá, they are its orphans. The anthropologist Sonia Montecino points out that in Chile the figure of the *huacho*, or foundling, has been pivotal in the nationalist ideology of *mestizaje*. Subverting this nationalist memory and freeing the foundling from its obligations to the state-as-surrogate-father entails acknowledging both the orphan's anger at being abandoned in the wake of conquest and colonialism and the possibilities inherent in being cut loose in a new world.[46] Perhaps this is the promise held onto in the orphans' song from the nitrate era: "A promise, yes, that will arrive, will come like a flower / liberty."

PART II *Conjunctures*

Dismantling Memory

STRUCTURING THE FORGETTING OF

THE OFICINA RAMÍREZ (1890–1891) AND

LA CORUÑA (1925) MASSACRES

3 In the 1950s Adelina Lara was forced to abandon one of the last nitrate-mining communities in the pampa and move to a small wooden cottage in the port city of Iquique. During an interview in 1993, she recounted what she knew of the La Coruña massacre.

> And there is also history in [La Coruña]. . . . At the entrance to the cemetery there is a grave my father told me about. They shot them at the grave tied up from behind, putting them in a line and throwing them in the grave. In these years they were bombarding in one part and terrorizing the people in another part. The communists have always been persecuted for trying to improve wages; the people have always been persecuted. My father told me that they would hold

meetings in the mining trenches by carbon lanterns because they weren't allowed to meet. My father told me about the grave; he showed it to me once. . . . Likewise, my husband told me about [the Escuela Santa María massacre of 1907], when they came to win the eight-hour day. The pampinos came down to Iquique. His father came down, too, but he was saved from the massacre because he was out getting drunk.[1]

While largely neglected in the dominant narratives of the Chilean Left, the story of the La Coruña massacre has survived in accounts of people like Adelina Lara who lived and worked in the nitrate region.[2] Her account reflects the primary mode of non-elite memory in the nitrate era: cathartic, that is, a direct link with moments of past suffering brought to the surface and reworked as a tool for change. Cathartic memory constituted militant working-class subjectivity and action. Subaltern memories, like that of the miners who survived by meeting secretly in the mining trenches or by getting drunk, have survived, tucked away in family and local history.

The La Coruña massacre, as with the Oficina Ramírez massacre of 1890, appears in history texts either submerged under more general accounts of nation-state crises or is never mentioned as relevant to the political history of the nation-state.[3] Yet consideration of these "secondary" events on the frontiers of nation-state history challenges understandings of "primary" crises, such as civil wars and diplomatic conflicts, conventionally seen as central, by showing how violence on the frontier has been vital to the making of the nation-state. Therefore, in this chapter I sketch the events of Ramírez and La Coruña and the politics of memory at work at the time. I then demonstrate the role of the state (through the competing branches of the military and education) in the forgetting of those events, a process that used nationalist rhetoric to foreground the memory of certain *other* forms of state violence and thus obscured instances of internal aggression and everyday forms of state violence.

Given the gap between histories of internal and external national conflict, the hollows of local histories filled with the stories of state repression and working-class persistence. As Adelina Lara commented, "And there is also history in [La Coruña]. . . . At the entrance to the cemetery there is a grave that my father told me about." In the words of Pablo Neruda, who represented Tarapacá in the Chilean senate,

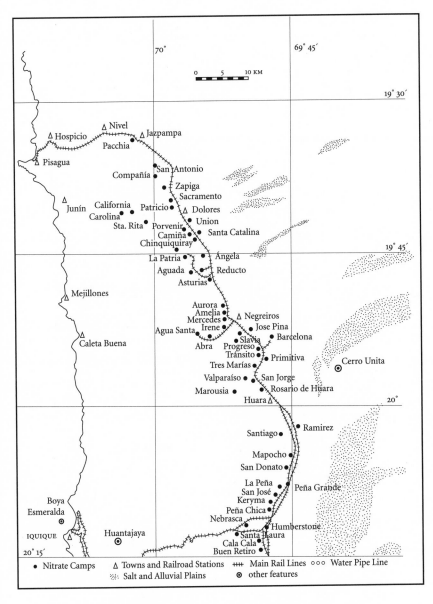

Map 2. Nitrate-era northern production sites. Based on map by Mark Somoza.

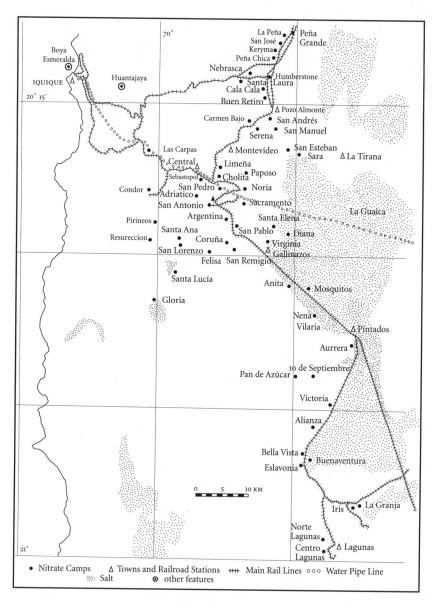

Map 3. Nitrate-era southern production sites. Based on map by Mark Somoza.

they were buried in darkness
or burned at night in silence,
heaped in mine shafts,
or their bones spit into the sea:

. . .

their executed hearts:
the Chileans smile:
the *pampas* valiant:
the captains of silence.[4]

Excavating the stories of these captains of silence uncovers not only the history of their struggles, but also the processes of forgetting, the burying and burning of memory.

In July 1890 and June 1925 the Chilean military launched full-scale military campaigns against nitrate-worker insurrections in Tarapacá. In both uprisings, laborers had seized the nitrate plants and run off foreign administrators during moments of profound crisis within the Chilean state. The general strike of July 1890 and its aftershock, the strike and repression of February 1891 during the Chilean Civil War, underscored labor conflict in the initial years of the nitrate era. The strike of 1925 reenacted the dramatic scenario of militant protest and repression during the constitutional crisis provoked by tensions between civilian politicians and the military. The vicious repression of strikers in the 1925 strike underlined the decline of the nitrate industry and the collapse of Chile's parliamentary system.

By situating these events not only in the history of the nitrate industry but also at the intersection of regional and national histories, one can see how a particular mode of forgetting — the obscuring and localizing of state violence — was critical to nation-state formation. Memories of events that unfolded in Tarapacá were key to Chilean state formation precisely through their elision, or partial erasure. These events were not hushed at the time they occurred; on the contrary, they received substantial commentary in both pro-state and non-elite press coverage. The marginalization of these events in the historical narratives of both the state and political parties points to the structure of forgetting on the frontiers of Chilean national memory. This mode of forgetting constituted an attempt to dismantle militant forms of cathartic memory.

The use of memory as catharsis among non-elite sectors entailed analyzing politics by drawing on an internationalist framing of class conflict, creating semiautonomous cultural and civic associations, and documenting state and industrial violence in both print and oral forms. For the Chilean state, this period saw an intensification of elite anxiety regarding political conflict, the strengthening of alliances between Chilean elites and foreign interests, and the counterbalancing of international, regional, and capital conflicts and crises. Multiple forms of violence constituted the Chilean state: wars, internal repression, and the violence of everyday conditions. Some forms of state violence — that is, certain episodes of internal repression — were necessarily obscured by the memorializing of the nation-state through the foregrounding of other memories of more "legitimate" state violence, such as wars of national conquest.

The legitimate control of violence has, in Chile, as in most modern states, formed a key component of the state's own story of nation making. Workers' explicit use of violence as a strike tactic both in material practices and in their rhetoric, especially in 1925, along with their traditionally strong internationalist current, further expelled them from the moral realm of the nation and thus voided their claims to citizenship.[5] Uncovering the processes of forgetting such acts of insurrection and repression reveals the centrality of violence within the nation-state and at the frontiers of national memories. State violence in the frontier zone of Tarapacá has been recognized nationally and internationally as particularly brutal. The key to understanding that brutality lies in the contradictions of regional memory as, on the one hand, the cradle of the labor movement, and, on the other, the consecrated ground of military history.

In the nitrate era, labor groups, the military, and newer contenders in the political system, such as educators and emerging political parties, used memory to spur social action both in the formation of state policy and in the mobilization of labor. As these groups have shaped the Chilean political system, memories of state repression have changed over time and have become part of the ongoing politics of present and future. Competing understandings of past state violence have profoundly informed the outcomes of conflictive moments. The processes of forgetting that mitigated the ramifications of the labor insurrections and resulting state repressions in 1890–1891 and 1925 frame a critical period of Chilean history — the nitrate era.

The Great Nitrate Era (1890–1930)

Nitrate, or saltpeter, lay in vast deposits on the surface of the Chilean desert. Miners dynamited, picked, and dug up the salted sands in the form of large chunks (*caliche*). In the processing plants young boys, called *matasapos* (figuratively, toad-killers), manually pulverized the caliche. Other workers then placed it into cauldrons of boiling water (*cachuchos*), after which the sodium chloride was poured away, leaving sodium nitrate deposits. Workers called *derripiadores* scraped away the deposits, sending sacks of the "white gold" by rail to the ports. From there it was shipped primarily to Europe, where it supplied the explosives and agricultural fertilizers necessary for European warfare and empire building.[6]

This production process required vast numbers of workers in an otherwise sparsely populated desert region.[7] In 1890 the nitrate provinces of Tarapacá and Antofagasta depended on 13,060 workers in fewer than fifty plants to export a million metric tons of nitrate. By 1925, ninety-six plants (out of 149 in existence) exported two million metric tons of nitrate and employed 60,785 workers.[8] The nitrate companies formed a cartel (Combinación), which regulated production to keep nitrate prices high. At any decline in the market, however, companies ceased production to avoid stockpiles; nitrate-industry strategies thus required an easily accessible and disposable labor supply. Most workers were recruited from Southern Chile, and they were shipped back south when sudden downturns in the market closed the camps, often overnight, then were brought back again when the industry picked up. The boom-and-bust cycles kept the camps and workers in a perpetually precarious position. Since the abrupt shutdown of operations often met with vehement protests from workers, nitrate administrators would appeal to the government for military forces to preserve "order."[9] They furthermore relied on the Chilean government to feed, house, and pay return passage south for the laid-off workers.[10]

Each nitrate company issued wages in tokens (*fichas*), which workers used to buy food, water, liquor, clothing, and tools at the company store. Alternatively, they could exchange the tokens at a discount for the chronically weak Chilean currency.[11] The token system both heightened company profits and restricted workers' mobility. From the strike of 1890 throughout the era of the nitrate industry, laborers constantly pressed the nitrate companies to pay them in

1. The evocative ruins of Oficina Humberstone, one of many nitrate ghost towns left on the pampa after the spectacular crashes of the industry. While most of the camps ceased functioning in the 1930s, this one lingered until the 1950s. Photo by Mark Somoza.

coins at a rate tied to the British pound sterling.[12] Protesting the unfairness of a cartel of employers, the early autonomous labor organizations — mutual aid societies called *mancomunales* — allied themselves in a new association, which they called Combinación (after the owners' cartel), thus pulling off a very serious satire of employers' tactics. Laborers organized in hopes of mitigating their vulnerability to fickle economic cycles.[13]

Nitrate was a volatile commodity in more ways than one. The state and the Chilean elite invested little of the nitrate revenues in diversifying the national economy, leaving the country vulnerable to fluctuations in world markets.[14] By the 1920s, in spite of the short boom brought on by World War I, the Chilean nitrate industry had entered its final decline, spurred by the German development of synthetic nitrates.[15] Whereas Chile previously had once supplied over two-thirds of the world's sodium nitrate, by 1925 its market share had fallen to less than a quarter.[16]

Eventually, the precarious swing of economic cycles crashed and nitrate mining was for the most part finished. For well over three decades now, the nitrate fields of Tarapacá have been virtually uninhabited except for a couple of dusty towns along the Pan-American Highway, a handful of camps that extract iodine from the residue of the old nitrate-processing plants, and a single intact yet abandoned nitrate camp — a ghostly reminder of the epic proportions of another era.

From 1890 to 1930, Chile earned over half of its wealth from its nitrate reserves, which it had acquired in the 1879 War of the Pacific, between Chile and a Peruvian and Bolivian confederation.[17] In winning that war Chile gained a quarter to a third of its current national territory, the mineral-rich provinces of Tarapacá and Antofagasta.[18] The War of the Pacific gave Chile control (albeit through concessions to European, primarily British, entrepreneurs) of the world's primary source of the single-most-important commodity at the end of the nineteenth century. A brutal Chilean civil war in 1891, fought in part over the degree of national control of the nitrate industry, resulted in continued foreign dominance of the industry.[19] In the face of overt international influence, the state adopted an increasingly vehement attitude of militarized nationalism toward the region and cemented this stance through official historical narratives. However, this national memory had to contend with the region's legacy of labor and political mobilization.

The Eliding of Memory

In the nitrate period, workers, nitrate companies, and the state all actively recalled, as part of their tactical maneuvers, past episodes of worker mobilization and state repression. In the 1924 commemoration of the 1907 Santa María massacre, for example, labor newspapers hoped that the improved organization of the labor movement and the shame of the massacre would prevent the current military from becoming "the assassins of the Chilean people like their predecessors."[20] After the 1921 San Gregorio massacre of striking nitrate workers in Antofagasta, nitrate companies used the specter of a militant strike to intimidate the state into making preemptive arrests of blacklisted agitators.[21] The state later explicitly used the memory of this same massacre to threaten other organizers, including Luis Emilio Recabarren, the founder of the Chilean Socialist and Communist Parties.[22]

Thus, during this time, the labor movement and non-elite political organizations situated prior cases of state violence as equivalent in importance to the most nationally famous incidents and acknowledged the particular aspects that distinguished them. Yet, since that period, the Ramírez and La Coruña massacres have been glossed over in collective memory, especially in dominant narratives of the Chilean Left. The eliding of memory offers a more precise characterization of this particular process of forgetting. For instance, when mentioned in later years, the La Coruña incident was generally referred to, almost in passing, as merely one in a series of massacres. It was also said to mark the end of the so-called heroic period of Chilean labor history. In official memory, the strikes and repressions of 1890–1891 and 1925 were subsumed under what were regarded as more central, constitutional crises as well as under issues of international relations. In this sense, the stories of what happened in the North, rather than silenced, were elided into national narratives. Both conjunctures, bookending the heroic period of Chilean labor history, constitute moments when the mass mobilization of working-class communities and their repression by the state shaped processes of Chilean state formation and the growth of oppositional cultures in Chile.

From the Strike of 1890 to the Civil War of 1891: Oficina Ramírez

In late 1890 nitrate workers led the first general strike in Chilean history. A few months before, President José Manuel Balmaceda Fernández had toured the northern nitrate regions; his denunciation of British monopolies in the nitrate industry were later seen as the basis for nationalist economic sentiment. At the time, his rhetoric helped him to forge an alliance with workers. His political adversaries accused him of having incited workers to strike in order to further his own political ends. Indeed, President Balmaceda seemed initially tolerant of, even sympathetic to, the workers' actions. On learning of the strike, Balmaceda demanded to know whether it was "against the government or against the foreigners" and what the political positions of key local journalists and newspapers were. He also wanted to know what the workers demanded and what "intelligent, reasonable and equitable" steps the intendente (regional governor) had taken.[23]

The 1890 strike began with dockworkers in the port of Iquique, supposedly incited by a local newspaper, *El Nacional* (Iquique edition).[24] Workers demanded that companies pay them not in tokens but in silver or its equivalent.[25] Companies calculated that this would in effect increase wages by 60 to 70 percent.[26] On July 7 the intendente announced that he could not guarantee the protection of property if companies did not meet strikers' demands. The companies agreed to pay in silver but immediately considered other ways to limit any newfound worker power, for example, slowing down production during times of labor unrest. Workers, rightly suspecting that these concessions were meant to stall the conflict, continued to agitate.[27] Strikers in Iquique attacked the offices of newspapers, such as *Industria* and *Voz de Chile*, that they viewed as allied with nitrate interests.[28] Nitrate miners seized plants and company stores and ran off foreign administrators all across the pampa.[29] The strike then expanded to sectors of Santiago and the central port of Valparaíso.[30] Under enormous political pressure, Balmaceda shifted policy and forcefully repressed the strike.[31]

By mid-1890, Balmaceda had become irrevocably embroiled in the collapse of elite consensus, which culminated in the Civil War of 1891. The war positioned the president along with some military officers against the congress, British nitrate interests, and most of the army. A dispute over the national budget and the collection of nitrate export revenues precipitated the civil war. President Balmaceda ordered the cessation of nitrate production as the North fell under the control of the congress, which named Iquique as the provisional national capital. Nitrate workers faced a de facto lockout without any support for their subsistence. Their attempt to bring their grievances to the president's attention resulted in the repression called the Oficina Ramírez massacre. Balmaceda faced grave consequences for not only denying support for workers' reparations but also brutally suppressing the workers; these actions contributed to the mass desertion of troops from Balmaceda's army due to their dismay over his use of state violence both in the 1890 strike and in the repression of workers during the civil war.

British nitrate interests, in the nitrate companies and the foreign office, heralded the coming of the civil war, predicting that the cessation of production would improve the European nitrate market by raising prices while using up stocks of nitrate. Yet the cessation of production caused chaos at the local level, as British agents predicted 10,000 out-of-work laborers.[32] Indeed, by February 1891, many workers found themselves without sustenance, trapped between fighting military forces.[33]

The most well-known account of the subsequent events, written by the historian Francisco Antonio Encina, was based on conversations with key political and military actors, the British consul, and the correspondence of the German consul.[34] According to Encina, the presidential forces arrived in Iquique to learn that 2,000 workers had gathered from across the pampa. The workers had headed for Iquique by train to protest their dire conditions and to demand that the almost daily battles cease.[35] The intendente arranged to have the train engine disconnected near the Oficina Ramírez, next to the town of Huara. Here, the workers came under fire from troops sent to intercept them. Some fled across the pampa while others surrendered or were captured. Encina reported that eighteen of the leaders were executed and argued that while the violence protected Iquique, it further propelled the workers on the pampa toward revolution. On 16 February, even the people of Iquique (the ostensible beneficiaries of state actions) rioted to protest the killings at Oficina Ramírez.

Non-elite accounts of these riots and the massacre circulated at the time through popular poetry.[36] The poet José Arroyo, for example, told of riots in Iquique that involved workers from the pampa and that were quelled by troops brought in on the ship *El Imperial*: "The troops did wonders / because they made a hundred dead."[37] Then, according to the poet, the disorderly people fled for the desert, but some 800 were captured and thus the port city was saved.

At that point, Iquique fell under the control of insurgent congressional forces, which attempted to subdue the public's anger without losing popular support.[38] By the end of February, newspaper reports from the zone were reassuring: "In the Pampas in the interior everything is quiet. All the 'peones' have been occupied by the Government, some making a road . . . and others having joined the army."[39] This confident pronouncement from the capital suggests that the government mistook the quiet for the silencing of workers' discontents. Yet in that quiet was preserved the memory of struggle and repression that would fuel workers' struggles throughout the nitrate era. That the repression of the general strike and the Oficina

Ramírez massacre may not have deterred workers from organizing but may have actually incensed their militancy is borne out in the labor conflicts that persisted during the civil war.[40]

After the nitrate era, the story of Balmaceda and the Civil War of 1891 became allegory: in the populist era the Left told it as an account of a popular regime that *also* (empathy) fought imperialist control of the national economy; during authoritarian military rule, the opposition told it as a fable (meant to elicit sympathy) of the national-popular utopia martyred in the 1973 coup. While the labor conflicts of 1890–1891 played a key part in shaping the political crisis rending the Chilean state, the subsequent resurrection of Balmaceda as a populist and nationalist mythical figure effectively silenced the public memory of those struggles, as leftist memories could not bear the seeming contradiction of the martyred president's role in state repression.[41] In conjunction with these images, rightist historiography portrayed Balmaceda as an impractical and even despotic ruler. In each of these versions, as in the elite accounts of the events at the time, the actions and aspirations of the worker-soldiers were assumed to be coterminous with political contests for the state.

Yet working-class communities in Tarapacá demonstrated a remarkable ability to sustain semiautonomous relations with the state and to foment alternative social and cultural realms. The repression at Oficina Ramírez was linked to both the general strike six months earlier and the subsequent exponential increase in working-class associative life.[42] In spite of the magnitude of repression workers faced in 1891, "the memory did not die," insists the historian Pinto Vallejos, although workers later strategically promoted the "myth of Balmacedism." The memory of the general strike of 1890 and "the largest massacre of workers occurring up until that date in the nitrate North," along with workers' militarization in the armies of the civil war, combined to serve as a political "apprenticeship." The mobilized cathartic memory of these experiences enabled the nitrate communities to organize as they never had before.[43] The workers' increasingly militant oppositional culture grew even in the face of ongoing nationalist militarization of the region by the Chilean state.

Along with labor unrest and national political turmoil, another key event in 1890 reinforced the contradictions of memory in Tarapacá as a militarized frontier territory. Coinciding with the general strike, national attention had focused on Tarapacá for one of the major state initiatives at détente with Peru since Chile's conquest of the nitrate fields in the 1879 War of the Pacific.[44] The Chilean state exhumed, honored as heroic, and repatriated the remains of Peruvian officers killed on the battlefields of Tarapacá a decade earlier.[45] Repatriation from conquered territory made possible the material eradication of the Peruvian natural presence from the northern landscape and the removal of possible nationalist sites of mourning for those in the occupied territory who still yearned for older allegiances. Still, Peruvian foot soldiers remained, both in the earth and as spirits wandering the battlefields and roads of the desert—like the ghost of an Afro-Peruvian soldier who, residents say, rests in his rocking chair at the edge of Huara, where he perished in combat.[46] Through specifically valorizing the Peruvian war dead as relics of another country's (i.e., Peru's) national honor, the repatriation initiative of 1890 corresponded with the Chilean state's early and ongoing efforts to "Chilenize" regional memory by positioning it in nationalist terms.

In addition to these battlesites from the 1879 War of the Pacific, Tarapacá's centrality in the political and military struggles of the 1891 Civil War further increased the region's prominence in Chilean military memory. Iquique's importance as the provisional national capital for the forces opposed to President Balmaceda remained a point of pride for pro-military residents, who would often point to the battle scars on the customs house as marks of military glory. After the civil war, the ongoing militarization of the region was reinforced further by the state's policy of employing retired officers in regional government positions.[47]

The constitution of a national memory founded in military feats faced the challenge of cathartic memory's cleavage along class lines. The loyalties evidenced in the workers' successful engineering of a general strike presented just such a direct challenge. The seizure of nitrate plants and ports and the general strike's rapid spread to other regions of the country led to an elite paranoia among the government officials and the upper classes of the North.[48] The fear of worker militancy and organization would in the future justify repression as a means to prevent the worst-case scenario: workers taking over the provincial capital, Iquique, including the nitrate barons' palaces, offices, and banks. These fears, etched in elite and state memory, were seemingly realized in the massive worker insurrection of 1925.

State Violence on the Frontier: La Coruña, 1925

The years leading up to 1925 were marked by great political up-heaval. In spite of Chile's reputation as the model republic of South America, by 1925 the stalemate of oligarchic parliamentary politics had collapsed under the weight of social tensions and military pres-sure.[49] The military had forced the parliament to pass a whole set of legislation, including an elaborate labor code and revised military budget.[50] A new constitution was under negotiation between Presi-dent Alessandri, political parties, and the military led by reformist officer and minister of war Carlos Ibáñez del Campo.[51] Relations between President Alessandri and the military under Ibáñez even-tually deteriorated further, and Ibáñez effectively presided over the Chilean state from 1925 until 1931, a period of authoritarian rule that coincided with the economic devastation of 1929.

Internal political crisis was exacerbated by ongoing international conflict. In the mid-1920s tensions between Chile and Peru had heightened over the border question left unresolved from the War of the Pacific. At the end of that war, Chile had received stewardship of the two border cities between Chile and Peru, Tacna and Arica. After a certain period, a plebiscite was to be held in the occupied territory and residents were to choose their allegiance at that time. Yet when and how this would be organized proved to be a chronic diplomatic challenge, and international war seemed an ever-present possibility.[52] Rumors of Peruvian gold being used to buy potential voters for a future plebiscite were prevalent.[53] Nationalist newspapers suggested that Peru was financing subversive activity in the region in order to destabilize Chilean rule and that subversive agents were fomenting unrest in the nitrate region on behalf of Peru.[54] Other rumors and state press reports suggested that dynamite-hurling "Bolsheviks" were attempting to construct a workers' soviet on the nitrate pampa. Infiltration by multiple foreign sources was called on to explain labor discontent.

Ironically, it was the military that, by forcing new labor legislation through congress, went beyond nationalist rhetoric to address social issues at the base of the economic and political crisis. The new codes restructured industrial relations, situating the state as the interme-diary between capital and labor. Labor organizations initially rejected this legislation, which aimed to heavily regulate union activity. Meanwhile, the nitrate companies ignored the legislation, and the reforms remained largely unimplemented.[55]

Still, the Chilean state persisted in attempting to assume the role of mediator. In March and April 1925, further unrest came in the form of railway and nitrate-worker strikes. The state arbitrated the strikes, but nitrate companies ignored the settlement, regarding the fact that workers had pressured the administrative employees to comply with the stoppage as a sign of outrageous strike tactics. Ultimately supporting the companies, the government summoned troops to the nitrate zone and called a battleship to the region.

According to British industrial intelligence reports at the time, agitators held a meeting of about 2,500 workers in Alto San Antonio and a simultaneous meeting of workers from another set of camps to plan a general strike across the entire nitrate region of Tarapacá. The workers resolved to demand the dissolution of the Association of Nitrate Producers; strict compliance with the colonization law; nationalization of the nitrate industry; and the removal of an abusive police officer. The intelligence reports also suggested that workers felt they needed to save up more funds and to declare simultaneous strikes in order to assure success: "Their idea is not to have a pacific strike, but to resort to strong measures. . . . [T]here was an idea amongst the men of storing up dynamite."[56] This strategy of direct action was bolstered by the nitrate workers' faith in the class solidarity of conscripts.[57]

In response to the growing tension, the intendente ordered the closure of all bars and prohibited the sale of alcohol during the strike.[58] Conceding to workers' requests, he also endeavored to set up arbitration even as he proceeded to send a cavalry regiment to the pampa.[59] The state's attempt to mediate industrial relations through brute coercion of workers and feeble persuasion of employers merely deferred conflict.[60]

The nitrate companies had insisted that the Chilean state rush an entire military contingent to preempt the strike.[61] During late April and May 1925, the governor of Pisagua, having jurisdiction over the northern nitrate sector, began to round up suspected labor leaders and to ship them to the Chilean capital, a preemptive move heartily approved by the British.[62] The national government in Santiago requested that local officials clarify their motives for the deportation.[63] Having been reassured, state officials in the capital then heartily commended the governor for taking vigorous preemptive measures.[64]

The governor's punitive action, together with the shutting down of the working-class press, provoked outrage in multiple sectors.[65] In closing the main working-class newspapers—the communist paper, *El Despertar*, and the anarchist paper, *El Surco*—the government attacked one of the pillars of Chilean labor organization and propelled workers toward a general strike.[66] Workers continued to organize and plan for a great general strike until, in early June 1925, localized conflicts precipitated mass mobilization of workers and troops.[67]

On the night of 3 June 1925, police interrupted a labor planning meeting in the nitrate railroad-station town of Alto San Antonio, where workers had just decided to participate in a national work stoppage the next day.[68] In the altercation that ensued, two of the policemen were killed.[69]

Accounts of the subsequent events vary wildly. After the deaths of the policmen, workers began to gather in key camps such as La Coruña. According to military reports, the workers had been led to form soviets by an anarchist worker-agitator, Carlos Garrido. Garrido called himself El Mariscal or Comisario, emulated Lenin, costumed himself in a red shirt and sash as "a symbol of destruction and blood," and attempted to "persuade new workers, ex-peasants, to hate the military and to destroy the right to private property."[70] He purportedly received a cryptogram from the Workers' Federation to intensify labor conflict, and he took that directive to its absolute limit: confident that the entire pampa would rise up, Garrido had given the order to combat.[71]

Despite these descriptions, the charismatic figure of Carlos Garrido is less prominent in regional oral lore, which suggests that he alone did not incite the conflict at La Coruña. Indeed, another version of the story implies that the struggle grew out of an altercation between the manager of the company store and the pregnant wife of a miner. After the manager beat the woman, he was knifed by her husband.[72] This account emphasized the strike as an extension of working-class defense of honor.

Accounts sanctioned by leftist political parties underlined conflictive social structures as the cause of the conflagration. A popular-history booklet told a story of inchoate rage: the government wished to incite trouble among workers, as it saw them making unprecedented gains in parliamentary elections. Therefore, just before the strike at La Coruña, unlimited quantities of alcohol were sold to the workers. During the strike itself, the sale of alcohol was prohibited, and the enraged, drunken workers shot the company-store manager, compelling the administrators to run for help. In Iquique none of this was surprising, given that the companies had purposefully incited the workers, who were gullible. The booklet concluded by recounting that the troops bombarded La Coruña and subsequently began to "palomear rotos" — to shoot workers down into the trenches like game birds.[73]

At that point, it seems, foreign administrators abandoned several of the camps and ran to call for help from the Chilean state.[74] Workers took over southern-sector camps as well as some northern-sector camps; at least a dozen camps observed the work stoppage, as did railway and some port workers.[75] Reporting that the proposed workers' soviet would assassinate anyone who stood in their way, the antilabor press offered a sense of what was at stake in the conflict: "The laws that bind this Republic never have been violated, nor even less have occurred attacks against property and the lives of the patron bosses, the likes of which have passed since last Thursday in the richest and most historically significant province in our history."[76]

The sense that much more than wages or working conditions was at risk also appears in workers' accounts of the movement. In an interview published in *El Nacional* just after the repression, the miner D'Aquini Pizarro explained, "The *federados* [members of the Workers' Federation] obliged us to strike because of the closing of *El Despertar* and the presence of military forces on the pampa; because, in truth, more than the closing of their paper, the communists protested against the arrival of the military in their domain."[77]

The Chilean government had responded to the labor mobilization by cutting off public access between the nitrate fields and the ports, then sending several regiments, complete with cannons and machine guns, to bombard the camps under worker control.[78] According to military reports, the workers reacted to the presence of cannons by hurling dynamite. A telegram from General Antonio de la Guarda to President Alessandri explained the military's subsequent tactics.

When the troops began to impose order, the workers took up convenient positions [and], after seeding the field with dynamite, violently resisted the troops, who due to their reduced number, saw that it would be impossible to attack. . . . In light of the failure of efforts to calm the rebels by pacific means, thus began the bombardment. . . . The rebels put up a white flag so that the troops would trustingly come closer and subsequently put up the red flag, obliging the artillery to redouble the fire. . . . The combat, deliberately initiated long-distance, produced scarce casualties, counted at first, in number, thirty-four. Afterwards other cadavers were found in caliche caves and on the roads of the *quebrada* [gulch] of Hatacondo, all of which sum to date fifty-nine. In spite of the state of siege, on the pampa [workers] have continued dynamite attacks against the troops charged with securing order.[79]

In the end, the military rounded up workers in a process that lasted several weeks and involved raids on nitrate camps and towns throughout the region.[80] The military summarily shot some workers. Hundreds more were herded to the port of Iquique, imprisoned, and subjected to military justice.[81] The "Bolshevik encampment" set up there was run by the military according to international laws for prisoners of war, although the military claimed that "agitators within the prisoners' camp continued to protest in a stubborn campaign."[82] Some prisoners were shipped south for trial and punishment, while others deemed less dangerous were offered as docile workers for the copper mines.[83] Beginning in mid-June 1925, President Alessandri declared a sixty-day state of siege in order to "clean up" the region.[84]

At this point, the elite press accounts invoked national memory to offer an interpretation that would become the dominant framing of the violence: shifting the problem from one of internal state repression to one of national security on the frontier. The extensive press coverage in support of the government and nitrate interests hailed General de la Guarda as a hero and praised the troops, through comparison with the soldiers of the War of the Pacific, as having embodied the nation's honor: "The Carampangue [Regiment] conscripts, with valorous resolution, patriotic determination, disposed to give their lives—not in a fight, straightforwardly, with a common enemy, but rather with bad Chileans and foreign elements—advanced like the legions of the brave Atacama with unequaled warrior struggle and dominated the situation."[85] Using the analogy of the War of the Pacific, the pro-state press portrayed the internal military campaign against workers as equally vital to national interests. Praise took on sharply ideological forms. For instance, *El Nacional* declared, "In Chile, fascism should be founded to drown criminal communism. . . . Italy, working in peace, has prospered. In Chile it's sure to do the same. Come, fascism, now we need it."[86] Further congratulations for the military poured forth from President Alessandri, Minister of War Ibáñez del Campo, and various military regiments.[87]

In dramatic contrast, Alessandri's words to the workers of Tarapacá were stern and chastising: "[The workers] should be made to understand that the Government in the future will not tolerate propaganda meant to alter social order nor slander the authorities. For that reason, if they want to improve their conditions, they must abandon the path followed up until today and embrace the benefits offered by the recently dictated social laws."[88]

Thus, in the politics of memory the 1925 labor insurrection was not forgotten in the sense of being simply covered up, but rather was drowned out by the preoccupations of the formal political system and then subsumed into the public-policy rhetoric known as the "social question" as well as the rhetoric of national integrity.

That the politics of forgetting do not always work through silencing can be discerned in the ways in which the various presses became central protagonists of the conflict. Newspapers, too, embodied the cathartic political culture of the time through the explicit recognition that the primary node of conflict was that of incommensurable class interests. Profoundly concerned with the struggle for political voice, the workers initially rose to defend their newspapers, the communist *El Despertar* and the anarchist *El Surco*. Later, the pro-state newspapers, *El Nacional* and *El Tarapacá*, as well as smaller papers, worked in conjunction with state efforts to recast the conflict as one of morally weak workers tragically led astray by foreign agitators.

The pro-state newspapers told a cautionary tale to both the regional and national elite and the working-class communities, painting workers as victims of their own ignorance and gullibility, and hence as redeemable by a stern but forgiving state and industry: "The tragic end of the agitators, of the ringleaders who induced the tranquil workers like docile lambs to revolt, will be remembered by many with bitterness and regret, and they will not wish again to seek adventure in such a dangerous situation that today we lament, and [they will remember] that the communist ringleaders are the guilty ones who in this city and on the pampa had [taken over] because the authorities gave them too much discretionary freedom."[89] Redemption entailed memory-work whereby "we" (the assumed-elite public) would allocate historical accountability for the violence. In this allocation the "ringleaders" are the sole bearers of guilt, thus absolving the otherwise "docile lambs." Indeed, the state was held to task for being too permissive and for not responsibly safeguarding both the docile lambs and the public readership of *El Nacional*. Pro-state newspapers seemed to be generating memory for their own purposes as the voice of the elite-state nexus: to emphasize the punitive consequences of working-class attempts to create semiautonomous realms of sociability and politics. Working people also were admonished to forget their heroes and utopian aspirations.

> Painful has been the final part of the job in which the military forced respect for order, safeguarded lives and property, guaranteed the freedom of work, etc., but we must frankly declare that this has been very necessary. It was the only way and manner to finish with the bad elements that were useful, neither for the *patria*, nor for humanity, nor for society.
>
> A spadeful of the earth of forgetting over the fallen!![90]

The state used the threat of forgetting to enforce a radically exclusionary discipline in the name of the nation as circumscribed to a particular place. Using cathartic gestures invoking intense emotion and violence, the newspaper describes a situation of radical distinctions: either one is "useful" for the patria or "a bad element" to be "finish[ed] with," in other words, eradicated. The pay-off for submitting to this discipline is incorporation into the nation. Thus, workers were taught to fear their own erasure from national memory.

State rhetoric immediately after the conflagration also centered on the regulation of dynamite and drink in the nitrate region, a paternalist management of vice that masked the state-sanctioned proliferation of quotidian violence.[91] The emphasis on regulation corresponded with the rhetorical concentration of conflict between elite and popular sectors under the rubric of the social question, which removed issues of injustice from the realm of political economy to that of a moral economy of vice and virtue. To counteract the flourishing working-class newspapers of the North, promoters of Catholic unions, inspired by Pope Leon XII's encyclical, founded an alternative paper, *Cuestiones Sociales*, with articles expounding the fine qualities and patriotism of Chilean workers, whose only downfall were vices such as gambling and drink and a susceptibility to "unhealthy doctrines and revolutionary propaganda."[92] The rhetoric of the social question, disseminated through the pro-state and industry press, further pacified labor by emphasizing workers' moral vulnerability to vice as well as to outside agitators—workers' concerns and actions were thus negated.

The barrage of state-positive press coverage elicited counternarratives.[93] In Santiago the Communist Party paper *La Justicia* offered extensive, if not firsthand, coverage of the events in the North. Even in Southern Chile, working-class newspapers declared that it was clear from the "bourgeois press" that there had been a massacre of unprecedented scale in the North, but that, "the worker's press can't even protest such injustice because in each case it is shut down."[94] Similarly, marginalized working-class narratives of the repression were subjected to the politics of forgetting—drowned out through an onslaught of state-sanctioned reporting that denied labor's agency in the insurrection leading to the repression.[95] The state set out to dismantle the cathartic force of subaltern memory and to subordinate non-elite cultural spheres to a militarized national memory.

Obscuring Cathartic Memory: The Military and Educators in the Battle over National Memory

The Office of Labor Inspection credited the calamity of 1925 with inciting nitrate producers and the government to renew their commitment to labor reforms.[96] State mediation between capital and labor seemed all the more imperative as "only a long process of education and effort to establish reciprocal courtesies might end or at least attenuate the state of things."[97] Thus, in the aftermath of the 1925 movement, the state asserted its command over the North and the workers via the intersection of two of its traditionally key arenas, both couched in adamantly nationalist terms: defense and education.[98] Colonel Ibáñez del Campo began the "long process of education," placing under military guidance programs of augmented civic education for both adults and children.[99] The military was to create good Chilean citizens by instilling in them an appreciation for the martial glories of Chilean history, thereby forging an official, national memory. Nation-state formation, even when it involved violent, authoritarian military intervention, required the creation of official histories and the delimitation of spaces in which those histories could circulate. Nationalizing memory in the North, a region devastated by state violence, entailed the destruction of alternative, oppositional cathartic memory. Thus began a new phase in battles over education, memory, and the nation.

In the Chilean political system, the military, through its rhetorically antipolitical positioning, was charged as the guardian of national memory over and above the particular interests of civilian politics. The military's sense of mission was heightened by the fact that nineteenth-century Chilean state formation was dominated by a series of international military engagements culminating in the 1879 War of the Pacific.[100] Commemorations of battles and war heroes constituted the major national holidays.[101] Foremost among them was Naval Day (May 21st), which honored Arturo Prat, hero of the Battle of Iquique.[102] Beginning in the nineteenth century, the military used public commemorations of national holidays as a form of civic education, especially on the northern frontier. Military officer Patricio Lynch, the first Chilean administrator of Tarapacá following its conquest in the War of the Pacific, considered primary education to be an ideal vehicle for, in his terms, "normalizing" and "making nicer" Chilean military occupation. He felt that the diverse nationalities of Tarapacá's populace could achieve greater mutual understanding by coming together in primary-level public school, where, moreover, "the Creoles of these populations would conclude by Chilenizing themselves."[103] Military bands later visited elementary schools to teach national hymns, which the children would then perform alongside military displays under an appropriate monument.[104] In the 1920s President Alessandri ordered the schools to participate in national commemorations in order to "stimulate patriotic sentiment as a primordial end of education in public establishments of learning." Specifically, for 18 September (Independence Day), the state required students to sing the national anthem at monuments designated by the governor or school inspector; schools also had to schedule annual visits to the monuments and tombs of the heroes and fathers of the patria and to nearby national historic sites.[105]

However, the military's prerogative to shape national memory did not go unchallenged. Teachers, as contending agents of the state, asserted an alternative vision of patriotic allegiance, thus risking excommunication from the nation as issues of class solidarity continued to be subsumed under a rhetoric of external threats to the nation-state. Given the military's influence on education and the renewed militarization of the North after the 1925 strike, it was all the more remarkable that many schoolteachers in Tarapacá manifested their

solidarity with nitrate workers by refusing to attend the public ceremonies commemorating significant battles.[106] When news of the repression reached Santiago, the Association of Teachers there issued a
formal protest against repressive state policy. In response, pro-state
newspapers called for a nationwide purge of teachers with revolutionary ideas, especially in the North.[107] Because the War of the
Pacific had ended without definitive territorial treaties, the North
remained a place of military insecurity where national identity was
potentially transferable. In 1926 the regional government, on behalf
of the plebiscite office, requested that the national director of education transfer two teachers of "Peruvian descent" to schools further
south, as their "origin and Peruvian sentiments" made them a danger
to regional security.[108] Officials further lamented, "It is not rare to
find establishments of instruction in which a Miss or Mr. Child-of-
Bolivian-or-Peruvian . . . has been assigned to teach the *Historia
Patria.*"[109] The annual provincial-education report further emphasized the general sentiment that all teachers should be of "decidedly
Chilean descent."[110]

Even after the intense state repression of La Coruña, some teachers
still refused to participate in national or military commemorations
and faced arrest and dismissal for their defiance.[111] In general, schoolteachers' allegiances to the labor movement in explicit defiance of the
state deeply worried the military and the political elite of the capital.
In Santiago the presidents of the political parties decried that a student center called Lenin had been founded in the North and that
communist theories were being propagated by teachers throughout
the country; they urged that the government "adopt repressive measures, eliminating those who don't recognize their responsibilities,
combating the established regime on which they depend and twist-
ing the mentality of their students." They continued, "These precep-
tors' propaganda is the most pernicious and, as such, is what should
be punished with maximum energy and without further contempla-
tion."[112] Elite anxiety over the reliability of educators as agents of
state interests and fomenters of national memory prompted and bolstered the increased role of the military in civic education under the
Ibáñez del Campo regime.[113]

The Ibáñez regime preoccupied itself with the project of regional
Chilenization in the contest with Peru over the anticipated plebiscite
to settle the border dispute. The military saw issues of national se-

curity and national identity as completely intermeshed, especially in dangerous frontier zones: Tarapacá was both a site of Chilean military glory and a vulnerable frontier zone. The Chilenization project was all the more remarkable since labor in the North was constituted primarily of Chilean nationals.[114] The state had begun to emerge from its more strictly oligarchic form and had recognized that in this period political identity carried a class component. Thus, a national memory had to be crafted to explain, discipline, and surmount class cleavages in order to make the nation the ultimate frame for subjectivity. To effect this, the state ideologically foregrounded a new protagonist of Chilean history: the roto chileno.[115]

The working-class communities in the North, while technically comprising Chilean nationals, engaged in ambivalent relations with the nation-state despite the ways in which the military conquests of the War of the Pacific had valorized the category of the roto chileno. *Roto* had long been a derogatory term for the broken and impoverished (often referring specifically to peasants), and it was applied to non-elite classes in general. While the term originally applied to Chilean soldiers in an earlier war with Peru (1839), enthusiasm for the bravery of those earlier soldiers peaked only in the wake of the War of the Pacific. Thereafter, the military revalued the term *rotos chilenos* to evoke nationalist fighting valor.[116] Nicolás Palacios, a physician in the nitrate region, published numerous articles in Iquique's newspapers proclaiming the courage of the roto as the foundation for the "Chilean race" and nationalist sentiment.[117] Palacios advocated pride in Chile's mestizo qualities as a key component of economic nationalism, not just in opposition to foreign monopoly over the nitrate industry.[118] Palacios demanded that Chile's political elite recognize the virtues of the roto chileno by dedicating resources for education and economic advancement, which would offer non-elite sectors a legitimate way into the national realm.[119] The racialized worker-soldier figure of the roto chileno was thus advanced as a new national protagonist. At times, workers themselves used the rhetoric of patriotism to underline their demand for state protection. For example, one workers' petition asking the state to attend to their situation ended, "God willing, you will respond to our petition and when the Fatherland needs us, we will be ready."[120] They thus attempted to benefit from their dual role as worker-soldiers.[121]

In spite of efforts to incorporate working classes into national memory and into a nationalist project, blatant neglect of working-class war veterans and several decades of fierce labor conflict during which the Chilean government repressed workers on behalf of foreign capital had bruised relations between non-elite sectors and the state.[122] The working-class communities of the North mobilized around primarily class-based allegiances, explicitly internationalist, as evidenced by their public commemorations, which included faithful observances of the Chicago Haymarket Massacre each May Day, and by the widely recognized alliances between Chilean, Peruvian, and Bolivian workers, including that during the 1907 nitrate strike. For many Chilean workers, loyalties other than those to the fatherland beckoned.

In an effort to nationalize May Day and through its commemoration to emphasize the state's new role as mediator of capital and labor interests, President Alessandri decreed 1 May a legal holiday to be observed by public, state events.[123] Further countering the strength of labor organizations, the Chilean state took steps to foment divisiveness among nitrate workers by appealing to latent—and often explicit—nationalist and racist sentiments among working-class sectors regarding competition between Chilean and foreign workers, especially Bolivians and the Chinese; however, the main appeal to nationalist allegiance pointed to the ongoing territorial conflicts between Chile and Peru, as expressed by the Chilenization project. Conflicts between nitrate companies and workers and the lack of national sovereignty over the nitrate industry were cast in anti-Peruvian terms. For example, a conflict over nationalist memory between the Peruvian consul and the intendente of Tarapacá with regard to the anniversary of the Chilean military's invasion of Pisagua (in the War of the Pacific) inspired a diatribe from the intendente to the Chilean Ministry of Exterior Relations. The intendente complained that the foreign consulates in Iquique were not staffed by nationals from the appropriate country, but often by Peruvians or by consuls with Peruvian wives. He then asserted, "The Chileans of Tarapacá occupy a secondary place in the conjunction of industrial, commercial and social activity." He feared that the wealthier and more influential foreigners, especially the British and Peruvians, were infiltrating and asserting their own "personality." Therefore, the intendente stressed the urgency of "detaining the absorption of the national spirit through laws or administrative policies to resolve the numerous pending problems affecting the well-being of the Chilean working class of the region, improving the situation of public employees and giving the authorities extraordinary powers to effectively do the work of Chilenization."[124] Thus, the regional government moderated labor conflict by insisting that the problems could be traced to corrupt Peruvian administrators and by counseling the nitrate companies to fire foreign administrators.[125] The state worked to redirect working-class affiliations and to cut off ties beyond the nation.

In conjunction with state practices of fomenting division among workers, the Patriotic Leagues became quite active in the north of Chile, harassing Peruvian and Bolivian residents and painting their homes with crosses in late-night raids. The leagues were private, sometimes armed, associations, and their activities corresponded with the Chilean state's efforts to remove as many Peruvians as possible from the North so Chile would stand a better chance of winning the anticipated plebiscite to determine the fate of the two border cities. But at times the government worked to contain the fervor of the leagues in order to negotiate better with the Peruvian state.[126] Although the Patriotic Leagues had declined in the 1920s, immediately after news of La Coruña reached Chile's central valley, the leagues of Valparaíso called for the strictest measures possible, as well as for revitalized and active state support of their organization.[127] In the midst of the strike and repression, the military officer in the Plebiscite Office of Tarapacá drafted a formal memo to the intendente, urging the formation of a "Patriotic Crusade" in the port and in the nitrate camps and towns to help "maintain order and security" and to "raise up the patriotic spirit of the region." With the aid of a press campaign, the crusade, which was to be led by the regional government and the nitrate companies, would "organize assemblies and public meetings to be attended by the authorities, schools, public associations, trade associations, Army and Navy."[128]

Regarding the era in which the events of La Coruña occurred, one must take quite seriously military and state anxieties over the danger to national security represented by highly mobilized popular sectors whose allegiances were not defined solely by national concerns. Two very different understandings of past state violence—the workers' cathartic remembrance of state repression as a basis for mobilization and the military's investment as guardian of a national memory that was grounded in nineteenth-century military glories and that constructed the working class as morally delegitimated in its ability to make claims beyond the nation — shaped the conflagration that took place in June 1925.

State Violence: The Epic and Everyday Dismantling of Memory

The dismantling of memory entailed dominant political sectors refusing to recognize certain forms of violence as problematic and thus containing the memory of a time when people were able to make connections between massacres and the violence of quotidian life. In oral histories, alternative narratives sometimes come full circle to show the ways in which epic state violence itself became mundane.

In 1994, in Pozo Almonte — once a mining boomtown of taverns, shops, and brothels, now a dusty rest stop on the Pan-American Highway — an elderly Chilean, Anisate Camacho, remembered the events of 1925.

> As I was a mechanic, there came along a contractor to dismantle La Coruña. . . . We all went by train, four or six carpenters and the contractor and a driver from here, and arrived by train there about three o'clock in the afternoon . . . and began to disassemble. . . . When we felt PUM! PUM! . . . The [military] had begun to bombard La Coruña, with cannons. . . . At this point a patrol arrived, they pounded on the door: . . . "We're going to take you to speak with the administrator." . . . There, I was chosen to talk with him. So then he said to me, "Listen, Camacho, . . . put yourself at the service of the captain until I need you." Right afterward we went up and went along picking up the wounded on one of the tall hills. There were wounded all over . . . in front of the cemetery there were the poor things in a mine shaft. . . . I saw how they placed them there and BRUM! So after everything ended, they called me and told me, "Watch what you say or else you'll fall here." I was quiet. They told me, "Get going." I left . . . and I went to convince the others that we should go. We were terrified. . . . They killed many people, many people. . . . I have seen such things and I don't know how I am still alive.[129]

The events Camacho saw were effectively eradicated from memory by processes that included terrorizing witnesses into silence, dismantling prior modes of collective memory, and obscuring the state's use of violence by instituting a militarized national memory that rhetorically incorporated those very sectors that had been so brutally put down. Even more than acts of state repression, forgotten were the allegiances and aspirations for which the workers had fought. The workers had holistically denounced both the overt abuse of state power and the state's collusion in the daily abuses of the mining industry.

"Tarapacá will be the tomb of the roto chileno" prophesied the cover of Mariano Martínez's 1895 novel, *Life on the Pampa: The History of a Slave*, in which the protagonist struggled with the vices of the frontier towns and the brutal working conditions in the nitrate camps.[130] His moral decline allowed the nitrate-plant managers to deem his fall into a boiling cauldron of nitrate a suicide and thus to rob him of his dignity even in death. Discourses of social vice deflected issues of industrial and state moral culpability. When people in Tarapacá talk about the nitrate era today, they often incorporate stories of everyday violence, even with regard to the later years, when living conditions were less precarious. With legislation that made compensation for injured workers compulsory, there arose stories of workers who would get drunk and cut off a finger to cash in on a claim (each particular finger carrying a specific value). In contrast with the early labor movement's insistence on the complicity of the state in everyday forms of violence, these stories of self-inflicted industrial violence provide a means by which to assert a privatized reading of that transgression. In other words, instead of recognizing that the state participated in creating a taxonomy of the value of a worker's body parts, contemporary memory in certain sectors displaced industrial violence onto the workers themselves, as a problem of avarice and moral decay. In this way, the quotidian violence of industrial relations, like the dramatic incidents of strike and repression such as La Coruña, vanished from political history into the nebulous realm of the social question.[131]

Given these everyday forms of violence together with ongoing state repression of labor organizers, one sees that the Oficina Ramírez and La Coruña massacres, rather than being exceptional, discrete events, formed part of a broader context of violence in the nitrate region. *El Trabajo*, the official newspaper of the mutual aid and proto-union organizations, ran editorials implicating the state in everyday forms of violence ranging from industrial accidents to the degradations of living conditions. The editorials noted high suicide rates among workers, often through the use of dynamite. Further

2. The "tomb of the *roto chileno.*" The crosses of this graveyard, which overlooks Oficina La Noria, one of the oldest mining camps, testify to the dangerous working conditions and state violence of the nitrate industry. Photo by Mark Somoza.

review of newspaper accounts throughout the nitrate period indicates that this method was especially favored by elderly, infirm, or alcoholic workers. The editors saw the question of worker suicide as political and economic in origin, as a product of horrid working conditions and the stress of boom-and-bust cycles.

Similarly, the working-class press and labor organizations constantly pressed for safer working conditions. As in Martínez's novel, especially terrible were the *cachuchos* (open boiling cauldrons of nitrate). Though legislation required that nitrate companies cover the cauldrons, this law remained unenforced; workers regularly fell into them and were either maimed or, more often, killed by the hot liquid. The working-class press held both the nitrate companies and the state responsible for these tragic accidents.[132] Furthermore, company and police corporal punishment of workers — from beatings to confinement in stocks — was also common.[133]

Other forms of violence — hunger, high infant mortality, and brutal living conditions — pepper the stories of people who lived on the pampa. One woman described her childhood: during the regional bread shortages, her mother would scavenge for moldy bread, then scrape off the mold, knead the bread with water, and re-bake it for her children.[134] High infant-mortality rates resulted in the practice, found throughout Latin America, of angel burials, in which the child's body would be adorned with an angel costume and propped up on a chair for a celebration with drinking and merrymaking.[135] The child's spirit (*duende*) would then haunt the region. In Tarapacá in 1913, one out of every four children perished before the age of one.[136] Infant deaths reflected the poor sanitation and housing that resulted in enteritis, fevers, meningitis, and pneumonia. The office of labor inspection estimated that 60 percent of the working class on the nitrate plains had tuberculosis and that almost all suffered from organ ailments related to malnutrition.[137]

The everyday and epic violence in the nitrate era fed cathartic memory, which called on the working classes to channel their rage into mobilizations directed toward the transformation of their everyday lives. Non-elite sectors were largely excluded from the formal political process and subordinated in dominant definitions of the nation. Dominant sectors also recognized class as an incommensurable cleavage. The empathetic memory of the populist period was, in contrast, meant to bind sectors across classes to political party projects to gain greater access to the nation-state as the central agent of change.

The forgotten contexts and acts of state violence echoed in the abandonment of Tarapacá after the economic crash of 1929. The remnants of the nitrate industry were reconfigured under the patronage of the Chilean state and U.S. investors, then dwindled steadily until the military dictatorship finally closed down and dismantled Tarapacá's last nitrate camp in 1978.[138] Linking lost memories of repression with the abandonment of an industry and region, the renowned poet Mario Bahamonde wrote,

Someone asked, perhaps, about the workers assassinated
at La Coruña or at San Gregorio, where they remained?
Instead, smiling, persuasive, as if excusing themselves
they tell us: Nitrate's finished, brother, the pampa's finished.[139]

Anachronism displaced accountability, and epic struggle moved on to more fertile grounds. Nitrate, with its generative (as fertilizer) and destructive (as explosive) properties, provides a fitting emblem of the contradictions of Tarapacá's history and place in national memory as a site of vibrant sociocultural and political creativity intertwined with relentless repression.

Come woman, let's go down toward the sea . . .

They say Iquique is as big as the salt flats . . .

—LUIS ADVIS, "Cantata Santa María de Iquique"

In December of 1907 there unfolded a great mining strike in the North. The nitrate workers opposed payment [of wages] in tokens and asked for less-miserable living conditions. . . . 30,000 workers participated in the movement. The nitrate workers of the interior decided to go down to Iquique to explain their demands and thus exercise greater pressure. Nearly 15,000 workers mobilized, asking the government to intercede in the negotiations with the companies. In the port itself, other worker's associations which had caused work stoppage joined the movement. A state of siege was declared in the zone, and the government sent General [Roberto] Silva Renard to take command of the situation. He, after several days of conflict, ordered fire over the Escuela Santa María, where workers and their families had gathered. The numbers of dead were estimated at 2,000. This event constituted a hard blow for the northern workers and the *mancomunal* [labor brotherhood] movement.—Taller Nueva Historia: Pedro Milos, *Cuadernos de historia popular: series historia del movimiento obrero*

Song of the Tragic Pampa

STRUCTURING THE REMEMBERING OF THE ESCUELA
SANTA MARÍA MASSACRE (1907)

4 Since 1907, the Escuela Santa María Massacre has occupied a central place in national memory. Though the incident has always been pivotal, the affective shape of memories of the massacre and their use in political struggles has shifted as the national political system has expanded and contracted in the violent conjunctures of state formation. The hugely popular "Cantata Santa María de Iquique," for example, was written and performed in the early 1970s during the socialist Popular Unity government, and told the story of the 1907 event as a metaphor for the then present struggle to inspire support for the Popular Unity as the vindication of "the people's" (*el pueblo*) struggles. In the cantata a nitrate miner invites his female companion to travel from the pampa to the port city, where they would petition the governor to arbitrate their strike with intransigent foreign companies. On the other hand, a popular educa-

tion textbook, *Cuadernos de historia popular*, which was developed by one of the nongovernmental organizations that emerged with international solidarity funding against the Pinochet military regime, emphasized the magnitude of the events, along with the just and pacific nature of the unified workers' demands and their martyrdom at the hands of a villainous general.

Although the Escuela Santa María massacre was but one of many incidents of large-scale repression in the nitrate era, labor historians and activists have defined it as the central symbol of repression that led to the formation of Chilean working-class consciousness, as in José Bengoa's important study of Chilean strikes: "The massacre of Santa María of Iquique in 1907 symbolizes the originary worker's movement: grand spontaneous masses that 'come down from the *pampa*' to ask for improved living conditions, finding themselves faced with a State that does not accept the 'insubordination of the *rotos*' and that utilizes military force. The workers, their leaders, their organizations took lessons from this massacre. Not only did they organize in brotherhoods and committees of resistance, they also began to build parties and attempt to act in the institutional field."[1]

But when, how, and for whom has the 1907 massacre been symbolically central? And why and how has the Escuela Santa María massacre become such a key organizing event in local and national historical memory of state violence? To answer these questions, it is necessary to look beyond the declared importance of the event to analyze the means and forms by which it contributed to collective organization and the struggle for greater justice in Chilean history. This chapter analyzes the historical conjunctures that have constituted the moment of violence and the memory of that moment over the course of the twentieth century.

In the nitrate era, the 1907 massacre formed part of cathartic memory, which called for ongoing, direct, and collective mobilization of non-elite sectors. These oppositional movements were largely absorbed into the increasingly successful populist political parties of the emerging Left for which memory entailed empathy, which foregrounded and yet subsumed the Santa María massacre under broader narratives of martyrdom and utopia. In other words, according to empathetic memory, Past struggle was the forbearer of—and culminated in—Present struggle, that is, the progressive unfolding of a more inclusive nation-state. Thus, the affective ties that bound the people together in their claim to the state were based on an empathy for past suffering and a disciplined, even stoic, resolve. During the dictatorship, the predominant mode of memory shifted to sympathy, which used the story of the Santa María massacre as an allegory for the overthrow of the Popular Unity government, a story that could elicit solidarity both internally and abroad. In postdictatorship Chile the story of this massacre formed a nexus in the contest between melancholy, nostalgia, and the vestiges of cathartic memory.

The creative uses of the Santa María story over time reveal the changing role of memories of state violence in nation-state formation and the place of memory in projects of transformation. In the oligarchic parliamentary period (the nitrate era), class was the recognized and obvious vector of organization, as volatile economic growth lent relative autonomy to both the elite and working classes, especially in Northern Chile. The 1907 repression was recounted as the epitome of ongoing conflict between incommensurable class interests in which the state failed to mediate and instead acted as the agent of elite sectors. In the subsequent populist period, ideological affiliations were expressed through the system of emerging political parties. An expanding notion of the nation necessitated the emergence of sectors, including the military, that could mediate class conflict. While the 1907 massacre was lamented as a result of the state's misplaced loyalty and the lengths elites would go to protect their position, the empathetic portrayal of a noble and long-suffering working class solidified the moral claims of populist parties whose strategies were presented as a more sophisticated culmination of the workers' cause. Thus, Chilean political culture generated national-popular projects that sought to channel the vitality of non-elite sectors by building cross-class political alliances organized around an explicit allegiance to the nation and committed to contests for the state. The parties at the heart of this political culture were brutally repressed under military rule but reasserted themselves in the return to civilian rule. While the national-popular project of that political culture has remained in rhetoric, in practice it has given way to the market-oriented mandate of the state instituted under military rule.

In this chapter, to foreground the changing modes of memory as it shapes and is deployed in political projects, I move back and forth in time, weaving an ethnographic tapestry — something like the famous arpilleras, the quilted scenes of state violence sewn with pieces of family clothing by the mothers of those who disappeared during the dictatorship. I quilt a sense of place and people across temporal spaces, exposing the nature of the boundaries and connections erected between those spaces. Most important, moving back and forth between Iquique and Santiago, I foreground the frontier to critically unsettle and thus elucidate processes of nation-state formation. The chapter begins with a brief retelling of the 1907 massacre. Then — by focusing on the emerging memories of the massacre during the nitrate era — it offers an analytic lens for understanding the structures of remembering that have kept this event central in Chilean national memory, a lens that frames issues of urban geography, temporal conjuncture, and historical protagonists. The remaining sections of the chapter continue to look at the changing place of the 1907 event: First I examine its originary moment as preserved in the cathartic memory that called for greater combative working-class mobilization. This cathartic memory gave way to empathic memory in populist state formation that called for the incorporation of non-elite sectors into the nation-state. This empathetic memory, crushed in the 1973 coup, then reemerged as sympathetic memory contesting the bureaucratic authoritarianism of military rule. Finally, the memory remains as a trace in the contemporary dual mode of melancholy and (especially) nostalgia in the civilian neo-liberal state.

The Massacre at the Escuela Santa María

The strike of 1907 covered most of the nitrate zone. Workers' demands echoed those of the 1890 strike: accurate scales in every company store to check the weight of goods sold; the end of trade monopolies on consumer goods; the abolition of payment in tokens; wage stability through established exchange rates for the peso; prohibition of movement of caliche without payment; prohibition of companies processing low-grade nitrate for which they had refused to pay the miner; accident prevention in the cachuchos and compensation for injured workers in general; job protection for striking workers; job security for striking workers; school buildings and free night-school tuition for workers; layoff compensation; and public ratification of any strike settlement.[2]

When the regional government refused to mediate between strikers and the companies, workers decided to converge on the provincial capital, Iquique, where striking port- and railworkers would join them. From prior experience, especially that of the 1890 general strike, the workers realized that merely sending a delegation would

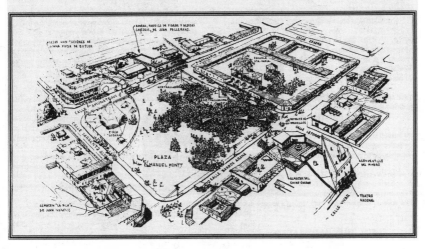

3. A bird's-eye view of the Escuela Santa María and the Plaza Montt on the day of the massacre. This illustration, which appears frequently in accounts of December 1907, depicts the circus that was in town that day and indicates where the workers may have been standing.

have little impact and thus decided to mobilize as many people as possible (somewhere between 8,000 and 11,000) to the regional capital.[3] This created panic among elites in Iquique, some of whom relocated to ships in the harbor. The intendente traveled to Santiago, and the deputy intendente, lacking authority, ineffectually attempted to mediate the labor dispute. The nitrate companies refused to negotiate and demanded that the Chilean state protect their private property; specifically, they demanded that the state militarize the nitrate fields with Chilean soldiers and police forces.

After the workers and their families arrived in Iquique, the government decided to concentrate workers from the pampa in the sporting arena on the outskirts of the city, in hopes of keeping them separated from the workers of the city (map 4). Members of the strike committee — among whom the most famous leaders were José Briggs and Luis Olea, who shared anarchist tendencies — demanded a more central location.[4] Eventually, the strike committee and the government settled on the Escuela Santa María, given its large interior courtyard, adjacent square, and ready access to local markets.

When the regional governor, Intendente Carlos Eastman, first returned to Iquique, he seemed amenable to mediating the conflict, but in what seemed to the workers to be a complete turnaround of attitude, he then declared a state of siege and ordered the workers to evacuate the school and move to the arena. They refused, fearing that the troops would arrest them once they left the confines of the school. Eastman sent troops to enforce the order. Having been notified by the Chilean government of the gravity of the situation, the foreign consuls of Peru and Bolivia visited the school to persuade their nationals to leave.[5] In a clear statement of class solidarity over nationalism, the foreign workers reportedly replied, "With Chileans we came. With Chileans we will die!"[6]

The military, under the command of General Silva Renard, fired on the workers and their families using machine guns and then advanced with bayonets.[7] The military dumped the dead into a mass grave. They marched surviving workers to the arena and from there shipped most of them back to the pampa. Defying efforts to force them to resume their old labors, many fled back to their places of origin: Southern Chile, Peru, Argentina, or Bolivia.[8]

Cathartic Memories of 1907 in the Nitrate Era: Urban Geography, Temporal Conjuncture, Character

Memories of state violence are constituted in part through historiographical and pedagogical narratives of both the presence and absence of agency and event. This interplay of presence and absence raises some comparative questions regarding the collective memory of several key events in the history of Tarapacá. Why, in contrast to the diminishment of the Oficina Ramírez and Oficina La Coruña massacres in Chilean labor and political history, was the repression of 1907 foregrounded in historical narratives as the paradigmatic scenario of state violence? Further, why have the events of 1907 been taken up in various projects to reshape the subjectivity of political actors, including the state? This dynamic of remembering can be understood along three interpretive tracks: the urban geography (where), the temporal conjuncture (when), and the character of the protagonists (who).

Urban Geography on the Frontier * The Escuela Santa María massacre is recalled so vividly in part because of its geographical context:

Iquique, the regional capital and point of departure from which nitrate was shipped abroad.[9] Due to the population density of the city, most long-term residents — regardless of class — had family history accounts of the massacre. The migration of workers immediately after the massacre ensured dispersion of eyewitness accounts in the rest of Chile. The Escuela Domingo Santa María, named for a nineteenth-century Chilean president, sits on Plaza Manuel Montt, which is located directly inland, east of the Iquique main plaza and slightly northeast of the secondary plaza. In spite of efforts to resituate the site of violence by demolishing then rebuilding the school with a new orientation and by building a market on the plaza, the efforts of labor organizations and other social movements ensured the site's significance in subsequent geographies of protest. Iquique's urban landscape attests to its contradictory place in national history as both a point of pride in national military conquests and as a cradle of labor organizations and emerging political parties.

The year 1907 has stood forth in Chilean memory — especially in contrast to the events of 1890–1891 and 1925 — for a number of reasons.[10] First, it embodied the worst fear of the elites: that workers would descend from the pampa and occupy their city.[11] Because they did occupy the city, there were many articulate witnesses to the events. The anxiety of elites who feared the workers' occupation of the provincial capital incited much discussion between state officials, diplomats, and business interests in the North and in the national capital, while the observations of professional doctors and journalists from the elite classes who directly witnessed and were horrified by the violence of the army generated compelling documentation of state abuses. Not only was abundant written documentation disseminated across Chile, but virtually every family that boasts three generations in Iquique has a story about the repression.

Thus, the prominence of the 1907 Escuela Santa María repression in political memory can in part be attributed to the spatial concentration of the events at the center of nitrate-industry power structures: the port where the processed nitrate was shipped off, where the state customs house garnered critical revenue, where the military celebrated several of its symbolically central battles and garrisoned key regiments, where nitrate barons located their homes and clubs, where workers' associations built their meeting halls and presses, and where the highest regional representatives of the nation-state governed.

The Temporal Conjuncture of 1907 * In addition to the geographic visibility of the repression, the 1907 massacre marked a particular temporal conjuncture in state formation — a moment of relative state stability at the height of the oligarchic parliamentary period. Therefore, the event in the North got the direct attention of national politicians and became itself a vehicle of intra-elite political positioning. This contrasts dramatically with the fate of other nitrate strikes and massacres, which were absorbed under the rubric of more generalized constitutional crises, namely, the Civil War of 1891 and the writing of a new constitution after military intervention in 1925.

Thus, the 1907 massacre marks a particular moment in which processes of class and state formation collided in Chile, processes further elucidated by looking at the forms that memory of the massacre took in the nitrate era. The cathartic memory of the nitrate era worked in semiautonomous realms, with a wide gulf between the ways memory was made and transmitted among non-elite sectors and among the elite, who dominated memory at the level of the nation-state.

The workers who arrived in the region in the years immediately following the massacre learned of the events from the accounts of their co-workers and neighbors just as successive generations in the region learned from the stories told by their elders. Elena Rojas, who had lived and worked in the pampa, told how she came to know of this history: "My father recounted that many people came down from the *oficinas* to Iquique. They were in the school and when the military arrived, they didn't surrender. There General Silva gave the order to kill. My father said that this [the school] was full, even though he didn't come down. But family of ours went by train. And those that remained alive, returned and told of what happened."[12] Many people from Iquique inherited stories about how their grandparents saved themselves by hiding under the cadavers, sometimes being hauled off with the dead and wounded to the cemetery, where they waited in the mass grave until nightfall to get to safety.[13] It is said that in the end the grave formed a small hill in the cemetery.[14]

The reproduction of cathartic memory in the nitrate era also occurred through speeches, poems, and songs. At political rallies, leaders of the emerging non-elite political parties often spoke of the repression.[15] By the end of the era, Communist Party events began with the singing of "The International" and "El canto a la pampa," which told of the strike and repression.[16]

I demand vengeance for those who came
Of the workers who bared their chests
I demand vengeance for the *pampino*
who, there in Iquique, learned to die.[17]

Just as *lira popular* (popular poetry) disseminated critical information and evaluation of the 1890–1891 strikes and repression, popular song played a similar role after 1907.[18] In the nitrate era the 1907 massacre was thus incorporated into the vibrant realm of non-elite culture using cathartic memory, which posited a direct identification between past and present peoples and struggles, to forge a community based on suffering and struggle.[19]

This community of struggle grew around flourishing civic associations that emerged from the rapid changes experienced by those who came to work in the nitrate industry from rural Southern Chile.[20] The arrival of these workers into the intensive, unmitigated wage-labor system of the nitrate zone entailed an intense shift in class position and the subsequent formation of new class identities.[21] Workers' organizations included mutual-aid societies, night schools for adults, "philharmonics" or cultural groups that put on shows and dances, popular theater troupes, and working-class newspapers.[22] Though vehemently anticlerical politics pervaded, the region also developed a thriving culture of popular religion. Working-class culture enjoyed a semiautonomous character complete with internal rivalries and processes of inclusion and exclusion.[23] At that particular historical moment, the Santa María massacre, integrated with stories of other repressions, formed a vital component of cathartic memory that bound working-class communities together in the pursuit of change.

Documentary accounts of the 1907 repression were published at the time by the distinguished public figures Nicolás Palacios and Leoncio Marín.[24] The repression's visibility among prominent members of the bourgeoisie, who were horrified by its brutality, facilitated the rapid dissemination and publication of nonstate accounts. Photographs taken both immediately before and after the repression provided another form of documentation.[25]

The state attempted to limit the political repercussions of the repression, immediately censoring newspapers throughout Chile and prohibiting public commemorations. Yet one cannot assume that state officials simply suppressed the history of the event; in fact, they processed the event as data. The director of the Oficina del Trabajo, the labor office in the Ministry of Industry and Public Works, sent a functionary from Santiago to investigate labor conditions. The ministry complained to the intendente that the office of labor statistics had never received the requested report on the 1907 strike: "Consequently, the event will pass into history leaving no testimony of the worker's cost of living during those months, the salary earned by each category of worker, the work accidents that occurred during the year and their causes; the conditions under which work was done; the limits imposed on free commerce; the use of wage tokens, etc."[26]

The state's preoccupation with "history" and "testimony" demanded memory-work to incorporate workers as a dimension of labor statistics. The ministry regarded data on the quantifiable conditions of workers' lives as critical given the importance of the industry for the state's income and the fact that it employed over 20,000 workers in "special work conditions: separated from the action of central power by the nature of the territory, subject to a rigorous climate of an arid land, a monotonous life and heavy labor"; these special conditions compounded the "constant danger that envelop[ed] Iquique [because] of an enormous mass of workers that live[d] at its gates" and because of citizens from bordering states who worked on the pampa.[27] The ministry reiterated its request for data on strikes in a form letter, sent to all intendentes, that demanded immediate notification of each strike, the day it began, the location, and the name of the company affected. The ministry defined a strike as a "suspension of all work in which more than twenty workers take part."[28] Although the office of labor statistics sought data to create a state-quantified memory of strikes primarily in order to circumvent fiscally damaging future conflict, the kind of data it sought to incorporate into "history" nevertheless documented exploitative conditions and recognized that the strike and repression made little sense without a context for worker grievances.

Thus, the massacre drew state attention to the problem of working-class dissent, which state officials attributed to a lack of incorporation in the national project promoted by the oligarchic parliamentary regime. Before 1907, the incorporation of non-elites into the nation had occurred only to a limited extent and largely under the rubric of soldier-workers, who had been condensed in the racialist category of the roto chileno, a term grounded in nineteenth-century wars of conquest and expansion. Such inclusion had suffered with the 1890–1891 strikes and repression and with the blatant neglect of veterans from the 1879 War of the Pacific. After 1907, the state began to apply explicitly xenophobic strategies (playing on national rivalries already present among the multinational workforce) to assert its leadership over the northern working class and its previously semiautonomous associations and solidarities. The project of strategic nationalism was made all the more difficult in the wake of the state's use of overwhelming force at the behest of a predominantly foreign-owned industry.

The repression of 1907 drastically weakened the incorporation of non-elite sectors into the Chilean nation. Nitrate workers' warnings to the state were reproduced in the 1913 congressional commission report on conditions in the nitrate-mining industry: "The authorities' bloody suffocation of the pacific strike of the 21st of December 1907, culminated the profile of the crisis of patriotism in the nitrate region." The report continued, "Half a century's systematic propaganda against patriotism by a thousand anarchists never would have produced the enormous destruction of morale in the sentiments of the workers that the authorities produced in only five minutes of fire and killing."[29] The workers underlined the report's admonition by noting that Chilean independence-day celebrations had all but disappeared on the pampa. Immediately after the troops attacked the strikers in 1907, Elías Lafertte, a nitrate miner and later head of the Chilean Communist Party, reported the workers' cries of indignation: "I'm no longer Chilean. . . . I'm leaving this place . . . assassin government. . . . I'm leaving Chile forever!"[30]

As a consequence of this crisis in civic allegiance provoked by the state's brutality, the historian Sergio González notes, "the process of chilenization that began from this date [1907] was compulsory and systematic," and it proceeded with "the social persecution and cultural assimilation of specific groups, thus destroying Tarapacá's plurinational and pluri-ethnic character."[31] State-supported compulsory patriotism was challenged by claims to the nation by labor and leftist political parties valorizing a different conception of patriotism (to a certain extent non-militarized).[32] Yet, after 1907, efforts to revalorize the nation remained within a framework that ultimately never questioned the nation-state's or the military's fundamental legitimacy. The Santa María massacre marked a critical conjuncture, a collision in what had been relatively distinct processes of class and state formation in Chile.

The Question of Character: Generals and Proletarians ∗ The 1907 massacre has remained an important part of national memory because the protagonists were characterized in the emerging narratives of 1907 in a way that specifically linked them to subsequent political figures and forms of agency. This is especially true of the dramatic portrayals of the military commander in the conflict, General Silva Renard, who absorbed and deflected depictions of the military and questions of attributing responsibility and exacting retribution for state violence. Populist labor and leftist political leaders—who increasingly favored a state-oriented and gradual electoral path to social transformation and the redistribution of resources—cast workers as orienting their strike tactics toward pacific and passive occupation of a neutral space, which constituted a model of proper collective political participation.

Throughout much of its history, the Chilean military acted as a nexus between non-elite sectors and the state. That this link was never severed, even after more than a century of intense repression, and that the integrity of the military as an institution and of the Chilean state as a whole have persisted intact constitute a remarkable historical puzzle. One piece of that puzzle can be found in the way in which certain historical figures depicted as exceptional preserved the stability of the institutions from which they seemingly sprang forth. The tenacity of the Chilean military as a whole in evading responsibility for state violence can thus, in part, be located in the way that individual generals served as targets of public wrath.[33]

General Silva Renard (rather than one of the thousands of workers who struck in the period from 1890 to 1970) is quoted in the introduction to the historian José Bengoa's study of Chilean strikes: " 'You do not fear for your life?' Silva Renard was asked several years after the events of Santa María de Iquique. 'No,' he responded, 'for many years now I have been dead.' " Bengoa agreed, adding that not only had the general who had ordered the troops to fire figuratively died, but so had many of the nation's fundamental organizing principles, namely, the ties of loyalty between rotos and patrons that had sustained the oligarchic order.[34]

In Bengoa's treatment, the pathetic figure of the general stands for a particular sociopolitical order that gave way to the proletarian question, as the working class assumed its "national vocation."[35] The general—embodying the military and the state as conduits of elite interests—channeled and redirected class conflict into the production of the nation. Through reference to Silva Renard's self-proclaimed symbolic death, Bengoa effectively nullifies the political importance of the more literal vengeance enacted on Silva Renard's body and the extent to which workers' aspirations to the status of national actors continued to contend with old configurations of oligarchic, military, and business interests.

The narrative of proletarians rising to the center stage of national politics has consistently accompanied the symbolic casting of generals as apolitical, neutral bodies through which political conflict could play out in the interests of national stability and order. This characterization began in the independence era, continued in the nineteenth-century civil wars, and persists to this day. Further analysis of Silva Renard as a historical figure suggests multiple and contradictory renderings of relations of alliance and domination.

Just before the attack on the workers, according to tales (circa the 1950s and 1960s) from the elders of Iquique's elite families, General Silva Renard had received a communiqué saying something like "Hold off," which he misread as "Hold fast."[36] The repression, the elders explained, had simply been an unfortunate mistake. The general had blamelessly upheld his duty as he understood it in a situation of immense danger: the unpredictability of the thousands of workers who occupied the port. For those elite families, Silva Renard remained a hero. In almost every account of the events of 1907, both those sympathetic to the state's predicament and those that were not, Silva Renard emerged as a central, if not the primary, figure of glamour and terror. How did this violent event in particular give rise to such a prominent figure and how did the attention given his agency — whether as hero or antihero — affect the ramifications of the events in political memory?

In his memoir Elías Lafertte depicted the general as an imposing figure, "mounted like Napoleon, on a white horse, for this unequal battle," who coldly directed the attack in spite of the white flags and who oversaw the cleanup afterward.[37] Without hesitation, Lafertte attributed the violence to Silva Renard: "All night the wagons lined up to move and make disappear the two thousand dead, victims of Silva Renard."[38]

The state, too, pointed to Silva Renard as the main actor in the events in the North.[39] In Santiago the repression presented an opportunity for positioning among the political elite at a time of relative state stability, a period of political stalemate of the oligarchic parliamentary system. The events in Iquique formed the center of debate between Minister of Interior Rafael Sotomayor and Representatives Bonifacio Veas, Malaqías Concha (who had actually interviewed witnesses), and Arturo Alessandri in an extraordinary session of the congressional body in late December 1907.[40] Sotomayor defended Silva Renard, saying that in addition to the provocations cited in the military officer's official report, the general had personally informed him that he had been directly threatened by the strikers. Silva Renard reported to congress that he had ordered his troops to fire because "I was convinced that it would not be possible to wait longer without compromising the respect and prestige of the authorities and the security forces, and I was compelled by the necessity to dominate the rebellion before the day ended."[41] The extensive treatment given the repression in Congress and transcribed in the state's public record further ingrained the event in official memory. Still, interest in the matter had passed by the time that ordinary congressional sessions resumed in 1908, and state officials involved suffered no repercussions.[42]

However, working-class cathartic memory during the nitrate era demanded vengeance, as in the "El canto a la pampa." Vengeance found General Silva Renard in the form of an anarchist who had lost his brother in the Santa María massacre: in 1914 Antonio Ramón Ramón stabbed Silva Renard in the eye as he left the munitions factory he supervised in Santiago.[43] Silva Renard survived. Legend has it that the attacker had coated the dagger with garlic so that the wound wouldn't heal.[44] Vengeance came, then, not only in the attack itself but also in its elaboration and persistence in non-elite memory. However, the way that vengeance for the degradation of the social body was condensed in the body of the antihero only further deferred the broader question of accountability and justice.

Thus, the phenomenon of generals serving as lightning rods, as Silva Renard did for the 1907 massacre, enabled the Chilean military to preserve its integrity as the primary keeper of national honor. Silva Renard's positioning as a foil absorbed and thus deflected the issue of accountability for state violence and minimized the impact of violent antecedents on the military and state as a whole.[45] The dramatization of Silva Renard's actions and character — whether he was viewed as a hero or an antihero — sealed the repression in the memories of Chileans.[46]

On the other hand, workers were characterized under the broad populist rubric of "the people," and their interests were assumed to be represented by emerging political parties in their contest for control of the state and by the expansion of the political system that began in the 1920s in the wake of the oligarchy's political collapse. The possibility of a fundamentally honorable armed forces loyal to the Chilean people was preserved in stories of those who, as veterans of the War of the Pacific, joined the 1907 strikers' front lines and were thus among the first to fall; popular accounts (substantiated by the British consul's report) told of soldiers who were shot down as they attempted to cross over to the strikers' side or who were executed for refusing to fire on workers.[47] The foregrounding of the roto chileno as a national protagonist further propagated the idea of an armed forces whose first institutional allegiance should be to the working classes from which the majority of the soldiers were drawn. The new populist political processes favored a vision of workers as martyrs, a vision which the Santa María massacre illustrated effectively.

The 1907 Escuela Santa María massacre took hold in dominant and contestatory (cathartic) memories in part due to three narrative components: (1) urban geography, that is, the fact that the events took place under the gaze of a cross-class public in a regional capital that was prominent in the national imaginary; (2) temporal conjuncture, that is, the fact that the events occurred during a lull in national politics and thus themselves became an arena for political contention, as the oligarchic state, which had excluded and neglected non-elite sectors, was forced to defend its decision to use violence at the behest of foreign capital; and (3) historical protagonists created by compelling portraits of military officials and workers, which dominated depictions of the event and were used to influence the allocation of historical accountability in subsequent political contests.

Empathetic Memory of the Escuela Santa María Massacre in the Populist Era

Hoping to redirect spatial memories of the massacre, the government built an enclosed market on the square in front of the original entrance to the school, thus cutting off both the view of the school from that direction and an open space for public gathering. In the 1930s the state tore down and rebuilt the dilapidated school itself, relocating the entrance to the opposite side of the block, which faced a narrow street. A former political prisoner of 1973, Elianira Escobar, remembered attending the school and how the children would tell stories about the ghosts of the massacre who inhabited the building

—ghost stories still in circulation even though the event as History was no longer taught in the school's classrooms.[48]

Political opposition shifted from a language of class conflict to one of cross-class alliance under the rubric of "the popular," the cultural realm inhabited by "the people." The Escuela Santa María massacre, as an event constituted through political memory, formed an interface between processes of class and state formation at various junctures in the twentieth century. The shape of that interface underwent dramatic shifts: from the documentary gestures and poetic projects for revindication that corresponded to a politics of catharsis, to the rallying cries of empathetic populist politics, to the highly evocative and allegorical historical narratives that pointed to a horrific present and invoked a politics of sympathy.

As Chile's economy contracted after the worldwide depression of 1929, the political system expanded, first with a series of short-lived, self-proclaimed socialist governments led by military officers, then with the election of the Popular Front, which governed for a decade and made major advances in state-initiated projects, the most important of which were education and housing.[49] In the late 1940s the Popular Front alliances collapsed under the weight of internal conflicts and of U.S. Cold War pressure.[50]

This international pressure, combined with subsequent presidents Gabriel González Videla's and Carlos Ibáñez del Campos's impatience with the limitations of coalition politics, led to the repressions of the late 1940–1950s. In spite of these purges, the model of coalition-based populist politics persisted in Chile, and even rightist presidencies had to present themselves as addressing—albeit through an ongoing paternalist rhetoric—the concerns of a wider national polity.

That the populist litany of martyrdom co-opted the 1907 massacre to exemplify sacrifice in service of socialist state formation did not go unchallenged by rightist voices that defended the state's use of violence as legitimate. In 1952 the current-events magazine *Ercilla* ran a debate between the brothers Silva Lafrenz and Valentín Sims, an Iquiqueño, which detailed the 1907 massacre's sequence of events and addressed whether or not the massacre could have been avoided.[51] In a similar spirit of debate, the columnist Joaquín Edwards Bello published two letters he had received regarding the massacre; he bemoaned the fact that there were only two versions of the events (Right and Left), both one-noted (*todos monocordes*), either "depicting the pampinos as angelitos" or depicting them as "human beings." The first letter, which Edwards Bello introduced by validating its position, was from Pedro González Acoz, the police inspector of Iquique and a participant in the 1907 events, who emphasized the provocative violence of the workers and characterized the reaction of the military as defensive. The second letter, discredited by Edwards Bello as "eloquent but poetic and with novelistic tendencies," was written by Juan Segundo Santibañez Lorca, who had witnessed the massacre as a child and who gave as his most potent memory the image of a half-naked child whose body had been cut in half by machine-gun bullets. Santibañez Lorca's letter opened with a verse from "El canto a la pampa" and underscored the pacific nature of the strikers: theirs "was a romantic movement that ended in tragedy." Laying blame on the military commanders, Santibañez Lorca closed with the question "Who gave the order to exterminate?"[52] Although Edwards Bello privileged the police inspector's account, he stated, "The truth will emerge a bit at a time from the grave of the passions [el foso de las pasiones], where it has remained buried," asserting the validity of History (objective) over memory (subjective).[53]

For people of Tarapacá, the assertion of a coldly rational History belied the pain of betrayal caused by the collapse of the populist political compact, which coincided with complete regional economic abandonment and isolation. *The Agony of Nitrate in the Pampa de Tarapacá*, Augusto Rojas Núñez's plea for regional economic development in light of the dwindling nitrate industry, ended by invoking the victims of 1907: "In pilgrimage, with bloody feet, and suffering even in their souls, they have returned to work, to continue to be subordinated to the sentence to which they have been condemned, not on holy wood, but rather in the tortures of premature aging [and] exhaustion, or in one of the daily accidents in their workplace."[54] Rojas Núñez equated the 1907 workers with the workers of his own time, the 1950s, and offered an antinarrative (re: modernist progress) of timeless struggle and a perpetual sentence of hard labor, in which the conditions of life, far from improving, deteriorated along with the nitrate industry.

Such despondent sentiments clouded all efforts to commemorate the 1907 event. The year 1957, the fiftieth anniversary of the Escuela Santa María massacre, was a bleak one in Tarapacá. Under state reorganization, the few nitrate camps that had survived the worldwide economic depression became vulnerable to shifts not only in market demand but also in state policy. From the 1950s to the 1970s, workers were forcibly removed from their homes as the camps were dismantled and sold for scrap in a concession granted to entrepreneurs. The people of the pampa demanded work and insisted that their communities not be destroyed. Drawing on the symbolic resonance of pampinos petitioning the government in 1907, the mining communities organized hunger marches to call attention to their plight, walking across the desert and down to Iquique. There they waited, hoping to negotiate with nitrate-mining officials. Odessa Flores, daughter of the prominent labor leader Epifanio Flores, marched to the port as a young girl along with her family; she recalled that the longer the workers waited for an audience with the regional governor, the more they feared a repeat of the Santa María massacre: "The tension [among the workers] was more than terror. The people feared that the same history would happen to them but [the government] couldn't do it and so some of the workers' demands were met and they ended their hunger strike and returned to the mining camps."[55]

The entire province was so economically devastated that, in protest, Iquique's municipal government dared the unthinkable: it refused to celebrate Naval Day, May 21st, which commemorated the Battle of Iquique in the War of the Pacific. The central government in Santiago — already in crisis from urban street protests that had occurred in March in Santiago and Valparaíso and that had been used as a pretext for harsh actions against political and labor activists and as a power play by General Gamboa — declared Tarapacá an emergency zone and threatened to arrest the mayor and entire city council for flying the flag at half-mast as a sign of regional mourning.[56] The region launched the "protest of the black flags," swathing Iquique in black mourning garb to symbolize destitution. In *El Tarapacá* a local poet declared that, although no one had complained of antipatriotism when the region had produced the nation's wealth,

Now that the pampa is desert without life
through the government's own decisions
the dynamite no longer breaks the silence
that was the sonorous song of national strength.

Tarapacá's citizens, "asking for work as [their] milk and bread," were called antipatriotic and threatened with imprisonment. The poet concluded, "Where is the sensibility of these people / who give jail when hunger cries for piety? / These people of Santiago, if they are antipatriotic and bad, / of what nationality will they be?"[57]

Given the breakdown of relations between the national capital and the frontier at the time, and because 1957 was also the fiftieth anniversary of the Escuela Santa María massacre, the unions built a small monument to victims of state violence beside the school. One person recalled the excitement leading up to the monument's unveiling: given a choice of whether to attend his graduation from secondary school or the inauguration of the commemorative marker, he chose the latter.[58] The unions led a dedication ceremony on May Day and again on the anniversary of the massacre, December 21st, thus asserting regional memory over national, or at least pointing to tensions and fissures between region and nation.[59]

Even facing abandonment, the North clung to its position as a generative space for political movements and successfully retained its role in the playing out of national political contests. This dynamic proved true with the regeneration of populist Center-Left coalitions in the form of the 1960s Popular Unity movement led by the recurrent presidential candidate Salvador Allende.

As "popular" sectors were increasingly incorporated into the political system, the Escuela Santa María massacre provided a rallying point in speeches, and the commemorative marker often served as a departure point for protests. The massacre was evoked largely to signify the pacific nature of the labor movement and the willingness of its adherents to sacrifice all for the revindication of workers' rights.[60] This interpretation coincided with the philosophy of social transformation undergirding the Popular Unity coalition, whose leaders advocated the redistribution of power and economic prerogatives through electoral, legal means. For example, in President Allende's 1972 May Day speech to university students, he devoted a section to the "Heritage of Sacrifice" (Herencia de sacrificio), emphasizing the indebtedness of consciousness between generations of activists and inviting the students to take their place in this lineage: "For this reason it must be understood that the historical process of the people's struggle . . . was marked with the sacrifice of thousands of Chileans in Ranquil, in San Gregorio, in the Escuela Santa María." After noting other state attacks on poor people, Allende concluded, "It has been this people's struggle and the consciousness of the popular parties connected to this struggle that has made possible the unity and within this a unified concept: to make possible the instrument necessary for the conquest of the Government and to advance to conquest of power."[61] According to Allende's linear metanarrative, violence became a transformative motor in the rise of the socialist state, clearly demarcating the intersection of class and state formation at the culmination of the populist era.[62]

With the mobilizations of the 1960s, especially the increasing organization of students and other young people into political parties, multiple cultural initiatives sought to recover the history of the 1907 repression: theatrical and musical works, most notably the "Cantata Santa María de Iquique" by Luis Advis; novels such as Volodia Teitelboim's *Hijo de Salitre* and Luis González Zenteno's *Los Pampinos*; and popular-education booklets from the series *Nosotros los Chilenos*, including Patricio Manns's *Las grandes masacres* and Julián Cobo's *Yo vi nacer y morir los pueblos salitreros*. The expansion of the political system continued until the coup of 1973, growing through the use of popular cultural forms and education; it culminated with the Popular Unity government, wherein popular history and memory converged with official history and memory.

In the North, specifically, national-popular blending manifested in academic studies and artistic works on regional history and experiences. A key focus of these social, cultural, and profoundly political movements was the recuperation of histories of struggle and repression. For example, in 1971 the University of the North mounted in Iquique's Casa de la Cultura a photographic exhibition on the "1907 proletarian strike and massacre," basing the show on the archive of northern social history compiled by Enrique Reyes Navarro, a regional historian and educator.[63]

Also in 1971 an Iquique theater group, under the direction of Jaime Torres and Cecilia Millar, produced Elizaldo Rojas's play about the 1907 repression. The protagonists included Juan, a strike leader, his fiancée, Sofía, and her brother, Juan, who had come to Iquique to do his military service. The reappearance of the roto in this play underscored the predominant effort to assert a popular identity for the military. Other characters included Intendente Carlos Eastman, General Roberto Silva Renard, and a representative "gringo," Mr. Lockett.[64] Another play by Elizaldo Rojas, *Recuento* (Retold), was revived in Santiago in 1971. Consistent with the general format of empathetic memory in the populist era, this work presented state repressions from the end of the nineteenth century to the 1960s — including the Santa María massacre — in the form of a litany, or chronology, of events. A reviewer noted that at its best, the play "shows, cumulatively, aspects often silenced in the history of Chile"; however, he felt that the work suffered from a problem characteristic of leftist theater, that is, that it took a schematic form and simplified the "complexity and dynamism of events," creating a flat portrait of the forces at play, not unlike a Hollywood western. Citing Brecht as a model, the reviewer concluded that Chilean authors needed to aim for such a "command of the ideological underpinnings of the themes they consider, and thanks to this, achieve a didactic simplicity, very different from the rustic-type simplicity of many committed works."[65]

Perhaps this reviewer would have considered more sophisticated Iquiqueño Luis Advis's "Cantata Santa María de Iquique," the opening bars of which have become an aural icon of the socialist experiment: they were used as Allende's campaign theme music. The band Quilapayún toured the country, including Iquique, performing cantata in 1969.[66] Advis recorded the cantata at the beginning of the Popular Unity years, and it was premiered at the second Chilean New Song Festival sponsored in part by the Universidad Católica in Santiago. The national folklore ballet company even set a choreography to the song. While serving as an homage to Pezoa's "El canto a la pampa" in sharing as its subject the 1907 massacre, in its use of the song-form, and in its incantation to travel from the desert plains to the provincial capital, the cantata is a complex concert-length piece that combines melodic songs with instrumental sections and spoken recitations.[67] A review in an Iquique newspaper lamented that while the Quilapayún recording of the cantata received much attention in Europe, it had not done as well in Chile because "its detractors don't care for the genre or don't understand it. This is the logical fate of all works that depart from the canons of descriptive traditionalism to incorporate new elements."[68]

In a typical attack on the cantata, a 1972 *El Tarapacá* editorial critiqued the Allende government and its attempts to strengthen alliances within the military. Mocking such government efforts, the editor wrote that the elevation of the military contradicted popular-history projects that emphasized the persecution of popular sectors. The editor suggested that some cases of state violence could not be so easily cast as victimization of the people; he pointed to the 1921 San Gregorio massacre, in which the first lives lost were among the "forces of order," who thus were provoked to justifiable violence. In other cases, he wrote, especially with regard to the Escuela Santa

María Massacre, memory was exaggerated. The editor then questioned the cantata for elevating the number of dead to 3,000, when
"according to history there were only 144."

> Certainly this was a tragedy that, God willing, will never happen again. But contribut-
> ing to it were a series of factors, among which have been placed first the disgrace or
> the misunderstanding of the supposed hatred of the armed forces at the service of
> the bourgeoisie or capitalism against the proletariat, as has been speculated. It is
> forgotten that its [the armed forces'] members are also of the people, and it omits
> the price paid by Colonel Silva Renard. . . . In the histories of all nations there are sad
> chapters, they form part of the total, and no Chilean should defame that, but the
> honest and really patriotic commemoration is pious silence. . . . [A]ll the rest only
> contributes to foment one-upmanship, hatred, and instability; above all, it makes it
> very difficult to construct a nation, unless the objective hidden behind all of the
> above is precisely this.[69]

The author underlined Advis's appropriation of the 1907 event as
an element of the ideological conflict between Right and Left during
the Popular Unity government. The editorialist argues that in order
to "construct a nation" such "sad chapters" are necessary: state violence is a foundational component of nation-making. The military
honorably absorbs the responsibility for that necessary force through
the duties assumed by its top officers, such as General Silva Renard.
The "pious silence" called for by the journalist is a form of commemoration particular to privileged sectors. Offered less than a year and a
half before the coup, the editor's defense of the military, in general,
and of Silva Renard, in particular, provides further insight into how
memory enables the Chilean military to preserve its position as the
guardian of national honor.

The military named a regiment in Southern Chile after General
Silva Renard; however, exactly whose memory the regiment honored
is uncertain, as there were two General Silva Renards, who were
brothers.[70] By the mid-twentieth century, however, the brother
charged with the Santa María massacre remained a vivid figure in
Chilean political memory, and many assumed that the regiment had
been named in his honor. A political activist and writer in Iquique
commented that, with fitting irony, in her view, the regiment had
been deployed to suppress the Movement of the Revolutionary Left
in the 1960s.[71] General Carlos Prats related this same incident in his
memoirs.[72] General Prats, too, was prominent in regional memory,

because his wife's family came from Iquique. Like his predecessor, General René Schneider (who died as a result of a right-wing kidnapping attempt), Prats served as head of the armed forces during the last months of the Popular Unity government, remained relatively loyal to Allende's presidency, and after the coup was assassinated along with his wife. Like Arturo Prat, Iquique's hero from the War of the Pacific, General Prats was remembered as an honorable military officer whose valor and loyalty were unquestionable. In the face of military dictatorship, such figures stood as pillars for a defense of the integrity of the Chilean military as an institution and thus were key to the military's political resilience. Even in the Catholic laypeople's February 1991 newsletter, a commentator elaborated the reasons why the civilian government's project of truth and reconciliation could not work unless it included treating the memory of Chilean military leaders with justice.

> We want to think that the armed forces have been always the pride of our country and have had men as marvelous as Bernardo O'Higgins, José Miguel Carrera, Arturo Prat, or a recent figure like the commander of the army, General René Schneider, that they would reeducate themselves and in a gesture of humility, of honesty, and, why not say so, of justice ask pardon of the mothers, wives, siblings, and children of the victims of this "dirty war," admitting their responsibility. . . . Only in this way could there ever be reconciliation, only in this way can all Chileans look anew with pride at our soldiers.[73]

For this commentator, such a justice, in distinguishing good and bad soldiers, could rescue the memory of an honorable military and thus could both implicate and redeem the military.[74]

An image that epitomizes the empathetic form of populist memory appeared in a national women's magazine in 1971: a full-page photograph of Fidel Castro in military fatigues, shaking hands with a tiny elderly woman in Iquique.[75] Bold letters explained the curious image: "For many that saw it, it was simply an old woman who carried a flag and greeted Fidel in Iquique's plaza. But Blanca Williams Delzo, 84 years old, was a living piece of history, survivor of that horrific massacre of workers at the Escuela Santa María in 1907. A chapter that the bourgeois teachers have tossed out, relived before the pampinos and their guest, when two historical moments met each other in Iquique."[76] (The phrase "two historical moments met each other in Iquique" served as the photograph's title.) The article recounted a conversation between Elías Lafertte and Luis Emilio Recabarren, the founders of the Chilean Communist Party, discussing the massacre just four years after it occurred, in November 1911. Lafertte said that he sometimes wondered if he would have preferred to have died in the 1907 massacre, because he could imagine no better way to die than in such fraternity. Recabbaren replied that the fraternity of living was even better, but he agreed that, since one must die, to die in the last battle would be the sweetest. Lafertte responded that if that were so, then his life had ended in 1907. Rejecting this millenarian assertion, Recabarren replied, "The people have no end. . . . In spite of the massacres, the people continue." The text sprang forward sixty years, to its present, November 1971, when Castro visited Iquique. When Blanca Williams Delzo and another elderly woman, Elsa Sánchez, greeted him on the stage and presented him with a memento, Castro embraced them and said that he was proud to greet two authentic representatives of the Chilean working class. The journalist thus offered the living body of the eyewitness as material proof of Recabarren's assertion that "the people have no end." Having forged that temporal link, the elderly women exited the stage, and Castro went on to give an hour-and-a-half speech.[77]

It would be difficult to find a better example of the populist period's memory as empathy. Castro visited Chile in empathetic support of the socialist regime and traveled to Northern Chile knowing he would find there Chile's "authentic working class," a testament to the symbolic power that the North continued to hold in the national political imaginary, even long after the nitrate era was effectively over, due to its position as a stronghold of leftist militancy. For the Latin American Left of the 1960s and 1970s, Castro epitomized the Socialist New Man, then the latest ideal of political agency. The New Man acted on behalf of the masses, as intellectual and (guerrilla) strategic leader. What better way to incarnate the people on whose behalf he should act than in the form of an elderly woman, a survivor of repression? The two moments of history that met were just that: two moments, distinct yet related. Empathetic memory maintained the discreteness between past and present struggles, wherein the actors of the present were emotionally inspired and morally authorized by prior suffering. As in the flashback to the musings of the Communist Party's founding fathers, the narrative of Castro's visit foregrounded chivalry and martyrdom to such an extent that it could be argued that Popular Unity was psychologically preparing the public for the likelihood of a civil war. In any case, the text assured its reader that even the most cataclysmic acts of state violence did not entail defeat but, rather, the resurrection and persistence of the people.

The article did not end there. Leaving Castro to his usual epic speech, the journalist accompanied Blanca Williams Delzo back to her house, where a very different kind of historical narrative unfolded. She turned out to be much more than a figure of victimhood silently bearing a flag (presumably the Communist Party flag, although that is not clear from either the photo or the text). Recounting how, as a child in 1907, she had stood very near to General Silva Renard, she claimed to have heard him give the order to fire. She then described how she had come to be a party militant but had remained quite shy until Lafertte had propelled her in front of an audience, saying, "Enough, *mierda*, you have to speak!" Knowing that Recabarren had once done the same to Lafertte to cure him of stage fright, Blanca Williams reported that from then on she was ready to give speeches and to debate. Detailing her arrest during the Gonzalez Videla period, she asserted, "I was rebellious. . . . They were so afraid of me that they called me 'la Tanque Rusa.'" The "Russian Tank's" cathartic historical narrative linked the present in a continuum of struggle and repression in which she continued to play a vital, active role. Thus, though empathetic memory animated the populist state's hegemonic project, cathartic memory persisted in this allied, yet counterhegemonic voice.

Dictatorship and Solidarity: Memory as Sympathy

As the most famous example of the Chilean New Song movement, the "Cantata Santa María de Iquique" played a vital role in forging links between folk traditions and political projects for transformation. After the 1973 coup, the movement's music and performers became the focus of direct repression, and the original master recording of the cantata was destroyed.[78] Abroad, the music was re-recorded and performed in live concerts to provide a point of affective appeal for the solidarity organizations of Chilean exiles, which publicized the repression in Chile and pressured for international isolation of the military regime. During the dictatorship, memory took a predominantly sympathetic form: a call for internal and international solidarity allying a spectrum of otherwise diverse political perspectives and social sectors.

Advis's cantata, because of its elaborate composition and its treatment of state violence in Chilean history, served as an especially evocative nexus for indignation against military rule. It was recorded in Paris in 1987 by the exiled group Quilapayún, with narration by the Chilean actor Hector Duvauchelle. The album notes proclaimed that the cantata's "symbolic power has to do with the patriotic and liberatory drive of the Chilean people to incessantly seek their unity and identity."[79] The notes also highlighted key performances that had garnered international support for Chilean exiles, including performance in Italy, France, Spain, Japan, Uruguay, Argentina, Germany, Finland, Mexico, Cuba, Canada, and even the United States.[80] International solidarity encouraged the diplomatic isolation of the military regime, and social movements fighting for democracy within Chile in the 1980s used subordinate histories as a source of oppositional consciousness. To this end, international agencies funded popular education and history projects coordinated by autonomous nongovernmental organizations.

Local history continued to be a particularly vital resource in Northern Chile. In Iquique during the military regime the monument at the Escuela Santa María itself became the point of departure for demonstrations and commemorations such as May Day and International Women's Day (March 8). In spite of the state's efforts to diffuse the memories encoded in the site, urban protests often began at Iquique's cathedral and ended up at the small memorial beside the school. The monument, which was about four feet tall and was painted blue and white with a bronze plaque that stated the bare particulars of the massacre, provided an anchor for subsequent urban protests. In 1993 the original 1957 monument was replaced by a larger, more elaborate one, which included a bronze relief of bare-chested nitrate miners with featureless faces. Both the massacre's anniversary and May Day have been commemorated there for a century, linking generations of suffering and struggle. The monument was maintained by various organizations, but the Association of Ex-Political Prisoners expressed a special sense of responsibility, as they saw themselves linked to the 1907 victims in a long history of state repression.[81]

Memories of the Escuela Santa María repression have undergone changes, as evidenced in their contexts of commemoration. After the

4. Monument beside the Escuela de Santa María to honor the victims of the 1907 massacre. Erected in 1993 and maintained by unions in Iquique, it illustrates the rotos chilenos as an image of masculinity idealized in nostalgic memory. Photo by Mark Somoza.

1973 military intervention, academic studies, artistic texts, and oral accounts forged sympathetic memory in their search for solidarity against the military regime, using the repression of 1907 as an allegorical event that pointed to more recent human-rights violations. The historian and philosopher Eduardo Devés proclaimed in his study of the Santa María massacre, "Neither should it be forgotten that the 21st of December 1907 wrote in miniature, [and its] defective pantograph would appear imprinted . . . [on] the morning of 11 September 1973. More or less the same contenders, more or less the same result, more or less the same dead, more or less the same shame, but now all on a gigantic scale."[82] As Devés's study exemplifies, allegory offered an important way to deal with political issues when the state had rendered impossible the necessary context for open confrontation and analysis.[83] Historical allegory mobilized to create sympathetic memory, however, tends to obscure the past, in a manner not unlike an eclipse, wherein the apparent magnitude of the eclipsed body (the past, specifically the 1907 massacre) is much smaller than that of the eclipsing body (the present, specifically the post-1973 dictatorship). As an act that privileges the present,

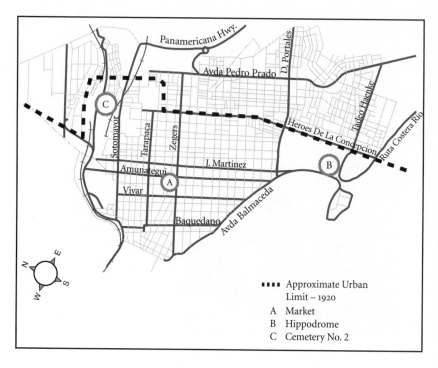

Map 4. Iquique, Chile, circa 1920. Map by Tamara Wilson.

sympathetic memory thus opportunistically eclipses the past, obscuring or subsuming the projects and aspirations of earlier peoples.

Since the nitrate era, the contradictions at the heart of Chilean history have continued to be evident in Iquique's urban geography. After the 1973 military coup, Iquique became known throughout Chile both as a location of especially intense repression and as General Pinochet's pet city, a place whose development via a free-trade zone exemplified the fruitfulness of military rule and neoliberal economic reforms. The general's affection for the city began in the Popular Unity years of the early 1970s, when he was stationed there as northern division commander.[84] Civilian and military realms were closely intertwined in Iquique.[85] In addition to the military installations placed throughout the city, housing for military families was similarly dispersed in civilian neighborhoods. Thus, since its conquest from Peru and given its continued strategic importance, Iquique has been an occupied, military city for at least as long as it has been a Chilean city.[86]

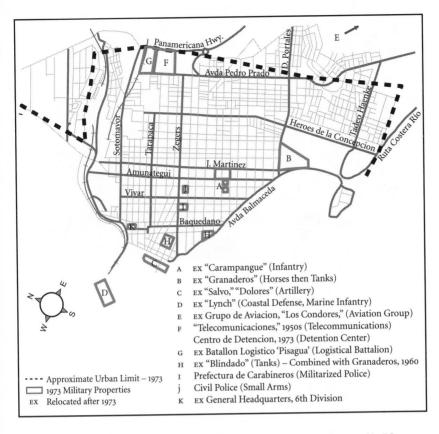

Map 5. Military properties within Iquique in 1973. Map by Tamara Wilson and Jodi Barnes.

Because of the military's fondness for Tarapacá, Iquique received special attention after the 1973 military coup. At the start of the military regime, Iquique languished in economic stagnation with a population of about 64,000. Paved, watered, urbanized, and blessed with a bounty of imported consumer goods, the city was a cornerstone in Chile's effort to ward off the negative effects of neoliberal economic restructuring in the late 1970s and 1980s. Due to the new infrastructure, the population neared 200,000 by the mid-1990s. Pinochet continued to retreat to this desert port when he felt assailed by the demands of democratic transition. Yet Iquique's streets and neighborhoods bear the scars of the dictator's attentions. Iquique being home to key garrisons and the stronghold of the northern frontier, military residential compounds were built around and within neighborhoods once famed as the cradle of the Chilean Left.

5. View of Iquique looking southwest from the Pan-American Highway. This image clearly demonstrates the legacy of the North's vicious economic boom-and-bust cycles and the consequences of neoliberal capitalism. Photo by Lessie Jo Frazier.

Neighborhoods and streets were renamed after aspects of the 1973 coup in an effort to erase the city's progressive legacy.[87] By renaming the city's landmarks, the regime inscribed a particular memory of military and national glory, for some — and one of terror, for others.[88]

Iquique still looks more like an encampment than a city. Its streets and buildings tell of a history of booms and busts, and the scars of abandonment and the tawdry relics of extracted wealth make palpable the contradictions of twentieth-century capitalism. The lack of rain encourages quick and easy construction, and the geographical limitations to building — the ocean and mountains — create an engorged real estate market. The old center of the city is filled with enormous homes built of Oregon pine shipped in by the nitrate barons in the early years of the twentieth century. Iquique is still often characterized as a frontier town of quick profits and shifting populace. Just as in the early years of nitrate exports, when corrugated tin shacks nudged up against wood palaces, today the government's cinder-block housing projects and particle-board shacks ring the old city center and the new luxury high-rises and "chalets" that stretch along the once public coastline.[89]

Melancholy, Nostalgia, and the Ghosts of Cathartic Memory

During the postdictatorship era, the Santa María massacre has been invoked in often ambiguous and contradictory ways that illustrate the political complexities of life in Chile after decades of military rule. The postdictatorship era for the most part embraced the related memory modes of nostalgia (celebrating a past clearly delimited from the present) and melancholy (mourning a past political possibility that holds no promise for the present). Both modes arise from a habituated sense of the "end of history," that is, a sense that the past is radically distinct from the present and that the future will merely elaborate the logics of the present. For some, memory entails a celebratory gesture, while for others it constitutes a prolonged state of mourning.

The Escuela Santa María massacre's centrality to the dynamics of political memory as melancholy is most evident in two examples, both of which date to 1997—just one year before General Pinochet's arrest in London rekindled the possibility of trials for human-rights abuses, and following seven years of civilian governments that had been unable to bring closure to the wounds of the past through a process of truth and reconciliation, which was presumed to entail some modest claims to retribution for human-rights abuses. First is the novel *El invasor* (The Invader), by Sergio Missana. Set in 1914, *El invasor* opens with Ramón Ramón's assault on General Silva Renard and follows the juridical process leading to the attacker's conviction.[90] Through a fictional dialogue between the defense lawyer and a powerful member of Chilean society, Missana explores the meanings of violent acts, justice, and revenge. Though ostensibly a dialogue, the more powerful party is silent and through that silence upholds the punishment of Ramón Ramón and suppresses public discourse on the question of justice for the victims of the massacre. Continuing a dymamic notable under the military regime, the 1907 event thus served as an allegory for the 1973 coup and repression. However, in the postdictatorship the temporal dimensions of the allegory expanded to include the scars and ongoing violent consequences of the massacre, including the rhetorical brutality of stifling discussion of justice in the civic sphere. The novel points to the inability of the post-1990 Chilean judicial system to accommodate investigations into human-rights abuses.

We might include in thinking about those legacies of retributive

violence the fates of those young people—often children of the executed and disappeared, or youths who grew up in exile—who became involved in armed movements to undermine the military regime; when the state apparatus was returned to civilian hands, those
young militants were transformed, almost overnight, from heroes
into "terrorists," not only by the dominant parties of the ruling coalition but even by the vestiges of the leftist parties that had recruited
them. While a few managed to build new lives for themselves, many
former guerrilla fighters succumbed to alcohol and depression and
ended up homeless, while others turned their training to banditry in
the narcotics industry or in bank heists.[91] The lack of a discursive
future, created by the silencing of public dialogue and by the redefinition and revaluing of justice and forms of political agency, rendered
the allegoric relation between the events of 1907–1914 and 1973–
1997 profoundly melancholic.

Also in 1997, to celebrate the ninetieth anniversary of the massacre,
prominent social historians from the nation's capital traveled to Tarapacá. In conjunction with a local scholar, they had organized a conference around the theme of the 1907 event; they later published the
proceedings.[92] A performance of the "Cantata" both in Iquique and
on the pampa (under the ruins of the nitrate-processing equipment
at the abandoned camp Oficina Laura) culminated the historians'
pilgrimage. Although, oddly, few papers presented at the conference
dealt specifically with the 1907 event, they did have in common a
critique of a state unresponsive to the demands and predicaments of
the majority of the nation's inhabitants, as well as a sense of justice
deferred. The historian Pedro Milos observed that the participants
used the conference as an occasion for recognizing a collective identity and memory, both regional and national: "Today, when we live
in a period in which the profound gulfs of inequality divide our
society, it is significant to feel oneself part of a common memory, that
authorizes us to continue believing in essential values like solidarity,
justice, and respect for others."[93] The historian Gabriel Salazar noted
that the conference signaled the will to remember: "Like a ghost
from the past, the social will to remember crosses Chile from north to
south." This will circulated "in flagrant opposition to the obvious
political will to forget or to commemorate only 'in terms of the
possible.'" Further situating the pilgrimage as exceptional in the contemporary political context, Salazar continued, "This will forms part
neither of political transitions nor of the fluctuations of the mar-

ket."[94] Through the historians' melancholic pilgrimage, the North once again served its historical role as a symbol of state abuse and abandonment. Furthermore, in continuing to commemorate early-twentieth-century working-class movements, these social historians mourned a loss of the sense of community-in-struggle.

In Tarapacá competition between sectors over the content of memory and the control of commemorations have constituted the pampa as a terrain of conflict and debate, even though some of those sectors promote a view of the nitrate past as uniformly harmonious. In Iquique there are roughly a dozen associations of people with roots in the old nitrate camps: the Hijos de Salitre (Sons of Nitrate). These organizations unite in various configurations to sponsor social activities and to stage Nitrate Week each November. However, many former pampinos reject these associations, maintaining that such groups represent the families of white-collar workers (*empleados*), not of workers (*obreros*), and that they indulge in nostalgia. Even those observers most cynical about the region's troubled past recall life on the pampa as "lovely" and "special" in spite of the injustices and terrible conditions of work and survival there. Understanding the call of the pampa and the persistence of its way of life requires a questioning of facile distinctions between nostalgia and a more overtly political stance—what one might recognize as the ghost of cathartic memory.[95] The tensions between these forms of memory are revealed in the uses of the Santa María massacre.

Efforts to organize commemorative events such as Nitrate Week and Tarapacá Week had occurred as early as the 1930s, after the industry had collapsed and been reorganized on a very small scale. The point of those early events was not to indulge nostalgia for "the past," but rather to rally enthusiasm for a much-hoped-for resurgence of the industry—a resurgence that never came. What did come under military rule in the 1980s were renewed efforts to celebrate aspects of regional history. Interest in Chile's nitrate heritage was backed by entrepreneurs such as Carlos Cardoen and Francisco Javier Errázuriz, who financed a number of publications such as *Historias de la pampa salitrera*, a collection of reminiscences. As Cardoen declared, "There is nothing more valid than the objective pursued by the nitrate committee in organizing the literary rescue of the fascinating history of the northern *pampa*, because it is time to save the remembrances for the benefit of posterity."[96]

Such rhetoric rang oddly optimistic, as efforts to celebrate Nitrate

Week reemerged just after the 1979 closing of the last working nitrate camp in the region, La Victoria (named in honor of Victory-in-Europe Day, which marked the end of World War II). La Victoria's demise definitively relegated nitrate in Tarapacá to the past. In 1984 various political sectors representing those interested in local history attempted to cooperate in planning events for Nitrate Week. However, vastly different understandings of nitrate-era politics and legacies and the constraints of operating under the dictatorship eventually derailed these efforts.

Specifically, certain sectors, including human-rights activists, wanted to use empathetic memory to recuperate nitrate-industry history as one of hardship and of fighting for dignity; they hoped that this recuperation would fortify and inspire people as they struggled through the dictatorship. For the nitrate associations, however, the nitrate era represented regional prosperity and community. Nitrate Week planning was eventually left to the Sons of Nitrate, a federation of civic associations for those who lived, worked, or were raised in the nitrate camps and towns. Still, the desire for communal solidarity remained important even for those who recognized that such solidarity coexisted alongside suffering and exploitation. These efforts to commemorate the nitrate era demonstrated the play of modes of memory that sometimes were inconsistent with the predominant mode of the day.

By the 1990s, however, nostalgia increasingly predominated, and the Sons of Nitrate flourished. Two competing federations emerged from the various Sons of Nitrate associations (each former nitrate camp had its own association). Competition between the groups became so intractable at times that, as in 1994, it led to parallel and only somewhat complementary Nitrate Weeks, placing local government officials in the delicate position of trying to appease both groups in their allotment of state support. One federation was led by an autocratic former schoolteacher, the other by a nexus of leaders among whom were many local-history aficionados. Both groups were often led by shopkeepers, office staff, supervisors, or teachers in the company towns as the groups took shape after the initial collapse in 1930.

In a conversation I had in 1993 with the president of the largest federation, a retired schoolteacher, I asked him to talk about his understanding of nitrate history. When he brought up the Santa María massacre, I asked about its relation to other incidents of strike and repression. He replied that, after 1907, there really hadn't been more strikes in Tarapacá—presumably negating the 1925 La Coruña strikes and repression.[97] In his narrative the 1907 strike and massacre, as a moment of conflict and rupture, was an aberration on the otherwise smooth cloth of nitrate-community life. The Sons of Nitrate reconstruct holidays as moments of cross-class harmony and community, when employees, managers, educators, shopkeepers, and workers— even manual laborers—can meet on common social terrain to celebrate the nation.[98] The popular, as it pertains to the people, was a political concept that emerged out of antifascist alliances formed from the 1920 to the 1940s, and it offered a way of building cross-class coalitions, movements, and political parties. At times, the category of the popular has been used to smooth over ongoing class and ideological conflict.

Nostalgia for working-class history is reflected in iconographic emphasis on the body of manual nitrate laborers, the roto chilenos, in statues, photographs, books, and other media—which is in sharp contrast with the current configuration of labor in Iquique, as male manual labor does not generally characterize the modern workforce.[99] The new production system implemented in the later years of the nitrate industry had eliminated one of the most strenuous occupations, that of the derripiador, the worker who scraped away the residue from the sides of the cauldrons. The figure of the derripiador became the foremost image of the pampino, a regionally specific variant of the roto chileno. The northern poet Andrés Sabella urged that Chileans enrich their collective memory by embracing the pampino, the "exceptional Chilean exalted in 1909 by Eulogio Gutiérrez as the 'most beautiful symbol of the energies of the race' and 'the most virile' of Chileans who 'makes the *patria*' with his spirit and blood."[100] Photographs of bare-chested derripiadores standing proudly with their shovels are framed and hung in homes and businesses throughout Iquique, even in the offices of recent congressional representatives from Tarapacá. During Nitrate Week in 1993, a man dressed in the typical costume of the derripiador—rough cloth pants, heavy boots, no shirt—posed for souvenir photographs. Some observers of the scramble for memorabilia remarked that when men actually worked as derripiadores, none of the souvenir seekers would have even sat at the same table with them.

The image of a strong, virile pampino stands on a monument at the entrance to Iquique, the culmination of the "nitrate park" alongside the access road to the city. The park consists of large relics from the nitrate industry, including a camp gazebo or bandstand, a transport wagon, and a water wagon. In the heart of Iquique, near Plaza Montt, the 1993 monument to the Santa María massacre displays a row of bas relief, faceless derripiadores. When I asked the monument's designer why he chose to represent the massacre in this manner, he replied that the derripiadores represented strength and that he had left their faces smooth so they could stand for everyone who had died in the massacre.[101] This was a further assertion of the masculine working-class figure as universal (national-popular) subject. When asked about the women and children who had died, the artist predicted a supplementary sculpture would eventually be raised.

Another monument to the pampino stands on the desert where the road to Iquique curves off the Pan-American Highway. Local historians had rescued this bust of a nitrate worker from an abandoned nitrate cemetery, where it had guarded a crypt built by one of the labor associations. In recent years the military had used the abandoned plains for maneuvers and target practice, and the crypt had made an appealing target for the fighter planes. Only the bust was left as a remnant of old allegiances. In its destructive attack on sites of regional heritage, the military in a sense continues to obliterate the more militant legacies of that heritage.

Claims to that heritage come not only from descendants of shopkeeper and working-class families but also from the descendants of mine owners and top administrators. A recent short-story collection, *Remolinos de la pampa*, by the granddaughter of British nitrate-mining administrators, is based on slightly fictionalized family lore.[102] While visiting one of the few remaining pampa towns (now nearly a ghost town), I met a young man with a British accent who explained that his interest in the region was more personal than that of the usual European tourist: he was the grandson of British nitrate barons. After the Chilean nitrate industry had collapsed, his family had moved themselves and their capital to Peru, where they had other investments. The radical 1970s Peruvian military regime had forced them to abandon their properties and return to the metropole. While the young Englishman spoke well of Chile, with a fond nostalgia for the era of his family's fortunes, he spoke angrily and resentfully of Peru, given what he saw as his family's economic exile and the end of their profitable adventures in Latin America. British and German film crews, similarly searching for traces of Europe's imperial heyday, came through the region in the early to mid-1990s to shoot documentaries on the glory days of nitrate and its demise with the Great Depression. Neocolonial capitalist nostalgia occupies a glamorous niche in the regional tourist industry.

In the same spirit as *Remolinos de la pampa*, which celebrated the glamour of the nitrate boom, a Chilean television station produced a 2001 telenovela set in a 1920s nitrate camp.[103] *Pampa ilusión* depicted the nitrate-mining camp as a small, cozy town whose inhabitants ranged from Europeans who indulged in social reform and the radical social practices of the flapper era (such as nonnormative behaviors for women, including one cross-dresser) to picturesque and comical miners and prostitutes. The plot centered on an elderly English nitrate baron trying to keep control of his unruly progeny and of the mining camp in general, but eventually giving way to progress and the economic collapse of the industry. As with its predecessors, *Pampa ilusión* told a story (albeit ambivalent) of national integration through mestizaje, depicting romances between the European capitalists and "Chileans."[104] While demonstrating the ongoing fascination with the former metropole, the series was designed to increase interest and tourism in the region. Some filming took place in the North, at Oficina Humberstone, the one remaining nitrate-camp ghost town. At the time the camp was privately owned but ill-maintained by a land speculator, and regional preservationists had long called for the state to purchase the camp and protect it as a historical park (which, by the end of the Lagos presidency, became a reality). The film crew's superficial renovations of the camp succeeded in re-creating some sense of the bonanza of nitrate's heyday, but at the expense of washing clean the material evidence of the longer history of abandonment of the region.

In addition to visiting the Oficina Humberstone, tourists can visit the nitrate museums opened in the last fifteen years by individual collectors in the towns Huara and Pozo Almonte. The most elaborate display on the nitrate industry resides in the government's regional museum in Iquique and includes a large photographic exhibit of workers and machinery that traces the changes in industrial organization caused by new processing techniques, portraits of leading industrialists and researchers, an extensive miniature model of a nitrate plant and company town, a reconstruction of an administrator's office complete with roll-top desk and account ledgers, and displays of hand tools. In the center of the largest exhibit hall are several free-standing cases displaying the company tokens, or fichas, issued by each plant to its workers.[105] The fichas, which were the single most continual point of grievance for workers, have become, by their number and variety, the most popular collectible for regional history buffs and tourists.[106]

Just as the museum displays emphasize the minutiae of nitrate production, discussions of the nitrate industry among history buffs in Iquique often entail hours of detailed elaboration of production processes and community rituals.[107] With a dual focus on the epic proportions of nitrate history and the details of daily life, the Association of Tour Guides offers an annual course to verse potential tour guides in regional culture and history.[108] The emphasis on detail and organization replicates the form of industrial extraction in which the labor process was highly divided and bureaucratically, scientifically managed.[109] Local aficionados of history palter over the particulars of the nitrate industry's past, thriving especially on debates about the number of people killed in the Escuela Santa María. They base their calculations on regional population, the square footage of the school courtyard, the rate at which machine guns of the day could fire rounds, the likely density of bodies in the courtyard, the various reports before and after the attack, and myriad other details. The minutiae of these debates allow the history aficionados to talk about production and state violence without reference to exploitation and repression.

A 1990s fourth-grade textbook included an account of the 1907 repression, but it, too, minimizes the significance of the strike and repression by dwelling on the question of the number of dead and assuming an impartial tone. The textbook explained, "At the end of December of 1907, there occurred in Iquique one of the bloodiest events in the history of social struggles. . . . The official statistics indicate between 130 and 140 as the number of dead and wounded. Extraofficial sources raise the number to 195."[110] This estimate is low relative to other available assessments. But, more important, fascination with calculating and debating the number of dead runs the risk of dehumanizing the event. The textbook account, as with other historical texts, assumes an impartial tone that while acknowledging the repression, diminishes its affective impact.[111] Although the historian includes the events of 1907 as a part of official history, he, like so many other practitioners of local memory, omits the demands and principles of the movement and thus depicts the workers as victims of a larger history rather than protagonists, agents of change.

In spite of the tendency to diminish the struggles of nitrate workers through nostalgic commemorative practices, it is no simple matter, as the historian Leo Spitzer notes, to distinguish between nostalgia and what he calls critical memory (reminiscent of cathartic memory), which refuses to relegate the aspirations and struggles of the past. In fact, nostalgia may at times work as a "creative tool of adjustment, helping to ease . . . cultural uprootedness and sense of alienation" by allowing for "the recall and recreation of aspects of the past within an institutional ambience" that reinforces "cultural and historical continuity."[112] The complex connections between nostalgia and forms of critical memory were apparent during Iquique's annual folk festival in 1993.[113] The festival features *estudiantinas*, musical troupes that originated in the nitrate camps in the early years of the twentieth century. They dress in turn-of-the-century white jackets and straw hats and sing of life in the nitrate pampa and ports. Although the songs are replete with romanticism about the olden days, on opening night the estudiantinas dedicated their performance to "the fallen of San Gregorio and La Coruña."

Another telling moment in the festival occurred during a performance by Kirqui Wyra, the city's folkloric ballet company, which each night staged an elaborately choreographed and costumed dance number portraying some aspect of life in the region's history. (One night, for example, they evoked the drama of the nitrate railways, ending the rousing scene with a life-sized train chugging across the stage and spewing steam.) On the very last night, the audience waited with great anticipation, and into the expectant silence rolled the famous opening bars of the "Cantata Santa María de Iquique." The troupe then danced the story of the Escuela Santa María massacre. I later asked the choreographer if he had been nervous about staging such a serious and politicized scene for the finale. He replied that his grandmother had witnessed the 1907 repression as a child and that her stories made him feel connected with the event as a fundamental part of his own, and the region's, past. How could he not include it in his review of nitrate history?[114] That last night of Iquique's international festival, after the dancers fell into their final poses, the audience sat in absolute silence for several minutes, a silence that continued even as the troupe began to take their bows.

Finally, the audience applauded and the show continued. The dance troupe had asserted the place and pain of the strikes and repression into an event filled with nostalgic elegies.

In the last part of this chapter, I pose and then question the distinction between melancholy, nostalgia, and the vestiges of cathartic memory as contending modes of political memory in late-twentieth-century, neoliberal Chile. Furthering the notion of nostalgia as a political problem, Roland Robertson points to Tom Nairn's suggestion that "willful nostalgia" marked political practices, especially among the emerging elite of industrial capitalist nations, in the decades between 1880 and 1930.[115] The concept of willful nostalgia echoes Renato Rosaldo's description of imperial nostalgia, "where people mourn the passing of what they themselves have transformed."[116] Robertson compares the nostalgia of end-of-the-nineteenth-century monopolistic capitalism with the kind of nostalgia that proliferates in late capitalism and requires a "universalization of particularism" and the "expectation of uniqueness."[117] The ethnographer Kathleen Stewart further elaborates the nuances of postmodern nostalgia.[118] Much like postnitrate Tarapacá, the postextractive industrial area of West Virginia where Stewart worked was marked by "a nostalgia . . . being inescapably haunted by the images they [the local people] dwell in."[119] It is this haunting that binds nostalgia to critical memory, virtually precluding any stance outside of the dynamics of pining.

The late-twentieth-century nostalgia for heroic histories highlights how the operations of nostalgia relate to earlier forms of connecting past and present memories and to contemporaneous modes of memory by delineating the distinctive and irretrievable blessings of past eras. The insistence on deep fissures in history entails, as David Harvey notes, the "creative destruction" necessary for capitalist restructurings.[120] The dismantling of histories of repression and opposition works by way of nostalgia's creative destruction.

Nostalgia is but one of the products of a century in which people and nation have, in part, been constructed through memory. The collision and mutual constitution of class and state formation reflect intersecting political projects that aspire to an organic synthesis of nation and people. Shifts in the modes of memory (catharsis, empathy, sympathy, and nostalgia) point to the kind of affective glue necessary to bind specific sectors together for specific kinds of political projects. These projects became increasingly and exclusively oriented around contests over the state grounded in rhetorics of nation. Populist projects asserting the broadest possible definition of the nation met with opposition from a persistent and adaptive Right who reasserted paternalist renditions of state and society. These contending voices were dominant or oppositional depending on their access to key state sectors at any given moment. Along the way, contestatory voices continued to assert other modes of memory, especially that of catharsis, to challenge the prioritization of the nation-state in political projects.

The Escuela Santa María massacre has continued to have relevance in contending mobilizations of memory because of its geography (in a regional capital under a cross-class gaze), its temporality (during a lull in national politics), and its protagonists (the military and working classes). Contending sectors continued to use the 1907 events to express the political conflicts of their time and to imagine new political positions. Certain conjunctures of state violence (e.g., 1890–91, 1925) were relatively forgotten because they played no role as models for later political mobilizations, given that the affective charge (cathartic memory) they offered was based on horizontal linkages meant to generate direct, passionate, radically oppositional action. Cathartic memory was thus not conducive to the emerging gradualist party politics prioritizing a vertical linkage to the state. As a moment whose memory shifted over time, the 1907 massacre illustrates how the memory of a single event was used to mobilize people and bind them together in ways appropriate to various political projects. It thus elucidates the continuities in Chilean nation-state formation that scholarship has treated as disparate moments. These continuities work because of the ways in which conjunctures of state violence were creatively taken up in memory-work. In this chapter I explored the long-range view of nation-state formation, illustrating various modes of memory and their concomitant state formations. In the next chapter I further explore the disciplines and deceptions of memory, from the 1940s to the present, as processes of remembering and forgetting intertwine in a single place, one of the most remote locations on the nation-state frontier.

How will it end, how will it end?

In Pisagua's night, jail, chains,

silence, the country debased,

and this bleak year, year of blind rats,

this bleak year of rage and rancor,

you ask, you ask me how it will end?

—**PABLO NERUDA**, "Accuse"

Geographically, Pisagua is a point on the Pacific Coast. In human terms, it evokes popular repression and persecution. Concretely, it is a natural prison for those that struggle for justice and freedom. The [political prisoner] of today and yesterday, standing with his back to the sea, only sees *cuadras* and an immense smooth hill 150 meters high. There is no need for bars.—**CECILIA ALLENDES**, "Pisagua"

Conjunctures of Memory

THE DETENTION CAMPS IN PISAGUA REMEMBERED

(1948, 1973, 1990) AND FORGOTTEN (1943, 1956, 1984)

Baldramina and I rode the night bus through the desert. We were headed from Tarapacá to a neighboring province to attend the 1993 inauguration of the tomb for those executed there in 1973, whose mass grave had been recently discovered and excavated.[1] As we rolled through the night, Baldramina quietly spoke of finally seeing her son Humberto's body as his remains were removed from the Pisagua mass grave in June 1990, during the earliest days of the new civilian regime. Because of the extreme dryness of the climate and salinity of the sands, the corpses had remained intact, and in the forensics laboratory she could clearly see his hands and feet, mangled by torture, and the bullet holes through his torso. The burlap bag over Humberto's head and shoulders had flattened and discolored his hair, and Baldramina protested to the coroner, "It's not right, his hair is not right." The coroner showed her a spot at the nape of Humberto's neck where his hair was as fine, dark, and curly as it had been when he was a baby. "Yes, this is my son's hair," she said, caressing the soft strands.

As a young woman, in 1948, Baldramina had helped her aunt work for the release of her uncle from the Pisagua prison camp, where he had been confined by President González Videla's government for being a militant Communist Party member audacious enough to dub his pharmacy in Iquique "Moscú." In spite of Baldramina's youthful dedication to her uncle's cause, she later, along with her husband, opposed the Popular Unity government and lauded the coup, despite their eldest son's open activism in a leftist revolutionary movement and despite the graffiti someone had painted on their house just one month before the coup: "Jakarta comes" (referring to the violent purge of communists in Indonesia).[2] In an essay that Baldramina distributed at an annual mass commemorating the executions at Pisagua, she recounted a 1973 conversation she had with Humberto just before the coup; he berated her, saying that she had no idea of what the coup would mean, of what was to come.

> "Mama, the day that the military takes power, all of Chile will cry, from Arica to Magallanes. The tortures that the Nazis applied, the fascists of the last World War, will be applied here and now will be even more cruel and subtle."
>
> "No, son, you're mistaken. They'll only topple the president and send him out of the country. . . ."
>
> "Mama, believe me. When the coup happens, then you'll remember your son."
>
> "You understood so well what would happen in Chile. For this reason, that night I saw you so sad and tired that I came close to you and caressed your head, not thinking that it would be for the last time."[3]

With Humberto's detention and execution, Baldramina renounced her right-wing beliefs and began to actively support the then underground political organizations of the Left.[4] She even assumed leadership of Tarapacá's human-rights movement, earning the Óscar Romero Human Rights Prize for her work.

After recounting her story on the bus, Baldramina turned to me and said, in a voice hardened with conviction, "If I had the power, I would obliterate Pisagua from the face of the earth, because just as my uncle was prisoner there and just as my son was murdered there, someday my grandson will be prisoner, too." She concluded

6. View of the prison and clock tower overlooking the tiny town of Pisagua and the beach. This photo captures both Pisagua's image as "a natural prison," which some hope to escape, and its modern attempts to make itself a resort town. Photo by Lessie Jo Frazier.

7. A map of Pisagua drawn on a rock there by the military, which indicates the town's significance in the military's imaginary. Photo by Lessie Jo Frazier.

that the use of Pisagua as a prison would always be irresistible to those in power.

The military never notified Baldramina of the location of her son's grave. Nor did they notify any family of the executed and disappeared of Pisagua. Yet, in spite of the close military watch kept over the semiabandoned port, in the 1980s ex-political prisoners and family made expeditions with increasing frequency to commemorate the events of the prison camp and to search for the graves of those killed there in 1973. In June 1990, less than three months after the inauguration of Chile's first civilian government in almost two decades, a team of visitors uncovered a mass grave in Pisagua and conducted the first excavation of such a site during the transition.[5] This excavation was a tactical political choice on the part of the new civilian regime, an effort to consolidate its position by launching a dramatic denunciation of state violence under military rule. The explicit narratives and imagery of the grave riveted the country's attention, particularly a photograph of a young man's face (Sanhueza) gripped in death agonies, which was reproduced in news magazines, books, protest posters, murals, and paintings throughout the country.[6]

The new civilian government took advantage of public outcry over the Pisagua grave in the timing of its reparations initiatives, while local groups used the furor to make demands on the state regarding the form and inclusiveness of reparations.[7] The excavation at Pisagua resonated in profound and often contradictory ways, evoking sets of memories that were linked across time but rife with inconsistencies and silences. To understand how dramatically the 1973 Pisagua executions affected the shift from dictatorship to formal democracy in 1990, one must understand as well the currents of memories about Pisagua that keep alive its place in Chile's history of state violence and tenacious opposition. Central to this history are the memories of Pisagua as a detention camp for communists and other political prisoners in 1947–1948 and for homosexual men. Also central are the forgotten moments of repression in Pisagua as a detention center for Axis nationals in 1943, as a prison camp for political and labor leaders in 1956, as a prison for so-called common criminals in the 1980s, and as a site of internal exile and detention in 1984. These moments layer into a hierarchy of deserving victimhood according to which forms of repression are remembered or forgotten. Thus, some are revindicated and others remain outside the boundaries of actionable suffering circumscribed by human-rights movements.

8. Mural depicting an executed person, Sanhueza, who was preserved in salt and pulled from the mass grave found at Pisagua in 1990. This image was ubiquitous in the media at the time. The mural was painted in the Pisagua town square in 1993. Photo by Lessie Jo Frazier.

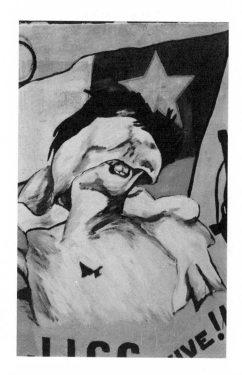

9. Another mural depicting Sanhueza. This was painted in Santiago, ca. 1990–91. Photo by Lessie Jo Frazier.

Particularly instructive and poignant has been the attempt of the Association of Ex-Political Prisoners of Pisagua to construct and defend their account of the past by linking Pisagua 1973 to other moments of repression in local history. Those linkages appear most clearly in the family histories of ex-prisoners whose forebears had participated in earlier social movements. The association's efforts to reclaim a history of struggle involved painful processes of reflection and conflict within the group, the broader community, and the state, ultimately leaving unresolved the complex intertwining of memory as a tool of domination and memory as a means of recuperating a history of struggle.

A Brief History of State Repression in Pisagua

Official and non-official memories of Pisagua as a prison site are replete with disjunctures, gaps, and conjunctures. The foregrounding of certain events in oppositional narratives has necessitated the absence of others. For example, in leftist accounts, emphasis on the 1947–1948 purge of communists has suppressed or neglected the Communist Party's nationalistic enthusiasm for the detention of foreign nationals in 1943. While accounts of the 1947–1948 prison camp by prominent political figures — especially Pablo Neruda's *Canto general* and Volodia Teitelboim's *Pisagua: La semilla en la arena* — have ensured the camp's heroic status in official oppositional memory, everyday aspects of camp life and their implications for state formation and militarism have been less elaborated.[8] Across various political moments, the shifting associations surrounding Pisagua's role in Chile's history of repression and perseverance reveals the complex and uneven layering of national memories.

Pisagua, initially a fishing settlement, has been populated since precolonial times. During the colonial and early national period, this stretch of coastline hosted whaling and guano extraction by Chinese indentured labor; on the coast south of Iquique lies a memorial to Chinese workers who were executed by cannon fire for defending themselves against the cruel demands of the labor bosses. When nitrate replaced guano as the prime fertilizer for export, the Peruvian state chose Pisagua as one of the first nitrate-shipping ports. Pisagua's population boomed. Due to a lack of real estate, a number of buildings were constructed over the water, including an elegant municipal theater where European opera companies and entertainers performed. As a nitrate-shipping port, Pisagua became a target in the Chilean campaign of conquest against Peru in the War of the Pacific. The landing of Chilean troops at Pisagua was a particularly fierce and proud victory for Chile and marked Pisagua in the rhetoric of nationalist history as a site of military valor and glory.

As Pisagua became an early casualty in the collapse of the nitrate industry, regional authorities proposed various alternative development plans. Government officials from Santiago, however, favored a scheme in which Pisagua would become a penal fishing colony, where prisoners would fish to feed themselves and generate income for the state. With a vertical mountain range towering over a small beach not more than 200 meters wide and being surrounded by unpopulated desert and ocean, Pisagua was seen by politicians and bureaucrats as a natural prison whose prisoners would require little supervision, thus keeping penal overhead to a minimum. Pisagua's residents, mostly fishermen at the time, protested the measure, fearing that it would mean the degradation of their already fragile community, reducing both the quality of daily life and the dignity of their national image. The state prevailed, however, and established a small colony of common prisoners at Pisagua. With the authoritarian regime of President Carlos Ibáñez del Campo, the policy of relegation, or internal exile, became standard state recourse, and Pisagua thereafter hosted political unfortunates.[9] Over the course of the twentieth century, Pisagua played a key role in the implementation of state projects by absorbing the excesses of the political system.

Though Chile had delayed formalizing an alliance in World War II, by January of 1943 it had ended diplomatic relations with the Axis powers. At the urging of center and leftist political parties and under pressure from Great Britain and the United States, the Chilean government imprisoned the few nationals from Axis countries who resisted deportation, confining some Japanese and Germans to interior oases and sending others to Pisagua for the duration of the war.[10] The state did so with the blessings of the unions and the Communist Party in Tarapacá, which had organized against fascism even before the beginning of the war.[11] In Tarapacá the party was especially incensed by the continued presence of one particular German national, Iquique consul Peter Müffeler.[12] The party campaigned tirelessly for Müffeler's surveillance, arrest, and deportation, but eventually contented themselves with his confinement to Pisagua.[13] The party's eagerness to call on the repressive apparatus of the Chilean state in the name of nationalist sentiment only became more fervent with Chile's declaration of coalition with the Allied forces.[14]

Perhaps inspired by Pisagua's convenience as a point of forced residence for Axis nationals, in 1945 Minister of Justice Enrique Arriagada returned to Santiago from a tour of Tarapacá with a proposal that the state develop Pisagua as a "Penal Fishing Industry City," where prisoners would bring along their entire families; he touted the plan as "an ideal solution to many problems in the penal system, and then Chile would have an opportunity to have a record of legitimate pride, the fact of possessing the first penal city of this type in the world."[15] Before bureaucrats could figure out the logistics and physical requirements of this ambitious development plan, Pisagua was filled with political and labor leaders and their families by President González Videla.

The Center-Left coalition that formed the post-war Popular Front government of Radical Party candidate Gabriel González Videla had continued those political alliances, both nationally and internationally, that had so enthusiastically used Pisagua as a place of detention during World War II.[16] With the collapse of Chile's near-monopoly on nitrate production, caused by the development of German synthetics around the time of World War I, nitrate and copper companies from the United States replaced Great Britain as the dominant economic and political influence in Chile; with the advent of the Cold War, the United States pressured Chile to ally with the "Free World." Accordingly, Chile severed diplomatic relations with the U.S.S.R., which President González Videla accused of inciting Chilean coal strikes with the goal of paralyzing the North American arms industry in a war that González Videla predicted would commence within three months.[17] In further compliance with the Cold War agenda, González Videla's regime agreed to sign the Rio Pact, the military agreement for hemispheric defense organized by the United States in 1947. This move was actively protested by pacifist, feminist, and leftist groups.[18]

At odds with the Communist Party over his pro-United States policy, González Videla also resolved to purge the party and its sympathizers from democratic politics.[19] This policy proved highly convenient for González Videla, who had resented communist demands for access to powerful positions within the coalition and was faced with increasing labor and social unrest in the dire postwar economic conditions.[20] Through the 1948 Law for the Permanent Defense of

Democracy (known on the Left as the Ley Maldita, or Damned Law), González Videla finally banned his old ally, the Communist Party, and had its members removed from all electoral roles, the civil service (including scores of teachers, government clerks, and the like), and positions of authority in government.[21] Additionally, González Videla had already purged Communist Party members and sympathizers from the armed forces, a key locus for political struggles within the state apparatus.[22]

Well before the culminating act of the Ley Maldita, in October of 1947 the government deemed labor activists to be security risks, and it rounded up and shipped to Pisagua Communist Party members, striking southern coal miners, and their families, as well as others who might oppose González Videla's policies (some 600 to 800 people), even though the port lacked the necessary facilities to house, feed, or provide medical attention for them. To protest the abject conditions of the camp and the complete denial of due process, the prisoners conducted three hunger strikes, and associations of prisoners' wives and families conducted hunger strikes and demonstrations in their home communities.[23] The death by starvation of Margarita Naranjo, the wife of a nitrate miner, came to stand for the determination of the hunger strikers. Her story assumed such prominence in part because Neruda relates it in his *Canto general*, wherein her ghost decries her husband's detention and promises to haunt the Chilean collective conscience: "There's so much betrayal, so much injustice, / that something like a sob that wouldn't let me live / rose to my throat."[24] Three prominent labor and political leaders and a number of small children also died for lack of medical attention and due to malnourishment.[25] Nonetheless, according to a British consular report, "the 'relegation' of some six hundred Communists to the isolated camp at Pisagua, to the North of Iquique, seems to have strengthened the *esprit de corps* of the Communists in the North as a whole," while "the inmates have exhibited a most unrepentant mentality and have successfully defied any attempts to get them to work or give up their attitude of passive resistance."[26]

As the notion that the military as a state institution should be held accountable for its role in political struggles was still foreign to most Chileans, both official and popular accounts of this period of Pisagua's history identified González Videla as a traitor to the Chilean political system. Social memory has never fully implicated the military, or the Chilean state in general, as a complicit institution.[27]

The state used the prison camps in Pisagua to suggest a profound disconnection between the place of detention and the nation, locating the prisoners geographically and symbolically as outside civil society, as political and moral outcasts, excommunicated from the nation, but still living within the purview of the state. For the Chilean military, the 1948 deployment in Pisagua constituted a formative moment. According to the memoirs of the future dictator Augusto Pinochet Ugarte, who had been a guard there, Pisagua exemplified the nation's need for the discipline and order the military could provide, and it offered a formative experience in his own training as a soldier.[28] However, in the official populist vision, especially in Pablo Neruda's *Canto general* and Volodia Teitelboim's fictionalized *Pisagua: La semilla en la arena*, Pisagua stood for the state's betrayal of the Chilean people and for the people's ability to endure and overcome repression. Together, these responses demonstrate the role memories of 1948 Pisagua would play in the conflictive years to follow.

Cold War politics of the 1950s further heightened Pisagua's role as a place where the heavily centralized state attempted to banish what Ibáñez del Campo called "disruptions from the syndical oligarchy."[29] As president, he cultivated the persona of a grand populist in the style of Argentina's Perón, including the use of anticommunist rhetoric to shore up his faltering policies. The economic crises of the early to mid-1950s led Ibáñez del Campo to invoke the Law for the Defense of Democracy, which had originally authorized the Pisagua prison camp in 1948. Ordering the minister of the interior to supervise the preparation of Pisagua to receive prisoners, Ibáñez del Campo confined a number of political and labor leaders there for the first two months of 1956.[30] This time, however, his drastic measures met with immediate scorn from Chileans across the political spectrum and received a great deal of negative publicity.[31] The centrist phalangists (predecessors of the Christian Democrats) actively participated in seeking the release of the prisoners, a Support and Pro-Liberty for the Relegated Committee formed in Iquique, and some of the nitrate unions formed commissions in solidarity with those relegated to Pisagua.[32] Soon the prisoners were being freed in small groups.[33]

Perhaps because General Ibañez del Campo's heavy-handed and blatantly ideological policy generated such ridicule and ended within two months, few references to the Pisagua camp of 1956 appeared in either political essays or popular representation afterward. Although Volodia Teitelboim, former general secretary of the Chilean Communist Party, had been a prisoner in Pisagua in 1956, he chose to relate instead the more dramatic experiences of the 1948 prisoners, in his widely read novel *Pisagua: La semilla en la arena*.[34] Regarding its connection with General Ibáñez del Campo, Pisagua was prominent less as a political prison camp than as a detention center for homosexual men, certainly during the general's first regime (1927–1931) and perhaps also during his second presidency. Ibáñez del Campo is characterized in popular memory as having been exceedingly, perhaps even pathologically, homophobic.[35] Leonardo Fernández, a scholar of Chilean gay history, has attempted to trace the fate of young men sent to Pisagua by boat from Valparaíso during Ibáñez del Campo's first presidency in the late 1920s, a number of those men having been cast overboard.[36] An elderly Pisagua local claimed to recall a group of about fifty young men being confined to Pisagua for some months, and the contemporary gay-rights organization in Santiago has cited the persecution of gays in Pisagua as an important marker in their history of repression and struggle.[37]

Still, little documentary evidence exists on the widely acknowledged policy of incarcerating homosexual men.[38] An exception is a 1942 editorial debate in *El Tarapacá* that discussed the Ministry of Justice's creation of a special homosexual section in Pisagua's prison, where professionals, using the most advanced techniques of psychiatric and rehabilitative care, would "reform" the prisoners. The first commentary in the published debate reacted to this policy and pleaded for its reversal

> But do not make this offense against Pisagua, which for its war-making traditions, with all of its national glories, merits the respect of the whole country as a sacred place. If the Sub-Tte. Barrientos, the patriot who placed the first Chilean flag on the Playa Blanca of Pisagua during the War of 1879, demonstrating his valor and fierceness for the fight to the whole world, could know all that has been done with this town—even to the point that its economy has been allowed to die—surely he would curse those that do not consider the respect that is owed the glorious lands of this country.[39]

The second and less negative editorial insisted that the director of prisons should indeed mobilize these new theories of rehabilitation, noting that "by analyzing the factors that create these insane, as they are called, we seek a humane solution, and we do not think for a minute that Pisagua's traditions of warfare, as with all of the national glories, could suffer diminution in the presence of a rejuvenating attitude such as that the Prison Service sustains. Let us not forget that its motto is 'Prison Service: Heralds of Reform.'"[40] As a reflection of local thought, this debate suggests that Pisagua, as a special site of national memory — of military and thus national honor — might well have been an ideal place to defend patriarchal heteronormativity, but it was also especially sensitive to the possibility of dishonor and contamination should that project fail. After the 1950s, the port of Pisagua languished in near-abandonment, left in relative peace to the small group of fishermen who lived there. Almost two decades would pass before Pisagua would be deployed again on a significant scale in defense of national honor.

Almost immediately upon the military coup of 11 September 1973, with little resistance, the military again filled Pisagua with so-called subversives (mostly authorities of the Popular Unity government and its supporters who the fascist sectors of the military defined as subversives), mainly from Iquique (Pisagua at this time was not the only prison camp in the country), including siblings, parents and their adult offspring, uncles and their nephews, and cousins. Some of those imprisoned in 1973 had also been prisoners in 1948. The military kept them locked up under intense and often brutal supervision, staged summary trials and executions, and used systematic torture in an attempt to justify the military coup by obtaining confessions of plots to take control of the country through an armed movement.[41]

By the early 1970s, although the notion of politics as war was a trope familiar to — and to a certain degree adopted by — actors across the political spectrum, it still clashed with most Chileans' understanding of their history as one of democratic progress toward a greater nation-state through a lively, open political system. While the military depicted the activism of the Popular Unity period as a prelude to civil war and thus as justification for the coup, the president of the Association of Ex-Political Prisoners of Pisagua argued for the fundamental innocence and pacific nature of political organizations of the period. He stated, "We gave ourselves as lambs," suggesting that people had such faith in the state, the military, and Chile's tradition of a relatively democratic political system that many turned themselves in when summoned instead of hiding, fleeing, or fighting.[42] On hearing that they were to be sent to Pisagua and remembering stories about camp life in 1948, when prisoners had roamed the port fending for themselves, some of the 1973 relegated even took along fishing tackle, so thorough was their inability—or unwilling-ness—to anticipate the brutality of what was to come. Collective national memory thus deceived many of those subjugated in the repression, especially nonleadership political-party militants, and thus made them all the more vulnerable to military will; for those allied with the military, the sweeping brutality of the coup provided opportunities to settle personal vendettas under the rubric of fight-ing the Cold War.

In the Cold War era the specter of armed revolution (as in Cuba and Vietnam) resided at the heart of National Security Doctrine, which provided the military with an ideological and tactical justifica-tion for filling the prison camp at Pisagua, a justification based on the military's own historical memory. The militarization of the camp and of the entire northern region was also justified by the threat of inva-sion by Peru. Potential conflict with Peru had long been the basis for armed activity in the region, and the generals who gained control of the Chilean forces feared that the Peruvian military would glimpse an opportunity in Chile's internal political crisis. The prospect of inter-national warfare heightened the Chilean military's sense of mission as the guardian of the nation-state, and the generals considered war with Peru imminent.[43] Ex-prisoners recalled the camp officers sug-gesting that an international war would present male political pris-oners a path of redemption as soldiers for the patria.[44] The military's institutional memory of conflict with Peru in the 1879 War of the Pacific colored their understanding of their own actions in 1973. Thus, Pisagua was explicitly organized from September 1973 until September 1974 as a military-style prison camp where the military treated male prisoners who were considered less dangerous much like conscripts.[45]

The experiences of the prisoners varied greatly depending on when they arrived at the prison camp and on their level of prior political participation. The military brought most prisoners to Pisagua from Iquique. Out of Iquique's population of sixty thousand, sixty women and nearly a thousand men were detained and sent to Pisagua be-tween September 1973 and February 1974: students, government authorities, civil servants, teachers, other professionals, union lead-ers, and working people, especially those employed by state-owned businesses.[46] The military transferred approximately 300 prisoners from Valparaíso, who remained in Pisagua for about three weeks, from the end of September to the beginning of October. The military isolated the region, especially the prison camp, eventually denying Red Cross and church officials access to the prisoners. The Red Cross visited the camp in October, December, and January, and on these occasions the military did its best to hide the most brutally tortured of the prisoners. According to surviving prisoners, on one visit a Red Cross official happened to look down through the staircase and see one of the hidden prisoners, Luis Toro, who was being kept in "the catacombs," and the official demanded to inspect him more closely. Despite this intervention, Luis Toro was eventually executed. The military stopped allowing such visits, in preparation for the large numbers of executions it anticipated with the courts-martial upcoming in February. Tarapacá is thus widely recognized as having been the focus of especially terrible repression due to its high levels of political participation, with the majority of its population having supported the Popular Unity government, and due to its strategic military significance, which led to a massive military presence: one navy, one air force, and five army regiments. General Pinochet even (symbolically) moved his government to Iquique for a short time to demonstrate his control over the region.[47]

Leaders of the political parties that constituted the Popular Unity coalition were systematically tortured, ostensibly in an effort to uncover each party's internal defense plan in the case of a civil war and to exact so-called confessions of treason (such as having stockpiles of weapons and food). The military's methods of torture included systematic beatings, electric shock, burning, the use of various hanging positions and forced postures, immersion, and mock executions. The party leaders were tried for treason in a series of courts-martial in which the time between the initiations of the trials and the executions of the prisoners ranged from less than 24 hours to a maximum of 48 hours. The regional commanding officer, General Carlos Forestier, acted as military judge with the right to modify sentences assigned by the court.[48] At least seven people were not given even the pretense of a trial. Military officers selected them, took them out of the prison compound, and machined-gunned them under the pretext of preventing an escape attempt. At least forty-four men were executed in Pisagua and Iquique (the location of twenty-two of the remains has yet to be disclosed).[49] Dozens of prisoners were condemned to sentences ranging from perpetual imprisonment to five years (the military junta eventually sent many of these people into forced exile). Over a hundred prisoners were condemned to jail-time of less than five years or internal exile (*relegación*).

The torture and courts-martial culminated in February, when the last court-martial resulting in executions in "time of war" was held in Pisagua.[50] One hundred fifty people were judged and condemned in only forty-eight hours. The planned number of executions was reduced, according to ex-political prisoners, by the intervention of Pinochet's top minister, General Oscar Bonilla, who was from Iquique.[51] One ex-prisoner memorized the following conversation between Bonilla and the cruel commanding officer Lieutenant Colonel Ramón Larraín Larraín, which took place during inspection.

> Bonilla: "Comandante, how is the prisoners' food?"
> Larraín: "They eat well, mi general."
> Bonilla: "Comandante, do you know the price of lying to a general?"
> To this, Larraín fell silent to avoid doing himself further damage.[52]

In spite of applying such pressure internally, the general publicly stated, "People are content. They play sports and swim in the ocean. It is a life that I am envying: it is making me want to go to Pisagua as a prisoner of war because even the climate is great."[53]

In addition to imprisoned government officials and party leaders, lower-level political party and union activists and government functionaries filled Pisagua; they arrived at various times during the year the camp was in operation and remained anywhere from a few weeks to several months. Pisagua was to have been the final destination for about 600 political prisoners from across Chile who were considered most dangerous to the military regime; those who were not executed would be held permanently in Pisagua. The military had contracted out the camp buildings to a German specialist.[54] The military used the political prisoners — already weakened by torture (including multiple fractures), generalized beatings, and malnourishment — to do the construction work. The first six prisoners who started the clean-up of the construction site were those marked for death. After being forced to do hard labor, they were executed at the site. (One prisoner had recently undergone major abdominal surgery, which made the work especially excruciating for him; a further point of cruelty was the commanding officer's choice of round-tip bullets for the executions.) After an East German film crew documented for European audiences the explicitly Nazi design of the camp and the plan for an ultimate point-of-destination camp for all of Chile, international pressure forced the military to abandon their plan and to shut down the Pisagua prison camp in 1974.[55] Higher-level prisoners were sent to urban prisons (many left Chile beginning in 1977, when international and national human-rights activists negotiated the exchange of prison sentences for forced exile); others were sent either into internal exile or parole in Iquique.

After the last of the courts-martial, the lower-level political prisoners who remained in Pisagua used their crafts, cooking, and, most important, theater collectives to build the ties of humanity that would enable them to endure their confinement. The theater — which had initially been forced on the prisoners by the military officials — created a vital space that called on the regional tradition of workers' theater from the nitrate era, allowed for a suspension of disbelief, and briefly gave prisoners the power of representation, with which they both drew on a body of cultural memories and shaped alternative memories of the prison camp, memories that went beyond the brutality of their captors.[56] At the same time, camp officers used the theater productions to demonstrate the military's benevolence for the benefit of Pisagua's villagers, visiting officials, and the officers' families.

Another vital component of the collective experience were the religious Masses. Lieutenant Colonel Larraín Larraín, having directed two rounds of brutal executions, ordered the first Mass to be held just before carrying out the death sentences of Socialist Party leaders. That many of the military officials, especially the commanding officer, and many of the political prisoners were devout Catholics generated a complex dynamic.[57] Former prisoners recall as especially moving the point in each Mass where the congregation chanted: "Cordero de Dios que quita los pecados del mundo, ten piedad de nosotros" (Lamb of God who takes away the sins of the world, have mercy on us). The relevance of this allegory of sacrifice seems to have been clear even to the officers. Prisoners noted that the officers' composure deteriorated as the killing and torture continued. By the time of the last court-martial in February 1974, when massive executions were anticipated, Mass was held both before and after the mock trials.

According to the ex-political prisoners, after a number of months, Lieutenant Colonel Larraín Larraín began to feel paternalistic toward the prisoners and to give speeches about how proud he was of the camp: he told them that Pisagua was "better than the American and Japanese camps" and, in reference to Spain's ongoing fascist dictatorship, that Pisagua would "last longer than Franco." He spoke of the prisoners' rehabilitation and increasing readiness to fight together in the coming war with Peru, when they could redeem themselves as good Chileans. His attachment to the prisoners was such that, long after the prison camp had closed down, he retired to Tarapacá, where he opened a bakery and nostalgically offered discounted bread to his former prisoners.

There was no single experience of Pisagua, for either the jailers or the jailed. Claims to so-called authentic accounts of Pisagua and ongoing commodification of that story create painful divisions among survivors, as each ex-political prisoner's experience is judged and ranked on a scale of suffering, and as books and scripts are marketed by people whose accounts of the prison camp are entirely secondary.

That experiences of Pisagua exceeded boundaries of time or space is evident in the ongoing connections between place, memory, and action for the ex-political prisoners. The theater in Pisagua continues to be an important place for the association of ex-political prisoners based in Iquique. The annual pilgrimage to Pisagua each October always includes a performance in the old theater, during a service that begins in the church and ends at the excavated gravesite in the cemetery. Critics of the group, including ex-political prisoners not affiliated with the association, claim that the members are trapped in the past and that they glorify a degrading experience to hide their inability to seize the opportunities offered by a free-market democracy. Nonetheless, the ex-political prisoners, their families, friends, fellow party militants, and those brought by curiosity walk through the port telling their stories, claiming their history: that this place belongs to them but that they no longer belong to it.

In many ways the ex-political prisoners are caught between nostalgia (for an era of political optimism and for the solidarity in the prison camp) and melancholy (at having their present overwhelmed by the past and the future that might have been). One consequence of this is the incommensurability of certain aspects of that past, memories about certain people that had to be left behind. This bind was crystallized in commemorative ceremonies that took place beside the excavated grave during an annual pilgrimage to Pisagua, when the association of ex-political prisoners presented framed certificates in honor of executed prisoners found in the grave to their relatives or to

10. The annual pilgrimage of human-rights activists to Pisagua. Activists begin at the entrance to the graveyard, where they display a visual litany of images of those executed at Pisagua. Photo by Mark Somoza.

11. Site of the mass grave excavated in 1990. Activists call out the names of their comrades buried in the grave and hold a service. Photo by Mark Somoza.

a proxy. The presentation echoed the traditional litanies of leftist parties, as a presenter called out the names of the executed—for example, "¡Compañero Pizarro!"—and the assembly responded, "¡Presente!" But the association reached an impasse when confronted with the presence in the grave of those presumably executed for their connections with a notorious protector of drug traffickers, Carlos Acuña. After the coup, Acuña was named military judge, and he used the coup to kill associates who could implicate him and his superiors and to assassinate Popular Unity officials who had been investigating the drug trade.[58] The traffickers' remains presented a conundrum for the ex-political prisoners. What to call them? How to acknowledge their suffering, even though they had not earned the status of compañero? In the end, the ex-political prisoners offered certificates to them as friends—"¡Amigo Mamani!"—and the assembly again responded, "¡Presente!" Other human-rights associations had also ignored these men and their families as unworthy of solidarity for the duration of the dictatorship and only confronted the limits of their own understanding of politics when presented with the evidence in the grave; in this way, they replicated the broader national dynamic to which they themselves had been subjected, that is, the questioning of the moral integrity and worth of those singled out for violence by the military.[59] Even further outside the dominant rubric of human-rights discourses were the so-called common criminals held in Pisagua, whom the ex-political prisoners acknowledge were often treated more brutally on a day-to-day basis.[60] The politics of memory under dictatorship led activists to parcel out solidarity stingily. And in the aftermath of the dictatorship, this silent history of the unrecognized victims of state violence has vexed the human-rights groups' efforts to build sympathy by staking claims on the sites of repression.

However, multiple claims have been made to those sites of repression. The regional civilian government, in a development plan to turn Pisagua into a tourist center, at one point named the Pisagua Foundation (the former Association of Ex-Political Prisoners) to oversee government funds granted to restore the old theater. The association also drew up (ultimately fruitless) plans to purchase the abandoned hospital in order to host human-rights summer camps, as well as plans to develop small aquaculture projects in conjunction with the local neighborhood council. The final irony of place and memory in Pisagua was that in selling state properties to raise funds, the former military government auctioned the old jail, which has since been converted into a private, relatively expensive hotel, complete with the bars on the cells and the prisoners' old graffiti on the walls. Ex-prisoners themselves, however, are often unwelcome at the hotel, especially during the annual pilgrimage when the prison-hotel is closed.[61]

Memories that "Burned like Fire": Dictatorship and Democratization

The contemporary struggles of the human-rights movement in Tara-pacá have been influenced by how human-rights groups formed during the dictatorship. Memories of repression were consciously used to mobilize opposition to the military regime, as human-rights groups employed their visions of the past to win sympathy and thus build support for their movement locally, nationally, and internationally. Organized protests by human-rights groups, labor, and students increased during the economic and political crises of the early 1980s and were made possible by the protection and support of the Catholic Church.[62] Nowhere was the church's role more vital than in the isolated North. Many of those executed in Pisagua had been devout and active church members (some had even been dancers in the troupes that rehearsed year-round for the annual festival of the Virgin of La Tirana); Catholic human-rights activists were thus largely defending the memory of their own.

Although the guiding principles of the budding human-rights organizations of Iquique emphasized solidarity and a willingness to become martyrs as essential to creating real change, the Catholic Church's Department of Laicos (laypeople), formally organized in July 1984, moved even further in that direction, propelling Iquique's church toward liberation theology, thereby appealing to church-goers' deeply felt religious beliefs and symbols in order to direct their work for peace and justice.[63] The lay people drew upon religious language to convey the depth of their loss to an often hostile public, as in this biblical passage, which they frequently cited.

Death has climbed in through our windows
and has entered our fortresses;
it has cut off the children from the streets
and the young men from the public squares.
. . . "The dead bodies of men will lie

like refuse on the open field,
like cut grain behind the reaper,
with no one to gather them."
—Jeremiah 9:21–22[64]

In reminding the people of Tarapacá that the coup had destroyed the hopes of an entire generation "like refuse on the open field," human-rights groups made a moral claim for revindicating the honor and ideals of that lost generation and challenged their communities to assume responsibility for gathering their memories and seeing that justice be done.

The year 1984 marked a significant turning point for the church and human-rights movements in other ways as well. In March the military regime publicly accused Father Ángel Fernández, a priest active in the human-rights movement, of subversion.[65] This attack led the bishop and the group of lay activists to pull together in a united front.[66] Events in Tarapacá reflected mobilizations happening all over Chile, which culminated in the 9th of August, nationally designated as Chile Defends Life Day by Cardinal Raúl Silva Henríquez and other human-rights leaders, a day for organizing activities "related to the defense of life, that is, against hunger, torture, murder, unemployment, exile, violence, and all the violations that affect Chile today."[67]

Later in 1984, reacting to the wave of social mobilization, the military reopened Pisagua as a point of internal exile and imprisonment for both political prisoners and so-called common criminals.[68] Recalling the horrific abuses of the 1973 detention camp, a new human-rights group, the Tarapacá Cultural Association, quickly organized themselves, compiled and circulated a mimeographed booklet that testified and documented the repressions of 1948 and 1973, and used street theater to perform the story of the 1907 Escuela Santa María massacre as an allegory for the suffering and struggles in Chile since the 1973 coup. Local human-rights organizations also formed an umbrella group, the Permanent Solidarity Committee, to coordinate efforts to create an oppositional community and to bring pressure on the military regime to close the prison in Pisagua. In part due to a law forbidding internal exile to nonurban places — a concession the military had recently made to the human-rights movement — the government acquiesced to the opposition's pressure and returned the political prisoners to urban prisons. This episode is alluded to in Leo Kokin's 1987 film, *La estación del regreso*, in which a woman travels north to find her detained husband, and in Diamela Eltit's novel *Por la patria*.[69] Both works, offered by nationally prominent artists, further underlined Pisagua's pivotal place in Chilean memories of state violence.

It was around this time of increasing social mobilization that some of the ex-political prisoners living in Iquique first formed their own association. Even their original name, the Association of Ex-Prisoners of War of the Concentration Camp at Pisagua, reflected the contradictions in the politics of memory around Pisagua. For example, the name appeared to contradict their professed opposition to the military's framing of the 1973 coup as a civil war, while simultaneously attempting to appropriate the loaded post-Holocaust connotations of calling Pisagua a concentration camp. Together with the Association of Families and Friends of the Executed and Disappeared, the ex-political prisoners began to make pilgrimages to Pisagua (opposed at first by the military), where they held commemorative events and searched for possible gravesites. They were driven by a sentiment much like that expressed by Pablo Neruda about the 1948 repression in Pisagua: "Beneath the nitrate and thorns / I found a drop of my people's blood, / and each drop burned like fire."[70] The search for the missing in the desert became a burning mission for local human-rights movements and a predominant theme in the writings, paintings, and protest graffiti created by members of the various human-rights groups and their families.

One artist who addressed the sad, consuming effect of the search for the dead was a young woman who depicted in painting the story of that quest as she herself had experienced it. She had been born into an elite family of white Russian émigrés who had made their wealth in Chile by exporting nitrate. Against her family's wishes, she had married a local judge committed to finding the graves of those executed in Pisagua. For years, she painted her husband's search in abstract, evocative works that suggested amorphous figures wandering the desert and hands reaching up from the sands. When the excavation of Pisagua's mass grave finally brought forth bodies of the missing, she began to paint graphic, detailed images of the site, documenting the crime by reproducing the forensic truths encoded in the remains. As her husband persisted in looking for other graves, they received threats, their home was vandalized, and he was demoted in rank as a judge, his career ruined. Driven to nervous collapse and an end of their marriage, he departed for Southern Chile, hoping to find peace and to preserve his memories by writing his memoirs. In despair, she destroyed her Pisagua paintings and began to paint brightly colored abstract compositions with which she hoped to appease her aggressors and to somehow heal her family — coloring over the painful past.[71] After her encounter with the compulsive aesthetics of remembering and the dangerously provocative force of those memories, she, unlike her husband, came to believe that she must rip the past away. If the judge sought the recuperation of memory in the permanency of its textual telling, the artist turned to healing through the destruction of mnemonic representations. The tension between these two modes of confronting memory and violence — to voice them or to paint them over — continues to haunt human-rights activists and civilian government officials as they struggle over the best way to build political projects for Chile's future.

In response to the military's claims to have won a civil war against the forces of global communism, the national human-rights movements worked to keep alive a long, specifically Chilean history of repression and struggle, using the excavations of mass graves as a mnemonic device, as in this chant from a Santiago protest march in which I participated, which offered a litany of places in Chile where the remains of the victims of the dictatorship had been found in mass graves.

> ¡Mulchén, it wasn't a war,
> It was a massacre, all were assassinated!
> ¡Lonquén, it wasn't a war,
> It was a massacre, all were assassinated!
> ¡Laja, it wasn't a war,
> It was a massacre, all were assassinated!
> ¡Pisagua, it wasn't a war,
> It was a massacre, all were assassinated!
> ¡Colina, it wasn't a war,
> It was a massacre, all were assassinated!
> They spilled the blood
> ¡Now they want to erase their guilt!
> There will be neither pardon nor forgetting in the earth
> ¡Pinochet is guilty!
> ¡Justice and punishment for all of the guilty![72]

This litany exemplified the struggle over whose history of the dictatorship would prevail and which regimes would come to be seen as legitimate representatives of the Chilean people. In this context, the exhumed bodies became artifacts of the struggle over history, as forensic scientists traced the stories of torture and execution encoded on the corpses. The human-rights movement in Tarapacá printed posters with photos of their executed and disappeared, captioned "Pisagua: And the earth spoke to demand justice." Each additional gravesite mapped out a topography of state terror, against which those struggling against the legacies of dictatorship — which included the unreconstructed military and police forces, the continued political advantages claimed by the military and its supporters, and the lack of a complete investigation of human-rights violations — could ground their protests in local, regional, and national places and thus constitute and connect communities of struggle.

During another Santiago protest that I joined, the members of the Sebastian Acevedo Movement against Torture lay along the main pedestrian thoroughfare, holding a sign for each of the gravesites, their silent presence representing the silencing of those excavated bodies. Provided an arena in which passersby could speak of their own histories, a woman cried, "Pinochet murdered my nephew, there is no pardon on this earth!" Other bystanders called back, "Calm down, here is the truth," referring to the activists' public documentation of that violent past. Through the geography of urban protest, the demonstrators and the crowd reshaped the public discourses of regime transition by evoking a history evidenced in the archaeology of state terror.

Pisagua assumed a central place in the Santiago protests as the site of the first mass grave excavated after the military regime, which lent it the greatest shock value. Abundant video and photographic documentation made the grave's impact on the public palpable and reestablished Pisagua's infamy as a detention camp. The discovery of the Pisagua grave impinged on the course of regime shift, the form of which had begun to take shape in the early 1980s, when economic crisis exacerbated by the increasing vulnerability of Chile's export-oriented economy to worldwide recessions, the social cost of neoliberal economic reforms, and increasing social mobilization against the military regime in the early 1980s combined to force the military to normalize its rule by adopting a new constitution. The constitution called for a 1988 referendum in which Chileans would vote either for Pinochet's continued rule or for a general election. After an intense campaign, the Concertación, a coalition of political parties ranging from the Christian Democrats to Socialists, won about 60 percent of the vote and thus the right to hold an election, which they also won by the same margin. Although the civilian government was inaugurated early in 1990, the shift to fuller democratic rule was less dramatic, slowed by General Pinochet's continued control of the armed forces (whose structure and personnel were unchanged) and by the fact that certain seats in the legislative and judicial branches were guaranteed for the military and parties of the Right. Also complicating the process were complex bureaucratic regulations left intact from the previous regime.[73] Thus, the shift to civilian rule necessitated a painstaking negotiation of state power at every level.

The excavation of the grave in Pisagua during this period served both to revindicate the claims of the antimilitary movement and to challenge the newly elected civilian administration to move, more quickly than it might have wished, to formulate its own relation to Chile's political past. In doing so, the now-civilian state set up the Chilean National Commission on Truth and Reconciliation to investigate the human-rights violations of the dictatorship; the commission recommended that the state "provide to families of the victims legal advice and necessary social assistance."[74] However, the commission pursued only those cases that had ended in death and did not fully acknowledge family members, who often had also experienced brutality, or other living survivors of imprisonment and torture. The government's reparation plan was intended primarily to appease those left behind (children, parents, and widows) and to thus provide closure on a painful period of history—in their metaphor, to turn the page of history.

In response to the state's reparation plan, human-rights groups demanded that perpetrators of state violence be brought to justice as an essential first step in the government's project of national reconciliation.[75] The civilian government attempted to regain control over the transition by curtailing the forensic investigation of Pisagua (a collection of remains from the grave are still unidentified and held in Santiago), by limiting access to information on the location of other graves, and by co-opting or forcing into silence those involved in the Pisagua excavation. When local human-rights activists pressured the state for official recognition of the significance of the grave at Pisagua, the government seized the political moment and initiated in Tarapacá a health-services pilot project for victims of the dictatorship, a program eventually known as the Human Rights and Integral Health Service Reparation Program (PRAIS).[76] Though the main emphasis was on mental health, PRAIS offered primary and specialized health-care services to families of the executed and disappeared, to returned exiles, and to ex-political prisoners and their families.[77] The program, along with other reparation initiatives, privileged the family members of those who had died, the executed or disappeared.[78] The process of recovery on which the reparation projects were modeled involved a clinically supervised mourning in which the family, as the foundation of civil society, was to come to terms with its loss and then move on — a key step in and mirroring of the national project of reconciliation. As with the Report of the Chilean National Commission on Truth and Reconciliation, this idealized process acknowledged neither survivors who had been detained, tortured, and exiled, nor family members who were themselves repressed for opposing the dictatorship. In other words, this model of reconciliation did not account for the fact that the military state oppressed people not as individual political victims to be mourned, but as part of collectivities to be sustained. In effect, the mental-health program was a component of the state's attempt to manage collective memory and, through that, the collectivities themselves. This program, of course, was mostly symbolic, as an acute lack of public-health resources meant that very little therapy actually took place, and certainly not in any ongoing or intensive way.[79]

Conflicts over what would be just reparation for the crimes of the dictatorship and over the role of reparation in dealing with the legacies of that repression were echoed in conflicts between medical staff and patients about the connection between the current complaints of a generally aging population and the physical and psychological traumas they had experienced over the past twenty years. The ex-political prisoners attributed diabetes, stress-related disorders, cancer, alcoholism, and other common illnesses to abuse and torture in the prison camp and detention centers, but the PRAIS staff hesitated to draw those conclusions; their skepticism frustrated the ex-political prisoners to the point where some refused to discuss past traumas or even current symptoms with the staff.

According to a committee of ex-political prisoners who wanted to put together their own book on Pisagua, torture was central to achieving the fundamental purpose of the camp: to force prisoners to betray and renounce their political loyalties.[80] That the military was unsuccessful—this is, that most prisoners had not told the military what they wanted to hear—represented in the minds of the committee members a victory for all prisoners. Yet when I asked the general physician of PRAIS in Iquique about the ex-political prisoners' insistence that their current maladies stemmed from torture in Pisagua, he replied that torture had not really been an issue there, because the camp had operated early in the dictatorship before methods of torture had been perfected and because most of the guards had been mere conscripts, overwhelmed by the situation and not trained in such tactics.[81]

When the state incorporated the PRAIS program into the Ministry of Health as the Mental Health and Violence Program, it was expanded to include victims of other types of violence such as domestic violence, violence against women, and child abuse. While this policy could have served to politicize domestic violence as a human-rights issue, it instead domesticated and subsumed what had been marked as political violence.[82] The stated intent of this shift was to emphasize the reincorporation of human-rights patients into society as they recovered from their past traumas (as would be expected of the new types of patients) and thus moved out of the health-care system. The Iquique branch of PRAIS refused to comply, protesting that their original patient population was not diminishing (and thus opening space for new patients), but in fact expanding as more exiles returned and more victims came forth who before had been too unsure of the stability of the civilian regime. Conceding the issue, the Ministry of Health was persuaded to relent, but only in Iquique.

In light of the tensions between regional and central state perspectives, perhaps the Iquique physician's inability to credit ex-political prisoners' claims of torture stemmed in part from having to represent the same state, albeit under a new regime, that had perpetrated the violence, despite his genuine commitment to caring for its victims. Likewise, often obeying under duress the imposition of policies from afar could undercut the very premise of the project and may have rendered real listening impossible.[83] Still, in at least partial alliance with the regional PRAIS staff, the ex-political prisoners forced the state to acknowledge the specificity of repression in Tarapacá. Furthermore, by defending their memories of state violence, they reconstructed themselves as historical actors and reclaimed their collective agency, not in opposition to the state (and national history) but in a particular and valued relation to it.[84]

Nonetheless, health as a metaphor for politics—and, in this case, as the safest means of dealing with the memories of state violence and enacting a politics of reparation—had certain troubling implications. Notions of political repression as pathology and of reparation as therapy do not necessarily confront the configurations of power that had caused a long-lived and somewhat popular dictatorship to take hold and endure. For example, a psychologist from a prominent U.S. treatment center for the victims of torture visited Tarapacá, where he attended a meeting of the Association of Ex-Political Prisoners; he suggested that ex-prisoners' mental-health issues did not mark them as mentally aberrant but rather as people who responded in a reasonable, normal way to extremely adverse circumstances. Furthermore, he commented, some widows of the disappeared, despite having turned their backs on the human-rights movement and even in some cases having remarried to military men, had recently laid claim to reparations money; those women, he asserted, simply required therapy, as they suffered from an over-identification with their oppressors.[85] After the meeting, I asked one of the association members what she thought of the psychologist's analysis of the promilitary widows' moral culpability. She leaned close and said, "It's crazy."

It's not surprising that she rejected the psychologist's dismissal of moral culpability as pathology, for if politics is pathology, then there are only victims: the politically subversive and those whose paranoia required their destruction. Still, one can imagine the possibilities if the PRAIS program had begun under the supposition that it was the military and its many supporters who needed psychological first aid before being reincorporated into moral, civil society. That process would have entailed a profound dismantling of structures of repression, a task made impossible in the regime transition as negotiated under a rhetoric of constant military threat.

Human-rights groups in Tarapacá, insisting on the historical specificity of their needs and relation to the state, saw this history as inscribed in the scars that the dictatorship left on their bodies, minds, and landscapes.[86] Similarly, they used the opened grave at Pisagua as a countermemorial supplementing the enclosed crypt built by the government. Yet early in the transition they demanded recognition for their martyrs so vehemently that they nearly condemned themselves to speak only through or in the name of the dead, rendering all the more complicated the relations between the land, the dead, and their own living bodies in the contemporary political order. However, this stance also allowed them to demand that the state, principally through the public-health system, facilitate not their efforts to recover from or get over the past and be incorporated into a seamless national narrative, but rather these efforts to recuperate the memory, agency, and integrity of their collective struggles.

While the Association of Ex-Political Prisoners prided itself on Iquique's centrality in the development of the mental-health and human-rights program, the group was even prouder of having negotiated a pilot program to address their economic concerns. The association was extremely conscious not only of its leadership throughout Chile as one of the first organizations of ex-political prisoners but also of its members being locally stereotyped as alcoholic failures and social outcasts. Entrepreneurial initiative offered one way to demonstrate their organizational direction and ability to contribute to Chile's so-called free-market miracle. The association negotiated state-sponsored small-business loans based on a model common in developing countries: the group was divided into smaller groups of three or four, and if one of the groups defaulted, the others would also be liable. While a successful model in many places, it failed to account for the economic havoc that two decades of political persecution had imposed on the ex-political prisoners' lives (interrupted education, unemployment, lost property, lost homes). Peer pressure combined with stiff repayment terms to make success difficult, especially for those without prior business experience. In the end, the riskiness of the individual small-business component of the project largely reinforced a rhetoric of failure already attached to the ex-political prisoners' lives.

The development program also included a collective component, a carpentry workshop for the entire association. With financing coming from Santiago, the municipality of Iquique had agreed to contribute space for the workshop and association offices. The mayor of Iquique delayed fulfilling this contract, offering possible locations and then withdrawing them under various pretexts; for example, he retracted an offer to include the ex-political prisoners' association in a complex with other social organizations, explaining to the group in one of its meetings that I attended that it would not be politically feasible, as people would say the mayor was "putting the Boy Scouts in with a bunch of drunken Communists." This justification hurt and offended the ex-political prisoners, and they considered drafting a formal complaint. One member disagreed, saying that they shouldn't be so hard on the mayor: "We're not white doves." The rhetoric of culpability and failure had so permeated political discourses left un-challenged from the dictatorship that the ex-political prisoners had no moral authority that was not contaminated by their own im-prisonment and survival, which left them no position from which to defend themselves. Sadly, the ex-political prisoners themselves ac-knowledged their less-than-authentic status within the official dis-course of human-rights victimhood: they had not died and thus be-come martyrs, and there had been no political process to revindicate their integrity and honor by recognizing that they had indeed been wrongly targeted by the military regime. The civilian state project of reconciliation left the ex-political prisoners behind as unfortunate living reminders of nearly two decades of repression.

Thus, in spite of the way in which the excavation of the mass grave at Pisagua changed the tempo of transition by corroborating a history of oppression, its potentially empowering effects for human-rights activists were mitigated by at least two factors. First, the new civilian regime appropriated the broad desire for justice inspired by the ex-cavations to garner authority without overstepping the limits im-posed by the military: on the national scene, the state's truth commis-sion promised the investigation and subsequent closure of a limited portion of abuses; on the local level, although the state offered repara-tion funds and political opportunities, it unfortunately based the program on arbitrary definitions of deserving victims, which made these resources vulnerable to appropriations of suffering.[87] Second, and perhaps more important, in spite of the efforts of human-rights groups, Pisagua continued to serve as a mnemonic site of exemplary class and ideological discipline: it still carries the connotation of being the place to which the state relegates delinquent and morally dan-gerous members of society and thus serves as a reminder and a threat as to where transgressors might find themselves.[88]

Thus inextricably linked with Pisagua and its ambiguous signifi-cance, the Association of Ex-Political Prisoners decided to remake that city. The innumerable difficulties they had faced in gaining a space for themselves in Iquique—where the economic boom and real-estate speculation had made land scarce and where the politi-cal alliances of regime transition had left them on the margins—

encouraged them to reclaim Pisagua, by then almost completely de-populated and economically moribund. They embraced Pisagua as agents of progress, rather than as victims of an unjust fate, and importuned the state to accept its responsibility to develop and incorporate the abandoned port into Chile's future. During an annual human-rights pilgrimage from Iquique to Pisagua, association members made a special effort to talk about their plans for Pisagua's development with the townspeople, a handful of families, many of whom were recent migrant fishers.[89] The ex-political prisoners were touched in turn by the way the residents had cleaned up the town and chapel for their visit and by the townspeople's attendance at the annual religious service and the performance in the theater.[90] Subsequently, the association met formally with Pisagua's neighborhood association and proposed to organize social and economic projects.[91]

The Association of Ex-Political Prisoners of Pisagua eventually stopped identifying themselves as ex-political prisoners — having earlier omitted the even more problematic "ex-prisoners of war" — to take on the almost philanthropic title of the Pisagua Foundation. They saw this shift as a way of broadening their membership to include their children and others in the human-rights movement. During the reorganization, membership did not depend on the notion of an authentic experience or even on solidarity.[92] Membership now depended on a collective memory reminiscent of catharsis (a shared identification with past struggles) and a shared commitment to a vision of the future, as full of contradictions as that vision may have been, contradictions that emerged from Pisagua's complex history: "City is this like none other in Northern Chile, it evokes a sumptuous past. These are not the magnificent ruins of disappeared civilizations. They are more than material ruins, the ruins of a remembrance, saturated with nostalgia."[93]

In this chapter, I moved through the "ruins of remembrance" to show how processes of both remembering and forgetting intertwine in the history of one peculiar place — often referred to as a natural prison because of its geographical features — thus naturalizing state violence. Foucault presented the rise of modern disciplinary institutions that have molded space to police the boundaries of rational order as a "geography of haunted places," in which edifices and processes of sociospatial separation mark the creation and then brutal separation of categories of persons, yet remain crucial to past and future histories of struggle.[94] Haunted places become critical sites of conflict between hegemonic and counterhegemonic projects. Accounts of Pisagua in 1948 and 1973 figure prominently in local and national collective memory, occulting other, more ambiguous moments. In the early days of Chile's shift to formal democracy, the excavation of Pisagua's mass grave reverberated throughout the country and impinged on the course and pace of regime transition by deflecting the state's attempt to gloss over memories of state repression. Throughout the dictatorship and transition to civilian rule, the human-rights movement's battles against the military deployed memories of the geography of repression and struggle to mark the field of opposition. Yet this oppositional memory was "saturated with a nostalgia" that demanded heroic narratives and excluded subjects who did not fit neatly within cultural notions of morally deserving human-rights victims: Axis nationals, homosexual men, common criminals, and often even those recognized as political prisoners. In addition, nostalgic views of past suffering at times deceived Chileans and encouraged them to give in more easily to state discipline. Finally, state-sanctioned remembrance implemented through a psychological model of therapy directed toward political reconciliation has threatened to obviate the political agency of many human-rights activists. Pisagua is a haunted place where the fields of opposition and alliance marking the history of state repression underline the conjunctures of memory, state violence, and emancipatory action.

The Melancholic Economy of Reconciliation

TALKING WITH THE DEAD, MOURNING

FOR THE LIVING

Memory has been a terrain of political struggle in defeating the dictatorship and in confronting its legacies.[1] Antidictatorship artists, scholars, and critics invoke memory, per se, in films, literature, political commentary, journalism, and scholarship where Memory represents a set of events and characters from the past that are violently excluded from the nation and whose words and stories must be reiterated, even though the general consensus among the Concertación (center-left to center-right parties) is that that past has only cautionary relevance for the present and does not offer positive models for current political mobilization. Starting with the first civilian president, Patricio Aylwin (Christian Democrat Party), military and political leaders have declared their desire "to turn the page of history," as the former president Ricardo Lagos (Socialist Party) put it, to "govern for the future."² Since the earliest years following the dictatorship, the civilian leaders of the Concertación, though genuinely and deeply concerned about redressing human-rights violations, have been quick to concede that President Allende's Popular Unity government was a failed experiment whose specific ideologies and policy initiatives have no relevance for present governance. Even sectors further on the Left that still hold those core principles (such as the state's responsibility for ensuring the equitable redistribution of resources) have found little space for their expression. Therefore, almost all of these public memory interventions share in the contemporary (neoliberal) dynamic of melancholy-nostalgia, in which there is a sense of radical rupture between the Present and an ultimately irrecuperable Past that has no practical life in the present beyond the cultural archive. In other words, people suffered and much was lost, but those projects have no bearing on present reality.

In terms of my own intervention, which may seem no less melancholic, I explore memory as not only content, facts, or pieces of the past, but more fundamentally as a way to relationally delineate moments in time and to assert affective ties as a basis for political projects in specific ways across time. By the late twentieth century and beginning of the twenty-first, memory-making as a form of sociopolitical action had become even more central to state formation. Administrations tried to develop technologies of memory to manage problematic psyches and sites in relation to the demands of social actors with multiple subjectivities and political projects of their own.

I do not presume to fully depict here all of those perspectives, nor do I offer a holistic ethnographic picture of Chile since military rule; rather, I explore the predicament of those actors who, by design or simply by their continuing presence, challenge the predominant dynamic of melancholy-nostalgia in nation-state formation and thus keep open the possibility that the past does offer substantive resources for more transformative political action in the present.

Identifying the Remains

In mourning, the crypt or grave localizes and contains loss. Until the body of Baldramina's son was located, she refused to join the pilgrimages to the former detention camp at Pisagua that took place during the second decade of the military dictatorship. She explained that with each step she might have been crossing Humberto's grave.

12. The "Para Que Nunca Más" (Never Again) mausoleum in Cemetery III in Iquique. Such government-built tombs attempt to close up gravesites and, by extension, the discourses they opened. Photo by Lessie Jo Frazier.

13. The niche tomb of Patricio Rojas Ramírez in Iquique's Cemetery I, the only remaining tomb of an individual victim of the Escuela de Santa María massacre. The mass grave and other individual graves in Cemetery II were demolished during the dictatorship, ending Popular Unity plans for a monument and memorial park. As a result, Ramírez's tomb has become a site for collective mourning. Furthermore, as someone who died a tragic death, Ramírez is believed to be able to intercede on behalf of faithful Catholics. In what is perhaps a modern echo of the ancient practice of making a death mask, his photograph is framed within the tomb's face. Photo by Lessie Jo Frazier.

Having no marker for his grave, he inhabited the entire terrain, haunting the national political culture from which he had been violently excised. His impinging on the Chilean political system both was mediated by and gave shape to his mother's political voice. With the discovery of the mass grave in June 1990, Baldramina assumed an even more prominent role as one of the leaders of Iquique's Association of Families and Friends of the Executed and Disappeared, which printed posters with the photographs and names of the dead captioned: "Pisagua—and the Earth Spoke to Demand Justice." Thus, while the mass grave remained clandestine the reclamation of the dead permeated the nation's subsoil. Even when some of the dead were found in 1990 and interred in a state-funded mausoleum three years later, the dialogue with the dead was neither finished nor contained. Some of this dialogue did occur, in quiet conversation, inside and on the steps of Iquique's chapel-like crypt with "Nunca Más" (Never Again) inscribed over the entrance.

On 11 September 1993, human-rights activists, center-left political parties, and some regional government officials met on the steps of the crypt for the commemoration of the twentieth anniversary of the 1973 coup. Military supporters in elite neighborhoods across the country toasted the occasion as the anniversary of deliverance from chaos into order. For this sector, the contest over national memory has been an endeavor to contain a past made unruly by the excess meaning of subversive political positions. In Santiago a mass demonstration against the abuses and legacies of the dictatorship filled the main avenue until the police violently dispersed the crowd. In Iquique ex-political prisoners and families of the dead solemnly milled about the steps of the crypt. Even ex-political prisoners and relatives who usually avoided public events appeared, including Raul Reyes, who arrived exhausted. He hadn't slept much the night before: each time he had closed his eyes, painful memories had swelled.

Nightmares often haunted ex-political prisoners. Iliana Ramírez, imprisoned in Pisagua along with her grown daughter, Rosa, had been besieged by nightmares. In May 1993 the military staged a *boinazo* (saber rattling) to protest both the civilian government's selective pursuit of human-rights cases involving high-profile victims and its investigation of a financial scandal involving the former military administration and relatives of General Pinochet.[3] While President Aylwin traveled to Europe to garner economic support and to persuade those still in exile to return to Chile, the military donned formal battle gear, rode in tanks into the Plaza of the Constitution, and entered the presidential palace; in effect, they reenacted a key scene from the 1973 coup, one widely remembered by Chileans — including pro-coup sectors who still proudly displayed photographs of the bombing of the presidential palace — and thus conjured memory-images that had festered for twenty years.[4] Ramírez felt despair at how closely her nightmares resembled the images she now saw on television news. She resigned her party membership, horrified that she had been coaxed by the promises of democratization into renewing her involvement in politics, again putting herself and her family at risk.[5]

By the coup anniversary in September 1993, Reyes's and Ramírez's memory-images had been reinforced, supplemented by documentaries televised in the preceding days. One showed previously censored footage from the dictatorship: bodies floating down the Mapocho River through Santiago, the four-hour bombing and siege of the presidential palace, the tanks in the streets, and President Allende's last radio address before his death. In contrast to the flurry of commemorative national media, a quiet mass took place on the steps of the crypt in Iquique, led by the longtime human-rights activist Padre Luza. Even political-party militants seemed more subdued in brandishing flags and shouting slogans.

Yet despite the performance of requisite acts of mourning and the consecration of an official site of memory for the recovered remains in the regional capital, the mass grave, now empty, has continued to act as a nexus for contending memories of the dictatorship. The grave remains important not only for human-rights movements but also for military personnel; for example, a career military officer brought his adolescent daughter all the way to Pisagua from Iquique, specifically to show her the mass grave and to explain the tragedy.[6] Human-rights activists, too, continue to make the annual pilgrimage to Pisagua, their dialogue ranging from fervent prayer to militant cries as they call for preservation of the site to commemorate the taking of life and the denial of justice. Without justice and redeemed honor, the activists assert, those who died and those who survived are in danger of remaining in a state of perpetual loss, or what Freud called melancholy, that is, failed mourning. Mourning, as a technology of memory, straddles structures of remembering and forgetting; it contains the past through a ritualized remembering that stands in for (forgets) the powerful emotions of loss, so that that loss does not interrupt the everyday task of living. In linking mourning to a call for revindication, some human-rights activists have challenged the dominant framing of mourning and thus the contemporary mode of memory as melancholy, refusing to locate grief solely in the corpse, the crypt, and rituals of mourning.

In contrast to the activists' mourning, the Chilean political leadership's version of mourning-as-reconciliation may not constitute the public memory-work required to create a viable path to a more democratic polity, a deficiency that is more palpable on the moral and politicoterritorial frontiers of the nation-state than at its center. Because frontiers are spaces of crossing and colonizing, they are indelibly marked by alterity, a radical demarcation of those who do and do not occupy a central position in the nation and of the distinguishing characteristics of that national territory. The definition of nation by denying the non-national political voice plays an especially important role on the frontier; more than offering habitation, the northern frontier of Chile has invited haunting, as in the case of Baldramina's son, whose spirit had wandered the desert for the duration of the dictatorship.[7] Moving in this chapter between Tarapacá, the frontier, and Santiago, I extend questions of nation-state formation and memory, with continued attention to the mutual production of personhood, place, and practices or — in the language of the nation-state — citizens, territory, and democracy.

These political components map onto the components of mourning that structure my account: the corpse and mourner (the person or subject), the crypt (place or sites of commemoration), and the mourning ritual (narrative acts or processes of closure). Focusing on the contemporary neoliberal market-state period, I argue that in Chile current technologies of memory manifest themselves most clearly in terms of psychology, political memorial sites, and the political process of "transition as reconciliation."

I first discuss the politics of memory in the postdictatorship period, as new civilian administrations have struggled to cope with the legacies of military rule. The state undertook two major national memory projects that book-ended the first decade after military rule: the Chilean National Commission on Truth and Reconciliation (1990–1991) and the Mesa de Diálogo (2000–2001). Subsequently, the state attempted to deal with the unresolved issue of survivors through the National Commission on Political Imprisonment and Torture Report, also known as the Valech Report (2004). I then consider localized state projects of memory discipline that operate on individual psyches and local development through sites of commemoration in the context of the emerging tourism industry. I conclude by pointing to the ways in which social actors in Chile's North have mobilized the vestiges of cathartic memory despite the predominant modes of melancholy and nostalgia nurtured in the present of the neoliberal market-state.

As research on human rights and state terror in Latin America asserts, withholding bodies of the executed and disappeared, as military regimes have so often done, torments the populace in a culturally specific way. The disappeared were those whom security forces covertly seized and then denied having in custody, making sure that the bodies were not recovered — though some mutilated bodies did strategically surface as cautionary examples. In addition to bodies of the disappeared, the bodies of those the military acknowledged having executed were also withheld. In Latin American, largely Catholic settings, where viewing the remains is central to rituals of mourning, the withholding of bodies places both the dead and the living in a liminal position, making verification and resolution of loss through proper mourning impossible.[8]

Indeed, in Northern Chile the location and identification of remains often allowed the social recovery of the person lost: their corporeal presence enhanced the possibility not just of mourning but also of dialogue with the living. In this dialogue remains were read by forensic anthropologists to tell the story of their suffering, and the recovery of bodies occasioned eulogistic acts of praise. These commemorations of the dead were performances of the mutual constitution of personhood: the dead as martyrs and the living as human-rights activists who revindicated their dead. The dialogic relationship between the living and the dead has become a culturally specific dynamic of political haunting. It has enabled conditional political action: the conferring of martyrdom on the deceased validates the activists who speak on their behalf even as it threatens to undermine activists' own claims (as survivors) to a morally grounded political agency of their own.

The tensions in the dialogic constitution of political agency for the living and the dead have been magnified in the political project of regime transition, a transition configured by the political elite of the antidictatorship parties, the Concertación, as reconciliation. The politics of reconciliation has a Catholic theological underpinning, one that reflects a shift from the term *confession*, which foregrounded the agency of the sinner, to the post–Vatican II term *penance*, which foregrounded the punitive and forgiving role of the priest and church, to the 1980s term *reconciliation*, which emphasized the relationship between the sinner and a forgiving community represented by the authority of the priest and church.[9] The political concept of reconciliation thus emerged alongside the new religious signification—not surprising, given that, in Chile, state and church have remained closely intertwined.

In this political context, reconciliation is understood as a process of societal forgiveness through the enunciation of truth about the past and through an exchange of contrition and forgiveness between perpetrators and victims (those presumed dead and represented by family members), which results in a peaceful and consolidated national polity. This exchange is core to the economy of reconciliation in contemporary Chile—economy in the sense of a system of ongoing social relations. Economies tend to operate in cyclical time, and each exchange ideally reinstantiates the system of relations. In the case of neoliberal reconciliation, it is a process that actually reanchors the state as arbiter of relations in the nation and market; this is in stark contrast to the state's own rhetoric of reconciliation, which refers to resolution, closure, and making the past the Past.

In Chile, a model for other nations with histories scarred by state violence, reconciliation has been offered as a way of collectively resolving past wrongs which—while regrettable—were necessary to build stable political and economic orders. In transitions to democracy, reconciliation is often understood as a form of mourning in which a truth commission documents the human-rights abuses of prior regimes so that the nation may confront its loss, process its pain, and move on. Reconciliation as a state project therefore reenacts the nation-state's tendency to promote a homogenizing subjectivity, that is, a unitary model of the national protagonist. Reconciliation glosses over the incommensurability of certain bodies and places, especially contested sites of violence, unreconciled ex-political prisoners, and unrepentant military officers. These actors, as vestiges of prior conflicts and because they play a critical role in the economy of reconciliation by absorbing collective social responsibility for the past, cannot fit neatly into the neoliberal present and are thus consigned to a kind of limbo, much like ghosts. The predicament of these political ghosts, both living and dead, compels my critical analysis of the neoliberal present.[10]

1990–Present: State Formation and Reconciling National Memory

In looking at how Chile's postdictatorship civilian regimes have negotiated memories of state violence even as they have remained within the process of neoliberal state formation begun under the military, one finds important differences among the first three presidencies. The first civilian administration (Aylwin), like those who organized against armed rule in the 1980s, tried early on to confront legacies of human-rights abuse through the Truth and Reconciliation Commission, out of which emerged limited reparations projects such as PRAIS but almost nothing in terms of judicial processes. By the second presidency (Frei), in the mid-1990s, the human-rights situation was moribund as leaders declared the transition over and tried to dismantle state human-rights programs as anachronisms.[11] At the end of the second presidency and the beginning of the third (Lagos), this impasse was cracked wide open by international intervention backed by human-rights movements within and outside of Chile that had persevered over the course of the decade and maintained a level of basic organization.[12] As these movements reinvigorated their demands on the state for reparations, including expanding the health-care program and access to judicial recourse, the civilian administration and the military resuscitated the rhetoric of reconciliation. The management of memories of state violence has thus been a central problem in contemporary nation-state formation, especially in the shift from military to civilian administrations.

As the historians Gabriel Salazar and Julio Pinto have argued, in nineteenth-century Chile the state consolidated well before the nation. This is reflected in the exaggeratedly legalistic character of Chilean political culture. The codification of even political breakdowns is key to the continuity of the idea of a single Chilean state with a coherent history.[13] After the 1973 coup, the military suspended the 1925 Constitution even while claiming to have acted constitutionally in defense of a nation at civil war. The regime ruled Chile through a series of arbitrary decrees backed by overwhelming force until the 1980 Constitution took effect, and though many of the old legal statutes were retained in the civil code, the military republished them in abridged editions edited to their convenience.[14] It planned for a plebiscite on armed rule at the end of the decade and its loss in 1988 led to presidential and congressional elections in 1989, with the Concertación assuming administrative rule in 1990. Thus began the period known as "the Transition" to democracy.

Yet, technically, the only transition of rule available under the military's 1980 Constitution was the shift from the postcoup military junta to the military's self-designated constitutional period, which they termed a "protected democracy."[15] According to the military's constitution, the shift in head of state from General Pinochet to civilian Patricio Aylwin marked a handing over of administration and a continuity of regime, not a significant change in the allocation of state power. In what scholars Pinto and Salazar have described as the "pragmatic politics" of the political parties, the civilian political elite accepted this framework.[16] For the decade and a half after military rule, the first three elected presidencies governed according to the military's constitution. The inability of civilian regimes to undo this constitution marked the structural continuity of the Chilean state from military to civilian rule, a continuity made possible by the concomitant continuity of elite-sector interest in the radical neoliberal economic restructuring begun under military rule. This continuity, however, stands in stark contrast to the Concertación's narrative of the coup as a historical aberration in an otherwise democratic history to which Chile then returned in 1990. Thus, in the civilian leaders' narrative, the military dictatorship was a blip in a longer, progressively more democratic historical trajectory, rather than a manifestation of other kinds of undemocratic historical tendencies that can be traced both in long-range history and in the specific question of state continuity between military and civilian regimes.

The military crafted state continuity by successfully packing the legislative and judicial branches with supporters and by protecting the structure and personnel of the armed forces.[17] The constitution further protected the military's stake in the state through the National Security Council, comprising military and civilian officials, with disproportionate voting power assigned to the military representatives. Since it took only two members to convene the council, the generals could readily invoke council power to challenge presidential authority, but such power would carry great political cost: it would humiliate the president and reveal the military's stronghold on the state to a national and international public. Thus, when the military wished to convene the council, it applied pressure on the president less publicly, a pressure intensified by what amounted to a military shadow-government. Even the civilian leaders most committed to challenging the legacies of authoritarian rule were impeded not only by the often explicit threat of military intervention but also by profound structural constraints.

The degree to which the transition entailed both change and continuity extended beyond formal, constitutional structures. In terms of key policies—the neoliberal economic model, in particular—and legal frameworks, the Chilean state manifested remarkable continuity. In terms of visible state personnel, the shift from a military dictatorship to an elected civilian-representative system did entail a change of actors, but the military had packed the courts and congress, protected its mid- to lower-level state functionaries, and preserved its own institutional organization and staffing. Long-term continuity of state structure echoed through the political culture in the resurgence of a tripartite political system of shifting alliances among parties that characterize themselves as Left, Center, and Right, and whose members are children of or actually were those who had been prominent political protagonists before 1973. For example, during the presidency of Eduardo Frei (son of the 1960s center-right president), I attended a session of the Chilean Senate, where I observed a debate that included Sergio Bitar (center-left senator for Tarapacá and Allende government figure), Evelyn Mattei (rightist politician and daughter of a pro-coup general), and General Pinochet himself (as self-appointed senator-for-life). As I looked around the senate chamber, I was struck by how many current senators had also been political figures in the past or were from political families that had been contenders for power nearly thirty years before. This practical continuity in political personalities and families has undergirded and been celebrated as the historically notable stability of the Chilean state as a cohesive and continuous entity, especially among economically and socially elite sectors.

Despite the relative seamlessness of regime transition from the political elite's point of view, a modern state's claim to democracy still requires a national body politic. By the 1990s, decades of political turmoil and an authoritarian regime had fractured the Chilean populace along lines of political ideology (pro-military intervention vs. civilianist opposition) and class (the old oligarchy, the newly rich, the military, and other beneficiaries of neoliberalism vs. the impoverished and people in declining economic positions, such as small-business owners and former state-sector employees).[18] Yet a political culture (especially of the Center and Left) that had been grounded in notions of solidarity (even among less formally mobilized sectors, like nonunion or party activists) became characterized more by generalized apathy and individualist interests. The decline of solidarity is viewed by many analysts as a mark of the widespread acceptance of the military's proclaimed antipolitical nationalism and neoliberal ideology (sometimes at odds with this very nationalism), which supplanted the primacy of the nation as the state's constituency in favor of a market made up of individuated consumers.[19]

Given the increase in neoliberal social fracturing, a language of democratization grounded in the long-standing claim of Chile as an inherently (historical) model democracy could have helped unite the polity in a viable project for effective political rule (hegemony). Theoretically, the democratization rubric could have empowered more people's claims to political enfranchisement than it obscured (for example, by whitewashing as anomalous the pre-coup political violence).[20] If so, such dynamics should be evident among groups that actually used the discourse of democracy to make emancipatory claims.

How a language of democracy could be mobilized in postdictatorship Chile was exemplified by a public event I attended in mid-1990, the first year of civilian rule. This event was sponsored by a group called Participa (generously funded by international aid), which had held extensive workshops for women on the nature of a democratic system and their right to participate in that system. Most of the women were from middle-sector to poor neighborhoods and had gathered in downtown Santiago in a university auditorium for a culminating conference. Prominent women leaders spoke on topics germane to women's issues in the newly democratic Chile. Sitting in the audience, I noticed the women around me growing restless. The session erupted when one of the audience members exclaimed that while the Participa workshops extolled democracy as participatory in contrast to authoritarian hierarchies, the conference itself privileged elite women's voices and limited so-called popular women's role to that of the chorus. As she finished, women all over the auditorium leapt to their feet, raising their hands to voice their own positions, much to the dismay of the organizers, who did their best to control the session. Though Participa organizers could have handled this episode in a way that symbolized Chile's return to democracy, they instead drew the session to a close by repudiating what they saw as a disruptive intervention. Participa — as with most of the nongovernmental organizations begun in opposition to the dictatorship—was ultimately folded into the state's new National Women's Service.[21] The scholar Lucy Taylor traced a drastic decline in direct citizen participation as well and found Chile's contemporary system to be radically depoliticizing in the service of elite neoliberal interests.[22]

Despite sharing Taylor's skepticism about the ways in which languages of democratic participation had been co-opted into the rebirth of an elitist-political-party-centered culture, I took back to Chile the question of whether the rhetoric of democracy—even in the face of persisting authoritarian structures and practices—had opened up political possibilities. A particularly articulate response came out of my interview with Patricia Ruíz, an artisan from a non-elite family (*clase popular*); she was part of the eighties generation that came into adulthood under military rule and had participated actively in social movements, eventually working for nongovernmental social organizations for poor neighborhoods. Patricia reframed the question of democracy as one of political economy: "Democracy and the economic model are distinct rivers and the question is whether they converge or in general if that is not possible. Even if this country does have a democratic state, daily life is the furthest thing imaginable." She continued, "We are always showing the superdemocratic face of the army, but fundamentally if you look at the daily life of a common person, things look very different."

Indeed, fissures in the rhetoric of democratization abound. In the campaign to defeat General Pinochet and in the presidential elections of 1989, the antimilitary coalition, the Concertación, drew on the mantra of the human-rights movement, "Truth and Justice," asserting that juridical justice would be key to a democratic state. Having won the elections, party leaders dropped the language of justice not only to bridge the pro- and antimilitary divide but also because justice was not practical given the military's ongoing power. Patricia, too, underlined key rhetorical connections between Democracy and Justice, even as she critiqued them: "The discourse is that we have completed the transition period. If this is so, what has marked this completion? The resolved emblematic cases [the high-profile human-rights prosecutions]? But for whom?" She continued, "For me, it is not a democracy when a person's basic rights are not secured because they are contrary to the [neoliberal] model: if we were more democratic, the model wouldn't work." Patricia then gave as an example the government's "labor flexibility" legislative agenda, which she attributed more to the requirements of the International Monetary Fund than to Chilean national needs. "We are in the neoliberal paradise. What we understand democracy to be, the model can't accommodate because the model is *so* crazy." She asserted the agency of the populace: "They say that people aren't interested in politics. Our culture *is* political but people reject the current way of doing politics because the dictatorship created this political system for us — our political imaginary was that it would be very different than the dictatorship." Still, there is a gap, she conceded, between the rhetoric of democracy and the exercise of citizenship. "People have less awareness of their citizenship in terms of basic rights and do not defend them."[23] Ruíz's critical narrative highlighted the continuity of the state, even as it signaled the increasing depoliticization and fragmentation of society. Similarly, the sociologist Tomás Moulian diagnosed postdictatorship Chile as a "simulacrum of democracy," divorcing form and content in the further atomization of the populace into consumers for neoliberal markets.[24]

In practice, mainstream political leaders of the Concertación, however sincere, have failed to foreground the discourse of democratization so as to provide the ideological glue to forge a unified national polity. In fact, as Salazar and Pinto argue, leaders largely have dropped democratization as a central mandate.[25] This is due, in part, to the economic conflicts of interests to which Ruíz alluded when she talked about "basic rights."

The fissure that increasingly shaped elite political discourse was the one that bisected more well-to-do sectors and thus threatened elite consensus: the ideological conflicts of the past (from Popular Unity through the dictatorship) had resulted in the violation of the rights of even middle-sector and elite actors by way of imprisonment, death, and exile, with the kind and extent of abuses circumscribed under the rubric of "human rights" in the narrowest sense. Indeed, even one of the Right's most successful political personalities, Joaquín Lavín, has a disappeared family member. Hence, the limited pursuit of so-called emblematic cases was politically necessary to promote elite cohesion. *Emblematic* is very much a neoliberal adjective, as it implies an undifferentiated liberal subjectivity (consumer-citizens in the case of neoliberal market-states), that is, that these cases can stand for all because all cases are basically the same; in fact, the cases that have received attention usually involve a victim from political and/or social elite — or at least middle-class — families. The economy of reconciliation is one of hierarchical suffering, in terms not only of the type of violation (death vs. torture, imprisonment vs. exile) but also of economic and social status. Chilean political leaders have not been able to negotiate that economy without great cost. Human-rights movements have still demanded the investigation and prosecution of particular regime violations while pro-military sectors have constantly pressured for a law (Punto Final) that would provide blanket amnesty and definitively stop further investigations.

In the face of conflict arising from legacies of human-rights violations in the political realm and from inherent economic inequalities (though not articulated as such), reconciliation as a model became even more central in political ideology—as became evident when the new civilian government shifted its slogan of "Truth and Justice" to "Truth and Reconciliation." This became the title of the 1990 human-rights report dedicated to uncovering the fate of those executed and disappeared after the coup. Reconciliation was supposed to accomplish what a rhetoric of justice could never do: bridge pro- and antimilitary regime sectors (about 40 percent and 60 percent of the electorate, respectively). Until the end of the 1990s, however, reconciliation as a project solely targeted the mobilized human-rights movement. Human-rights sectors were asked to forgive pro-military sectors pragmatically, given the moribund status of legal and political avenues for justice in the first decade of civilian governance and in spite of the insistence of pro-coup sectors that there was nothing much to be upset about, as officers justified their actions as the imposition of order for the sake of ultimate economic prosperity.

Catapulting Chilean politics out of this stalemate, the British government detained General Pinochet in London—where he had traveled for minor surgery—for extradition to Spain to be tried for crimes against humanity. Pro-military sectors began to vigorously promote national reconciliation to rally support for the former leader, defining that support as a question of national sovereignty against foreign intervention in Chilean affairs. Despite vigorous human-rights protests demanding justice within Chile and internationally, President Frei's administration adopted the Right's position and sent diplomats —some of whom had themselves been victimized by the military—to England to lobby for Pinochet's release; Frei argued both that Pinochet was immune from prosecution as a former head of state and that Chile could solve its own problems. The state grounded this demand in the premise that travel to the authentic site of the nation-state would reveal and resolve the Past, making it accessible for national reconciliation.

Pinochet's forced exile in England lasted for 503 days, punctuated by landmark British decisions that applied to former state leaders the principle of international trials for crimes against humanity. As Pinochet's political and legal situation weakened, he was forced to resort to desperate measures: medical examinations, conducted by British doctors, determined that he was mentally unfit to stand trial. This conclusion reinforced a public-relations campaign to transform Pinochet's image from that of imposing and all-knowing general to that of the nation's benevolent grandfather.

Public debates in Chile and abroad centered on who was responsible for what events leading up to and following the coup and how responsibility for state violence would be assigned. Even while Pinochet was still under house arrest in England, the idea of a Chilean juridical forum for assigning historical accountability suddenly seemed more feasible when a Chilean court upheld previous rulings and decided that the disappeared, lacking proof of death, had been kidnapped, a crime not absolved by the military's self-amnesty for most actions committed before 1978. The court therefore allowed those cases to be prosecuted. With Pinochet still in London, the military (especially the head of the navy, acting through the minister of defense) promoted the idea of an official roundtable, the Mesa de Diálogo, its purpose being to determine once and for all the fate of the disappeared and to formulate an official historical interpretation of what had happened in Chile before and after 1973.[26]

National Mourning and the Economy of Reconciliation

The Mesa de Diálogo was to attribute agency within the economy of reconciliation that was already underway in postdictatorship Chile. Languages of agency assigned, exchanged, and deferred guilt in the so-called dialogue between the military and civil society (especially human-rights movements). The Mesa was organized by civilian state and military officials as a way of negotiating the military's release of information about the fate of the disappeared and the bodies of the executed. The military's choice of the term *dialogue* may have arisen from their particular subculture. As one civilian specialist in military affairs told me, in the 1950s and 1960s, whenever Chile entered into negotiation with Bolivia to settle the (to this day) unresolved border issues from the 1879 War of the Pacific, Chilean officers would say, "With Bolivia we will always dialogue but never negotiate." Whatever the various notions of dialogue may have been, the organization of families of the disappeared used silence as a political statement; they declined the invitation to participate in the Mesa because of the legal immunity offered to military officers willing to provide such information. The official dialogue nevertheless did take place between military officials and some human-rights lawyers, along with state-appointed "representatives of society."[27] In forums over the nature of past political conflict—had it been a civil war or an unleashing of abusive, illegitimate violence?—the military insisted that the Mesa come to a consensus, that there be only one official national history. The historians and other social scientists acting as "representatives of society" retorted that there were multiple histories and that the nation could and would have to accommodate incommensurable versions of the past. A more cohesive part of the negotiations involved allotting actors, both dead and alive, quotas of guilt and responsibility for political conflict.

In the economy of reconciliation, the dead—who cannot speak but must be spoken for—were to assume and absorb the guilt of the living, a burden mitigated by a cultural framework in which, as one ex-political prisoner noted, "All *muertitos* [dear little dead ones] are good." This conviction was intensified in Iquique, where many aspects of Catholic popular culture were magnified by a long tradition of vibrant popular religiosity, especially the belief that anyone killed tragically, whether they had been good or bad, whether their death had been accidental or not, could become an effective intercessor for the living. For example, flowers often appeared at one soldier's gravesite in Iquique's municipal cemetery, indicating requests or expressions of gratitude for favors granted; according to locals, the soldier was executed for mistakenly shooting an innocent person while on guard duty. Similarly, flowers were often placed at the only surviving grave of a 1907 massacre victim (Figure 13). Thus, the work of the dead in assuming a disproportionate quota of guilt and responsibility was consistent with their obligations toward the living. In the work of absorbing culpability, the dead were to be accompanied by the other political ghosts, less worthy for not yet being physically dead: those ex-political prisoners who refused or were incapable of incorporation into the fabric of elitist party politics.[28]

Some families of the executed and disappeared have refused to equate physical remains with the lost social person and have thus questioned the Mesa's goal of locating bodies, especially since it came at the cost of the perpetrator's anonymity (the state's concession to the military) and a fuller recovery of the integrity of the victim. Even so, the state — including the military — has persisted in attempting a sleight of hand whereby the body is mistaken for the personhood of the dead in order to forestall the question of justice. In the cases of the living survivors of human-rights violations, the demand to restore social and political-juridical personhood would be even more impossible to evade.

Indeed, some ex-political prisoners have pushed back against the economy of reconciliation. As is evident in the PRAIS mental-health and human-rights reparations program, the objects of psychologistic state discipline in contemporary Chile are not passive, but answer back. The Santiago chapter of an organization for the beneficiaries of the PRAIS program evaluated the recent, in-depth program guidelines and concluded, "We have made a detailed study of the guidelines that the health authorities have given the PRAIS centers, and therein no relevance is given to the human-rights situation and, of course, we are very concerned about this." Asserting the centrality of their position as a diagnostic for Chilean democratization in general, they added, "This sums up the government's attitude of wanting to give the impression — both within the country and abroad — of a successful Chile, with almost all of its problems resolved, little shy of decreeing reconciliation — without justice."[29] As the scholars Michael Lambeck and Paul Antze observed, "collective guilt is evaded through the medicalization of individual experience. The overall result has been a shift in moral focus from collective obligations to narratives of individual suffering" and, I would add, pathology.[30]

The economy of reconciliation has entailed the distribution of guilt and the delimiting of the past by negotiating who needed to heal and who would bear the guilt of the past. This distribution and negotiation worked, in part, through politics of mental health broadly conceived and through the ongoing model of reconciliation as collective mourning, initiated with the Truth and Reconciliation Commission and continued with the Mesa de Diálogo. Even as the political system was framed by dominant sectors, both in terms of state institutions and the economy, the transition in Chile had already happened: from ideologically national-populist projects serving a model of "paternalistic state capitalism" to a neoliberal political economy.[31] As the market dissolved economic frontiers, this dissolving has produced a form of hysteria over the integrity of the nation. The mental-health program PRAIS was arguably the key resource in the civilian government's painfully limited ability (whether by lack of resolve, by complicity, by circumstance beyond their control, or by some combination) to mediate between the military and the populace, between the national-popular and neoliberalism, between the past and the present.

However, others — like the Spanish judge Juan Garzón, who requested that Britain extradite Pinochet to Spain for trial — refused to so gently resolve past and present or to concede that the Chilean nation-state was only actor with the prerogative to pursue questions of justice; they instead favored a horizontal (even cathartic) claim, that is, that the allocation and defense of the most profound human rights concern everyone, irrespective of national ties. Jude Garzón's determination to extradite Pinochet from England on charges of crimes against humanity, especially torture, opened up new possibilities in the international politics of justice: that such crimes could be tried anywhere, since they concern all.[32] The British House of Lords ruled that Pinochet could be extradited to Spain for trial for the crime of torture; the dramatic testimony of torture survivors before the British authorities was critical for this verdict (though the Chilean media did not transmit these accounts). The Chilean state sent government officials to argue against this decision in the name of national sovereignty, thus reasserting the state as the only appropriate mediator of what had been essentially a national conflict only resolvable on national soil.

In the end, the negotiated rationale that the general was too ill to stand trial saved him, and he was returned to Chile with the tacit stipulation that the Chilean judicial system would at least begin to prosecute him for human-rights crimes. However, subsequent criminal investigations of military officials in Chile did not deal with cases of torture, but rather with disappearances, legally interpreted as kidnapping, and with illegal executions. At the same time, civil cases on behalf of some families of the disappeared and executed have made claims for damages against the Chilean state, which puts the civilian administration in the awkward position of legally defending the state's actions under military rule precisely because it *is* the same state.

While in Britain torture constituted the central grounds for the pursuit of justice, by and large in Chile torture survivors were silenced in public discourse on justice by the civilian state, the military, and most human-rights lawyers.[33] One prominent lawyer explained to me that it would be too difficult to win cases in which the victim had survived, that their situations couldn't compare to the plight of families whose loved ones had died, and that such cases therefore were not worth pursuing. Some ex-prisoners, when I passed along this opinion, responded that many lawyers anticipate large cash settlements from the civil cases against the state, which leads to the emphasis on high-profile victims, especially ones with ties to prominent families. In other words, class permeates the economy of justice in Chilean human-rights struggles. Indeed, public attention to torture emerged in the dominant Chilean media for the first time only at the beginning of the second decade of civilian governance, and it did so when an investigation into the fate of a Frei family cousin disappeared in Northern Chile turned up a surviving fellow prisoner, who recounted his own and the dead man's torture. In public discourse on torture, the living exercise moral voice primarily through their association with the dead.

Renewed pressure from former political prisoners and other activists resulted in the 2004 Valech Report on torture under military rule, in which the state still tightly circumscribed the scope of investigation (excluding the names of perpetrators and sealing possible legal evidence for fifty years) and the implications of the report. Although the report dramatically recounted tens of thousands of cases of torture at a thousand different sites, it met with strong critiques from survivors who pointed to the need to "recuperate the dignity" or personhood of the tortured and to confront the issue of the ongoing privileges of those responsible.[34] For example, the state offered, in the words of then president Lagos, "symbolic" reparations in the form of pensions well below national poverty levels while omitting from official discourse the fact that former military personnel continued to receive generous pensions and health care. The sole emphasis on the importance of symbolic or politically meaningful recognition elided material policy continuities.

Still, the Valech Report served as a node for ongoing and reinvigorated contestations by associations of ex-political prisoners and other human-rights organizations. The report also, like the Mesa fiasco, embarrassed sectors of the Right and further propelled their efforts to disassociate themselves from the Pinochet regime. Rather than representing a synergetic relationship between human-rights organizations and the state, the torture commission reflected the degree to which human-rights sectors—given conjunctural openings—forced the state to address the past. The state did so in ways which continued to protect the fiction of reconciliation, that is, by focusing exclusively on validating the moral personhood of so-called victims and by enforcing silence with regard to both the direct perpetrators of violence and the wider political culture that made those violations possible.

In 2004 I asked Judge Guzmán—the person most credited for pushing forward legal cases against Pinochet and other military officials—whether, in the wake of the report on torture, he planned to prosecute that crime. Guzmán responded that it was more important to pursue cases of wrongful death, since that was the more serious crime and more urgent to resolve while family members were still alive to see justice.[35] Guzmán's response was interesting for two reasons: first, because it illustrated the deployment of a logic that ranked victims and furthermore made human rights a zero-sum game that recognized only certain victims as deserving of justice; second, because the urgency rationale would seem to apply more to torture survivors, the most direct victims who were still around to see justice carried out. Once again, the dead and their representatives were prioritized over the living.

While Judge Guzmán was at least willing to recognize the suffering of torture survivors, they themselves live in a society that daily questions their claims to moral personhood. I accompanied an ex-political prisoner, Miguel Rojas, to the public hospital's emergency room three days in a row. He asserted his right to health care as a reparations-program beneficiary and fought to gain adequate medical attention. During one visit, after a nurse had made two unsuccessful attempts to draw blood, Miguel explained that she would have more luck getting the needle in if she switched to his other arm, which had suffered multiple fractures as a result of torture sessions. As she jabbed the needle under his skin, she said, "Well, you must have been political [thus interrogated for a reason]. What party were you in?"[36]

Ex-political prisoners affected by the politics of the past bear legible scars. Due to having a criminal record (*punctuario*) from the court-martial, a large number of ex-political prisoners have repeatedly been denied markers of citizenship (including the right to vote or to obtain a passport) and modern personhood.[37] Ex-prisoners have been told that they must produce copies of sentencing records to have their names cleared under the 1978 (military) amnesty law, yet the Report of the Chilean National Commission on Truth and Reconciliation verifies that the military acknowledges that many records were burned (purportedly in a "terrorist attack" on the military archive). Even ex-political prisoners who succeeded in getting themselves reinstated on voter rosters have often found themselves invalidated simply by being removed from the roster in the subsequent election. The civilian state, like its predecessor military administration, has juridically disappeared these ex-political prisoners. They are dispossessed as citizens because their documents were disappeared, leaving them to circulate as ghosts in the present. One ex-prisoner, Alfredo Ríos, told of his shock on election day 2000: when he passed the voting center, having yet again been denied his right to vote, he saw one of his former torturers installed as an election official.

Another ex-political prisoner, Juan Sánchez, recounted a conversation he had with a prominent (Communist Party) psychiatrist who heads a European-sponsored nongovernmental organization for the psychological treatment of torture survivors (thus sharing the potential patient population with PRAIS). In the course of that conversation, the psychiatrist posited some 400,000 torture survivors in Chile. Sánchez interpreted this as an assessment of the availability of raw material waiting in line to be processed by mental-health professionals for the international human-rights market. Juan suggested that the increased interest in torture survivors was a guild-oriented movement driven by professionals looking to keep themselves employed in an industry with relatively low overhead (as opposed to the much higher cost of treating the physical legacies of torture). While Sánchez's assessment of health professionals' motivations was ungenerous and not necessarily true, it aptly critiqued the psychological reading of the ex-prisoners' mental-health situation not as an explicitly political process, but as an emerging market niche in the general commodification of health. In contrast to such exploitation of ex-prisoners' stories, the forensic reading of bodies recovered from mass graves, though also a medicalized process, became a state-sanctioned (albeit problematic) avenue through which human-rights activists could assert political voice.

In the economy of reconciliation, healing has been defined as burying the past to leave no visible scars. Scars on dead bodies can be buried more easily than those on the living. Furthermore, the living are seen as inscribed with psychic scars. Whereas physical problems can be more easily attributed to external events, mental illness is often diagnosed an internal, individual pathology.[38] If the political state were to give attention to ex-prisoners' physical health, it would see the scars and thus have to admit that the past and its effects continue. (Recognition of torture-induced physical limitations would also provide critical evidence should there ever be a political opportunity for ex-political prisoners to press for reparations.)

The narrative of reconciliation, most clearly articulated in the work of the Mesa de Diálogo, is premised on a vision of past trauma as the result of abuses by a few pathological individuals who committed excesses; it assumes that victims were guilty of subversive political activity but didn't merit death. Overenthusiastic military officers, in other words, killed in an (possibly good-faith) effort to rid society of the cancer of subversion—a logic that demands the victims accept some guilt. Moreover, the victims had to have died in order for their families to be redeemed as innocent and securely incorporated into the nation. There is an exchange of guilt between the dead victims and the military's acceptance that some in their ranks were culpable. This exchange excises guilt and buries the past such that family members and the military as an institution remain innocent and resolve the past. The past is dead, and the dead past is located and contained in the bodies of the victims, who must be reburied so that this kind of conflict never happens again: "Para que nunca más," the slogan inscribed over Iquique's mausoleum for those in the mass grave. The past must be buried. The dead are guilty, and with them gone, the debt is to be paid to their living family. The dead and a few military officers have to share in the responsibility for past conflict if the state has any possibility of continuity as an entity in which key sectors of Chilean society can still invest.

Because the survival of the state itself is ultimately at stake in the economy of reconciliation, the government has mediated the process, most prominently during the Mesa de Diálogo. The impetus for conjuring up the Mesa de Diálogo was the internal and external political crisis provoked by General Pinochet's detention in London. Because the Chilean state was so successful in negotiating the international arena, Pinochet returned to Chile. He landed with his old sense of impunity: on arrival he hopped out of his wheelchair to embrace military officers waiting as guarantors of national memory and honor, the symbolic of kissing national soil. However exuberant his arrival, Pinochet encountered an eroding base of support. In his own efforts to defend himself, he had betrayed his subordinate officers, violating the sacred principle of chain of command by claiming to have shifted responsibility for crucial decisions to regional officers. As Pinochet's political position weakened and he became intransigent in negotiating the internal settlement of the political crisis, efforts to try him proceeded. He was stripped of his immunity from prosecution, charges were filed against him, and he was placed under house arrest.

In the midst of this crisis the Mesa de Diálogo resumed its work. In January 2001 it released a report that purportedly revealed, once-and-for-all, the fate of the missing. As exposed by a (likely intentional) leak, the report declared that the military had hurled many of the missing bodies from airplanes into the ocean. This manner of disposal presented a tidy solution to the problem of the disappeared's juridical status as "kidnapped," since their death could be presumed even without a body, which obviated the possibility of a forensic reading in which the dead could speak for themselves. But the airplane explanation was clearly untrue; many cases cited in the report's claim had already accrued solid documentation pointing to quite different fates.[39]

Though limited and improbable, the report resulted in unforeseen and ironic consequences for Chilean politics and for the distribution of political accountability and agency. It was a poetic justice. The civilian politicians had ostensibly approached the Mesa as a good-faith endeavor, presupposing the honorable intent of the military despite the objection of their constituency (i.e., human-rights groups). The fact that the military handed them a basket of lies made the administration look gullible, and the civilian leaders were forced to attend more to the demands of human-rights movements, including moving forward with court cases. The military also paid a political price for its participation. The right-wing sectors most loyal to the military had doggedly denied for decades that anything untoward, excessive, or at least undeserved had happened; they were left out in the cold, politically, by the military's admission (albeit with false particulars) that atrocities had in fact happened. The project of reconciliation gave way to the Mesa's even more pragmatic call for "coexistence" (*convivencia*).

The failure of the state to build a single, encompassing narrative of the past that would resolve current conflicts in the nation revealed the state's ongoing complicity with a market-driven model that makes so clear the limits of common interest between the state (including the military) and the nation. In the wake of this failure, the state turned to two kinds of localized projects through which it bureaucratically managed persons and places identified as sites that condensed tainted memories: (1) the taming of victims and perpetrators of human-rights abuses subject to psychological intervention, and (2) the taming of contested sites of violence sanitized through official commemoration. This return to localized state discipline entailed an effort to make the past the Past and thus available only in certain, contained ways.

These efforts reveal the complex ways in which the positions of various government functionaries are mapped on the remarkably homogenous position that both scholars and laypeople recognize as "the State," which comprises its own logic and interests. The scholars Thomas Blum Hansen and Finn Stepputat note that states generate frameworks "to incorporate communities in a hierarchically organized yet homogenous nation-state through strategies that relate certain identities to certain spaces, time sequences, substances. . . . Who belongs to the past of the nation, who belongs to the future?"[40] Refusing to be relegated to the Past, the ability of various actors to elude this state discipline has constituted political haunting.

Places of Official Commemoration

While Northern Chilean human-rights activists have used the mass grave at Pisagua as a critical site of memory, the Chilean state has more recently attempted to reshape Pisagua as an official site of national commemoration. The scholar Eric Santner argues for the importance of "a context for historical actualization" in which places of mourning are both constituted by memory and themselves provide the conditions of possibility for memory, structuring and containing those memories as forms of action.[41] Indeed, as in Chile, official projects to shape places of mourning represent political efforts to contain "historical actualization," though some degree of it may happen anyway, as nonstate actors participate in and contest the making of the terms of those commemorative projects, especially at key moments in the political process.

In 2001, an election year, the senate races included a contest for the seat for Tarapacá. Public projects can seem to move quickly in election years, and the Ministry of Housing and Urbanization had been commissioned to oversee the rebirth of Pisagua and "reinforce its touristic connotation and territorial integration," including construction of a monument at the mass grave in Pisagua.[42] Why would such a project fall under this particular ministry?[43] Principally, because it was part of a long-standing plan to develop a tourist industry in Pisagua, a plan made more realistic by the supposedly impending completion of a coastline road that would pass through Pisagua and connect the two principle cities of the far North, Arica and Iquique. Potential visitors would travel more easily, quickly, and scenically than they could on the Pan-American Highway, with its tedious and sinuous roads. The coastline—formerly protected from private development as part of the national patrimony—could now be carved up into plots of land, which were to be sold and developed as vacation homes and hotels. Given the proper infrastructure, Pisagua's dramatic beaches and small town square, with its quaint nitrate-era buildings of Oregon pine, had the makings of a resort town. Ex-political prisoners had asserted their agency by advocating local development in terms of small-scale aquaculture projects for the artisan fishers who had been forced out of the bigger ports and recently settled in Pisagua; they had also established human-rights centers in the old prison, market, school, and theater, where international workshops and symposia could be held. Pisagua's scenic qualities would make it all the more appealing for what one might call political tourism. As the president of the ex-political prisoners' association at that time, Nelson Calderón, repeatedly said to me, with a small smile, "After all, *we* know those beaches better than anyone."

The most pleasant of those beaches sits just below the old cemetery. The mass grave marks the outer boundary of that cemetery, just beside a location perfect for a parking lot to service the beach.[44] A proper site of commemoration could solve the problem posed by having a mass grave next to a tourist beach by sanitizing that space enough to secure—precisely because it straddles the boundary between sites of martyrdom and politics—the boundaries of the sacred and the secular in the delimited space of the nation-state.

The local offices of the Ministry of Public Works presented an initial summary of the plan to human-rights groups in Iquique. It gave them one week to review the plan and, as had been also the case with the "Nunca Más" crypt, asked for their blessing rather than for actual participation in planning and design. (The ministry told the groups that the project required immediate action because it had to use up funds allocated for the year or risk losing them.) At a heated meeting that followed, ex-political prisoners and family members of the executed voiced their dismay.[45] In addition to objecting to the project's fundamental philosophy (including equating human-rights issues and tourism) and political practices (including the fact that it limited activists to "debating a few details"), one ex-political prisoner was particularly aggrieved by a proposal to place a canopy over the empty grave to shade tourists as they read the marker; he explained that, having been subjected to a mock execution staged at the edge of the open grave, where he could smell the bodies of his compañeros, he knew that any person facing execution at that spot would try to catch at the edges of the blindfold for a glimpse of the blue sky. He told me, "I even asked other ex-political prisoners [who had also endured mock executions] and they said that they, too, had strained their heads up toward that sky." Covering the gravesite, he felt, would not be true to the experiences of those who had died there, even though it might more readily accommodate their visitors and mourners. Moreover, as before, the state project completely failed to recognize the suffering of the ex-political prisoners as part of that site.

Ex-political prisoners further objected to the "conceptual definition of the monument" and its three goals, which, together with the "high level tourism (resort type)" aspect of the project, seemed to reshape the meaning of Pisagua in local and national memory. The first two of the three objectives raised relatively little concern: the first was to recognize those who were "unjustly and inhumanely executed" at the site; the second was to offer Pisagua as a "symbol before the world of something that should never be repeated, something like Auschwitz," in other words, as a generic commemoration of human-rights victims everywhere. The third—and most problematic —objective was to create

a positive message of reconciliation, through which Pisagua looks to revindicate itself before the national community, without negating its past but demanding its right to project itself in the future with a different image.

In this way, the monument will convert itself into a pivot, a gateway between the past and the future. A past burdened with negativity that is closed but that one does not forget is there, a future of life and hope, into which the visitor is invited to enter by means of this gateway. In addition, the project involves not just structures and objects, but also a space and a passage, where an atmosphere for reflection, remembrance, and encounter is generated. Something like the park built by MINVU [Ministry of Housing and Urbanization] in the ex-Villa Grimaldi [a torture center in the Santiago area]. This conceptualization is fully compatible with the other projects [for tourism development] outlined above and makes it possible to convert Pisagua into a representative place on a national (or worldwide) scale in terms of the theme of human rights. For example, the Pisagua Theater appropriately restored could constitute a continental center for human-rights events.

Lastly, the point is to reclaim the image that the North has of Pisagua, which goes beyond the images of horror spread by TV, through which this locality could constitute itself as a site of relevant cultural events commemorating the times of nitrate splendor—all of which could combine well with the typical attractions of the bay, an adequate hotel infrastructure, and good accessibility by land and sea.[46]

Horrified at this effort to recast Pisagua's history, the human-rights activists addressed the young state functionaries who represented the Ministry of Housing and Urbanization and were not from the region, describing Pisagua's long history as a site of state repression and the history of state violence associated with the "times of nitrate splendor," thus challenging attempts to cast that history as nostalgia. The activists left the meeting with the perception that the state representatives had formulated the project hastily and without understanding the broader historical context, to which they seemed ultimately sympathetic; the activists furthermore felt that the meeting had concluded with the state — via the young technocrats — agreeing to postpone the project indefinitely due to the serious concerns raised.

In addition to this verbal agreement, the project's official document stated that "this project can not be accomplished without the necessary participation of the institutions related to the defense of human rights, the associations of families of the political executed, organizations of ex-political prisoners, and state employees who lost their careers after the coup [*exonerados*]."[47] Nevertheless, in September 2000 these very organizations were notified that a group of artists was being flown from Santiago to visit the site and prepare proposals for a monument to be inaugurated by President Lagos in late October as part of his Caravan of Life — a play on the infamous 1973 Caravan of Death — which was essentially a campaign tour for the parties of the Concertación.[48] At that moment, the Caravan of Death case looked like it might become one of the first cases, and possibly the only one, actually tried against Pinochet; it thus represented a legitimized indictment of the Chilean state, both in terms of the problem of state continuity and in terms of the ultimate failure to carry through the task of democratic justice through a fully independent judicial procedure. These political repercussions required containing.

To this end, the 2001 Caravan of Life was to take the form of a pilgrimage of consecration and healing in which, as in all pilgrimages, the sacredness of the sites visited would confer moral authority on the pilgrims. This pilgrimage was to be life affirming in its project of reconciliation (understood as healing and closure). While the mass grave at Pisagua clearly resonated with great political sacrality, it was problematic, for it also marked radical political difference and rupture, a potential signification that required reshaping. The government chose to do this by building an official, state-authored monument, which the president was to consecrate — as a final act of mourning, as a final tombstone. These gestures were to temporally delineate the time of personal (including ideologically sectarian) mourning from the ritual time of official national memory. In planning the monument at Pisagua, the state implicitly acknowledged that the work of mourning had not been accomplished by building the "Nunca Más" tomb in Iquique, where the actual bones came to reside. As in other significant moments in Chilean history (like the Civil War of 1891 and the coup of 1973), the center of the nation-state, this time in the body of the president, once again moved to the frontier in order to establish the nation's sovereignty vis-à-vis the past, thus ratifying a new initiative in nation-state formation. The point was not to silence Pisagua, but rather to appropriate it as a particular kind of space for state enunciation and for the affective interpellation of state subjects, no longer mourners (especially with the generational culling achieved by the passing of time) but now tourists partaking of a great national tragedy.[49]

Psychology: The Modern Technology of Memory

On the back cover of his 1993 book, the Chilean psychiatrist Claudio Naranjo proclaimed, "Just as the Italian Renaissance centered itself in art, our actual renaissance will have to center itself in psychology and in the new religions."[50] Why psychology? Why psychology on par with spirituality? And why now, in many places, but especially in Chile?[51] Political battles to shape the memories of particular political actors have taken on the language, tools, and form of psychology at the same time that psychology and psychologists have taken on increasing prominence in public life.

Psychology long has been regarded as a useful tool for understanding politics, beginning with Freud's own commitments to intervening in the world (for example, in *Civilization and Its Discontents*). In Chile one finds many examples of this perspective, from notions of the collective psychology of politics, as found in Alfonso Stephens Freire's *El irracionalismo político en Chile* (1957), to examinations of the psychology of those in power, as found in Hernán Ramírez Nechochea's 1963 article "Un estudio psicológico: Gabriel González Videla," where he links the former president's betrayal of the Popular Front alliances and enactment of state repression to an inferiority complex.[52] Such examples are consistent with the history of psychology in general, in which collective and individual identities are each used to talk about and understand the other.[53]

While in using Freud's analytic insights I certainly follow this tradition, I also explore the disciplinary role that psychiatry, psychology, and, even more precisely, psychologism—the appropriation of psychological terms and practices as part of hegemonic state projects—have played in contemporary politics as a modern technology of memory. In terms of governmentality (technologies of governance), psychology may be one of the few viable ways to confront the continuing entanglements of events and people, which the political elite wishes to relegate firmly to the past—a position consistent with neoliberal ideology's refusal to engage with or acknowledge the validity of collectivities. Psychology aids neoliberal individuation in the radical commodification of social life, and psychologistic intervention has become critical for the ideological work of making politically intelligible the personas and agency of state actors. How those actors, with their complex personal trajectories, become interpellated into the unitary position of "the state" or refuse to do so illuminates the ongoing processes of state formation.

To explore such interpellations, I conducted two interviews: the first, in August 2000, was with the geriatric psychiatrist who returned from exile in Canada to determine whether or not General Pinochet was mentally fit to stand trial in Chile; the second, in February 2001, was with another health professional, a top official in the Chilean Ministry of Health, who talked about PRAIS, the mental-health and human-rights reparations project.

Interview 1: Mental Health and Human Rights: Who Is Sick? * In August 2000, just after the Chilean Supreme Court stripped Pinochet of his immunity from prosecution as self-appointed senator-for-life, I interviewed Dr. Elena Espinoza, a high-ranking national official in the Ministry of Health.[54] The Ministry of Health was headed at that time by Dr. Michelle Bachelet (later minister of defense and now the president of Chile). As she is the daughter of a prodemocratic military officer tortured to death after the coup, many human-rights activists expressed a particular affinity for Bachelet's leadership. I introduced myself to Dr. Elena Espinoza, who had been one of Bachelet's top staff members at the Ministry of Health, explaining that I wanted to ask her about PRAIS so as to better understand the state's position. Espinoza looked taken aback and said, "I'm the state?" She then explained to me that in addition to serving as a high-ranking state official, she had worked with a prominent nongovernmental organization that helped ex-political prisoners during and after the dictatorship. Furthermore, she herself was an ex-political prisoner. Espinoza concluded wryly that all she lacked in order to be completely representative of the problem at hand was to have been a torturer as well.

In occupying multiple and mutually exclusive positions at once, Espinoza was representative of the many government officials who had become part of the postdictatorship state after a long history of working to make possible the end of the dictatorship. As members of a coalition government, these officials came from various parties and social movements. Many of them experienced personal conflict in assuming the duties of government officials, given that many state policies contradicted not only the democratic practices they had espoused as activists but also their own interests as subjects of state abuse. That struggle was intensified by the remarkable structural and ideological continuity between the military and civilian regimes. The compromises required by the pragmatics of governance were more than many could tolerate; however, as professionals they found few options outside the state, which by then had incorporated not only the personnel, but also the work and international financing (such as it was) of previous organizations. And even the surviving organizations and think-tanks relied on state contracts and grants. Whereas the former activists had once prioritized the needs of human-rights and other disenfranchised sectors, they were required as government officials to prioritize the state's interests in dealing with those sectors.

The project of reconciliation, in particular, took precedence. The conflicted position of mental-health professionals and other human-rights activists now working within the state is evidence of what the scholar Francine Masiello has noted as the widening gap between intellectuals and "popular" sectors, with the close alliances forged during the dictatorship being squandered as a result.[55]

More generally, these contradictory positions are part of the push-pull (dialectical) processes whereby the shape of the state is nego-tiated. Espinoza's predicament embodies the contradictions of the postdictatorship state writ large. While the state comprises multiple actors — from individual officials to institutions — in Chile, a country with a remarkably stable state, these actors coalesce into an entity that elides its own internal tensions. For example, along with the criminal cases brought against former military officials, monetary-damage claim cases have been brought against the state for crimes committed by the military regime, which the civilian regime — as the current incarnation of the state — must now defend. State continuity and the famed stability of the transition exact a high price: former activists cum officials now embody the same state they fought against.

After congratulating Espinoza on the ongoing existence of the PRAIS program and reporting from my fieldwork that human-rights activists in the North took pride in having piloted the project, I pointed out that other newly democratic nations look to Chile as a model for reparations initiatives. We then discussed the place of PRAIS in the overall policies of the Ministry of Health. Near the end of the interview, I suggested that since the program was based on the insight that those subjected to state violence were normal people reacting in a normal way to the extreme circumstances produced by a "sick" society, it was ironic that the program had also, however in-advertently, construed the victims as a "problem" population that required reintegration into Chilean society. Would it not be more consistent to say that the military was the entity that required proper reinsertion into a democratic society? She thought for a moment and then agreed, saying that the state should offer therapy to military personnel as well as to victims but that that was not a tenable political position in Chile at that time.

She then switched voice from that of a Ministry of Health official to one of a mental-health professional, thinking through the techni-cal challenges. She explained that there were two competing modali-ties for diagnosis of mental illness: one which defined illness by underlying *causes*, and another which defined illness by *symptoms*. Given these very different systems for classifying patients, how would a state program encompassing both victims and victimizers work in practice? In a diagnostic scheme based on underlying causes, one would have different treatment procedures for those whose mental status resulted from having acted as torturers and executors than for those whose mental suffering derived from having been tortured and from having had one's family and friends killed and disappeared. In a diagnostic scheme based on symptoms, all those who exhibited the same symptoms (for example, paranoia) would be treated identically, regardless of their roles, perhaps even ending up in the same group-therapy sessions. Satisfied with neither solution, the Ministry of Health official cum mental-health professional cum human-rights-victim began sketching intricate diagrams that imagined an intersectioning of the two systems.

Interview 2: General Pinochet: A Little Senile or a Little Crazy? * The British released Pinochet on "humanitarian" grounds after medical examiners found that he was too sickly for Spain to extradite. The British and Chileans negotiated Pinochet's return to Chile behind closed doors, quite likely through Masonic channels, with the understanding that the Chilean government would have to in some way prove their claim that Chile could handle its own past. As a result, in Chile Pinochet was stripped of immunity from prosecution as a senator, placed under house arrest, and again forced to prove himself infirm—and worse, mentally deficient—to avoid prosecution. He was examined by a negotiated team of doctors, including his own military physicians and doctors appointed by the government. One of those appointed was an Iquiqueño, as I learned in January 2001 during a phone conversation with an animated colleague, who, as a native of Iquique, expressed pride that a hometown son had been one of the examiners and who urged me to meet with the doctor.

Dr. Luis Fornazzari graciously agreed to talk with me.[56] I began by saying that it was an honor to meet with him since he was an illustrious son (*hijo ilustre*) of Iquique. He replied,

I'll tell you something I haven't told in other interviews. When the examination time with Pinochet began, the general was wheeled into the room in a wheelchair and almost everyone (his doctor, Ferrer, and the Medical Legal Institute people) swarmed around him in a fawning way, not in the professionally courteous way one should treat a patient. I held back and he came toward me and broke the ice by saying, "I know who you are, you are from Iquique." (Clearly, he had been coached before entering the room that I would be the unknown party and who I was, and so forth). Still I was a bit taken aback, but I responded, "Yes, you and I are two illustrious sons of Iquique." He pulled back and was clearly surprised and disconcerted by this—as if, "Obviously, I'm illustrious, but you?"

When I asked Fornazzari whether he had said this to test the general's faculties, he replied, "I'm not so clever as to plan such a thing in advance, but I did see it as an opportunity to test him a bit, to take him off his guard. He did seem a bit disoriented at first by my response." Overall, though, Pinochet showed an amazing degree of stamina: "We would ask him if he was getting tired—after three hours of examinations!—and he would pull himself up and say, 'A soldier never tires' [un soldado nunca se cansa]."

It was a diagnosis by consensus. His personal, military doctor kept insisting on looking for some physical issue. He also tried to say that subcortical dementia doesn't exist. At this point, the two doctors from the University of Chile and I said that psychiatry has advanced in the last thirty years and that this is a completely accepted [and diagnosable] condition. Furthermore, memory is the last thing to go in this condition, especially biographical and long-term memory. With this condition, any examination is likely to get a 70 to 80 percent chance of getting an adequate answer. This doctor (who by the way persecuted many people directly after the coup, including people in the hospital where I had worked) insisted that 'la memoria es una sola' [there is only one memory], and I said, 'Pardon me, but there are seven memory systems.' And he got very angry and said, 'Let's go outside and discuss this memory thing,' as if we were to go outside for a fistfight! The first day I realized that he didn't have Alzheimer's, but the London report said that there had been no strokes so I was puzzled. What was going on here? Then through that first day as he got more tired his answers began to deteriorate, and I began to worry a lot that it was bad dementia and that we would be supplying his defense with an excuse to get him off. But the next day was not so bad. So I left Chile very satisfied with the work I had done. CNN tried to interview me in the airport but I was very restrained. Guzmán [the investigating judge] had insisted that we formally sign a document with the final diagnosis, which was slight to moderate dementia, before leaving on January 15th. So I came back to Toronto and resumed my usual work. Then, on a Friday, I got a call from the [Chilean] consul asking me to come over and look over the final report. I got there and they gave me a sealed envelope and said that, if I agreed, I should sign every page and reseal the envelope and it would be taken by diplomatic pouch back to Chile. If I disagreed, I was not to make any marks on the papers but to submit a separate response. I was not allowed to photocopy any of the report; however, I could take notes *for myself. When I saw that they had changed the diagnosis to just moderate [from slight to moderate], I was completely indignant and furious. I protested that I could not submit a response at that precise moment because I had not come prepared with all of my files on the case (with the test results, etcetera), as I had assumed all would proceed in good faith. This is why I decided to make my protest public, because I worried that they would lie and say that I had signed the document or create further problems—as they were so clearly capable of falsifying the results and so forth. Since it was the weekend, I went ahead and sent my response to Guzmán and the human-rights lawyers so that when the diplomatic pouch arrived on Monday morning, they would already be on the alert in case the government [tried anything suspicious]. The Ministro de Justicia immediately defended the general's side on two levels: defending the Instituto Médico Legal [the leading state medical office], and defending the Majesterial Servicio Judicial because the legal secretary had signed [notarized] both the original document and then just a few days later the document with the different conclusion. They had also changed the relative importance given the interview with the professional caretaker versus the wife for data about the level of dementia. The caretaker is always going to be much more reliable and the general's had said that the general picks out his own clothes, writes greeting cards, handles his bank account, writes checks, etcetera. On the other hand, the wife painted a much more dire picture of the level of deterioration: his outfits are a mess, etcetera. But a spouse's testimony is always complicated by emotional factors, such as their distress at any level of deterioration in their spouse, etcetera. The Instituto had thrown out the professional caretaker's testimony in favor of the wife's.*

I asked Dr. Fornazzari about the diagnosis, subcortical vascular dementia. He explained that the team of examiners, representing both the defense and the state, had agreed in advance on the procedures — which tests, which diagnostic parameters, who would do what — and they could not be changed once they had begun. This became problematic because the doctor who conducted the psychological interview — and who, it turned out, had worked as a psychologist for the police — did an atrocious job. "This was the worst psychological interview imaginable: repeating questions from the ICD [International Classification of Diseases], but misstating the question. It was boring and irritating not only for the other doctors but even for the patient!" Fornazzari at first thought that the psychologist was truly incompetent, but later decided that his ineptitude was intentional. "What a wasted opportunity, finally here was a chance to find out what lay behind the public persona to answer the questions, 'Why did he do what he did? What is this man? Narcissist? Paranoid?

What is the basic personality profile? What motivated him?' But with such a terrible psychological interview, we learned nothing."

Asked about how the experience of examining Pinochet had affected him, especially as a Chilean exile, Fornazzari replied, "It was an incredible experience." The medical team used an interview technique, wherein the first hour and half is used to determine whether the patient has Alzheimer's.

Once it was clear that he didn't, I was very happy. Then came the question of the degree of subcortical dementia and in the afternoon I began to worry. Also I could see that he was getting tired and I began to regret not having negotiated for more precise tests that could have more precisely specified his dementia. You see, until that moment nobody knew what state his health was really in because the London examination was so poorly done. He was examined together with his own doctors, who acted as his translators for the British doctors, so many psychiatrists outside thought that he had faked the exam or that his doctors had fixed his answers, fooling everyone. Happily, everything turned out okay. He does have a problem but certainly nothing that would prevent him from standing trial, physically or mentally. His dementia is no more than any typical of someone his age, and he has a bit of trouble walking and with one arm affected by the minor strokes, but otherwise he is very healthy. He has as good or better a command of his long-term memory as any of the doctors examining him.

I was struck by the faith that these two interviewees — each complexly connected to and constitutive of the state's workings — placed in psychology as a mechanism that could address issues on at least two fronts. First, both suggested that psychological intervention could answer the major questions of contemporary Chilean history and of their own personal histories: why did the military embark on such a violent and long-lasting regime? Why did I end up in prison? Why were my children raised in exile? Second, both interviewees participated in and imagined ways in which psychological technologies could help solve fundamental political dilemmas: how should historical responsibility be assessed? How could the state, in all its multidimensional complexity, mediate fundamental fissures between diametrically opposed sectors? Espinoza's question (and exclamation) "I'm the state?" perfectly expressed how such actors become invested in the state's position in spite of their own contradictory commitments, the complexities of all that constitutes "the state," and the ambiguities that they face in sustaining that position. For Chilean officials (though not for U.S. scholars), their contradictory positioning is a part of and produces the solidity of the idea of a singular, continuous, and cohesive state in Chile and the ways actors become interpellated into that state position.

Remarkably, both interviews suggested an almost complete absence of public discourse regarding perpetrators of human-rights abuses as potential subjects of state biopower (mechanisms of discipline habituated in and on bodies). In applying or contemplating the application of psychological technologies to actors across the political spectrum, both interviewees revealed the ways in which psychology can obscure differences between individual actors.[57] In this leveling process, the Present (as lingering effects or legacies of previous torture) is made part of the Past, a sanitized version of which is woven into national memory. Psychology, as a primary mechanism of contemporary politics, has become the privileged venue, even replacement, for the work of politics in the market-state.[58] This is, in part, because neoliberalism assumes the autonomous and undifferentiated liberal subject and refuses to recognize collectivities that may have incommensurably distinct interests. Thus, any sector that asserts such interests must be pathologized and removed from society for clinical treatment on individual bases. The unreconciled (non-Concertación) Left has mocked the new role of (mental) health — and the medical clinic as an ironic site of political intervention in general — as impoverished political practice: during Pinochet's house arrest in London, as the government and military scrambled to reinvigorate a politics of reconciliation and to recast the former dictator as a sickly and slightly forgetful elder statesman, *La Clínica*, a maverick satiric weekly, hit the streets.

To be sure, there is still a need for mental-health services that base clinical practice on an understanding of the connections between psychic suffering and political, social, and economic injustices. This need is urgent for those most directly affected by state violence ("the victims") and those implicated in systems of state abuses ("the perpetrators"). Numerous physicians have reported to me a marked increase in people who had worked in or with the military regime appealing for help with their mental anguish.[59] Even human-rights groups find themselves locked in a rhetoric of monsters and victims; this precludes an engagement with the fact that many sectors of the populace colluded with the military regime in complex ways. It will be nearly impossible to address the needs of suffering populations as long as human-rights discourses rely on humanist dichotomies of monsters and victims to press claims for justice and as long as psychology is used to depoliticize social fractures and render collective experiences individual.[60] Effective clinical practice for dealing with the legacies of human-rights violations still requires a political project.

Melancholy and Mourning

Here I arrive full-circle at the importance of psychological processes for dealing with the past and mourning as a model for confronting national trauma. Freud argues that mourning and melancholy are related processes, equally important for individuals and for collectivities. Mourning involves a gradual detachment in reaction to the "loss of a loved person, or to the loss of some abstraction, which has taken the place of one, such as one's country, liberty, an ideal, and so on."[61] Memory plays a key part in the work of mourning, as each memory of the lost love confronts and thus confirms the reality of absence.[62] Melancholia, as failed mourning, carries with it the uncertainty of what exactly has been lost, making the resolution of suffering difficult.[63] Melancholic uncertainty introduces a "conflict of ambiguity," which makes melancholia dangerous and potentially destructive.[64] Much of the ambiguity occurs (subconsciously) through countless minute struggles in "the region of the memory-traces of things."[65]

Even before the Pisagua mass grave was excavated in 1990, an artist in Tarapacá had accompanied her husband, a judge, as he searched for the remains of the 1973 coup. Her paintings depicted the shock of memory: hands reaching up through the sand and amorphous forms haunting the desert. In an analogous way, the human-rights movement used old, blurred snapshots of the missing, along with songs and poetry, to sustain the memory-traces of their lives and political projects. In her paintings the artist contributed to the forensic documentation of the mass grave at the same time that documentary video and photographic portraits of the mummified cadavers illustrated human-rights protests in the nation's capital. This mobilization of memory occurred at the historical conjuncture of regime transition, where the pragmatics of reconciliation scoffed at demands for justice and exacted the price of sanity: when her husband's career was destroyed by more powerful sectors of the pro-military judiciary, the artist destroyed all of her work in atonement for conjuring the past. The human-rights movement, having identified some of the remains and officially marked appropriate sites of memory, for the most part lost its political direction. Identification of and with the dead offered no easy resolution. Mourning gave way to melancholy. As the cultural critic Eric Santner comments, "The repetition compulsion that is melancholy emerges out of the struggle to engage in the labor of mourning in the absence of a supportive social space"; thus, "melancholy is a sort of chronic liminality" for those lacking such a space.[66] Yet it remains unclear what an adequate space for the labor of mourning would look like, or even if such a space is possible in the midst of a long history of state violence.

In questioning the limits of commemorating atrocities with memorials, the historian James Young notes that remnants of the past too often "are mistaken for the events from which they are taken." In the politics of the past, "authentic historical artifacts are used not only to gesture toward the past, to move us toward its examination, but also to [impose and] naturalize particular versions of the past." Memory-traces condense around affectively charged artifacts. "Pieces of charred brick, a broken bone seem to endow their arrangements in museums with the naturalness of their own forms." Young cautions that "at such moments, we are invited to forget that memory is, after all, only a figurative reconstruction of the past, not its literal replication."[67] The remains (physical memory) of a few of the executed and disappeared may be recovered, identified, and placed in consecrated ground, but should they be mistaken for the recuperation of the lost person, of lost solidarities? Should one expect to mourn at their crypts?

This is the problem of the memory-trace, Young explains: "The archivists' traditional veneration of the trace is tied directly to their need for proof or evidence of a particular past."[68] Recent scholarship tends to embrace this lack or trace at the heart of modern politics. Yet it would not do to become too enamored of loss without questioning the evacuation of memory that sustains it. Those who feel the loss deeply may be subject to what the cultural critic Marianne Hirsch calls "postmemory," in which one is so inhabited by the memories of previous generations that one is unable to generate memories of one's own.[69]

The subject denied a context for historical actualization, Santner argues, "will be unable to mourn and integrate the losses necessary to becoming a self and will instead engage in repetitive rituals of exorcism and purification, hopeless efforts." There's a compulsivity to these rituals that can become numbing, "performed again and again in the absence of a space in which genuinely elegiac rituals of mourning could be enacted and brought to some sort of completion."[70] I am dubious about the claim that even a genuine elegy could and should lend itself to political transformation, especially under the rubric of completion.[71] Memory raised solely in elegy cannot transform the conditions of life.

Psychologistic models have come to pervade contemporary political discourse, and mourning as a path to social reconciliation has proven inadequate for the politics of memory in Chile's postdictatorship period.[72] Human-rights movements, on the other hand, have used funerary rituals with implications far beyond a politics of mourning. Although the conflicts of ambiguity in these events reveal the conjuncture of melancholy and modernity in Chile, one nevertheless finds, in the resilience of a few, lingering possibilities for cathartic memory.

Countermourning: A Response to Melancholy

My ethnographic research in Chile began and has continued to be punctuated by funerals. The contrasts among three of the many funerals I attended illustrate the possibilities and limits of culturally meaningful political action in regime shift to a civilian-governed neoliberal state.

The first funeral was a June 1990 protest in the national capital while formerly clandestine graves were being excavated. These excavations, which took place across the length of Chile, mapped the national territory with evidence of previously denied state violence. The role of the church in coordinating the excavations and in opening sanctified spaces as protected realms for protest exemplified the connection between the church and human-rights movements during the dictatorship. The 1990 ceremony, one of my first fieldwork experiences in the Chilean capital, was a double funeral for two political activists murdered during the dictatorship. Their families had recovered remains near the national capital during the nationwide excavations, which had been spurred on by the discovery of the mass grave in Pisagua.

Earlier in the week, I had followed a protest march in downtown Santiago. The marchers were mostly young people, members of the Sebastián Acevedo Movement against Torture, who proclaimed the discovery of yet more mass graves and demanded the condemnation of the perpetrators of the violence.[73] At the end of the march, I approached one of the demonstrators; he suggested that I show up at a large church on the northeast side of the city for an important funeral that was to take place a few days later—which I did. As I approached the church, I spotted the Sebastián Acevedo demonstrators chanting and marching down the street with a large banner and signs. I fell in step with the slow procession. They chanted, "No hubo guerra, fue matanza, todos fueron asesinados, justicia para todos los asesinados," that in 1973 there had been not war but a massacre of the Chilean people. Again, they demanded justice. Other groups arrived at the church, including the associations of families of the detained, disappeared, and executed. All available space in the church had filled with journalists, human-rights activists, political figures, and those who had known and cared for the two men being remembered. The service reiterated many of the themes the human-rights groups had chanted outside. I began to realize that such funerals could reverberate in many ways simultaneously—as lament for the dead and as political protest.

The second occasion was the 1993 wake and funeral of Luis Silva, an ex-political prisoner who had wasted away. Although the ex-political prisoners' association had struggled to finance and build a collective mausoleum, it was never built, so Silva was to be buried in a rented niche—the only recourse, other than a common grave, for poor people unable to purchase a plot. The proposed mausoleum was to have contained the remains of those executed in the prison camp of 1973 (the official martyrs) as well as those political prisoners who died in later years (the survivors). Because neither the state nor nongovernmental organizations showed interest in the project, the mausoleum's progress had halted at the stage of preliminary drawings discussed at association meetings. Silva's funeral exemplified the problem of abandonment and the pining that marked the experience of those who were unwilling to drop the past in favor of moving forward, as the state characterized it, with the transition to civilian rule.

This second funeral occurred early in my stay in the Chilean North. I walked with Sara, the wife of another ex-political prisoner, to the small, wooden house that had been Silva's home. The wake was held in the living area, where family and guests sat in chairs that lined the perimeter. The room barely held the chairs, and the plain wooden coffin filled the center floor space; Luis lay in the coffin, bloated from the lack of embalming and the multiple pathogens that had slowly killed him. As we took our seats among the mourners, Sara told me how her husband, Manuel, too, had nearly wasted away in obscure neglect a number of years before. Manuel had survived the Pisagua detention camp, a period of internal exile, and subsequent personal economic devastation, only to find his memories consuming him as he lost kilo after kilo. In desperation, Sara had taken him over the border to a specialist in Peru, who diagnosed his condition as one of acute stress. He told them that Manuel would collapse within two months unless they followed the doctor's specifications. In compliance, the family sold all of their possessions, and Sara and their three small children moved in with her mother while Manuel went to live in a tent on an uninhabited beach. There, he fished and exercised for two years until his hands stopped trembling and his weight stabilized. Concluding her account, Sara explained that given her own family's experience, she felt particularly deeply for the widow in whose parlor we sat, whispering.

Later we all walked with the coffin to the municipal cemetery where, after a brief ceremony, Luis was placed into a niche in a wall that was six slots high and about twenty long. The cemetery had dozens of such walls, much like bookshelves in a library. One can walk along the walls reading, like books, the covers of each niche for inscriptions. Some were carved in stone, indicating that the family had had the resources to purchase the niche; others were painted on trawled plaster, indicating that the family lacked funds for better material or that they could only afford to rent the niche, as was true for Silva: he could rest there as long as his family kept up with the rent, but would otherwise end up in the unmarked common grave of the very poor or the forgotten.[74] Still, for now, family, friends, and fellow ex-political prisoners, forming a special honor guard, carried Luis to his own consecrated space, accompanied by a band playing the same pampino songs and processing in the same manner that had characterized working-class funerals in Tarapacá since the nitrate-mining era.

The third funeral was for another ex-political prisoner who had been a city councilman and Socialist Party leader. His wake in city hall under the populist mayor's administration became a celebration of regional history, with an honor guard made up of ex-political prisoners and Socialist Party militants. A caravan of buses and cars accompanied his remains to one of the old nitrate cemeteries up on the desert, for he had also been raised in the mining camps. The funeral proceeded in the style of those of the nitrate era, when the North formed the heart of the labor movement and challenged the authority of the liberal state to submit Chile to the whims of world markets. Surrounded by torches in the crisp desert night air, hundreds of people sang political anthems and folk songs from the labor era. At this funeral, mourners wove together a long history of struggle and persistence.

The funeral, according to common understandings of the Freudian model, serves in the work of mourning as a temporal hinge, just as the crypt or gravesite spatially localizes loss; by spatially and temporally containing loss, mourning enables the representation of absence, which allows the mourner to act as a living agent in a world otherwise unchanged by the loss. Yet quite different processes constituted each of these three funerals, processes that insisted on indelible connections between these deaths and the larger world that (at least potentially) might transform that larger world. In the first, the recovery of remains confirmed loss and provided, through the conventions of the funeral procession and oration, the opening of a space for political protest against state policies of reconciliation as the denial of justice. The second funeral underlined the complete abandonment of those who, as survivors of state violence, could not claim martyrdom; ex-political prisoners had been so tarred by the politics of the preceding twenty years that, for the civilian state and reconstituted political parties, they represented a deformation on the margins of national political processes. Social death, marked by an impoverished burial, acted as a causal factor in their physical wasting away. The third funeral broke the temporal restrictions of regime transition to connect one life and death to a longer lineage. This political lineage, which spanned the twentieth century, offered a source of strategy and strength for constituting a collectivity.

A culturally specific model of mourning, akin to the Freudian ideal, framed national reconciliation as enacted by the political parties of the Concertación and some sectors of the military; for both it served to smooth over the national tragedy of the Chilean coup and military dictatorship as a "problem." Many involved in human-rights movements and associations have, by contrast, linked intimate processes of mourning with political action. While I do not want to homogenize or collapse the array of responses to the terrible losses of that coup, I do want to add a caveat to the scholarship on violence and memory by cultural theorists, who draw so heavily on Freudian models of mourning. In contexts of dire societal trauma, mourning itself—as a particular process of healing that specifies places of commemoration, narrative processes and time frames of lament, and roles for both the dead and the living—may not be sufficient for politics, even if it does or might work for other types of loss. In other words, the political model has claimed that the nation can reconstitute itself as a whole through a common experience of mourning. In characterizing the dominant mode of memory in Chile's postcoup administrations as melancholy, I draw on the notion of failed mourning as melancholia, where the living are left behind in a kind of emotional limbo; I heed the call of some sectors of the human-rights movement, that healing requires that the dead and those they have left behind obtain histori-cally and culturally relevant forms of justice. However, foreground-ing family members as the paradigmatic human-rights activists has impoverished political possibilities. It boxes the national subject, as an ideological proposition, into the category of mourner. Like the citizen, the liberal subject of modernity, the mourner—in spite of the inventiveness of Chilean countermourners—threatens to even more tightly constrain political agency, subsuming under the rubric of rec-onciliation those in the various sectors within Chile and outside Chile whose lives have been tattered or have benefited from this history of violence.

A scene of anti-mourning occurred at the point in the Pinochet saga when the Chilean Supreme Court was ruling on whether to remove his immunity from prosecution as senator-for-life. The court delayed in making its verdict public so as to fine-tune the ruling through political negotiations. In Iquique anxious human-rights groups organized a vigil in the Plaza Condell, a site of non-elite mobilizations since the early part of the twentieth century. Day and night, the Association of Families and Friends of the Executed and Disappeared displayed homemade collages of print media docu-menting regional deaths and presenting a biography of General Pi-nochet that explicitly invoked his self-promoted image as omnipo-tent persona and military man and assigned him historical agency and accountability for state violence. Together with a younger gen-eration of leftist-party and social-movement activists, association members held silent, candlelit vigils punctuated by the rhythms of a Brazilian-style drum corps of teenage boys and girls. Milling about and occasionally joining in were ex-political prisoners. Like a wake, this vigil entailed collective reflecting on a person abstracted from the group and on the role that person had played in social life. One painted banner waving over the vigil depicted Pinochet as a large, Kafkaesque beetle, and the caption read "A Bad Pest," rendering Pinochet not so much a monster as a subhuman political anachronism. The vigil in Iquique merged protest styles, slogans, music, and iconography of the current ludic antiglobalization movements, of the 1980s antidictatorship actions of "relámpago" street theater, of 1960s radical movements, and of labor activism from the first half of the twentieth century. This internal Chilean mobilization, together with international pressure, kept the possibility of justice politically alive. When the Supreme Court finally released the decision to revoke Pinochet's immunity, the vigil erupted into full-scale — and cathartically vindictive — jubilation, no longer a site of either mourning or melancholy.

From Transition to Evolution and Reconciliation to Coexistence?

By the beginning of the 2000s, President Lagos was forced to recognize publicly that the transition, especially as reconciliation of the past, had been a chimera. Instead, he expressed hope in what he called evolution, and he declared his desire to govern for the future.

Indeed, the political culture has shifted with time and the military's 1980 Constitution has presented new ironies in the face of current political, economic, and social configurations. In other words, mechanisms set up to safeguard the interests of the pro-military regime Right may come to work against it. For example, the electoral system, designed by the Right to insure disproportionate representation for the minority coalition, has seemed increasingly inconvenient given the growing popularity of certain right-wing candidates who espouse a conservative populism reminiscent of Ibañéz del Campo. The Right has also begun to wonder whether or not they can continue to count as allies the military's "designated" senators, especially as under neoliberalism class and national(ist) interests do not always overlap. Furthermore, the military has been engaged in a steady process of de-Pinochet-ization, mostly motivated by a drive toward a "modern" military of a smaller, better-trained force, capitalized with high-tech equipment (in contrast to a conscript-based, bottom-heavy structure, mostly useful for internal repression). Pinochet's disavowal of responsibility in the chain of command and the subsequent vulnerability of subordinate officers has taken its toll. His successor, General Óscar Izurieta, brought with him an "honorable" military lineage; he also promoted the "Schneider" doctrine of military-civilian relations, invoking General René Schneider, martyred before the coup, who had insisted that the military should not intervene in civilian rule nor be unduly subject to the whims of civilian politics.[75] These policies were supported by his successor, General Juan Emilio Cheyre. The new leadership had a warm working rapport with President Lagos's minister of defense, Michelle Bachelet, the daughter of a martyred anti-coup general and as of 2006 president herself.

These structural shifts culminated in the dramatic 2005 constitutional reforms, which dismantled many of the most egregiously authoritarian components of the 1980 Constitution: namely, the military's overrepresentation in the Security Council, presidential authority to force military-commander retirements, and the appointment of lifetime senators. However, Chilean constitutional scholars such as Francisco Zúñiga point to the ways in which — contrary to the state's press statements — these changes ultimately remain *reforms* negotiated in closed-door meetings and do not represent the kind of fundamental changes called for by sectors who supported a constitutional assembly to replace the military-imposed 1980 Constitution. For example, the binomial electoral system remains in place, benefiting large coalitions and excluding smaller parties. As Paulina Weber of the Movement for the Emancipation of Chilean Women commented in December 2005, "Pinochet's constitution is congenitally deformed." Proposals from such organizations call for, among other reforms, proportional representation, greater popular participation in decision making through plebiscites and referendums, more formal mechanisms for recognizing indigenous populations, and constitutional weight for international treaties. Scholars point to what Zúñiga calls the "heart" of the Pinochet constitution: the free-market neoliberal model. The connection between structural mechanisms such as the constitution and the role of affect in political culture is aptly described by Eric Palma, who represents an organization pressing for a constitutional convention, when he points to the role of the constitution in the daily lives of common people and imagines a process of crafting a new constitution that could be "a space for coming together, one of fraternity, joy, affection, solidarity, cama- raderie, love, essentially respect for others."[76]

Other shifts in the political culture have altered political dynamics to an extent. For the rightist leadership, in general, Pinochet and his most loyal supporters became something of an embarrassment—as when the media televised right-wing women throwing chicken bones and vulgar racist slurs at the mothers of the disappeared outside one of the court hearings—especially with the release of the Valech Re- port, whose very existence marked a shift in the terrain of struggle.[77] In terms of state policy, however, key features of the Pinochet legacy remain intact as now even Socialist Party leaders continue to sink Chile more deeply into global markets and to ground domestic con- tentment in debt-based mass consumption, thus heightening Chile's position as linchpin in broader macroeconomic stability and aug- menting the ideological debt of Chilean political culture to mili- tary rule.[78]

In the shift to civilian rule, political parties reasserted themselves as the dominant force in civil society and committed themselves almost exclusively to contests over the state. The center-left parties of the Concertación of necessity drew on skilled professionals and leaders nurtured in the antidictatorship think-tanks and social movements (inside and outside of Chile proper), even as the international soli- darity funds that had sustained those spaces dried up. Any remaining international funding was, by law, directed through the state. Thus, in terms of human capital and resources, civic culture was drained in favor of state building. This left the far (pro-dictatorship) Right as virtually the only opposition and thus deprived the civilian state of a loyal opposition (one which invested in the general health of the system but was not on the same side). The unreconciled Left and some sectors of the human-rights movement flailed about on the margins, having few financial resources and even less cultural capital until global intervention—by way of the application of international law to Pinochet—opened up spaces for political contestations.

I spoke to many people after the 2006 election of Chile's second socialist president since the return to civilan rule. An internationally known Chilean artist commented, "Well, they will still have to deal with corruption—the Left can steal just like the Right—and solve the problem of the disappeared." This comment is illustrative of two problems: first, ongoing faith in the state but distrust of political agents (in part the legacy of the military's antipolitical ideology); and second, an insistence on the role of the disappeared as a fundamental lack (a missing insurmountable component) in Chile's process of democratization. The degree to which this presents the political leadership with an impossible task—both politically and logistically—marks an insistence on something like countermourning, in which the ongoing impact of the past on the present belies the neoliberal claim to a radical break between past and present, the suggestion that it should be possible and desirable to complete the Concertación's project of "turning the page of history."

Healthy democracies cannot rely solely on dissention from within the state, but rather require a dynamic civic sphere to nurture alternative visions, including more assertive demands on the state, as well as perspectives not wholly state-centered. This is particularly true for a society such as Chile, where a small political elite still hold inordinate access to the state. However, the problem is not just one of political will but also that subordinate countries such as Chile must struggle to find options and resources for sustaining both a strong, competent state and a dynamic civil society. This is an especially acute problem given the demands of the neoliberal global economy to prioritize economic niches, divest from and commodify social services such as education, and rationalize state structures in the interests of the market.

Democratic nations (in the most inclusive sense) require spaces for contestatory voices that open up political debates by virtue of their very ability to question dominant framings of political culture. I have prioritized a search for contestatory voices—specifically, the vestiges of cathartic memory—not because they preserve a prior form of political mobilization (from the Past) per se, but rather because they posit a transformative political vision based on proximate (overarching temporal divides) and passionate commitments.

In contrast, the currently dominant depoliticizing mode of memory narrates a radical break between past and present in the dyad of nostalgia and melancholy and obviates as anachronism any perspective that questions this framing. Still, some optimistic analysts have suggested that the numerous and vibrant thirtieth-anniversary commemorations of the coup, along with public events that took place in the wake of the 2004 Valech Report, do constitute a new widespread politics of memory akin to cathartic memory.[79] However, my periodization of the politics of memory describes the predominant structures of memory emerging from and constituting nation-state formation. Thus, it remains to be seen whether these trends in the political culture will result in or reflect a definitive transformation of the nation-state. At the moment falling far short of definitive transformation, what President Lagos called evolution looks less like a prognosis for a better future and rather more like the playing out of the neoliberal End of History.

Coda: Retiring to the North

Still, unfolding events suggest that there are, in corners of outlying places, passionate refusals. In those cathartic refusals one finds a kind of ironic justice.

Political conflict has been particularly terrible in the North because this frontier region has been the locus for contradictory affective meanings and alliances in Chile: from the military conquest of new territories and defense of the nation from outside, to the legacies of working-class militancy, to state violence against non-elite and oppositional sectors, to political party formations across the political spectrum, to symbols and sites of national glory in military history, including very personal connections to major figures in Chilean political history. In fact, Tarapacá and especially Iquique continued to serve as Pinochet's haven (prior to his death in December 2006) from political pressures to answer for the past.

The justice served on Pinochet was worthy of a novel of magical realism: the former dictator, who had worked so hard to legitimize his rule legalistically, is caught in perpetual loops of litigation. When he returned to Chile from London in 2000, he used senility as a reason to not stand trial. Pinochet assumed that, after thwarting prosecution, he would return to public life as senator-for-life. Yet some of the most potentially damning human-rights cases against him were not dropped but rather suspended as a technicality due to his ill health. Though senility is not usually a curable condition, Pinochet was informed that any attempt to act as a public figure would constitute evidence that he had recovered, and thus he would be considered fit to stand trial. By this brilliant move, Pinochet was silenced politically and reduced, ironically, to becoming the persona the Right had already crafted for him: a slightly daft grandfather to the nation.[80]

The Sunday after what seemed at the time to be the final suspension of Pinochet's court proceedings, his son declared to the elite press that his father "want[ed] to catch a flight to Iquique in order to recover in his apartment, in a temperate climate that would suit anybody." Although his doctors had not yet authorized "the warrior's" travel to "his winter barracks," his son anticipated that in the future the general would spend the winter in a place like Iquique, "just as any elderly person might wish to do."[81]

Pinochet viewed Iquique as a possible refuge not only because of its temperate climate but also because he and his wife had lived there in the years preceding the military coup. He had been well-liked there by many across the political spectrum, especially the local pro-coup Right, who had benefited disproportionately from the military state's investment in local economic infrastructure and the distribution of booty seized during the coup. On his arrival in Iquique, supporters indeed welcomed Pinochet and helped the general and his wife, Lucia, settle in a luxury apartment near one of the urban military installations. Camped outside, however, were the local human-rights organizations, which loudly protested the retired general's presence and the warm welcome extended to him by other locals. Pinochet, Lucía, and their hosts met even more conflict when they ventured from the apartment.

Two public incidents, the first of which received national attention, epitomized the couple's growing discomfort. One day Pinochet and his bodyguards drove to a military monument at the city's northern edge. As they pulled up to the monument in an otherwise deserted spot, they noticed some adolescents with guns. Pinochet's bodyguards roughed up the youngsters, ostensibly in the general's defense. When the police arrived to arrest the boys, the youths exclaimed that they had been hanging out at that remote spot to harass seagulls, not retired dictators. In light of this incident, local human-rights groups filed a legal complaint. They used the general's sense of entitlement, as demonstrated by his proactive aggression against the youths, to argue that his presence in the city was endangering the public. In lodging this complaint, activists asserted that the past was not over but still influenced power dynamics and struggles, including ongoing human-rights violations by state and non-state agents.

The second incident gained no media attention, but was related to me informally. Elena, a middle-aged returned exile, was window-shopping in Iquique's U.S.-style Mall of the Americas. The mall is a monument to Pinochet's vision of Iquique as a leading city in Chile's transformation into a neoliberal economy of modern consumers. In the re-creation of Iquique's British-nitrate-built clock tower, which is located in the food court as the new central plaza, the shopper encounters a nostalgic gesture to the past's dominant rendition of the community translated for the commodified, privatized present of the market. As Elena rode down the mall escalator, she found herself passing Lucia de Pinochet, who was on the up escalator. Before Elena knew what she was doing, she found herself yelling, "You shameless bitch!" At the bottom of the escalator, she was grabbed by security guards, who asked, "How dare you insult the general's wife?" With her heart pounding, and again without stopping to calculate her words, Elena retorted, "How did she know I meant her?" Finding no way to fault Elena's logic, the guards released her. In this story, historical accountability is like a magnet: a force persistently binds it to the appropriate subject. The general and his wife soon retreated to their secluded estate outside of Santiago, no longer welcome in Iquique's civil society, which human-rights activists had reclaimed from pro-Pinochet sectors, if only for that moment.

Anger erupted—both among groups mobilizing formally and people acting spontaneously—against Pinochet's attempt to claim Iquique as a refuge. This anger also implicated the postdictatorship state: in the first incident, filing a legal complaint even while knowing the state would never label Pinochet a public hazard was a way of calling the state on its ineptitude and/or refusal to guard the public's well-being; in the second incident, the state's inability to mete out justice to Pinochet produced a reaction that asserted a horizontal tie—even in the form of conflicting interests—that precisely pointed to the state's irrelevance as the actor who mediates conflict. Furthermore, both Pinochet and his wife still partially embodied the state and themselves called on the state to defend them as such (e.g., a personal insult amounted to sedition). The angry gestures were about severing those ties.[82]

Angry actions such as these have served as cathartic gestures in the face of a tepid politics of transition as reconciliation-mourning, otherwise characterized as nostalgia-melancholy. Psychologistic models apply to emotions the modernist binary of order-chaos to posit mourning as a temporally delimited process wherein one moves through a logical progression of affective states (such as sorrow, anger, passionate love for the lost one—seen as dangerously chaotic in and of themselves) in order to arrive at an emotionally neutral point of functional stability. The cathartic mode of memory disrupts this model by sustaining passionate emotions in ongoing, quotidian practices of struggle. The vestiges of cathartic memory as political practice have emerged as passionate refusals to relegate human-rights actors and accountability for human-rights abuses to the past.

Conclusion

DEMOCRATIZATION AND ARRIVING

AT THE "END OF HISTORY" IN CHILE

Ethnographies, this one included, often open with scenes of arrival.[1] Yet I want to end with the trope of arrival as well, not only to think about my own experiences as a researcher but also to contemplate the nature of living "the present" right now.[2] The term "ethnographic present" characterizes the ways in which anthropologists conventionally portrayed their subjects of study as "peoples without history" who lived in static states of "culture," which the ethnographer could empirically study for the space of a few months or years in order to extrapolate general principles about those peoples.[3] Thus, it was the ethnographer who arrived to study these timeless worlds, which were understood to embody the past of modern civilized nation-states.[4] Arrival constituted a privilege of the knowing, active (imperialist) Self and was never a possibility for the (postcolonial) Other. José

Piedra explores the contradictions entailed in the critical knowledge produced from the position of otherness, in other words, playing the game of arrival from a nearly untenable position.[5] Reflecting on Colombus's so-called discovery of the New World, Piedra characterizes the mutual discovery of the Self and Other as the game of critical arrival.[6] More than a temporally defined and encapsulated event, arrival in this sense can become a transformative process of contingency and possibility.

Arriving at the "End of History"

I first traveled to Chile in 1990, a time understood by prominent participants in the Chilean political process as beginning "the transition" from military dictatorship to civilian democracy. During the decade that followed, each of the three civilian presidents at some point in their term of office declared the transition to have ended, signaling Chile's arrival as a modern nation-state—each declaration was later retracted. I was struck by the centrality of historical narrative in Chilean political discourse, specifically the problem of periodization in terms of the political ability to delineate moments in the past in relation to the present. The inability of each of these presidents to make their claim of arrival stick is symptomatic of the contradictory factors that have rendered the problem of the present particularly elusive for me as a committed critic. Transition has proven a useful political category precisely because it rhetorically creates a liminal arena, pragmatically leaving a great deal of indeterminate room for negotiation, a degree of temporary tolerance of ongoing antidemocratic practices. The term *transition* suggests a kind of preliminary, incomplete arrival at an already known and predetermined destination. This paradoxical place exacerbates melancholy-nostalgia, the contemporary dual structure of feeling wherein the modernist narrative of linear official History suggests a radical break between past and present, rendering the past either anachronism or curiosity.[7] For subordinate states, the intensely desired goal of arrival is elusive, in large part because the ideal type, the North Atlantic state, is not a static entity, but rather a shifting set of privileges and practices— a moving target—whose cachet must be understood in relation to subordinate nation-states predefined by terms like *developing* or *emerging*.[8] Thus, for subaltern nation-states, playing the game of arrival *now* entails negotiating a particular nexus of geopolitical space and neoliberal time that puts postcolonial nation-states in a paradoxical place, making claims to modernity while perpetually marked as alterity vis-á-vis the North Atlantic nation-state. Neoliberal rhetoric of globalization depicts a world system which seems to be coeval and geographically integrated, at the same time consigning most places to peripheral positions with their only room for maneuver being to maximize their comparative advantage.

Yet, in some respects, in the 1990s Chile had arrived. Within the span of a few years, Chile became a prototype for regime transitions from authoritarian to civilian rule, and specifically for the model of truth and reconciliation commissions (for South Africa, for example). Concomitantly, Chile served as a model for neoliberal economic structural reorientation, especially in relation to former Soviet bloc countries.[9] The Chilean press often quoted a Russian politician who had said that what the former Soviet Union needed to pull itself together was a Russian Pinochet. Along these lines, a 1991 *New York Times Magazine* feature, "Prosperity Born of Pain," declared in bold-face type, "The Pinochet regime in Chile trampled on human rights and revitalized the economy. Now under democratic rule, Chileans find it good business to put the past behind them."[10] The Chilean story has been used to support the conclusion that state violence is regrettable but ultimately justifiable if the end result is a market-driven economy. In Chile, arguably more than anywhere else in the world, neoliberalism has been pursued methodically to the limits of its logic, with the privatization of even the most basic services and resources. In 1992, as part of a decade-long effort by U.S. Presidents Bush, Clinton, and Bush to "fast-track" Chile into the North American Free Trade Agreement (NAFTA), George Bush Sr. said, "Today Chile gives hope to an entire hemisphere. With market-oriented reforms, you've led by example."[11] As such, Chile has served as a model not only for so-called developing economies, but even in relation to places like the United States, as in the case of state-pension privatization debates. In a mid-1990s report on plans to reform Social Security in the United States, *Time* featured a story headlined "How Chile Got It Right."[12] Given such praise, and echoing the popular claim that since the late nineteenth century Chile had been the "England of Latin America," in the 1990s the Chilean business and political elite often called Chile, with reference to East Asia, the economic "Tiger of Latin America." Therefore, although the key concept in the dominant narrative of contemporary Chilean political history was regime transition with the assumed outcome being democracy, albeit very generally defined, this period in Chilean politics happened at the same moment as neoliberal ideologues were victoriously proclaiming "the end of history"—and they came to Chile to do so.[13] Among the high-profile ideologues, politicians, and capitalists who traveled to Chile to herald the arrival of the end of history were former British Prime Minister Margaret Thatcher, Francis Fukuyama, and Jean Baudrillard.[14]

Francis Fukuyama, a U.S. State Department deputy director and RAND Corporation analyst, resurrected Hegel's concept of the end of history to describe the post–Cold War era as it was emerging in the years between 1989 and 1992.[15] He argued that "liberal democracy remains the only coherent political aspiration that spans different regions and cultures around the globe. In addition, liberal principles in economics—the 'free market'—have spread, and have produced unprecedented levels of material prosperity." For Fukuyama, "modern liberal democracy and technologically driven capitalism" work hand in hand, though they are not necessarily synchronized.[16] In short, there is no alternative to this model, and any residual "injustices and serious social problems" are the fault of an "incomplete implementation." Yet, Fukuyama added a second critical problem: using Plato's and Hegel's formulation that the desire for recognition, which he glossed as "self-esteem," generates a battle to the death between self and other, Fukuyama claimed that the key impediment to this utopia lay in the realm of culture, specifically in cultural hierarchies based on prestige, including nationalism. The privileged subjectivity produced by liberal democracy was the "last man" willing to forgo personal prestige for the greater virtues of equality; however, such sophistication entailed a debilitating loss of passion.[17] Thus, Fukuyama's vision of the end of history involved a kind of millenarian chaos (ethnic conflict, etc.) that betrayed the promise of prosperity that should come with the rational implementation of neoliberal democracies. While he credited decolonization movements with forcing Europeans to consider (due in part to fear of death) a world built on equality—ostensibly the pinnacle of European-based civilization—he suggested that multicultural relativism threatened apocalypse through the excessive and differentiated passion of the other.[18]

Like Columbus, Fukuyama played the game of arrival through voyaging in the New World, from the University of Chicago colloquium where he first presented his essay to the Chicago School of Economics' protégé: Chile. On his November 1992 visit to Chile, Fukuyama admitted that, in writing his book, even he had underestimated the magnitude of the process of economic transition in the former Soviet bloc countries and the development of an "exacerbated nationalism."[19] Still, he emphasized that not all nationalisms are bad and pointed to Canada's effort to resolve Quebec's desire for recognition as an appropriate, "healthy" expression of national identity. Turning to the topic of development, Fukuyama emphasized that the problem was not capitalism but rather the lack of enough capitalism, and he praised Chile's economic development as "extraordinary" because it led to the "autolegitimation" of the market. In spite of the assumed correlation between development and democracy, Fukuyama admitted that Chile was an example of the greater possibilities for economic growth under authoritarian governments than under democratic regimes. Thus, Fukuyama emphasized that the market was nonnegotiable and warned his Chilean audience that stable democracy depended on development through the free market.[20]

About six months after Fukuyama's visit, one of the preeminent philosophers of postmodernity, Jean Baudrillard, arrived in Chile. He was described as a "skeptical observer of the world, our societies and our tragi-comic rituals" by the premier Chilean elite newspaper, which published an interview wherein Baudrillard posited that although things continue to happen, there is no plot, only the "acting out" of recycled characters and conflicts, and hence "no place" and "no history."[21] Baudrillard elaborated his views on the millenarian, post-Soviet world in *The Illusion of the End* (1992), in which he denied any purposeful element to history: there is no frontier, nothing to be discovered. What had ended were the conditions of possibility for modernist historical narrative, so historians must imagine writing histories "without end."[22] Baudrillard's relinquishing of the modernist narrative of emancipation reinforced both the triumphalist neoliberal ideology of the Chilean elite and the pragmatist neoliberal policies of the governing political parties. The possibility of historical efficacy having been evacuated, the "tragi-comic" work of politics was consigned to ritual time.[23]

A third voyage from north to south that marked the end of an era was former East German leader Erich Honecker's 1993 arrival in Chile. Released for ill health from war-crimes prosecution in a unified Germany, Honecker had come to die, of terminal cancer, in the care of his daughter's Chilean in-laws, with the support of the thousands of Chileans who had found refuge in East Germany after the military coup.[24] The journalist Ascanio Cavallo ranked this event as Chile's new civilian government's "most prolonged and dramatic diplomatic crisis."[25] In spite of crucially significant differences, some aspects of that crisis foreshadowed the Pinochet extradition crisis at the end of that decade: appeals for clemency based on contradictory medical examinations, precedent-setting implications for international law (on expulsion and extradition, treatment of former heads of state, etc.), the Chilean government's stance that at stake in each crisis was its international dignity vis-à-vis Europe, serious threats to the alliance of political parties within the ruling coalition, and moral and juridical debates over the question of justice under new geopolitical conditions for both prominent Cold Warriors.[26] Both cases entailed the invoking of memories of state violence (and debating the legitimacy of that violence), public contestations over history at the level of fundamental categories of analysis and the assignment of culpability, and efforts to contain and curtail such public debates because the historical questions raised implicated all involved—accused and accuser alike. In spite of Russia's rather disingenuous statement that Honecker's initial refuge there amounted to a threat to its national security, in both cases (Honecker and Pinochet) the decrepit bodies of the former heads-of-state represented anachronistic vestiges of the past that required the sanitizing operations of juridical and ultimately medical interventions to bring resolution and closure to political conflicts—whether valorized or demonized by the many parties involved—defined as *over*. Ascanio Cavallo drew his account of the Honecker crisis to a close with a melancholic image of an act of embodied memory: Honecker, being forcibly taken by security forces from his initial asylum in the Chilean embassy in Moscow, paused in the doorway and raised his left fist "like his worker father, like Margot's [his wife's] worker father, like the millions of German workers of other years, the proletariat of a whole century, now defeated." Cavallo juxtaposed this image of defiant mourning with the dispassionate gazes of the German, Russian, and Chilean officials, who were "men of State, on missions of State," agents of a new pragmatic political system from which emotional drive had been evacuated.[27]

The Chilean scholar Tomás Moulian has argued that what has become naturalized (a subtle and insidious form of forgetting) in

Chile today is a particular understanding of the relationship between past, present, and future: "Even though it is denied, the hypothesis of the 'end of history' permeates the thought of many Chilean intellectuals who — because they have accepted the purported impossibility of change — no longer see any need to propose it."[28] In support, neomodern and postmodern thinkers arrived in Chile to confirm the impossibility of alternative projects for the future, a future emptied of connections with past. Further nullifying the past is the dominant narrative of reconciliation. Civilian political party leaders apologize for what they call the mistakes made under the Popular Unity's experiment of a nonviolent transition to socialism, and they acknowledge that time has revealed that there is no alternative to this particular form of capitalism as defined by the logic of the market. This defeatist rhetoric concedes all but the moral high ground of human-rights discourses that denounce the so-called excessive brutality of the military coup; it thus leaves unchallenged — for practical purposes — the military's subsequent rule, as well as its political, economic, and social legacies — and even continuities — which have dominated national life for nearly three decades now.

Memories of State Violence in Nation-State Formation

I have endeavored to show how state violence forms, in multiple and complex ways, an integral part of hegemony in processes of postcolonial nation-state formation. This approach interrogates the legitimacy of certain forms of state violence, forms that may even come to be seen as foundational to the state. The shift from military to civilian rule in Chile has been accomplished with minimal restructuring of the state and virtually no disruption of the military's internal order. Human-rights groups insisted that military rule and state violence included both overt destruction of life and daily degradations that dismantled people's lives. The three funerals I attended illustrated this problem and suggested that not only did people themselves understand state violence in this way but also that they were adept at using scripted forms of marking death as opportunities for political critique. Yet their insights have yet to succeed in helping them disrupt the current pragmatist framing of regime transition, and of politics more generally.[29] One is left to wonder how the Chilean state and its military managed the transition so as to retain their integrity over time.

Since its independence at the beginning of the nineteenth century, the Chilean state constituted the key locus of struggle and focus of aspirations in its political system. The Chilean cultural critic Bernardo Subercaseaux has argued that Chile not only has a vibrant political culture but that, especially compared with its Andean neighbors, culture in Chile has become overdetermined by the political.[30] The eminence of the state in political culture has worked, in large part, through contests over national memory. Official memory— memory generated, endorsed, and policed in the conflicts over consolidation of the state—was never fixed but always subject to and constitutive of hegemonic processes. In turn, projects for hegemonic control encountered countermemories, which together with the official memory of any given moment formed part of the tussle for position in the formal political system. Conditionally positioned on the margins of this system were rhetorically antipolitical sectors, such as the military, the Catholic Church, and certain social groups and movements. Through an array of shifting alliances, these political and antipolitical sectors fought to mobilize, shape, and contain national memory.

Increasingly over the course of the twentieth century, Chilean politics became oriented toward a multiparty system organized around the contest for the state. These parties were united in their aspirations for national memory grounded in the forging of a national-popular hegemony.[31] At times, memories circulating among non-elite sectors intersected with the projects of the various political parties and were taken up in national-popular projects. Still, in the multiple elite and non-elite sectors, strands of memories persisted which were incommensurable with that dynamic hegemony.

I have worked, sometimes against the grain of my own research topic, to avoid stigmatizing as sites of violence Chile, or Latin America, or even the so-called developing world, which one might locate on all hemispheres as the one-third of the world's population that lives in poverty. In fact, my argument has been precisely to the contrary, suggesting that the reason scholars and activists concerned with social justice in places other than Chile have cared so much about this little country—fourteen million people located on the southeastern edge of the Americas, in a world in which power is mapped from north to south and west to east—is not because the state violence there was more horrific than other places in a century characterized by total warfare: hot, cold, and proxy. That would enter into murky and ultimately dehumanizing rhetorics of economies of suffering.[32] Rather, Chile's importance stems from the creative achievements of its peoples, whether in the Popular Front model, democratic reforms (Alliance for Progress), the democratic (non-armed) road to socialism, democratization, or even the restructuring to a neoliberal political economy.[33] In each of these, imperialist powers, especially the United States, promoted Chile as a laboratory for particular political-economic models. In each of these, dominant international sectors underestimated the creative and transformative work that goes on in a laboratory wherein models are not merely applied but innovated on and recrafted.[34] Consequently, Chile's very success in its role as a laboratory for technologies of modernity has magnified the scale of the tragic repercussions of these remarkably successful experiments. In line with my emphasis on violence as broadly conceived to break down dichotomies of physical and representational violence and as spanning from large-scale coups and massacres to everyday forms of violence, I argue that contestations and deployments of memories of violent "events" are integral to struggles for power.

Furthermore, when discussions of violence and memory center only on the danger of forgetting acts of extreme violence, they risk colluding in the occulting of that which those very acts sought to destroy. In contemporary Chile, mistaking the struggle over memory as being primarily about the memory of atrocities from the 1973 coup on elides the concomitant forgetting of the hegemonic gains made by years of political organizing and struggle that made the coup necessary from the point of view of domestic and international elites and their military allies. Hence, even given this long history of violence and sorrow, I focus on the generative capacities not of violence per se, but rather of those groups most subjugated to that violence, who have historically responded by culturally appropriating prior instances of state violence to forge their struggles anew and to keep alive the possibility of a different future.

The historical transformations of memory both reflect and constitute regional, national, and transnational political processes. The Chilean story, told through this regional historical ethnography, has played a sentimental and strategic role in the imagining of political projects for peoples around the world. Looking at memory as praxis (rather than as text only) requires specifying the place of memory as meaningful action in the possibilities for histories and subjectivities.

Memory includes intertwined processes of remembering and forgetting in varied dimensions. The specific tactics of forgetting appeared in the strikes and repression of Oficina Ramírez and La Coruña, which were emblematic of a working-class politics of catharsis that would be domesticated into the Chilean political system as that system incorporated a wider social base. The scale of insurgency and repression covered much of the nitrate plains. Yet as outside the direct gaze of the political and economic elite, their cathartic memory would be dispersed and subsequently elided, even as the state shuffled many of the surviving workers to other regions and subsumed the events into narratives of state crisis due to international conflict and constitutional turmoil. Despite this officially sanctioned forgetting, dispersion and elision created the possibility of sustained memories embedded in working-class family stories and cultures throughout the nation.

In contrast, I explored the politics of remembering through an event that became a key interpretive locus in the politics of memory in Chile. The largely pacific and communal cast of the Escuela Santa María strike and urban occupation by nitrate workers lent itself especially well to later empathetic appropriation by populist political movements, which stressed electoral revindication of (loosely defined) non-elite interests in reshaping the Chilean state. Empathetic and later sympathetic and nostalgic memories of this event both enabled and precluded forms of popular mobilization and state discipline at key conjunctures during the twentieth century.

Having considered case studies of processes of forgetting and processes of remembering, I showed the interrelatedness of these dynamics by bringing together the analysis of the structuring of remembering and forgetting through the sinuous history of Pisagua — a place at once outside of the everyday course of Chilean politics and yet marked by a history, both heroic and infamous, that played a key role in the formation of the nation-state. In showing the (selective) interplay of memories in the foreground and shadows of both official and countermemories, I argue that just as the relegation of people (internal exile) became a form of ideological discipline favored by the state, the relegation of memories of certain forms of state violence attempted to render them available and yet containable. The state used internal exile to define and defend the frontiers of citizenship. The North played a dual role: first, it symbolized the state's use of force to delimit the nation; second, through its commemorations of military history, it represented the territorial forging of the nation through violent conflict. Tarapacá is thus a paradoxical place, where even the very barren landscape and the dry clear air of the desert seem to magnify the present predicament of Chile and, more generally, of other subaltern nation-states.

In casting the predicament of subordinate nation-states in terms of place and power, I heed Gavin Smith's critique of the current predominance of spatial metaphors in social analysis (too often replacing metaphors of production) as revolving around notions of inclusion and exclusion, center and margin.[35] Smith argues that this use of the spatial tends to emphasize agency as individual resistance to structures, rather than emphasizing action in relation to and emergent from social relations of power. Memory has been a key aspect of hegemonic contests over the nation, as revealed by the relationship between a centralizing state and a region designated as a frontier occupied by groups of people (for example, the ex-political prisoners) who have often been the subjects of state discipline. These struggles, grounded in a particular place, have exceeded the dichotomies of margin-center, inclusion-exclusion.

My methodology for exploring the relationship between the state and the subjects of its constitution—the people-nation—questions dominant framings of citizenship in contemporary Chilean politics, wherein this relationship has become mediated by the market. This model of citizenship has entailed the depoliticization of an only technically entitled population.[36] Bernardo Subercaseaux cites as a central challenge to democratization in Chile the "absence of diverse cultural expressivity" capable of projecting national identities.[37] This situation has facilitated the interpolation of market citizens as the public space of the nation is threatened by the expansion of the market—enabled by the state—into almost all sectors of life such that one might even term the new unit of political economy a market-state rather than a nation-state.[38]

In Chile the most prominent case of a sector attempting to impede the encroachment of the market in the 1990s involved the Chilean military. This may seem suprising, since in the 1970s and 1980s the military dictatorship had enforced the neoliberal restructuring of the economy by, among other measures, disciplining the labor force and privatizing key industries and resources. The primary ongoing dispute has been the privatization of copper, a vital resource, the nationalization of which began in the 1960s under the Christian

Democratic government and was finalized by the socialist state. The nationalization of copper—together with the agrarian reform that initially heralded the break-up of the oligarchy's static grip on agriculture, but that later enabled capitalist rationalizing of export agribusiness—arguably made the economic growth of the mid-1980s through 1990s possible given favorable conditions in the international economy.[39] The military continues to garner 10 percent of all copper revenues and has impeded efforts by the postdictatorship civilian regime to completely privatize the industry. Thus, the apolitical rhetoric the military deploys in its self-appointed role as the guardian of national memory and intrinsic integrity has been bolstered by its defense of this key component of national patrimony.

In further claiming a particular national memory, it is no accident that in the wake of the court ruling that effectively terminated the attempt to try General Pinochet in Chile, the principal elite newspaper ran a story commemorating General Carlos Ibáñez del Campo, Pinochet's role model.[40] It also ran "Dresden, Death and Resurrection: The Other Western Barbarity," a story about the Allied bombing of Dresden in World War II, which culminated, during Pinochet's arrest in London, in a lively series of letters-to-the-editor on the topic of Dresden.[41] Conceding a political rhetoric of the nation to the military armors a homogenizing fascist lineage, which, in Chile as in other places, has maintained remarkable continuity over the course of the twentieth century.

Given this context and the particular predicament of the Chilean state and political system in general, I support the scholar Pheng Cheah's concern that much of the postcolonial theory on the nation casts it as a political form irredeemably contaminated by imperialist logics. Remarking on horrific cases of state violence in the modern era, Cheah notes that "the nation's seemingly inevitable affinity with death is paradoxically inseparable from the desire for life," and suggests that the postcolonial nation is "a specter that haunts global capital, for it is the undecidable neuralgic point within the global capitalist system that refuses to be exorcised."[42] Focusing on refusal, persistence, and resilience, I have argued that social actors in Northern Chilean working-class and human-rights movements have mobilized memory to forge semiautonomous collective political subjectivities around a sense of the North's place in the nation *in relation to* the state rather than necessarily seeking to create a space apart from the nation-state. This is an ongoing mobilization of memory for action (the vestiges of cathartic memory) in spite of the predominant structure of feeling predicated on a radical break between the past and the present with no future alternatives (operating dually as melancholy and nostalgia). This models practices of democratic, participatory citizenship through historical narratives that create a space for their own agency in the forging of a more just world.

Remembrance of certain historical incidents have influenced official memory and even countermemory. Thus, nineteenth-century military glories became, in a manner virtually unquestioned, foundational to a political memory that sought national prominence and cast the military as the guardian of that honor. Those memories of state violence inconsistent with nation-state memory took the form of aberrations or flaws in what was presented as an otherwise whole cloth of national memory in a functioning political system. Countermemory was woven into that cloth to the extent that oppositional movements accepted the general framework of the Chilean statist political system. Yet, as in Serge Gruzinski's metaphor of the "net torn apart"—which referred to the rending of the social fabric in histories of conquest and colonialism that leaves indigenous peoples tenaciously holding together their sociocultural threads—the rhetorically whole cloth of national histories can be read not only against the grain but in their very weave.[43]

However, as a model for understanding the relationship between what might be termed subaltern memory (non-elite) and official memory, Gruzinski's metaphor and methodology for elucidating subaltern cultures present a problem similar to what Rosalind O'Hanlon critiqued as the Swiss-cheese approach to hegemony.[44] In this problematic model, hegemony is viewed (rightly) as always partial, and thus one should look for the counterhegemonic projects, sometimes called resistance, that wriggle up through the holes. So discouraging has this insight been that some scholars have declared that looking for resistance is helpful only to the extent that it provides a diagnosis for power.[45] Thus, subaltern memory can do very little to challenge the terms of official memory other than to reveal its gaps. As O'Hanlon argues, this model ignores the possibility that hegemonic and counterhegemonic projects are mutually and, to a certain extent, simultaneously constituted. Hegemony, as Antonio Gramsci formulated the concept, has always been about multiple and overlapping tugs and pulls. Furthermore, especially in postcolonial contexts, the relational interplay among multiple locales of power (the local, national, global, and others) further complicates the play of power, often leading to "scattered hegemonies."[46] And so, multiple subaltern memories and official memories temporally and spatially share a terrain of struggle.

This articulation of hegemony resonates with Walter Benjamin's description of the play of involuntary memory: "And is not this work of spontaneous recollection, in which remembrance is the woof and forgetting the warp, a counterpart to Penelope's work rather than its likeness? For here the day unravels what the night has woven. When we awake each morning, we hold in our hands, usually weakly and loosely, but a few fringes of the tapestry of lived life, as loomed for us by forgetting. However, with our purposeful activity and, even more, our purposive remembering each day unravels the web and the ornaments of forgetting."[47]

Memory offers an avenue for exploring the multiple tugs and pulls of hegemony both over time and because time, as an ideological entity, forms one of the "force fields" of hegemony.[48] A focus on memory contributes to a historical understanding of multiple pasts and their trajectories, some of which may have been cut short or woven in a variegated pattern. While historians have labored to demonstrate that history is always a particular assemblage of what becomes constituted as facts and stories, the relation between history and subjectivity remains cumbersome. Memory, as an analytic focus, carries with it the suggestion of differential subjectivity as continuously reconstituted in each present. Subjectivities, in turn, are always highly located, situated both metaphorically, as intersecting vectors of possible subject positions, and more literally in time and spaces.[49]

Focusing on memory in the dynamics of nation-state formation can provide an avenue for going beyond the homogenizing modernist narrative of History in which progress is achieved through the proper production of the Self and the Nation whose ultimate rational self-consciousness is manifested in the State. Because political memory entails particular structures of feeling, or key modes of affectively constituting political subjects through connecting them to visions of the past and future, a history of memory offers a way of considering multiple subject positions, especially in terms of collectivities such as the nation, with multiple pasts and futures.[50]

Such are the politics of memory at work in the disjunctures of Chile's transition from military to civilian rule. In political mourning, political subjectivities are defined by loss, but not subjugated to it.

Like the poet's subversion of memory, politicized mourning acts as a response to the dominant mode of melancholy by insisting on a perpetually oppositional dialogue with the dead for the pursuit of justice. The state-built mausoleum for the martyrs of the military coup constitutes a terrain negotiated through the pragmatics of regime transition; the dead are mistaken for the history of state violence, and their bones for their agency as human beings. Politicized funerals provide a context for a haunting that allows human-rights activists, including ex-political prisoners, to speak through the dead. The danger is that—especially for the ex-political prisoners, whose narrative of everyday forms of state violence and its legacies cannot fit into the state's story of transition—speaking through the dead can foreclose taking any other form of political agency. Northern human-rights activists have been most able to deploy memory in the politics of mourning in the moments and spaces in which collective memories of regional histories of struggle exceed the historical narratives promoted in the state's transition of regimes and its preservation of its own institutional and moral integrity.

Keeping these considerations in mind, I have examined memory as historical praxis from complementary vantage points on the particular historical geography of Tarapacá and created an ethnography of the located subjectivities of the people who have lived and struggled there. Historical ethnography is also a kind of Penelope's work: it must face the problem of memory not only as an intriguing puzzle or sleight of hand but also as a matter of fidelity and commitment.

Engaging in something like the game of critical arrival, I have sketched the different ways in which past and present have been linked in projects for the future at particular conjunctures, not so that one might replicate them as such; rather, the effort to recover the methodologies of memory practices can help one formulate a politics of memory adequate for the making of one's own future. As Pablo Neruda asked, in a "bleak year of rage and rancor," in the despair of history's betrayal, "How will it end?"[51] Lacking a definitive answer to this question, one still can hope to draw from the past a methodology for action.

The question of memory is generally framed in terms of the nation—who makes it, who owns it, who silences it. I have been particularly attentive to the question of who owns history because, as a scholar from the United States (a state which has so often instigated, armed, and sustained regimes of terror), I have often asked myself and been called on to justify my work on difficult topics, such as antidemocratic or authoritarian practices, political and family violence, and even the humiliating ways in which people participate in their own subordination.[52] Without discounting issues of privilege —especially imperialist and ethnic privilege—I wonder why my citizenship status and ethnicity should be enough to authorize or deauthorize this account? Innovative scholars such as Daniel James have posited as relevant other avenues of connection, such as one's class origins and political convictions and commitments.

The literature on memory, in particular, often offers scholarship as a form of witnessing. Claims based on any sort of authentic identity (by virtue of the author's position as witness, his or her expression of identity, or who he or she cites) are impossible to defend in any absolute sense because nobody is ever authentic enough.[53] Furthermore, all scholarship is some kind of political intervention, even if not recognized or claimed. While the cultural critic Gary Weissman critiques what he calls "fantasies of witnessing," I suggest that scholarship as witnessing is problematic as a relatively weak (sympathetic) action, since witnessing as a kind of sympathetic gaze downplays the scholar's role in framing the account (vis-à-vis their subjects), takes an advocacy role ("giving voice to the voiceless") vis-à-vis the presumed underdog status of subjects of study (what about those who also look at ambivalent actors, the powerful, or even people whose politics they abhor?), and characterizes the political action as derivative ("I'm just a transparent conduit relaying your project").[54] However, there is a fatter mode of witnessing understood as active example by word or deed (as in the work of the human-rights group Witness for Peace). Heeding the call to move beyond describing to changing the world invites one to question the power dynamics between scholars and subjects while forging political projects based on explicit alliances with—and commitments to—not just particular sectors of the peoples one researches, but, more important, with transformative projects.

I offer this account in the spirit of engaged scholarship, with my point of departure being the struggles of non-elite sectors I encountered through archival and oral-history research on working-class communities and through participant-observation with human-rights groups. John Burdick has argued for anthropology's potential contribution to both the study and practices of social movements, positing that the "power of ethnography, anthropology's key methodology, lies precisely in its ability to reveal and explore local patterns of social heterogeneity."[55] By refusing to idealize social movements as seamless communities but rather looking at their internal dynamics in relation to broader struggles, scholars can provide tools for activists that may allow them to better gauge the possibilities for mobilizing their presumed constituencies and to better diagnose potentially destructive conflicts within particular movements. Through a lens of "hopeful realism" offered by the ethnographic research of "committed critics," movements can grow and change in dynamic relation with their social and political contexts. Furthermore, Burdick concludes, ethnography offers a way to move beyond the current dichotomy in scholarly analysis between social movements and everyday forms of resistance. In sum, ethnographies of social and cultural movements can unpack their quotidian dynamics in terms of social relations, constructions of meanings, and negotiations of shared and contested languages of struggle. In this work, I have enacted this kind of scholarly analysis by looking at constraints and contradictions, by pointing to both current and as-yet-untapped cultural and social resources, by offering diagnostics of tensions within political movements, and by identifying potentially fruitful methodologies for constituting and sustaining communities of struggle.

"La reliquia de la huella" (the relic of the trace) was the nickname that the novelist Nicomedes Guzmán gave to the grizzly character of "the old fighter from days gone by" in his tale of working-class degradation in Iquique after the collapse of the nitrate industry.[56] The old man "could be found still in the breach, dreaming and fighting." His acerbic observations and doting affection for the heroine, a young girl, provided the narrative glue of the tragic novel. The paternal abandonment of the child and her laundress mother echoed the Chilean state's neglect of Tarapacá in the wake of the fickle desertion of capital once nitrate had served its purpose and profit.[57] Still, "In the *camanchacas calientes* [hot mists] of his soul, companionate blood and sweat boiled there still, nurturing his old age, injecting it with something like the centenarian dawn of struggle."[58]

Arguing for a praxis that configures memory as social action, I have characterized the play of memory in the Chilean political system as at times the dismantling of histories of such struggle. This entailed parceling out bits of the story of history's production in the minutiae of nostalgia, much as the hungry state and scavenger entrepreneurs sold off for scrap the mining machinery and company towns of the nitrate industry. Conditioned by an economy historically tied to chronic boom-and-bust cycles, the orphans of extractive capitalism have insisted that their land, the desert plains declared wastelands fit only for military target practice, holds untold riches for those bold enough to once again work the minerals in the sands and the subterranean rivers. Clinging to this conviction, they linger in the desert ghost towns and make do in the speculative, consumptive ports.[59] They sustain their dreams on the remnants of recalled communities. In the forging of breaches, inhabited by these stubborn relics of history's traces, the work of memory has persisted in desperate optimism.

Doing the work of memory, I have protested the inadequacy of lament: "I don't come to weep here where they fell: / I come to you, I repair to the living," writes Neruda.[60] Neoliberal euphoria threatens to consign the struggles of ex-political prisoners and others who refuse to forget and forgive to the hinterland of anachronism. Inspired by the way in which the scholar Carolyn Steedman strategically recuperated working-class lives and therein "found a psychology where once there was only the assumption of pathology," I have searched for a politics even where official psychology had pleaded reconciliation.[61] In doing so, I have joined a path already worn by the steps of so many who have fought and persevered. Having inhabited this haunted place and "searched beneath the nitrate and thorns," one can no longer weep for the dead whose memory "burns like fire."[62] In the wake of this history, one has called out their struggles and damned their traitors so that one need mourn no more for those who are left.

Notes

Introduction

1 For an assessment of the limits of South Africa's Truth and Reconciliation project with regard to its failure to connect with popular ideas about justice, see Richard Wilson, *The Politics of Truth and Reconciliation in South Africa: Legitimizing the Post-Apartheid State* (Cambridge: Cambridge University Press, 2001); also Lars Buur, "The South African Truth and Reconciliation Commission: A Technique of Nation-State Formation," in *States of Imagination: Ethnographic Explorations of the Postcolonial State*, ed. Thomas Blom Hansen and Finn Stepputat (Durham, N.C.: Duke University Press, 2001), 149–81; and Heidi Grunebaum-Ralph, "Re-placing Pasts, Forgetting Presents: Narrative, Place, and Memory in the Time of the Truth and Reconciliation Commission," *Research in African Literatures* 32, no. 3 (fall 2001): 198–212. Tina Rosenberg argues for the need for truth commissions in the former Eastern bloc specifically drawing on the Chilean model (*The Haunted Land: Facing Europe's Ghosts after Communism* [New York: Vintage, 1995], 352–353). Similarly, John Borneman suggests that Eastern and Central European countries that did not have specific discourses of

justice paid a political price in terms of popular retribution (*Settling Accounts: Violence, Justice, and Accountability in Postsocialist Europe* [Princeton: Princeton University Press, 1997]). For a comparative approach from someone involved in formulating models of transition justice, see Priscilla B. Hayner *Unspeakable Truths: Confronting State Terror and Atrocity* (New York: Routledge, 2001).

2 Fernando Rosenberg offers a complex point of reference for thinking about affect as a political dynamic when he posits "indifference" as "an affective consequence of the nation-state." Indifference is not actively felt but rather is "the background of every feeling, as a primary separation" prior to the "distribution of roles operated by the nation-state, before the assignment of identity markers" possibly overcome by "an equalitarian friendship that moves away from the politics of empathy and incorporation." Indifference points to "untamable desire for community." See Fernando Rosenberg, "The Geopolitics of Affect in the Poetry of Brazilian Modernism," in *Geomodernisms: Race, Modernism, and Modernity*, ed. Laura Doyle and Laura Winkiel (Bloomington: Indiana University Press, 2005), 87.

3 I distinguish *frontier* from *border*, since border has become the conventional term in the historiography of the United States to indicate a shift from outpost to domesticated space. In Chile "the North" is a frontier: a space only partially absorbed into the nation. "The North" is a term commonly used in the region and by many in the national capital to refer to Tarapacá, which encompasses both the coastal ports, especially Iquique as capital city, and the nitrate desert plain, but often implicitly excludes the indigenous Andean people of the altiplano. The North is more difficult to apply as a geographical or historical analytic term. The Norte Grande also includes Arica (on the Peruvian border), Antofagasta (to the south), and the Atacama Desert copper-mining area. As noted by the geographer Doreen Massey, the elasticity of terms like the North is common to ideas about place in general. Furthermore, the elasticity of place names underscores, especially in this particular case, the instability of categories of subjectivity.

4 Prasenjit Duara, *Rescuing History from the Nation: Questioning Narratives of Modern China* (Chicago: University of Chicago Press, 1995). Also see Derek Walcott, "The Muse of History," in *The Post-Colonial Studies Reader*, ed. Bill Ashcroft, Gareth Griffiths, and Helen Tiffin (London: Routledge, 1995), 373; Amitav Ghosh, *In an Antique Land* (New York: Alfred Knopf, 1993).

5 For helpful overviews of theories of state formation, see George Steinmetz, "Introduction: Culture and the State," in *State/Culture: State Formation after the Cultural Turn*, ed. George Steinmetz (Ithaca, N.Y.: Cornell University Press, 1999), 1–49; Thomas Blom Hansen and Finn Stepputat, "Introduction: States of Imagination," in *States of Imagination: Ethnographic Explorations of the Postcolonial State*, ed. Thomas Blom Hansen and Finn Stepputat (Durham, N.C.: Duke University Press, 2001), 1–38; and

Michel-Rolph Trouillot, "The Anthropology of the State," *Current Anthropology* 42, no. 1 (2001): 12, 25–38.

6 Timothy Mitchell, "Society, Economy, and the State Effect," in *State/Culture: State Formation after the Cultural Turn*, ed. George Steinmetz (Ithaca, N.Y.: Cornell University Press, 1999), 76–97.

7 Like many authors, I place quotation marks around certain terms when I want to question their common-sense definitions, and I capitalize some words—for example, the Past—to point to the way in which they take the form of particular social facts or things: I use *History* to refer not to what happened before, but rather to a particular version of the past that is asserted as "the way things were" and, hence, "the way things are."

8 Bernard S. Cohn, *An Anthropologist among the Historians and Other Essays* (Oxford: Oxford University Press, 1987).

9 Mamphela Ramphele has critiqued appropriations of the grief of family members by political movements that claim the dead as their martyrs, a problem replicated all too often by anthropologists who tend to think more about collective processes of mourning ("Political Widowhood in South Africa: The Embodiment of Ambiguity," in *Social Suffering*, ed. Arthur Kleinman, Veena Das, and Margery Lock [Berkeley: University of California Press, 1997], 99–117).

10 Henry Krips, *Fetish: An Erotics of Culture* (Ithaca, N.Y.: Cornell University Press, 1999), 87.

11 Florike Egmond and Peter Mason, *The Mammoth and the Mouse: Microhistory and Morphology* (Baltimore: Johns Hopkins University Press, 1997), 205. Lawrence Sullivan also offers a convincing case for morphological analysis in his comparative study of South American religions in *Icanchu's Drum* (New York: Macmillan, 1988), 20–21.

12 Michel de Certeau, *The Writing of History* (New York: Columbia University Press, 1998).

13 Homi Bhabha rightly notes that "to be obliged to forget—in the constitution of the national present—is not a question of historical memory, rather it is the construction of a discourse on society that *performs* the problematic totalization of the national will" ("DissemiNation: Time, Narrative, and the Margins of the Modern Nation," in *Nation and Narration*, ed. Homi K. Bhabha [London: Routledge, 1990], 311).

14 Over a century ago, Ernst Renan noted, "Suffering in common unifies more than joy does. Where national memories are concerned, griefs are of more value than triumphs, for they impose duties, and require a common effort." He continued, "A nation is therefore a large-scale solidarity, constituted by the feeling of the sacrifices that one has made in the past and of those that one is prepared to make in the future" ("What Is a Nation?" in *Nation and Narration*, ed. Homi K. Bhabha [London: Routledge, 1990], 19).

15 Paul Antze and Michael Lambeck explore the usefulness of Bakhtin's notion of chronotope—"the spatio-temporal dimensions particular to a

narrative convention"—for situating the meanings of memories within "conventions" and "discursive contexts" ("Introduction: Forecasting Memory," in *Tense Past: Cultural Essays in Trauma and Memory*, ed. Paul Antze and Michael Lambeck [London: Routledge, 1996], xvii–xviii). In the same volume, see also Michael Lambeck, "The Past Imperfect: Remembering as Moral Practice," 235–54. My kindred analysis explores the shape of memory not as the product of particular chronotopic conventions, but rather (or also) as a chronotopic practice itself.

16 Steve J. Stern, *Remembering Pinochet's Chile on the Eve of London 1998* (Durham, N.C.: Duke University Press, 2004); Steve J. Stern, *Battling for Hearts and Minds: Memory Struggles in Pinochet's Chile, 1973–1988* (Durham, N.C.: Duke University Press, 2006); Elizabeth Jelin, *State Repression and the Labors of Memory* (Minneapolis: University of Minnesota Press, 2003).

17 Terry Eagleton, *Walter Benjamin, or, Towards a Revolutionary Criticism* (London: Verso, 1981), 147.

18 Ibid.

19 Michel Foucault, *Madness and Civilization* (London: Tavistock, 1967), 57. On Tarapacá as a hinterland for a centralizing state for which it has been difficult to "percibir al *hinterland* como una entidad que cuente más allá de mera realidad productiva," see Luis A. Galdames Rosas, "Los que no cuentan (Escuela Santa María de Iquique 1907)," in *A los 90 años de los sucesos de la Escuela Santa María de Iquique*, ed. Sergio González Miranda (Santiago: Lom Ediciones, 1998), 79–81.

I Memory and Chilean Nation-State Formation

1 In the wake of Jaime Guzmán's assassination, the civilian government ceased its public-information campaign on the Report of the Chilean National Commission on Truth and Reconciliation (known as the Rettig Report) and drastically curtailed its human-rights initiatives in general. It has been speculated that the former secret police may have indirectly facilitated the assassination because, during the course of the dictatorship, Guzmán had become increasingly uncomfortable with the rampant and blatant human-rights violations and had thus made an enemy of the secret forces. He was eventually buried near President Salvador Allende in the National Cemetery. For a clear and concise early review of the constraints and limits of transition, see Juan J. Linz and Alfred Stepan, *Problems of Democratic Transition and Consolidation* (Baltimore: Johns Hopkins University Press, 1996), 205–18.

2 Unless otherwise specified, I gathered all ethnographic observations and interviews during various research stints in Chile (1990, 1991, 1992–1994, 1998, 2000, 2001, 2002), in addition to numerous interviews I conducted from 2000 to 2006 within and outside of Chile, in places such as San Francisco, Amsterdam, Toronto, Chicago, Mexico City, St. Louis, and Berlin.

3 In their extended essay on memory and modernity in Latin America, William Rowe and Vivian Schelling claim, "The major limitation to the concept of hegemony, with its basis in consent obtained by non-violent means, is its lack of or at least diminished relevance to situations of violence" (*Memory and Modernity: Popular Culture in Latin America* [London: Verso, 1991], 10). I take this to indicate a limitation of the scholarship on violence and hegemony to date, *not* a limitation of the concept of hegemony. Hegemony deals precisely with the violence of consent as well as of coercion.

4 For a concept of national memory as a constantly reinvented rhetorical field inside which political actors operate, see James Fentress and Chris Wickham, *Social Memory* (Oxford: Blackwell, 1992), 127.

5 Rather than depicting Chile as more democratic per se than other Latin American countries, I join other historians of Chile, such as Gabriel Salazar and Julio Pinto, in framing Chilean stability as a result of the early consolidation of the state apparatus under the militarized authoritarian rule of Diego Portales and the subsequent ability of that state to secure the confidence of increasingly broad sectors of the populace in terms of state coherence and ability to act decisively. Many Chileans, including historians, have complex views of their nation-state and its deployment of violence, the subtleties of which I address throughout this book.

6 For the history of international human rights, especially in the wake of the Holocaust and African decolonization movements, see George W. Shepherd Jr. and Ved P. Nanda, eds., *Human Rights and Third World Development* (Westport, Conn.: Greenwood, 1985); C. Claude and Burns H. Weston, eds., *Human Rights in the World Community: Issues and Action* (Philadelphia: University of Pennsylvania Press, 1989); Robert F. Drinan, *Cry of the Oppressed: The History and Hope of the Human Rights Revolution* (San Francisco: Harper and Rowe, 1987); and Hurst Hannum, ed., *Guide to International Human Rights Practice* (Philadelphia: University of Pennsylvania Press, 1992). For inquiry into the historical relevance of human rights that follows the cross-cultural questions already raised by anthropology, see T. E. Downing and G. Kushner, eds., *Human Rights and Anthropology* (Cambridge, Mass.: Cultural Survival, 1988); A. A. Naim, ed., *Human Rights in Cross-Cultural Perspective* (Philadelphia: University of Pennsylvania Press, 1992).

7 Olaff Olmos F., "La explotación del guano y esclavos chinos en las covaderas," *Camanchaca* no. 6 (fall–winter 1988): 12–16; Mario Zolezzi Velasquez, "Los establecimientos guaneros de Tarapacá y el movimiento obrero (1898–1910)," *Camanchaca* nos. 9–10 (spring 1989): 70–75.

8 Of the large and growing literature on the nation and memory, the following studies, in addition to works cited elsewhere, have been helpful for my work: Shahid Amin, *Event, Metaphor, Memory* (Berkeley: University of California Press, 1995); John Bodnar, *Remaking America* (Princeton: Princeton University Press, 1992); Jonathan Boyarin, ed., *Remapping*

Memory (Minneapolis: University of Minnesota Press, 1994); Alon Confino, *The Nation as Local Metaphor* (Chapel Hill: University of North Carolina Press, 1997); Yoshikuni Igarashi, *Bodies of Memory* (Princeton: Princeton University Press, 2000); Daniel James, *Doña María's Story* (Durham, N.C.: Duke University Press, 2000); William Kelleher, *The Troubles in Ballybogoin* (Ann Arbor: University of Michigan Press, 2003); Alaina Lemon, *Between Two Fires* (Durham, N.C.: Duke University Press, 2000); Liisa Malkki, *Purity and Exile* (Chicago: University of Chicago Press, 1995); Jeffrey Olick, ed., *States of Memory* (Durham, N.C.: Duke University Press, 2003); Luisa Passerini, *Fascism and Popular Memory* (Cambridge: Cambridge University Press, 1988); Joanne Rappaport, *The Politics of Memory* (Durham, N.C.: Duke University Press, 1998); Henry Rousso, *The Vichy Syndrome* (Cambridge, Mass.: Harvard University Press, 1991); Marita Sturken, *Tangled Memories* (Berkeley: University of California Press, 1997); David Sutton, *Memories Cast in Stone* (Oxford: Berg, 1998); Ted Swedenburg, *Memories of Revolt* (Minneapolis: University of Minnesota Press, 1995); Greta Lynn Uehling, *Beyond Memory* (New York: Palgrave, 2004); Jay Winter, *Sites of Memory, Sites of Mourning* (Cambridge: Cambridge University Press, 1995); Lisa Yoneyama, *Hiroshima Traces* (Berkeley: University of California Press, 1999).

9 A dramatic exception is Licia Fiol-Matta, *A Queer Mother for the Nation: The State and Gabriela Mistral* (Minneapolis: University of Minnesota Press, 2002). Though memory is not a central category for Fiol-Matta, she does develop a theory of "melancholic nationalism," in which affect and state formation are linked in profound ways. She argues that this melancholia emerged from the 1930s to 1950s in a state-centered political culture grounded in lack in the psychoanalytic sense.

10 See George Mosse, *Nationalism and Sexuality: Middle Class Morality and Sexual Norms in Modern Europe* (Madison: University of Wisconsin Press, 1985); Thomas Lekan, *Imagining the Nation in Nature: Landscape Preservation and German Identity, 1885–1945* (Cambridge, Mass.: Harvard University Press, 2004).

11 For works that posit memory as profoundly historical, though still largely in terms of genres or formats of memory, see Fentress and Wickham, *Social Memory*; Matt Matsuda, *The Memory of the Modern* (Oxford: Oxford University Press, 1996); and Rowe and Schelling, *Memory and Modernity*.

12 Lila Abu-Lughod and Catherine Lutz look at the historical and cultural specificities of languages of emotion in "Introduction: Emotion, Discourse, and the Politics of Everyday Life," in *Language and the Politics of Emotion*, ed. Lila Abu-Lughod and Catherine Lutz (Cambridge: University of Cambridge Press, 1990), 1–23. See also Lila Abu-Lughod, *Veiled Sentiments* (Berkeley: University of California, 1986); Laura Ahearn, *An Invitation to Love* (Ann Arbor: University of Michigan Press, 2001); Lauren Berlant, ed., *Compassion* (London: Routledge, 2004); Jill Bennett, *Em-*

pathetic Vision: Affect, Trauma, and Contemporary Art (Stanford: Stanford University Press, 2005); Catherine Lutz, *Unnatural Emotions* (Chicago: University of Chicago, 1988); William Reddy, *The Navigation of Feeling* (Cambridge: Cambridge University Press, 2001); Renato Rosaldo, "Grief and a Headhunter's Rage," in *Text, Play, and Story*, ed. Edward M. Bruner (Washington: American Ethnological Society, 1984). I push the notion of the everyday to include the realm of the state and formal politics, much as in Ann Stoler, *Carnal Knowledge and Imperial Power* (Berkeley: University of California Press, 2002) and Lauren Berlant, *The Anatomy of National Fantasy* (Chicago: University of Chicago Press, 1991).

13 As in the concept of a class *for* itself vs. a class *of* itself. While one can imagine affective ties grounded not in historical narrative — especially narratives of struggle — but rather in structural relations (e.g., relation to means of production), once those relations are established, it is very hard to sustain them without a narrative about past struggle, especially when consolidating and not rendering political gains. Though some would discount my emphasis on affective ties in favor of structural position (e.g., rational-choice theories) as the groundwork for political cohesion, I argue that there are no objective interests outside of or not mediated by affect, ideology, and culture. The modern nation-state is completely predicated on memory-projects because of its foundationalist, autochthonous framework, which scholars refer to as the traditional-modern dichotomy in that ideology.

14 For further discussion of this case, see Catherine Holland, *The Body Politic: Foundings, Citizenship, and Difference in the American Political Imagination* (New York: Routledge, 2001).

15 Tarapacá, like the rest of Chile, is very narrow. Given good roads, a two-hour bus trip could take one from the beach to the Andean highlands.

16 The association of the camanchaca with passion appears in Nicomedes Guzmán's populist novel extolling the tenacity of a nitrate miner's political convictions: "The old fighter from days gone by . . . could be found still in the breach, dreaming and fighting. Between the *camanchacas calientes* [hot mists] of his soul, companionate blood and sweat boiled there still, nurturing his old age, injecting it with something like the worldly dawn of struggle" (El viejo luchador de otros tiempos . . . se encontraba todavía en la brecha, soñando y bregando. Entre las camanchacas calientes de su alma, sangres compañeras y sudores amigos bullíanle aún, nutriendo su vejez, inyectándole albores seculares de lucha) (*La luz viene del mar* [Santiago: Ediciones Aconcagua, 1951], 50–51). I have translated all passages unless otherwise noted and have provided the original Spanish text in those cases of literary merit or particular interest.

17 While I use the history of memory as the thread spanning that historiographic collapse, Castro uses the history of access to water in "Cuando el susurro del agua se acalló en el desierto" (master's thesis, University of Santiago, 1999). See also Luis Castro, "Las otras luchas sociales en el Tara-

pacá salitrero la defensa de los Quismeños del agua de Chintaguay," in *A los 90 años de los sucesos de la Escuela Santa María de Iquique*, ed. Sergio González Miranda (Santiago: Lom Ediciones, 1998), 45–78.

18 An important exception is the work of Elizabeth Lira and Brian Lovemen, who document the long-standing use of ideas of reconciliation in Chilean political culture during the nineteenth and twentieth centuries, showing the resiliency of elite political culture as it generated state mechanisms, especially political amnesties, to reintegrate contentious political rivals in the name of nation-state stability. See Brian Loveman and Elizabeth Lira, *Las suaves cenizas del olvido: Vía chilena de reconciliacíon política 1814–1932* (Santiago: Lom Ediciones, 1999); Brian Loveman and Elizabeth Lira, *Las ardientes cenizas del olvido: Vía chilena de reconciliacíon política 1932–1994* (Santiago: Lom Ediciones, 2000).

19 Until World War I, Chile was the only substantial source for the world's nitrate. As the basic ingredient for fertilizers, gunpowder, and explosives, nitrate was arguably the most important commodity of its time, essential to European industrial and colonial expansion.

20 Florencia E. Mallon, "Cuando la amnesia se impone con sangre, el abuso se hace costumbre: El pueblo mapuche y el Estado chileno, 1881–1998," in *El modelo chileno: Democracia y desarrollo en los noventa*, ed. Paul Drake and Iván Jaksic (Santiago: Lom Ediciones, 1999), 435–64.

21 Gabriel Salazar and Julio Pinto, *Historia contemporánea de Chile I: Estado, legitimidad, ciudadanía* (Santiago: Lom Ediciones, 1999).The same can be argued for the United States with regard to the role of the Mexican–American War and the frontier wars against indigenous peoples. See Deborah Cohen, "Bordering Modernities: Race, Masculinity and the Cultural Politics of Mexico-U.S. Migration" (unpublished manuscript, n.d.).

22 William F. Sater offers a rich account of the foregrounding of Arturo Prat, a naval officer killed in the Battle of Iquique in the War of the Pacific, as a key national hero (*The Heroic Image in Chile: Arturo Prat, Secular Saint* [Berkeley: University of California Press, 1973]).

23 Julio Pinto-Vallejos, "A Desert Cradle: State, Foreign Fntrepreneurs, and Workers in Chile's Early Nitrate Age Tarapacá, 1870–1890" (Ph.D. diss., Yale University, 1991); Julio Pinto-Vallejos, *Trabajos y rebeldías en la pampa salitrera: El ciclo del salitre y la reconfiguración de las identidades populares (1850–1900)* (Santiago: Universidad de Santiago, 1998).

24 For a detailed discussion of the central role that historian and statesmen played in nineteenth-century Chilean state formation, see Allen Woll, *A Functional Past: The Uses of History in Nineteenth Century Chile* (Baton Rouge: Louisiana State University Press, 1982). See also Gertrude Yeager, *Barros Arana's Historia Jeneral de Chile: Politics, History, and National Identity* (Fort Worth: Texas Christian University, 1981).

25 The historiography of the nitrate industry and the role played by British capital is exceedingly rich and varied; however, because most histories of the North revolve around nitrate, virtually nothing has been written

about the region after 1930. This book strives to connect processes from that period to later ones. See, among many others, Charles Bergquist, *Labor in Latin America: Comparative Essays on Chile, Argentina, Venezuela, and Colombia* (Stanford, Calif.: Stanford University Press, 1986); Michael P. Monteon, *Chile in the Nitrate Era* (Madison: University of Wisconsin Press, 1982); Carmen Cariola Sutter and Osvaldo Sunkel, *La historia económica de Chile entre 1830 y 1930: Dos ensayos y una bibliografía* (Madrid: Instituto de Cooperación Iberoamericana, 1982). On foreign interests, see Alejandro Soto Cárdenas, *Influencia Británica en el salitre: Origen, naturaleza, y decadencia* (Santiago: Editorial Universidad de Santiago, 1998); Charles Pregger-Roman, "Nineteenth-Century Chile: A Case Study: Subordination, the Class Process, and the Relative Autonomy of States," *Latin American Perspectives* 67 (1991): 113–35.

26 Arthur Lawrence Stickell, "Migration and Mining Labor in Northern Chile in the Nitrate Era, 1880–1930" (Ph.D. diss., Indiana University, 1979).

27 Cohen, "Bordering Modernities."

28 Sergio González Miranda used extensive oral-history interviews to compile the social history of the nitrate era in *Hombres y mujeres de la pampa: Tarapacá en el ciclo del salitre (primera parte)* (Iquique: TER, 1991). The flourishing of working-class theater from the nitrate era to the present has been studied extensively by Pedro Bravo Elizondo in *Cultura y teatro obrero en Chile, 1900–1930* (Madrid: Ediciones Michay, 1987).

29 Eduardo Devés, *Los que van a morir te saludan: Historia de una massacre: Escuela Santa María Iquique, 1907* (Santiago: Nuestra America Ediciones, 1988); Crisostomo Pizarro, *La huelga obrera en Chile 1890–1970* (Santiago: Ediciones SUR, 1986).

30 While international trade in general decreased by 25 percent, Chile's exports dropped 76 percent and imports 82 percent. Dietmar Rothermund notes that, even in the wake of this catastrophe, Chilean industry did manage to grow over the course of the Depression era (*The Global Impact of the Great Depression, 1929–1939* [London: Routledge, 1996], 105). See also Michael Monteon, *Chile and the Great Depression: The Politics of Underdevelopment, 1927–1948* (Tempe: Center for Latin American Studies Press, Arizona State University, 1998).

31 Paul Drake, *Socialism and Populism in Chile, 1932–52* (Urbana: University of Illinois Press, 1978).

32 For example, pilots from Tarapacá who had flown for the nitrate companies were sent to Cuba after the revolution to help train the Cuban airforce.

33 Frederick Nunn, *Chilean Politics, 1920–1931: The Honorable Mission of the Armed Forces* (Albuquerque: University of New Mexico Press, 1970); Jorge Rojas Flores, *La dictadura de Ibáñez y los sindicatos (1927–1931)* (Santiago: Dirección de Bibliotecas, Archivos y Museos, 1993).

34 On the role of the middle class in nation-state formation, see Patrick

Barr-Melej, *Reforming Chile: Cultural Politics, Nationalism, and the Rise of the Middle Class* (Chapel Hill: University of North Carolina Press, 2001). See also Timothy Scully, *Rethinking the Center: Party Politics in Nineteenth- and Twentieth-Century Chile* (Stanford, Calif.: Stanford University Press, 1992).

35 On the Popular Front period, see Karin Rosemblatt, *Gendered Compromises* (Chapel Hill: University of North Carolina Press, 2000); Corinne Antezana-Pernet, "Mobilizing Women in the Popular Front Era" (Ph.D. diss., University of California, Irvine, 1996); Paul Drake, "Chile, 1930–1958," in *Chile since Independence*, ed. Leslie Bethell (Cambridge: Cambridge University Press, 1993), 87–128; Paul Drake, *Socialism and Populism in Chile, 1932–52* (Urbana: University of Illinois Press, 1978); Verónica Valdivia Ortiz de Zárate, *El nacionalismo chileno en los años del Frente Popular, 1938–1952* (Santiago: Universidad Católica Blas Cañas, 1995).

36 These, too, could find themselves in unlikely alliances, such as the Nazi Party's alliance with the Center-Left against Alessandri, whom they held responsible for the massacre of Nazi youth in 1938 in the Seguro Obrero building in Santiago. For a comparative perspective on the Chilean Right, see Sandra McGee Deutch, *Las Derechas: The Extreme Right in Argentina, Brazil, and Chile, 1890–1939* (Stanford, Calif.: Stanford University Press, 1999). For an analysis of the Right in later years, see Margaret Power, *Right-Wing Women in Chile: Feminine Power and the Struggle Against Allende, 1964–1973* (University Park: Pennsylvania State University Press, 2002).

37 Luis Emilio Recabarren founded the Chilean Communist Party in the North and, later, the Socialist Party. Both Radomiro Tomic and Eduardo Frei Montalva served as editors of *El Tarapacá* and founded the Falange Party, precursor to the Christian Democrat Party. See Cristián Gazmuri, "Eduardo Frei Montalva en Iquique 1935–1937," in *A los 90 años de los sucesos de la Escuela Santa María de Iquique*, ed. Sergio González Miranda (Santiago: Lom Ediciones, 1998), 83–91.

38 This betrayal caused the decline of the Radical Party and nullified its role as the mediating party in Chilean politics, a role which the Christian Democrat Party tried to assume even though its more right-wing elements continually pulled it away from a centrist political position. Their mid-1960s platform would be progressive in today's terms, due in part to internal party dynamics, including the Chilean church's long-standing interest in organizing non-elite sectors to insure moderation, and in part to John F. Kennedy's Alliance for Progress, which was meant to forestall revolution.

39 By the mid-1950s, the few people remaining in the region began organizing to protest their economic abandonment by the nation-state, which culminated in the "black banner" protests of 1957, when the region went into symbolic mourning. State responses included the Green Revolution-backed development of the fishmeal industry (which not only initiated the fortunes of the most wealthy families in the region but also

spawned national dynasties such as that of Angellini) and the legislation (aimed at importing affordable food to the desert) that eventually led to the free-trade zone.

40 Raúl Pizarro Illanes, *Los intocables: La ruta del contrabando y la historia de la mafia* (Santiago: Quimantu, 1972).

41 General Pinochet spent the first years of the Popular Unity government as the northern commander and as acting regional *intendente* (governor) as the civilian intendente was often in Santiago on personal business.

42 Pre-coup tensions were exacerbated by Fidel Castro's visit and by the armed actions of leftist guerilla movements not participating in the Popular Unity coalition, which provided rhetorical pretexts for the United States and its Chilean allies. Center-Right parties that called for the military intervention argued that there existed an impasse that could not be resolved within the bounds of the political system—a highly debatable position given the Popular Unity's electoral successes in the generally well-run elections of 1972 and the Allende government's efforts to work through negotiation and broad alliances.

43 A much more nuanced story remains to be told about the complexities of Chilean military culture as a part of the wider political culture at the time of the coup, including the populist-era internal competition between Freemasons (like Pinochet and many army officers) and staunch Catholics (especially predominant in the navy). The fact that Pinochet betrayed Allende—who was not only a fellow Mason but also higher-up in the Masonic order—made him a pariah in the international Masonic world and possibly led him to switch alliances to favor conservative Catholics and to impose a glass ceiling for military Masons. The air-force officer corps, as the younger branch of the military, was more anti-coup in general, which caused a large number of air-force officers to be purged, detained, tortured, and disappeared after the coup.

44 For a compelling ethnographic analysis of urban movements against the dictatorship in Santiago, see Cathy Lisa Schneider, *Shantytown Protest in Pinochet's Chile* (Philadelphia: Temple University Press, 1995). An excellent companion ethnography that looks at urban issues in postdictatorship Santiago is Julia Paley, *Marketing Democracy: Power and Social Movements in Post-Dictatorship Chile* (Berkeley: University of California Press, 2001).

45 In the case of the Communist Party, Chilean exiles and their children were used or participated as combatants in other Cold War conflicts, such as those in Angola, Afghanistan, and Nicaragua, which ostensibly provided the military experience Chileans would need to someday liberate their country. It is quite likely that the Soviets timed their encouragement of armed agitation in Chile to geopolitical moments when it was desirable to annoy the United States. This is not to take away from the very real—and often ultimate—sacrifices Chileans made in supporting what were indeed just causes in other places. Unfortunately, with the return to civilian rule,

such sacrifices were disavowed or ignored by many of the same political leaders who had called on fellow Chileans to make them.

46 Bernardo Guerrero J., ed. *Vida, pasión y muerte en Pisagua* (Iquique: CREAR, 1990).

47 A major explosion at the Cardoen cluster-bomb plant in 1984, which resulted in the deaths of at least twenty people, marked another point in the landscape of violence.

48 The military used the framework of 1950s import-substitution industrialization blueprints and legislation but encouraged the importation of finished consumer durables and nondurables rather than machinery and other productive tools. Alejandro Soria (former regional governor of Tarapacá), interview by author, February 1994.

49 The terrain of the conjunctural, to use Antonio Gramsci's concept, is the balance of political forces that exists at a particular historical moment; it forms the context for political strategy and action. These political tactics must be understood in the context not only of an immediate crisis but of what Gramsci describes as the incessant and persistent efforts taken to defend existing structures of power, including, if the crisis is severe enough, the creation of new hegemonic forms to re-entrench the dominant position. Roger Simon, *Gramsci's Political Thought* (London: Lawrence and Wishart, 1991), 39.

50 This model for historical writing owes much to Alberto Flores Galindo's work on Andean worldviews and uprisings, *Buscando un Inca* (Lima: Editorial Horizonte, 1988).

51 Geoffrey Bennington, "Postal Politics and the Institution of the Nation," in *Nation and Narration*, ed. Homi K. Bhabha (London: Routledge, 1990), 121.

52 As Rowe and Schelling observe, populism entails "the political use of the popular as a definition of national identity" where the people serve as "on the one hand an alibi of identity between state and nation, on the other a way of referring to the condition of political availability of a large mass" (*Memory and Modernity*, 151, 166).

53 One prototypical populist character, the roto chileno worker-soldier, was drawn from northern Chile. Populist and labor leaders attempted to reclaim this character as an icon of the people without having to deal with the military as the final arbiters of national honor and memory. The collapse of the political system and initial shutting down of civil society following the 1973 military coup forced the innovation of what scholars came to call new social movements, whose actors could include those who had been regarded as auxiliaries in previous configurations of political agency (e.g., women, the poor, neighborhoods). Human-rights movements have posited the broadest claims for political subjectivity.

54 This formulation draws heavily on Gramsci's ideas about hegemony and common sense and on Pierre Bourdieu's model of doxa, orthodoxa, and heterodoxa.

55 Memory is a useful way to talk about the uses of the past because it implies subjectivity in acts of remembering or forgetting, and because it is temporally indeterminate.

56 Quoted in Pedro Bravo Elizondo, introduction to *Santa María de salitre* by Sergio Arrau (Iquique: Editorial Camanchaca, 1989), xiv.

57 Many of my examples are poetic in nature, due not only to poetry's particular role in twentieth-century Chilean history but also to its usefulness in countering the tensions of historical narrative and the drive to periodize. On poetry and politics in Latin America, see Mike González and David Treece, *The Gathering of Voices: The Twentieth-Century Poetry of Latin America* (London: Verso, 1992). On poetry and trauma, see Susan Gubar, *Poetry after Auschwitz* (Bloomington: Indiana University Press, 2006).

58 The view of memory as social action is an extension of the school of thought that sees language as social action, that is, that focuses on what language does, rather than what it is. See J. L. Austin, *How to Do Things with Words* (Cambridge, Mass.: Harvard University Press, 1962); Mary Louise Pratt, *Toward a Speech Act Theory of Literary Discourse* (Bloomington: Indiana University Press, 1977); John R. Searle, *Speech Acts: An Essay in the Philosophy of Language* (London: Cambridge University Press, 1969).

59 Raymond Williams, *Marxism and Literature* (Oxford: Oxford University Press, 1977), 132–33.

60 Raymond Williams, *The Long Revolution* (New York: Columbia University Press, 1961).

61 Williams, *Marxism and Literature*, 133. For Williams, structures of feeling are primarily emergent "social experiences in solution," as opposed to either dominant or residual forms that have precipitated out and thus are more readily available to social actors. Greta Uehling, too, uses the structure of feeling to think about memory, although she cautions that the word *structure* can carry unhelpful assumptions (e.g., an essence-surface dichotomy), despite the fact that, often, "recollections and sentiments are socially constructed in some very public and surprisingly superficial ways." She underscores the emergent aspects of memory: "Even as structures of feeling create the mood of a generation, sentiments and narratives are still in the process of development" and when "formalized, new structures of feeling are in formation" (*Beyond Memory* [New York: Palgrave, 2004], 13).

62 Speaking particularly of art, Raymond Williams states that a structure of feeling is "distinguishable from other social and semantic formations by its articulation of *presence*" (*Marxism and Literature*, 134–35). Analyzing the history of memory formations as indicative of feeling structures aids in uncovering the proliferation of presents in the past.

63 Louis Althusser, "Ideology and Ideological State Apparatuses," in *Lenin and Philosophy and Other Essays*, trans. Ben Brewster (New York: Monthly Review, 1971), 127–86.

64 Barbara Bowen, "Untroubled Voice: Call and Response in *Cane*," in

Black Literature and Literary Theory, ed. Henry Louis Gates Jr. (New York: Methuen, 1984), 187–204.

65 I have appropriated these terms from theatrical analyses of the event-relationship between performer and audience inspired by Aristotle's exploration of the possibilities in tragedy for catharsis generated by fear and pity (*Aristotle's Poetics*, trans. James Hutton [New York: W. W. Norton, 1982]).

66 John Hall, "Introduction: The Reworking of Class Analysis," in *Reworking Class*, ed. John Hall (Ithaca: Cornell University Press, 1997), 4. Sonia O. Rose provides a helpful overview to thinking about the connections between vectors of class, ethnicity, gender, and nationalism in "Class Formation and the Quintessential Worker" in *Reworking Class*, ed. John Hall (Ithaca: Cornell University Press, 1997).

67 Furthermore, the export-oriented political economy of this region entails an understanding of a century-long, but never unidirectional, processes of globalization in the conditions of possibility for various forms of political memory. See Michel-Rolph Trouillot, "The Anthropology of the State in the Age of Globalization: Close Encounters of a Deceptive Kind," *Current Anthropology* 42, no. 1 (2001): 12, 25–38; Michel-Rolph Trouillot, *Global Transformations* (New York: Palgrave, 2003).

68 Doreen Massey, *Space, Place and Gender* (Minneapolis: University of Minnesota Press, 1994), 120.

69 Johannes Fabian, *Remembering the Present: Painting and Popular History in Zaire* (Berkeley: University of California Press, 1996), 273.

70 Massey, *Space, Place and Gender*, 121.

71 This is true especially as the military component of regional pride implicates this northernmost region in the centralizing processes of the nation-state.

72 Silvio R. Duncan Baretta and John Markoff, "Civilization and Barbarism: Cattle Frontiers in Latin America," *Comparative Studies in Society and History* 20, no. 4 (October 1978): 587–620.

73 Geoffrey Bennington, "Postal Politics and the Institution of the Nation," in *Nation and Narration*, ed. Homi K. Bhabha (London: Routledge, 1990), 121. Anastasia Karakasidou presents an intriguing comparative case study on the ethnic nationalization of a frontier zone during the same time period examined herein (*Fields of Wheat, Hills of Blood: Passages to Nationhood in Greek Macadonia 1870–1990* [Chicago: University of Chicago Press, 1997]).

74 Ana Alonso, *Thread of Blood* (Tucson: University of Arizona Press, 1995), 15. Although northern Chile and northern Mexico offer many points of comparison, they represent very different configurations of militarism, frontier, honor and ethnicity: perhaps the most important difference is their hegemony over their neighbors.

75 Elderly woman, interview by author and Patricio Rivera O., Huara, Chile, December 1993.

"Veinte años, cien años de salitre amasaron el alma del / pampino. / Y ahora, al cabo de tanta historia, de tanta alborada / herida, / que me cuentan, vengan a ver a mi tierra, vengan a ver las / calaminas rotas, / las oficinas muertas, la tierra abandonada. / Vengan a escuchar el silencio en los fríos cementerios / de la pampa. . . . / Mi tierra es un paisaje arrepentido en medio de una / historia heroica. . . . " (Mario Bahamonde, "Les vengo a contar," *Tierra y sol: Homenaje a Mario Bahamonde* [Antofagasta: Colecciones Hacia La Tierra/El Hombre/La Poesía 1980], 22–23).

1 Huara resident, interview by author and Patricio Rivera, Huara, Chile, January 1994.

2 For a similar assertion, see Augusto Rojas Núñez, *La agonía del salitre en la Pampa Tamarugal* (Santiago: Imprenta Astudillo, 1960), 33.

3 All the forms of memory I offer as my template — sympathy, empathy, and catharsis — are transformative in that they relate to the production of relationally constituted subjectivities; however, catharsis often has the greatest transformative potential. The term *catharsis* as a way of talking about the production of political subjectivities further resonates in the debate between Bertolt Brecht and Georg Lukács over the praxis of revolutionary art. Brecht argued against Aristotelian catharsis (as he understood it): that the work of affect in politics should be not to incite identification between the audience and the characters in order to purge pity and fear, but rather to incite an estrangement that would provide the basis for critique. In calling this "one of the most sensitive spots in all dramatic history and theory," Frederic Ewen, a literary critic and Brecht biographer, provides a helpful assessment of the ways in which Brecht may have misread Aristotle on catharsis precisely around the question of whether catharsis is about purging or transforming the subject (*Bertolt Brecht: His Life, His Art and His Times* [New York: Citadel Press, 1967], 214–25). Ronald Gray similarly argues that Brecht misunderstood Aristotle and cites Humphry House's argument that Aristotle did not see catharsis as referring principally to the purging of painful emotions but rather to producing pain rightly (*Brecht the Dramatist* [Cambridge: Cambridge University Press, 1976], 80–85).

4 A moment which, as Sue Golding explained, "is always actively political and one not divorced from history," though unfettered by the ideology seemingly necessary to account for the contradictions of the present. Golding conceded Gramsci's enormous contribution in "emphasizing that we create . . . not only the very notion of what it is to be human but also what it ought to be, as such and for whom," a vision linking a dynamic history to the possibility of a transformed future. See Sue Golding, "The Concept of the Philosophy of Praxis in the *Quaderni* of Antonio Gramsci," in *Marxism and the Interpretation of Culture*, ed. Cary Nelson and Lawrence Grossberg (Urbana: University of Illinois Press, 1988), 543–63. On anthropological uses of Gramsci, see Kate Crehan, *Gramsci, Culture, and Anthropology*

(Berkeley: University of California Press, 2002). For a discussion of Gramsci and his usefulness in thinking about Chilean politics, see Antonio Leal, *Gramsci: La ciudad futura* (Santiago: Ediciones Documentas, 1991).

5 By locating the affective alliance in temporally located action, catharsis as a mode of mobilization need not rely on a politics of sameness, but rather on mutual commitment to a project, thus moving political strategy beyond the identicality-difference dichotomy of identity politics. See Antonio Gramsci, "Problems of Philosophy and History," in *Selections from the Prison Notebooks of Antonio Gramsci*, ed. and trans. Quintin Hoare and Geoffrey Nowell Smith (New York: International Publishers, 1971), 323–77. Also quoted in Golding, "The Concept of the Philosophy of Praxis," 557.

6 Terry Eagleton, *Walter Benjamin, or Toward a Revolutionary Criticism* (London: Verso 1981), 148.

7 "Hay una memoria que retorna, se clava y hunde en los 'hechos' que atraen la recordación. Pero hay otra que, desde allí, avanza en longitud y latitud hacia los procesos que construyen la realidad futura: es la memoria para la acción. La memoria 'de' los hechos es una. La memoria 'para' la acción, que engloba la anterior, es otra. El poder surge de la primera, pero 'madura' cuando la primera se funde con la segunda. La memoria 'para' la acción es, pues, la memoria histórica del poder" (Gabriel Salazar, "Voluntad política de matar, voluntad social de recordar: A propósito de Santa María de Iquique," in *A los 90 años de los sucesos de la Escuela Santa María de Iquique*, ed. Sergio González Miranda [Santiago: Lom Ediciones, 1998], 291–302).

8 This is plausibly true for both elites and non-elites. Maurice Zeitlan provides accounts for continuities in Chilean elite allegiance in *Landlords and Capitalists* (Princeton: Princeton University Press, 1988).

9 On the importance of "combative poets" and journalists in this period, see M. Angélica Illanes, "Lápiz versus fusil, las claves de advenimiento del nuevo siglo Santiago-Iquique, 1900–1907," in *A los 90 años de los sucesos de la Escuela Santa María de Iquique*, ed. Sergio González Miranda (Santiago: Lom Ediciones, 1998), 193–208. On popular poetry, see Jorge Núñez Pinto, "Los sucesos de Santa María de Iquique en la poesía popular," *A los 90 años de los sucesos de la Escuela Santa María de Iquique*, ed. Sergio González Miranda (Santiago: Lom Ediciones, 1998), 225–35.

10 Elias Lafertte, *Vida de un comunista* (1957; repr., Santiago: Editora Austral, 1971), 80.

11 A. Acevedo Hernández, *Los cantores populares chilenos* (Santiago: Editorial Nascimento, 1933), 216–17.

12 "Canto a la pampa la tierra triste / reproba tierra de maldición, / que de verdores jamás se viste / ni en lo mas bello de la estación. . . . / Sublimes víctimas que bajaron / desde la pampa llenas de fe; / y a su llegada lo que encontraron / la ruin metralla tan solo fue" (reprinted in Claudia Aranda B. and Ricardo Canales A., eds., *Páginas literarias de los obreros socialistas [1912–1915]* [Santiago: Ediciones ICAL, 1991], 86–87). The song may have ap-

peared in first print as "Song of the Strike" (to the tune of "La Ausencia"), which was written by an anonymous author and published in *El Despertar de los Trabajadores* on 20 December 1913.

13 "Hasta que un día como un lamento / de lo más hondo del corazón, / por las callejas del campamento / vibró un acento de rebelión: / eran los ayes de muchos pechos, / de muchas iras era el clamor, / la clarinada de los derechos / del pobre pueblo trabajador. . . . / Pido venganza por el valiente / que la metralla pulverizó / pido venganza por el doliente / huérfano y triste allí quedó. / Pido venganza por la que vino / de los obreros el pecho a abrir / pido venganza por el pampino / que allá en Iquique, supo morir" (reprinted in Claudia Aranda B. and Ricardo Canales A., eds., *Páginas literarias de los obreros socialistas [1912–1915]* [Santiago: Ediciones ICAL, 1991], 86–87).

14 Juan Segundo Montoya N., ed., *Cancionario libertario* (Talca: n.p., 1946). This work includes "Canto a la Pampa," called simply "La Pampa," and several other songs with lyrics by Pezoa, such as "La cancion sonora," "El guitarrico libertario," and "Coplas."

15 Acevedo Hernández, *Los cantores populares chilenos*, 59–60.

16 Increasingly, the state's "Chileanization" project insisted that such doubled allegiance was untenable, that is, that the workers could not be both internationalist (specifically, in the sense of a class identity) and Chilean. This rhetorical position was exacerbated by Cold War anticommunist ideology. The idea of doubledness is from W. E. B. Du Bois's *The Souls of Black Folk* (1903) (selection anthologized as "Double-Consciousness and the Veil," in *Social Theory*, ed. Charles Lemert [Boulder, Colo.: Westview Press, 1994] 177–82). Du Bois insists that doubledness was not a strategy chosen by subordinates, but rather a trap in which they were caught. In *The Souls of Black Folk* Du Bois also links identity to song, moving from classical mythology to spirituals as analytical catalysts.

So as not to romanticize this period, in which the structure of feeling called for a politics of memory as catharsis, it is important to note that populist and fascist movements also perceived the potential force of this early-twentieth-century mode and attempted to harness it and channel it toward the capture of nation-states.

17 Luis Polanco, "Mensaje a la pampa del futuro," in *Poesía popular chilena*, ed. Diego Muñoz (Santiago: Quimantu, 1972), 157–58.

18 Poor people's access to political power and the redistribution of resources would in "the Chilean road to socialism" be achieved through electoral successes and subsequent legislation. Peter Winn's historical ethnography of the contests between the workers of the Yarur textile factory and the Popular Unity government explores the dynamics and consequences of distrust between workers and the political organizations and linkages of the Left (*Weavers of Revolution* [New York: Oxford University Press, 1986]).

19 Building on anti-imperialist critiques of sympathy and sisterhood, Doris Sommer questions the possibilities for empathy and interrogates the

effectiveness of appeals to empathy which she finds at the core of feminist politics. See Doris Sommer, "Resisting the Heat: Menchu, Morrison, and Incompetent readers," in *Cultures of United States Imperialism*, ed. Donald Pease and Amy Kaplan (Durham, N.C.: Duke University Press, 1993), 407–432. Empathy, in feminist ethics, entails the validation of experiences of subjugation. Yet experience, as Joan Scott emphasizes, does not rest somewhere outside of discourse in its broadest definition; empathy based on authenticating experience of subordination is always mediated by the politics of language. See Joan W. Scott, "Experience," in *Feminists Theorize the Political*, ed. Judith Butler and Joan W. Scott (New York: Routledge, 1992), 22–40. Ruth Frankenberg offers a rich analysis of this problem in *White Women, Race Matters: The Social Construction of Whiteness* (Minneapolis: Minnesota University Press, 1994). For a concise critique of empathy as a gendered category and the ways in which U.S. masculinity is predicated on a cruel kind of empathy with those already "like" oneself, see Judith Kegan Gardiner, "Masculinity, the Teening of America, and Empathetic Targeting," in *Feminisms at a Millennium*, ed. Judith Howard and Carolyn Allen (Chicago: University of Chicago Press, 2000), 248–52. Kegan Gardiner offers an extended discussion of empathy in *Rhys, Stead, Lessing, and the Politics of Empathy* (Bloomington: Indiana University Press, 1989).

20 The northern poet Andrés Sabella wrote, "Como si la pampa salitrera fuese una mano con cinco dedos ensangrientados: huelga de Tarapacá, en 1890; baleo de Antofagasta, en 1906; matanza de la Escuela 'Santa María' de Iquique, en 1907; San Gregorio, en 1921; y la masacre de 'Coruña,' en 1925." In Sabella's litany, these "cosas de la sangre" served as a national conscience more than as a source for consciousness: "¡Qué mano de varón hirsuto y resuelto! Mano que podría desalojar del cielo a todas las estrellas: mano que se metería a través de la tierra, abriendo un túnel tenebroso a los satélites de la muerte; mano que si se agitara dentro del mar haría saltar lejos a todas las posibles cortes de sirenas" (*Norte Grande* [Santiago: Orbe, 1944], 163–64). For a discussion of Sabella's work on state violence in the North, see José Antonio González Pizarro, "Andrés Sabella y la historia social de Chile y del Norte Grande," in *A los 90 años de los sucesos de la Escuela Santa María de Iquique*, ed. Sergio González Miranda (Santiago: Lom Ediciones, 1998), 119–37.

21 The gendering of "the people" as male has been explored by a number of scholars who have puzzled over the Popular Unity's inability to incorporate and ability to alienate (even working-class) women. See Camilla Townsend, "Refusing to travel La Vía Chilena: Working-class Women in Allende's Chile," *Women's History* 4, no. 3: 43–63; Michele Mattelart, "Chile: The Feminine Version of the Coup d'etat," in *Sex and Class in Latin America*, ed. June Nash and Helen Safa (New York: Praeger, 1976), 279–301; Karin Rosemblatt, *Gendered Compromises* (Chapel Hill: University of North Carolina, 2000). In this sense, populism remained consistent

with liberal political thought in its gendering of citizenship. On citizenship in political philosophy, see Carol Pateman, "The Fraternal Social Contract," in *Civil Society and the State*, ed. John Keane (London: Verso, 1988), 101–28.

22 Pigmalión (pseud.), "Los aparecidos de la Santa María," *Camanchaca* special ed., nos. 9–10 (spring 1989): 28.

23 In a discussion compatible with my own model, Douglas Chismar argues that empathy is the more general category of involuntary vicarious emotion, whereas sympathy requires agency in making an identification. Chismar argues that getting people to sympathize with others is an unrealistic goal because of the multiplicity of possible combinations of comparable experiences. He argues instead for empathetic education, which would inculcate the general capacity to connect with others whether or not similar experiences have been shared. See Douglas Chismar, "Empathy and Sympathy: The Important Difference," *Value Inquiry* 22 (1988): 257–66.

24 This is something close to the Manichaean allegory, wherein minority cultures "are forever consigned to play the role of the ontological, political, economic, and cultural Other," an allegorical relation that "seems the central trope not only of colonialist discourse but also of Western humanism" (Abdul R. JanMohamed and David Lloyd, "Introduction: Toward a Theory of Minority Discourse: What Is to Be Done?" in *The Nature and Context of Minority Discourse*, ed. Abdul R. JanMohamed and David Lloyd, [Oxford: Oxford University Press, 1990], 2). For earlier formulations of the critique of allegory, see Abdul R. JanMohamed, "The Economy of Manichean Allegory," *Critical Inquiry* 2, no. 1 (1985): 59–87; also see Aijaz Ahmad, "Jameson's Rhetoric of Otherness and the 'National Allegory,'" *Social Text* 17 (1987): 3–25, in which he debates Fredric Jameson's critique of discourses of post-colonial nationalism as being ultimately allegorical for "the West"; (Fredric Jameson, "Third World Literature in the era of Multinational Capitalism," *Social Text* 15 [fall 1986]: 65–88).

25 Walter Heynowski, Gerhard Scheumann, and Peter Hellmich, *Anflug auf Chacabuco* (Berlin: Verlag der Nation, 1974). Walter Heynowski, interview by author, Berlin, June 2002.

26 Frank Graziano has identified the inspirations for the Argentine military's conduct of state terror in the 1970s as coming from the Spanish Inquisition and Nazi Germany, in *Divine Violence: Spectacle, Psychosexuality, and Radical Christianity in the Argentine "Dirty War"* (Boulder, Colo.: Westview Press, 1992).

27 For a depiction of the rise of a model of citizenship through consumption in the United States, see Lizabeth Cohen, *A Consumer's Republic: The Politics of Mass Consumption in Postwar America* (New York: Vintage, 2003).

28 This model of rebirth for the political system relied on a pragmatics similar to Chantal Mouffe's concept of an extended democratic movement of solidarity, that is, a chain of "democratic equivalences" between struggles, in which any given struggle would be just one of many ("Hegemony

and New Political Subjects: Toward a New Concept of Democracy," trans. Stanley Gray, in *Marxism and the Interpretation of Culture*, ed. Cary Nelson and Lawrence Grossberg [Urbana: University of Illinois Press 1988], 89–101). Similarly, Alberto Melucci identified the problem of "society without a future" in the decline of politics in "'post-industrial' democracy" as requiring social movements based on the "recognition and autonomy of individual and collective signifying processes" in the democratization of everyday life ("Social Movements and the Democratization of Everyday Life," in *Civil Society and the State*, ed. John Keane [London: Verso, 1988], 245–60). The model of political projects based on a chain of sympathetic alliances between equivalent and (semi)autonomous entities brings up issues similar to those raised by theorists who, questioning the colonialist antecedents of feminist movements, have challenged the presumption of cross-cultural sisterhood that neglects the differentials of power between subordinate groups that can compel, condition, and inhibit alliances. See Gloria Anzaldúa, ed., *Making Face, Making Soul: Haciendo Caras* (San Francisco: Aunte Lute, 1990), especially the contributions by Lorna Dee Cervantes, Pat Parker, and Audre Lorde; Avtar Brah, "Questions of Difference and International Feminism," in *Out of the Margins*, ed. J. Aaron and S. Walby (London: Falmer, 1992); Hazel Carby, "White Women Listen! Black Feminism and the Boundaries of Sisterhood," in *The Empire Strikes Back*, ed. Centre for Contemporary Studies (London: Hutchinson, 1982); Angela Davis, *Women, Culture, Politics* (1989; repr., New York: Vintage Books, 1990). Although asking for and offering solidarity can be mutual, sympathy as a mode of political action can reinscribe asymmetrical power relations.

29 In retracing the idea of melancholia in Sigmund Freud's thought, Eng shows that, for Freud, melancholia forms the basis for all subjectivity, as people take pieces of the past (by definition, lost) and incorporate them into their understandings of themselves. However, using recent work on racism, Eng argues that for sectors subordinated by gender, race, class, imperialism, and so on, melancholia becomes pathological. See David L. Eng, "Melancholia in the Late Twentieth Century," in *Feminisms at a Millennium*, ed. Judith A. Howard and Carolyn Allen (Chicago: University of Chicago Press, 2000), 265–71.

30 Guillermo Ross-Murray Lay-Kim, "Diario" (unpublished manuscript, n.d.), quoted in Sergio Gaytan M., *14 autores nortinos* (Antofagasta: Universidad Católica del Norte, 1993), 71. To date, parts of the diaries have circulated primarily among Ross-Murray Lay-Kim's friends. He is planning to publish an edited and annotated version.

31 Gaytan, *14 autores nortinos*, 71. Similarly, Ross-Murray Lay-Kim's manuscript "Animal desamparo" comprises over forty poems spanning the coup of September 1973 to the June 1990 excavation of the mass grave in Pisagua.

32 Guillermo Ross-Murray, "Trenos" (unpublished manuscript, n.d.).

33 As the Chilean political system constitutes itself in everyday life, the language of high politics reverberates in quotidian language as well. Roberto Rojas, who in 1992 returned to Iquique from exile in England, commented that in spite of having lived through Thatcherism, perforce immersing himself in the rhetoric of conservatism, he was still startled by the drastic change in Chile after two decades of neoliberal restructuring (personal communication, February 1994).

34 This was the Congreso de Escritores del Norte, which I attended at Guillermo Ross-Murray Lay-Kim's invitation.

35 Guillermo Ross-Murray Lay-Kim, "Proyectos culturales del estado" (paper presented at the Congreso de Escritores del Norte, Iquique, October 1993). On the ways in which the invocation of "culture" is intrinsically implicated in forming citizens for the modern state at the expense of working-class radicalism and contemporary social movements (in a cautionary notice to cultural studies as a field), see David Lloyd and Paul Thomas, *Culture and the State* (New York: Routledge, 1998).

36 For earlier efforts to pressure the government in Santiago to provide "cultural" services to region, see: Partido Socialista *Resoluciones adoptadas. Primer congreso regional del Partido Socialista en la provincia de Tarapacá* (n.pl.: Departamento de Publicaciones, Secretaria Nacional de Cultura, 1939), 26–27.

37 For more on the broad-based movements that opposed military rule, see Taller Nueva Historia: Pedro Milos, *Cuadernos de historia popular: serie historia del movimiento obrero* (Santiago: Centro de Estudios del Trabajo CETRA/CEAL, 1983). These projects adopted principles inspired by the pan–Latin American popular-education movement led by the Brazilian Paolo Freire, which stressed more participatory pedagogical strategies. See Paolo Freire, *Pedagogy of the Oppressed*, trans. Myra Berman Ramos (New York: Seabury Press, 1970).

38 The historian Germán Palacios Ríos also argued for the structural complementarity of liberal and Left historiography in the "sublimation of the past (in its double denotation: to exalt and to evaporate)" in his study on the agrarian massacre of 1934 in the southern frontier town, Ranquil. Palacios Ríos pointed to the ways in which what he termed liberal historiography hid the reality of conflict and guarded the silence around the conditions out of which conflict emerged, in this case, distorted land distribution. On the Left, sublimation provided a way of "enhancing social struggle, rescuing some elements that through the generality of social movement history identify themselves with the repression and massacre." But this appropriation, Palacios Ríos maintained, failed to attain those general principles which could be "applied to other situations, or to do projective analysis that permits the visualization of new conjunctures and possible ways to confront them considering the new reality in its particularity

and historical experience." See Germán Palacios Ríos, *Ranquil la violencia en la expansión de la propiedad agrícola* (Santiago: Ediciones Institutos de Ciencias Alejandro Lipschutz, 1992), 11.

39 David Forgacs "National-popular: Genealogy of a Concept," in *Formation of Nation and People*, ed. Formations Editorial Collective (London: Routledge and Kegan Paul, 1984), 83–98.

40 Terry Eagleton, *Walter Benjamin*, 147.

41 In her formulation of the problem of the relative autonomy of states, Nora Hamilton noted, "The fate of the Popular Unity government in Chile demonstrates the limits to the possibility of utilizing the state to effect a transition to socialism in the context of a capitalist society . . . [and] the rapidity with which previously fractured interests and segments of the dominant class can achieve unity and cohesion when the class structure is threatened" (*The Limits of State Autonomy: Post-Revolutionary Mexico* [Princeton: Princeton University Press, 1982], 15).

42 Michel Foucault, *Language, Counter-Memory, Practice: Selected Essays and Interviews*, trans. Donald F. Bouchard and Sherry Simon (Ithaca, N.Y.: Cornell, 1977).

43 On subaltern intellectuals, writers, and historians in Latin America, see Florencia Mallon, "Local Intellectuals, Regional Mythologies, and the Mexican State, 1850–1994: The Many Faces of Zapatismo," *Polygraph* 10 (1998): 39–78; Rosario Montoya del Solar, "Liberation Theology and the Socialist Utopia of a Nicaraguan Shoemaker," *Social History* 20, no. 1 (January 1995): 23–43. Johannes Fabian deals with the question of the historical narrative of a painter in Zaire, in *Remembering the Present* (Berkeley: University of California Press, 1996).

44 Derek Walcott, "The Muse of History," in *The Post-Colonial Studies Reader*, ed. Bill Ashcroft, Gareth Griffiths, and Helen Tiffin (London: Routledge, 1995), 373.

45 Ibid.

46 Sonia Montecino, *Madres y huachos: Alegorías del mestizaje chileno* (Santiago: Editorial Cuarto Propio, Ediciones CEDEM, 1991).

3 Dismantling Memory

1 Adelina Lara (resident of Iquique), interview by author, Iquique, Tarapacá, February 1994. Her comments were remarkable in that I had not asked her about state repression of labor, but rather to tell me about her experiences in women's civic associations in the mining communities.

2 Amelia Cofre told me that even though she arrived in the North in 1927, just two years after the massacre, and in spite of her active participation in popular theater and political organizations, she only learned about the repression of 1925 from the whispered stories of her neighbors (Amelia Cofre Quiroz (former resident of the pampa), interview by author, Linares, Chile, November 1992). The persistence of the massacre in non-elite

memory in the region is especially remarkable as the nitrate-area population was severely disrupted immediately after the events of June 1925, due
to the mass exodus of workers either fleeing repression or being forcefully
deported from the zone by nitrate companies that refused to rehire workers
they saw as contaminated by radical organization; however, this exodus
spread stories of the North throughout Chile. For example, papers reported one ship of 320 "subversives" who had been expelled from the
region on 17 June alone (*El Tarapacá*, 17 June 1925, p. 5). On refusal to
rehire workers, see Vice-Consul Gudgeon, Iquique, to Consul of Antofagasta, no. 65, 27 June 1925, PRO, FO 132/278.

3 Especially since the historiography glosses over labor history by framing it as particular to the "acquisition of a 'class consciousness' for the
proletariat" (Sergio Villalobos R., *Historia de Chile* [1974; repr., Santiago: Editorial Universitaria, 1990],727). Recent works by younger scholars show renewed interest in the 1925 events, possibly in relation to current
disillusionment with the ability of postdictatorship civilian regimes to pursue justice. Alberto Harambour Ross, noting the silencing of 1925 both in
conservative history and in the official history of the Left, posits that the
lives lost then "no apostaron a la negociación" (didn't lend themselves to
renegotiation) of elections, nor constitutions, nor the military apparatus,
nor official unionism; thus, in a new form of struggle, "elevaron su protesta
contra el Estado, contra los empresarios, pero también contra los Tribunales Arbitrales, contra la integración a la democracia burguesa donde una vez
asimilados no pudieron escapar de la cooptación, dejando de luchar por la
tan anunciada revolución social" (gave rise to their protest against the
state, the entrepreneurs, also against the arbitration tribunals, against integration into bourgeois democracy, where once assimilated they could not
escape cooptation, no longer fighting for the proclaimed social revolution); "Ya con los manos vacías (huelga) y sangre obrera en el Alto San
Antonio los 'sucesos' de la Coruña, Junio de 1925," in *A los 90 años de los
sucesos de la Escuela Santa María de Iquique*, ed. Sergio Gonzalez Miranda
[Santiago: Lom Ediciones, 1998], 181, 191). For an extended work based
largely on newspaper accounts and a few key oral histories, see Luis Espinoza Garrido, *De Coruña a Maroussia: El levantamiento pampino del 1925*
(Iquique: Colección Historia Tarapacá Obrera, 2001).

4 Pablo Neruda, "The Massacres," *Canto general*, trans. Jack Schmitt
(Berkeley: University of California Press, 1991), 187.

5 Judicial Depositions, "1925 strike in Tarapacá and Antofagasta," AN.

6 Michael Monteon, *Chile in the Nitrate Era: The Evolution of Economic
Dependence, 1880–1930* (Madison: University of Wisconsin Press, 1982);
Thomas F. O'Brien, *The Nitrate Industry and Chile's Crucial Transition, 1870–
1891* (New York: New York University Press, 1982); Enrique Reyes Navarro, "Salitre chileno, mercado mundial y propaganda (1889–1916),"
Cuadernos de investigación social 11, no. 17 (March 1986): 181–214; Enrique Reyes Navarro, *Salitre de Chile: Apertura, inversión y mercado mundial,*

1880–1925 (Santiago: Universidad Católica Blas Cañas, 1994); Óscar Bermúdez, *Breve historia del salitre: Síntesis histórica desde sus orígenes hasta mediados del siglo 20* (Santiago: Ediciones Pampa Desnuda, 1987).

7 On nitrate and labor, see Julio Pinto Vallejos, *Trabajos y rebeldías en la pampa salitrera* (Santiago: Editorial Universidad de Santiago, 1998); Charles Bergquist, *Labor in Latin America: Comparative Essays on Chile, Argentina, Venezuela, and Colombia* (Stanford, Calif.: Stanford University Press, 1986); M. Angélica Apey Rivera, "El trabajo en la industria del salitre, 1880–1930," *Dimensión histórica de Chile* no. 2 (1985): 63–141; Manuel A. Fernández, *Proletariado y salitre en Chile, 1890–1910* (London: Monografías de Nueva Historia, 1988).

8 Arthur Stickell, "Migration and Mining: Labor in Northern Chile in the Nitrate Era, 1880–1930" (Ph.D. diss., Indiana University, 1979), 341, 310.

9 For example, see Oficina Lagunas to Intendente, 8 January 1896; Huanillos to Intendente, 4 July 1896; Pozo Almonte to Intendente, 30 June 1896, AIT-S, 331/1896 Subdelegaciones.

10 Security Police, Prefect of Iquique to Intendente, no. 139, 8 June 1897, AIT-S, 340/1897 Notas de la Policía. Regional government officials appealed for funds from Santiago and even from the public (Iquique Prefect to Intendente, no. 139, 8 June 1897, AIT-S, 340/1897 Notas de la Policía).

11 Marcelo Segall, "Biografía social de la ficha salario," *Revista Mapocho* 2, no. 2 (1964): 97–131.

12 Between 1912 and 1925, real wages dropped almost 30 percent (Stickell, "Migration and Mining," 341, 310).

13 For example, in March 1925 the Chilean Worker's Federation appealed to the president of the republic, demanding that the workers be given one month's warning before a nitrate camp suspended production, one month's salary as compensation for being laid off, free passage to the place from which they had been contracted, and a guarantee that the government would intervene to halt the companies' contracting (*enganche*) of workers from the south while the industry's fate remained uncertain (*El Tarapacá*, 29 March 1925, p. 5).

14 The nitrate and iodine (a byproduct) industry generated over half of the national fiscal coffers from 1880 until about 1920. According to the historian Óscar Bermúdez, the expansion of mining in this period shaped incipient finance capitalism, which became intertwined with profound socioeconomic changes in Chile, especially with regard to class relations as the possibility of rapid wealth challenged old social hierarchies. Nitrate rents financed the expansion of the state and, consequently, the multiplication of political parties and the rise of new value systems. See Bermúdez, *Breve historia*, 42–43.

15 Overproduction of nitrate in 1928–1929—by over a half million tons, according to Bermúdez—caused prices to fall and production to

cease. Production froze almost completely between 1930 and 1933. See ibid., 46.

16 Enrique Reyes Navarro, "El mercado del salitre y yodo en las décadas de 1920–1940: Un muerto que gozaba de buena salud," (unpublished manuscript, n.d.). Professor Reyes was exceedingly generous in sharing this and other invaluable materials.

17 On Chile's wealth, see Bermúdez, *Breve historia*, 42–43. On the 1879 War of the Pacific, see Robert N. Burr, *By Reason or Force: Chile and the Balance of Power in South America, 1830–1905* (Berkeley: University of California Press, 1965); William Sater, *Chile and the War of the Pacific* (Lincoln: University of Nebraska Press, 1986).

18 As a result of military campaigns spanning South America, Chile gained independence from Spain in 1817. Both local and international political commentators characterized Chile as having an early and relatively stable and centralized state structure. See Simon Collier, *Ideas and Politics of Chilean Independence, 1808–1833* (Cambridge: Cambridge University Press, 1967).

19 The degree to which economic nationalism figured in the Civil War of 1891 has been intensely debated. See, for example, Hernán Ramírez Necochea, *Balmaceda y la contrarevolución de 1891* (Santiago: Universitaria, 1972); Hernán Ramírez Necochea, *Historia del imperialismo en Chile* (Santiago: Empresa Editora Anstral, 1960); Harold Blakemore, *British Nitrates and Chilean Politics, 1886–1896: Balmaceda and North* (London: Athlone Press, 1974); Maurice Zeitlin, *The Civil Wars in Chile* (Princeton: Princeton University Press, 1984). A more recent study is Alejandro Soto Cárdenas, *Influencia Británica en el salitre: Origen, naturaleza y decandencia* (Santiago: Editorial Universidad de Santiago, 1998).

20 *El Obrero*, 21 December 1924, p. 4.

21 Hernán Castro Nordenflycht and Armando González Pizarro, *El proceso de San Gregorio por los sucesos del 3 Febrero de 1921, contexto de la defensa*, 2d ed. (Antofagasta, Chile: El Socialista, 1921). On the repression of the labor movement of that same time, see Agustín Torrealba Z., *Los subversivos: Alegato ante la Iltma: Corte de Apelaciones de Santiago en el proceso contra la sociedades I.W.W.* (Santiago: Imprenta Yara, 1921). For an account of San Gregorio from the point of view of the military a few years later, see Carlos Silva Vildósola, ed., *Las fuerzas armadas de Chile: Album histórico* 2d ed. (Santiago: Atenas, ca. 1935), 707. The nitrate companies in effect used the reminder of prior state repression as a lever to make the state repress labor again, reporting to the Chilean government that "the administrators have heard conversations between workers like, 'Here we're going to have [a situation] like "San Gregorio," but a "Great San Gregorio." We have to be united and if they don't respect us, we're not obliged to respect anyone. Down with capitalism'" (Gildemeister and Co. to the Intendente of Tarapacá, 14 March 1921, AIT-1, 1921/no. 16–1921/Ejército, Armada, Carabineros y Gobernación Marítima). At least one of the labor organizers,

José M. Ramírez, was subsequently arrested for allegedly attempting to mobilize memory as a tool for organizing (Memo, Cuerpo de Carabineros I. Grupo Escuadrón "Iquique" Tenencia "Huara" to Juzgado de Subdelegación, Huara, 16 March 1921, AIT-I, 1921/no. 16–1921/Ejército, Armada, Carabineros y Gobernación Maritima).

22 In the nitrate era the notion of violence as an integral part of an innate clash of interests between capital and labor informed the rhetorical place of state violence in political maneuvers. President Arturo Fortunato Alessandri Palma commanded that the local head of the police, the *carabineros*, make it clear, privately, to Recabarren that he would be "held personally responsible for whatever disorder or whatever hecatomb analogous to what occurred at San Gregorio. . . . Do not have any consideration whatsoever for Recabarren — treat him with special and effective rigor and count on my unconditional support" (Alessandri to Intendente of Tarapacá, 28 June 1923, AIT-I, 1920–1922–1923/Confidenciales Enviadas y Recibidas, Criptogramas y Telegramas Enviados y Recibidos).

23 Balmaceda to Intendente, 3 and 4 July 1890, AIT-S, vol. 206/Ministerio Interior 1890. The president sent a series of such telegrams on the 3rd and 4th of July trying to ascertain the truth of rumors heard in Santiago about the strike.

24 *La Libertad Electoral*, 15 June 1890, p. 2; *El Amigo del Pueblo*, 10 July 1890, p. 3.

25 *El Comercio* (Lima), 11 July 1890, pp. 3–4. The Peruvian paper reported a demonstration on 5 July of 5,000 workers in Plaza Prat (14 July 1890, p. 4).

26 Copy of extract from report to board of directors of the Nitrate Railways, 14 July 1890, PRO, FO 16/299.

27 "This concession . . . has only been adopted with a view to temporize with the strikers and rioters and cannot be long continued so that a renewal of disorder is apprehended" (Kennedy in Santiago to Marquis of Salisbury, London, no. 57, 21 July 1890, PRO, FO 16/299).

28 *El Ferrocarril*, 6 July 1890, p. 2; *El Comercio* (Lima), 14 July 1890, p. 4; *El Comercio* (Lima), 18 July 1890, p. 4; *El Comercio* (Lima), 21 July 1890, p. 4; *El Comercio* (Lima), 22 July 890, p. 2.

29 The company stores completely overtaken included Oficinas San Donato, Constancia, Ramírez, Tres Marías, Sacramento, and Estación de Zapiga (Intendente to Judge Vital Martínez Ramos, 29 September 1890, AIT-S, 183/1890 Libro de Oficios no. 2). Other oficinas affected included Zapiga, Peña Chica, La Palma, Primitiva, and San José (*El Amigo del Pueblo*, 10 July 1890, p. 3). In claims for damages against the Chilean state, British administrators later told of their fear and escape during the uprisings and how their appeals for assistance from the authorities went unattended (Affidavit: Charles Fern, 28 July 1890; statement of injury: George Oswald Lancashire, 15 July 1890; affidavit: Robert Jackson; affidavit: John Boyd Harvey; report: "British claims for losses incurred during Chilean riots and

strikes in July 1890," 20 February 1891, PRO, FO 16/299). As late as 19 July, workers in plants near Jazpampa went on strike (Riofríos to Gobernador Pisagua, 19 July 1890, AIT-S, vol. 191/Gobernación Pisagua).

30 Sergio Grez, "La huelga general de 1890," *Perspectivas* 5 (December 1990): 127–67.

31 By 7 July, Balmaceda began sending troops North and asking whether strikers wouldn't like to travel south (Balmaceda to Intendente, various telegrams on 7 July 1890, AIT-S, vol. 206/Ministerio Interior).

32 However, they reasoned that "the men who will be thrown out of employment will doubtless be looked after by the Government, and it is probable the majority of them will be utilized to swell the ranks of the army which is already beginning to assume respectable proportions" (*Chilean Times*, 24 January 1891, PRO, FO 16/264).

33 *El Comercio* (Lima), 26 February 1891, p. 2.

34 On the role of nitrate workers in the civil war and on the repression known as the Oficina Ramírez massacre, see Julio Pinto Vallejos, "El balmacedismo como mito popular: Los trabajadores de Tarapacá y la Guerra Civil de 1891," in *La Guerra Civil de 1891: Cien años hoy*, ed. Luis Ortega (Santiago: Universidad de Santiago de Chile, 1991), 109–26.

35 Peruvian accounts indicate that in early February workers in the camps around Pisagua began to rise up, and a protest in Pisagua's plaza was dispersed violently by the military, resulting in a number of injuries, deaths, and imprisonments. Laborers reconvened and commandeered trains to take them to the provincial capital, Iquique. Sergeant Marío Larraín intercepted them near Oficina Ramírez, where his troops were fired on by the workers, thus obliging him to use great force against them (*El Comercio* [Lima], 26 February 1891 [news dated 13 February], p. 2).

36 A key form of popular political expression in Chile, publications of popular poetry (*lira popular*) flourished from the mid-nineteenth century until the early decades of the twentieth century and spawned an ongoing, vibrant tradition of popular poetry in Chile. In her study of the figure of Balmaceda in popular poetry, Micaela Navarrete Araya shows how initial non-elite support for Balmaceda turned into a loathing that lasted through the end of the civil war, at which point he was transformed into a martyr for populist and nationalist politics due the political and economic debacle of the subsequent government (*Balmaceda en la poesía popular, 1886–1896* [Santiago: Centro de Investigaciones Diego Barros Arana, Dirección de Bibliotecas Archivos y Museos, 1993]). See also Marcela Orellana, "Lira popular: Un discurso entre la oralidad y la escritura," *Revista chilena de literatura* no. 48 (1996): 101–12; Diego Muñoz, ed., *Poesía popular chilena* (Santiago: Quimantú, 1972); Jorge Nuñez Pinto, "Versos por rebeldía: La protesta social en la poesía popular (siglos 19 y 20)," *Mapocho* no. 43 (1998): 127–44.

37 Jose Arroyo, [title cut off], no. 103, vol. 3, CA. The poem refused sympathy for the workers and seemed to support the government's use of

force. However, the last stanza offered a sarcastic twist: "The news arrived here / by a very fast telegram / every dude and every lady / bought the supplement." Arroyo concludes, "The news circulated / with much haste / and in less than a two and three / the press sold / more supplements to count / than it had ever sold before." This strange ending comments on the politics of reporting on the violent confrontation between populace and state in the North. The poet's rendering of the consumption of tragedy as titillation perhaps underscores the ways in which examples of President Balmaceda's abuse of power fueled intra-elite competition at the expense of further distancing the actions, passions, and sorrows of the people on the frontier.

38 Francisco Antonio Encina, *Historia de Chile* (Santiago: Sociedad Editora Revista VEA, 1988), 54:29–30.

39 "The Fighting in Tarapacá (by an Eyewitness), Iquique, February 25," *Chilean Times*, 7 March 1891, enclosure 1, in no. 2, PRO, FO 16/264. A telegraph in mid-March also reassuringly stated that in Pisagua many people had returned to the pampa to resume their labors (Gobernador Zavala to Intendente, no. 51, 14 March 1891, AIT-S, 220/1891 Subdelegación Pisagua).

40 The historian Enrique Reyes Navarro has critiqued the labor historiography of the general strike of 1890 and has argued that the strike and the repression of Oficina Ramírez formed two moments of "disencounter" between Balmaceda's regime and nitrate workers. See Enrique Reyes Navarro, "Los trabajadores del área salitrera, la huelga general de 1890 y Balmaceda," in *La Guerra Civil de 1891: Cien años hoy*, ed. Luis Ortega (Santiago: Universidad de Santiago de Chile, 1991), 85–108.

41 To a certain extent, the conjuncture of the civil war's centennial with the period of regime shift in the 1990s allowed Chilean historians to begin to dismantle indirectly the allegorical web binding Balmaceda, Allende, and recuperative history. However, the critical reevaluation of conflict and violence under state regimes — especially those that had been central to the Chilean Left's historical models of social transformation — magnified the post-1990 transition politics of melancholy. The refusal of heroic historical narratives has coincided with an absence of cathartic political imaginings of what might take their place. This vacuum of political creativity has reinforced an increasingly dominant, pro-pragmatist, cautionary narrative of a history of hopelessly utopian and ultimately failed emancipatory projects. In the absence of cathartic memory, melancholy tears away as illusory even the most cherished of political memories in a chronicle of failure and betrayal.

42 Serio A. González Miranda bases his account on a letter from the pampa dated 22 February 1891 and published in *El Nacional* ("La matanza en la Oficina Ramírez y la participación obrera e inglesa en la crisis de 1891," *Campus Iquique* [August 1991]: 3–8).

43 Julio Pinto Vallejos, "En el camino de la mancomunal: Organiza-

ciones obreras en la provincia de Tarapacá, 1880–1895" (unpublished manuscript, Universidad de Santiago de Chile, n.d.), 42.

44 MacKenna, Ministry of Exterior Relations to Intendente, 7 June 1890, AIT-S, 555/1890 a 1895 Min. Rel. Exteriores. Carlos Paz Soldán, *El Perú y la guerra civil en Chile* (Lima: Impresa Liberal de F. Masís y Ca., 1891).

45 Subdelegación de Tarapacá to Intendente, no. 39, 30 June 1890, AIT-1, 1890/197/Subdelegación Tarapacá; *El Amigo del Pueblo*, 8 July 1890, p. 3; Iquique Consul to La Paz, no. 41, 9 July 1890, AMRE-LPB, Cuerpo Consular Boliviano en el Brasil, Colombia y Chile 1889–1893/0021. Extensive discussion of this process took place in Lima's premier newspaper, *El Comercio*, from 4 June to 30 June 1890, and included remarkable accounts of commemorative acts held at various battlesites in Tarapacá.

46 Though abandoned by diplomats (who did not press for their repatriation), the remains of these Peruvian veterans (along with those who fought for Chile), preserved in the dry salt, have reappeared over the course of the twentieth-century, excavated by construction projects and by graverobbers searching for war relics to peddle. Simon Collier and William Sater note that Chilean war dead "received approximately the same veneration as that accorded a medieval leper": common soldiers, for example, "were dumped naked into graves with indecent haste." This practice, apparently notorious, even caused one Valparaíso workers' society to send delegates to insure respectful burial. See Simon Collier and William F. Sater, *A History of Chile, 1808–1994* (Cambridge: University of Cambridge Press, 1996), 138.

47 As in the case of Col. Eduardo Hurtado R., who was appointed police chief of Pisagua (Gobernación Pisagua, no. 830, 25 August 1893, AIT-S, 259/1892 Gobernación de Pisagua.

48 Reporting elite worries about the possibility of workers taking over Iquique in 1891, one Peruvian journalist observed, "The fearful and even those who aren't, repeatedly look toward the sea and then toward the mountains, above which the workers are gathering. Indescribable is the terror suffered by the women, and the fathers of families don't know what to do. Many have horrible visions, as it already seems that columns of bandits are coming to pillage and enact all other sorts of crimes" (*El Comercio* [Lima], 26 February 1891, p. 2). After the massacre of workers, these fears were validated further by the elite press: "The insurgents' plan was to arrive in Iquique to engage in pillage and sacking" (*El Comercio* [Lima], 26 February 1891, p. 2).

49 On Chile's reputation as a model republic, see excerpt from the *Chilean Times*, 24 January 1891, PRO, FO 16/264. The repression of 1925 emerged from a conjuncture of factors and interests: British (and other foreign interests') insistence that the Chilean government protect their nitrate investments; the long-standing territorial conflict between Chile and Peru, stemming from the War of the Pacific; and, most important, state and industrial fear of the strong labor movement, which, with its internationalist, class-based allegiances, had built a semiautonomous cultural

realm in the North. In this context different understandings of the past formed a particular conjuncture out of which emerged an unprecedented full-scale military operation. The position that the repression of 1925 resulted from shifting class alliances and the changing composition of the political system, which instigated progressive labor laws and necessitated foreign investment, was passionately argued by the British journalist Arnold Roller in "White Terror in Liberal Chile," *Nation* 121, no. 3145 (1925): 415–16.

50 David Bari M., *El ejército ante las nuevas doctrinas sociales: Trabajo premiado en el concurso del Club Militar de Chile* (Santiago: Talleres del estado Mayor General, 1922). Moisés Poblete Troncoso, *Legislación social obrera chilena (Recompilación de leyes y disposiciones vigentes sobre el trabajo y la prevision social)* (Santiago: Imprenta Santiago, 1924).

51 On the process of drafting the Constitution of 1925, see Federico G. Gil, *The Political System of Chile* (Boston: Houghton Mifflin, 1966), 58–59.

52 "Peru Prepares for War" (a story sent from Santiago) and "Peruvian Espionage in Tarapacá," *El Nacional*, 2 June 1925, pp. 2–4. General John J. Pershing and the U.S. marines had come to Northern Chile to oversee the proposed plebiscite. Their mission failed to moderate the conflict, and the rowdy marines merely contributed to the violent disorder in the zone. The Chilean press noted that labor troubles in the North began the day after U.S. President Calvin Coolidge's diplomatic failure in mediating the conflict between Peru and Chile (*El Tarapacá*, 9 June 1925, p. 2).

53 Consulate Antofagasta to British Legation in Santiago, 12 May 1925, PRO, FO 132/278.

54 The Chilean government fueled these rumors—for example, by claiming that Peru was involved in dynamite attacks against carabinero garrisons in Zapiga—having "encountered documentation that clearly corroborated the part that Peru . . . had in the frustrated uprising in the moments prior to the plebiscite" (*El Tarapacá*, 16 June 1925, p. 2).

55 For example, the state inspector's report on nitrate camp Oficina Gloria noted complete noncompliance with the social legislation, especially in the commercial monopoly of the company store, housing, and working conditions (4 January 1925, AIT-I, 1926/Inspección del Trabajo).

56 Copy of letter A. W. F. Duncan to D. Blair, Iquique, 7 May 1925, PRO, FO 132/278.

57 "They also seemed to be of the opinion that the troops which had been sent up to the pampa would not take action against them, and that if it came to the fatal moment of action having to be taken, the troops would go over to the men" (Confidential memo, Santiago to Foreign Office, 17 May 1925, and no. 142, 25 June 1925, PRO, FO 132/278).

58 *El Tarapacá*, 8 April 1925, p. 2.

59 The provincial junta of Antofagasta, having received a delegation from workers of Iquique, urged Santiago to set up strike arbitration (Telegraph from Secretary Junta Provincial Ocampos to Ministry of Interior,

10 April 1925, AN, 1/Ministerio del Interior/Providencias/8/1925/3400–3899/6340). With regard to the cavalry regiment, see Intendente to Local Nitrate Junta, no. 512; Intendente to Comandante General de Armas, no. 510; and Intendente to Gobernador Marítimo, no. 509, 9 April 1925, AIT-I, 1925/no. 7–1925/1930/Copiador Oficios.

60 The Ministry of Interior attempted to intervene by strictly regulating all meetings and gatherings in the nitrate regions (Decree no. 2823, 1 June 1925, AIT-I, 1925/no. 8–1925/1381/Ministerio 1° Semestre).

61 The nitrate companies even purchased extra insurance policies in anticipation of the strike (Confidential memo, Santiago to Foreign Office, 17 May 1925, and no. 142, 25 June 1925, PRO, FO 132/278). Gildemeister, on behalf of nitrate interests, reported that he had personally warned President Alessandri that "if their oficinas had to close down through labor troubles, it might be some considerable time before they opened up again. . . . [T]he Government would naturally suffer seriously in consequence" (A. W. F. Duncan to D. Blair, Iquique, 7 May 1925, PRO, FO 132/278). Also see Sir Thomas Hohler to Foreign Office, Despatch no. 97 (confidential) draft, 17 May 1925, PRO, FO 132/278; Telegram no. 20 from Graham, 5 June 1925, PRO, FO 132/278. Realizing the threat of the workers, the London directors announced on 1 June the closure of Oficina Santiago, giving as their justification the insecurity stemming from "the insolent attitude and open disrespect on the part of the workers" (*El Nacional*, 1 June 1925, p. 2).

62 Gobernador of Pisagua via Intendente to Santiago, translation of cryptogram, n.d.; telegraph from Pisagua to Intendente, 31 May 1925, AIT-I, 1924 y 1925/Confidenciales Recibidas y Enviadas.

63 Officials in Santiago explained that, meanwhile, they'd been telling the Worker's Federation in Santiago that workers were deported because of an antipatriotic campaign and because they had sold out to Peru (Telegram, Santiago to Intendente, 3 June 1925, AIT-I, 1924 y 1925/Confidenciales Recibidas y Enviadas). In a session presided over by President Alessandri himself, the cabinet decided that of the thirty-three "subversives" deported from Pisagua — they were held aboard ship for weeks, with some becoming so ill they required hospitalization — would be sent to the Isla Más Afuera of the Juan Fernández Islands, and the rest would be set free, their innocence having been indicated by a military report (*El Tarapacá*, 27 June 1925, p. 7; *El Tarapacá*, 26 June 1925, p. 5).

64 He had even investigated certain mining administrators whom he felt should be prosecuted just like the workers; he pronounced that if his stern example were followed throughout the country, all worker unrest would be taken care of (*El Tarapacá*, 23 June 1925, p. 1).

65 The governor justified the treatment of "communist and Peruvian leaders," saying, "The vast majority were deported, they had been sold out by Peruvian gold and fooled by false Soviet apostles even to the extreme of getting indignant before the national flag." The prisoners deported from

Pisagua were first sent on the ship *Mapocho*, whose crew refused to cooperate in the deportation but were forced to sail by the military guards. See *El Tarapacá*, 9 June 1925, p. 7. Similarly, the crew of the ship *Antofagasta*, which docked in Valparaíso, were arrested and removed by the navy for having threatened their bosses. The press in the capital also attributed this incident to merchant marine solidarity with workers in the North (*El Tarapacá*, 4 June 1925, p. 5).

66 *El Nacional*, 2 June 1925, p. 2; *El Tarapacá*, 3 June 1925, p. 2.

67 A telegram to the British Foreign Office reported, "The Nitrate [Producers] Association glad that crisis has come" (Telegram no. 21, 5 June 1925, PRO, FO 132/278).

68 "The workers of Oficina Argentina" section of the F.O.CH. to the administrator of Oficina Argentina, 3 June 1925, PRO, FO 132/278.

69 *El Nacional*, 17 June 1925, p. 7. Iquique's Club de la Unión collected funds for the widows of the two sentries killed in Alto San Antonio (Intendente to the President of the Club de la Unión, 22 June 1925, AIT-1, 1913–1925/no. 1–1913/1925/Copiador de Cartas del Ministerio). Also on the deaths of the two police, see Coronel Muñoz Sepúlveda, "25.-Sucesos de Alto San Antonio y La Coruña (4 de Junio de 1925)," in *Oficial de carabineros y su misión*, 2d ed. (Santiago: n.p., 1964), 406–10.

70 *El Nacional*, 6 June 1925, p. 2.

71 *El Nacional*, 8 June 1925, p. 2.

72 This version was related to me in interviews and can also be found in Juan Cobo, *Yo vi nacer y morir los pueblos salitreros* (Santiago: Quimantú, 1971), 87–89.

73 A practice mentioned often in oral accounts and in some texts, where it was sometimes noted as having originated with La Coruña. See Guillermo Kaempffer Villagran, *Asi sucedió 1850–1925: Sangrientes episodios de la lucha obrera en Chile* (Santiago: Arancibia, 1962), 10, 257.

74 According to the pro-government press, "After the managers of La Coruña had fled . . . the revolutionaries sang in chorus the *International*, standing out among the thousand voices, the voices of women and children" (*El Nacional*, 8 June 1925, p. 2).

75 Telegram no. 18 from Graham, 4 June 1925, PRO, FO 132/278. The southern and northern nitrate sectors were demarcated by the nitrate railway as it tracked into the desert directly above (and roughly at the same latitude as) Iquique. Early reports indicated that workers had taken over numerous camps besides La Coruña, including Esmeralda, Resurrección, Pontevedra, Barrenechea, Argentina, Felisa, Santiago, Mauroussia, Santa Lucia (Telégrafos del Estado from Intendente Amengual to Ministry of Interior, 5 June 1925, AN, 1/Ministerio del Interior/Providencias/11/1925/4900–6099/6343).

76 "What has happened in two days in Tarapacá is unprecedented in this country's history, which has been distinguished above all by the order, patriotism, and respect of its citizens" (*El Nacional*, 6 June 1925, p. 2).

77 *El Nacional*, 12 June 1925, p. 2.

78 *El Tarapacá*, 4 June 1925, p. 2; *El Nacional*, 4 June 1925, p. 2. President Alessandri sent a telegram requesting special protection for the "American" camps Peña Grande and Paposo, saying that he would regard any incident in those places as a "personal disgrace" (Telegram, Alessandri to Intendente Amengual, 5 June 1925, AIT-1, 1925/no. 8–1925/1381/Ministerio 1° Semestre/).

79 *El Tarapacá*, 19 June 1925, p. 5. The publication of the entire telegram was remarkable both in the degree to which the state in crisis felt compelled to account for the use of violence and in the wide dissemination of this official version of events.

80 Ibid., p. 2. There was also a general purge of troublemakers from various nitrate camps such as La Granja (ibid., p. 6). On the severity of punitive action pursued by the Chilean state, British observers noted, "It appears that a considerable number of people lost their lives, according to some estimates over 300, and that a large number of those who were considered undesirable by the authorities had been shot after a trial by court martial." From the British perspective, "the Chilean Government have jumped rather too rapidly from an extreme tenderness towards Communist agitation to one of extreme and violent hostility, a process which is always more liable to produce injustice and exaggerated severity, than a continuous policy combining the iron hand and the velvet glove." See memo no.143, British Legation, Santiago to Foreign Office, 25 June 1925, PRO, FO 132/278.

81 Oral-history accounts recall how the prisoners were taken from the pampa by train, unloaded at the city's water tanks, and marched from there to the velodrome. See also *El Tarapacá*, 12 June 1925, p. 2. The military prosecutor Don Arturo Picón was sent north to preside over the military investigation and prosecution of over 700 prisoners guarded by the regiment Granaderos (*El Tarapacá*, 25 June 1925, p. 2).

82 *El Nacional*, 12 June 1925, p. 2.

83 In declaring a state of siege in the northern provinces of Tarapacá and Antofagasta, President Alessandri repeated his decree of September 1924 that all threats to the "interior security of the State" would be submitted to military jurisdiction (Telegram, Alessandri to Intendente, Decree no. 2860, 5 June 1925, AIT-1, 1925/no. 8–1925/ 1381/Ministerio 1° Semestre). Some prisoners awaited processing until as late as September 1925, and the regional government relied on the Chilean state and the charity of the nitrate companies for the funds necessary to feed the prisoners and to settle bills relating to the cost of hosting several regiments (Intendente's decree [authorized spending of the 1,500 pesos per day allotted by the Ministry of the Interior], 17 June 1925, AIT-1, 1925/Copiador Decretos, p. 159).

84 Decree no. 2868, 12 June 1925, AIT-1, 1925/no. 3–1925/Copiador de Oficios, p. 218.

85 *El Nacional*, 6 June 1925, p. 2. The authorities worried in the weeks

before the campaign whether the military conscripts would obey orders to fire on workers. In addition, earlier reports of fraternizing between workers and some units already in the region had worried both officials and nitrate producers (A. W. F. Duncan to D. Blair, Iquique, 7 May 1925, PRO, FO 132/278). Authorities were on alert for possible political organizing among troops and police in the nitrate region. A 1920 missive from the minister of the interior to the intendentes and *gobernadores* of the country relayed the minister of war's anxiety over possible radicalization of troops, especially those patrolling at railway stations (Circular reservada no. 5, 26 July 1920, AIT-I, 1920/no. 21–1920/1228/Ministerio del Interior). Workers themselves hoped that the troops would refuse to fire on them and would even join them (Messrs Gibbs and Co., Iquique, to the Whitehall Trust, Ltd., London, 12 June 1925; A. W. F. Duncan, Iquique, to D. Blair, Valparaíso, 7 May 1925, PRO, FO 132/278).

86 *El Nacional*, 19 June 1925, p. 2.

87 *El Tarapacá*, 9 June 1925, p. 5; *El Tarapacá*, 27 June 1925, p. 7; *El Tarapacá*, 12 June 1925, p. 2; Telegram, Minister of Interior Jaramillo to Intendente, 9 June 1925, AIT-I, 1925/no. 8–1925/381/Ministerio 1° Semestre.

88 *El Tarapacá*, 24 June 1925, p. 2; *El Nacional*, 24 June 1925, p. 2.

89 *El Nacional*, 6 June 1925, p. 2.

90 *El Nacional*, 8 June 1925, p. 2.

91 Such propaganda stressed workers' inability to manage either their liquor or such a powerful tool of progress as explosives. Regarding drink, see *El Tarapacá*, 20 June 1925, p. 2. Regarding dynamite, see *El Tarapacá*, 30 June 1925, p. 2.

92 "The Chilean Worker," *Cuestiones Sociales*, 3 November 1921 (vol. 1, no. 36), sec. "National Culture," p. 1. At the high point of worker militant action, the governor of Pisagua wrote to the nitrate administrators and the regional government to solicit support for the Pisagua newspaper *La Ley* as a vehicle for a press campaign against communist and socialist influences (Gobernador of Pisagua to Intendente of Tarapacá and various Oficina administrators, 5 June 1925, AIT-I, Gobernación de Pisagua Año 1925). Another newspaper of this sort was *La Razón*, published in Huara, whose "altruistic" goal was to "counteract the Communist campaign and attempt to maintain harmony between capital and labor" (Letter, Sr. A. Arellano C., Huara, to E. J. B. del P., 25 June 1925, AIT-I, 1925/no. 3–1925/ Copiador de Oficios, p. 293). More specifically, "The painful events occurring on the nitrate pampa, now having happily ended, have provoked the natural and logical commentaries, especially in workers' circles, many of which — shamefully — are responsible for the repression ordered by the Supreme Government" (Letter, Sr. A. Arellano C., Huara, to E. J. B. del P., 25 June 1925). The newspaper highlighted its own place in asserting order and reason: "But now that such commentaries are the daily bread, it is precisely that the worker can understand perfectly that it was his fallen

companions who created their own disgrace" (*La Razón*, 18 June 1925 [vol. 1, no. 2], p. 1).

93 At least one protest of the massacre appears to have taken place in Argentina (protest flyer, Agrupación Anarquista Vervo Nuevo, "Contra la reacción en Chile: Mitin de protesta," August 1925, MN, 378, folder 4).

94 "Shame!" *La Voz del Paria*, 7 June 1925, p. 3. While only traces of these alternative accounts persisted, details from official versions — for example, the assertion that "Commissar Garrido" used women as a shield against the military to promote a full-scale insurrection — appeared as late as 1936. See Carlos A. Alfaro Calderón, *Reseña histórica de la provincia de Tarapacá* (Iquique: La Semana Tarapaqueña, 1936), 58–61. I explore the gendering of labor and military conflict in this period in "Desired States: Gender, Sexuality, and Political Culture in Chile" (unpublished manuscript, n.d.).

95 Chilean workers, rather than being protagonists with their own vision of the future, were the victims of foreign agitators (Bolshevik and Peruvian) or were so influenced by alcohol and other vices that their actions were the result of inchoate aggression.

96 Cristomo Pizarro credits the repression of 1925 with nullifying any positive effect which the labor legislation of 1924 and the Constitution of 1925 might have had on labor relations in Chile (*La huelga obrera en Chile* [Santiago: SUR, 1986], 96). The intendente of Tarapacá and leading citizens attempted to take advantage of the national attention by lobbying cabinet ministers who visited the North and by sending a citizens commission, which included the mayor of Iquique, to the capital to make local concerns clear to the president (Telegram, Intendente Amengual to the Minister of the Interior, no. 279, 28 June 1925, 1; Ministerio del Interior; Providencias; 13; 1925; 6900–7999; 6325, AIT-S).

97 Reforms would "give workers' life in the nitrate industry a character more humane, just, cordial and friendly, we might say, to eliminate from it all that is violent and bitter" (Ministerio Higiene, Asistencia, Previsión Social y Trabajo, Iquique, "Memoria de la Inspección Regional del Trabajo de Tarapacá — 1 Enero de 1926 hasta el 14 Marzo de 1927 — Para la Intendencia de la Provincia," p. 9, AIT-1, no. 13–1926/Memorias Oficinas).

98 The state made plans to build up the militarized police contingent by providing them with the latest in military hardware, trucks, and machine guns, so they might better control the region. One article documented the arrival of seventy-five carabineros to create a new squadron for the northern sector (*El Tarapacá*, 25 June 1925, p. 2). As minister of war and later as president, Ibáñez del Campo promoted a militarized police force as a foil for the military proper; this may account for the fact that, despite the military occupations of Tarapacá during the nitrate era, the police had a worse reputation than the military among workers (Carlos Maldonado Prieto, "Los Carabineros de Chile: Historia de una policía militarizada," *Ibero-Americana* 20, no. 3 [1990]: 3–31).

99 As president, Ibáñez del Campo applied this strategy throughout the country, but his tactics may have been influenced by his own experiences as police prefect of Tarapacá (1919–1923) and as minister of war during the labor upheavals of the mid-1920s (Alessandri/Ministerio del Interior to Intendente of Tarapacá, copy of decree no. 4855, 29 December 1920, AIT-1, 1920/no. 21–1920/1228/Ministerio del Interior). Thus, like General Pinochet, Ibáñez del Campo served in Tarapacá before assuming a national role. See the full text of Ibáñez del Campo's internal memo to the carabineros from 24 June 1925, in which he explained his interpretation of the workers' movement and its connection to issues of nationalism and education, specifically with regard to the influence of foreign schoolteachers (Carlos Silva Vidósola, *Las fuerzaz armadas de Chile: Álbúm histórico*, 2d ed. [Santiago: Atenas, ca. 1935], 994–1004). On the question of public schooling and nationalism, see Patrick Barr-Melej, *Reforming Chile* (Chapel Hill: University of North Carolina Press, 2001), 192.

100 Frederick Nunn, *Chilean Politics, 1920–1931* (Albuquerque: University of New Mexico Press, 1970); Frederick Nunn, *The Military in Chilean History: Essays on Civil-Military Relations, 1810–1973* (Albuquerque: University of New Mexico Press, 1976). Also central were the wars against the indigenous peoples of the south.

101 The tense negotiation of civil and military cooperation in public holidays appeared in a document from 1914 in which the regional military commander complained of breaches in protocol for national independence-day celebrations and emphasized that while the intendente had the right to call on the military for a given purpose, the execution of this request should be left to the discretion of the armed forces themselves. Comandante Jeneral de Armas to the Intendente, no. 449, 16 September 1914, AIT-1, 1914/no. 12–1914/Ejército y Armada y Carabineros.

102 Prat's name and figure dominate the urban geography of Iquique (see William Sater, *The Heroic Image in Chile: Arturo Prat, Secular Saint* [Berkeley: University of California Press, 1973]). Yet, virtually all military engagements since 1879 have been internal wars, and the military has found it more difficult to incorporate these internal conflicts into the rhetoric of military honor and official memory in general.

103 Lynch to Ministry of Public Instruction, no. 88, pp. 51–53, 17 July 1880, AIT-1, 1881/vol. 1/Jefatura Política de Tarapacá.

104 Comdte. Jeneral de Armas to Intendente, no. 152, 28 April 1914, AIT-1, 1914/no. 12–1914/Ejército y Armada y Carabineros; Comdte. Jeneral de Armas to Intendente of Tarapacá, no. 326, 10 August 1922, and no. 367, 1 September 1922, AIT-1, 1922/no. 26–1922/Comandante Jeneral de Armas.

105 Ministry of Public Instruction, Decree no. 5582, 31 October 1921, transmitted as Intendente's decree no. 3210, 6 December 1921, AIT-1, 1926/Visitación Escuelas.

106 Telegram, Moneda/Ministerio de Instrucción Pública to Intendente

of Tarapacá, 23 May 1925, AIT-1, 1925–1926/1–1925/1926/Ministerio de Instrucción Pública; also *El Nacional*, 9 June 1925, p. 4.

107 The political activism of Emilio Uzcátegui, an Ecuadorian teacher at Iquique's Commercial Institute, provoked special wrath: "Persons entrusted with the education of tomorrow's men should be fundamentally Chilean and absolutely patriotic" (*El Nacional,* 10 June 1925, pp. 2, 4); Emilio Uzcátegui was said to have authored pamphlets found in the offices of the newspaper *El Despertar*, and other materials found there were said to implicate various teachers (*El Tarapacá*, 10 June 1925, p. 2).

108 Confidential from Tarapacá to Santiago, no. 1665, 19 November 1926, AIT-1, 1926/no. 28–1926/Confidenciales Enviadas y Recibidas.

109 Puga to Plebiscite Office of Tarapacá, no. 681, 30 June 1926, AIT-1, 1926/no. 28–1926/Confidenciales Enviadas y Recibidas.

110 "Memoria 1926" Visitación Provincial de Educación Primaria to the Director General de Educación Primaria, Santiago, p. 15, 31 January 1927, AIT-1, 1926/no. 13–1926/1926/Memorias Oficinas Públicas, AIT-1.

111 For example, the Emma Venegas Puga incident. See Petition, Citizens of Alto San Antonio to Intendente, 20 September 1926; Memo, Military officer and subdelegado of La Noria to Intendente, 18 September 1926; Memo, Schools supervisor to Intendente, 27 September 1926, AIT-1, 1926/Visitación de Escuelas. A large proportion of teachers were women; on teacher's unions at this time, see José Pablo Silva, "White-collar Revolutionaries: Middle-class Unions and the Rise of the Chilean Left, 1918–1938" (Ph.D. diss., University of Chicago, 2000).

112 *El Tarapacá*, 19 June 1925, p. 5.

113 Created in the North in 1923, Boy Scouts and Girl Guides [in English] also became resources in civic education, as when the provincial primary-education supervisor sent the scouts of the Brigada Arturo Prat, acting as representatives from Iquique, to the pampa to "stimulate the development of civic and patriotic duties among schoolchildren" and to visit the site of the Battle of San Francisco, which took place during the War of the Pacific (Memo, Visitación Provincial de Educación Primaria to Intendente, no. 286, 18 November 1926, AIT-1, 1926, Visitación de Escuelas).

114 Carl Solberg, *Immigration and Nationalism: Argentina and Chile, 1890–1914* (Austin: University of Texas, 1970).

115 Oreste Plath, "Epopeya del 'roto' chileno," in *Autorretrato de Chile*, ed. Nicomedes Guzmán (Santiago: Editorial Zigzag, n.d.), 133–47. The term is often given dual etymologies, both of which are, not incidentally, mestizo: first, from a Qhuecha and Auracanian term for a fighter; second, from a term applied to colonizing Spaniards who were often otherwise destitute adventurers. *Roto chileno* has furthermore had a series of variations and applications, including one for women who fought in the late-nineteenth-century wars and one for Chilean men who followed the export of Chilean wheat to the California gold rush. See also J. Rafael Carranza, *La Batalla de Yungay: Monumento al roto chileno (recuerdos históricos)* (Santiago:

Imprenta Cultura, 1939); Roberto Hernandez C., *El roto chileno: Bosqujo histórico de actualidad* (Valparaíso: Imprenta San Rafael, 1929); Mariano Latorre, "El huaso y el gaucho en la poesia popular," in *Memorias y otras confidenciales*, by Mariano Latorre, ed. Alfonso Calderón (Santiago: Editorial Andres Bello, 1971). For an analysis of Joaquín Edwards Bello's 1920 novel *El Roto*, see Barr-Melej, *Reforming Chile*, 123–24.

116 The historian Sergio Grez T. pushes this point further, arguing that this "psychological revolution" was one of the key factors in the "geometric progression . . . in revindicative movements of artisans, workers, and miners" ("Balmaceda y el movimiento popular," in *La Época de Balmaceda*, by Sergio Villalobos R., Eduardo Devés V., Bernardo Subercaseàux S., Gerardo Martínez R., Sergio Grez T., and Ricardo Couyoumdjiam B. Santiago: Dirección de Bibliotecas Archivos y Museos, 1992), 80.

117 Óscar Bermúdez, "El Dr. Nicolás Palacios y la industria del salitre," *Revista chilena de historia y geografía* 136 (1968): 209–49.

118 Palacios also advocated against renewed efforts by the state to draw colonists to work the nitrate fields of the North and the agricultural fields of the south that had been accessed by the military campaign against indigenous peoples at the end of the nineteenth century. Palacios worried about racial contamination by Asiatic people contracted to work in the North and about the "cultural" aberration posed by Italians. While more favorable toward the German colonies of the south, Palacios complained that they had isolated themselves too much. He also warned against the policy of using retired military officers as colonists and civil bureaucrats, as he felt that the state should strictly limit the purview of a properly professionalized military. For a feminist critique of the ideology of mestizaje in Chile, see Sonia Montecino, *Madres y huachos: Alegorías del mestizaje chileno* (Santiago: Editorial Cuarto Propio, Ediciones CEDEM, 1991).

119 Nicolás Palacios, *Raza chilena: Libro escrito por un chileno y para los chilenos* (1904; repr., Santiago: Ediciones Colchagua, 1988). Palacios's treatise was first published the same year that a congressional commission traveled to the nitrate region to document work conditions and the aspirations of labor organizations. The next edition appeared in 1918, at the height of the mobilization of the Patriotic Leagues. The most recent facsimile edition was sponsored by internationally infamous arms manufacturer Carlos Cardoen (whose interest in the North was grounded in his cluster-bomb plant there). In his prologue, Cardoen claimed indirect kinship with Palacios and ideological kinship as an advocate of national capitalists. His mnemonic calling on Palacios is fascinating: Chileans should reread Palacios so they might learn "to look in the mirror with love" and appreciate the bountiful "opportunities for material wealth" in "the length and width of the fatherland." Any social, political, or economic problems had their root only "in mental mediocrity," and Chile's future offered limitless opportunity if Chileans would "habituate themselves to think in terms of triumph and not of failure" (xi).

120 "The workers" to the Intendente of Tarapacá, n.d., AIT-I, 1918/ Huelga de Pisagua.

121 Chilean workers' xenophobia and racism cannot be completely attributed to the success of the state's effort to instill national memory and foment nationalist divisions. Further research remains to be done on the question of the extent to which national subjectivity was generated by migration to the North — as a frontier zone in which by definition questions of national distinctions flourish — by non-elites, either as soldiers in the War of the Pacific and/or as nitrate workers.

The now classic debate over whether the War of the Pacific forged a national subject for Andean peasants should be extended to Chile as well. See Heraclio Bonilla, "The Indian Peasantry and 'Peru' during the War with Chile," in *Resistance, Rebellion, and Consciousness in the Andean Peasant World*, ed. Steve J. Stern (Madison: University of Wisconsin Press, 1987), 213–18; Florencia Mallon, "Nationalist and Anti-state Coalitions in the War of the Pacific," in *Resistance, Rebellion, and Consciousness in the Andean Peasant World*, ed. Steve J. Stern (Madison: University of Wisconsin Press, 1987), 219–31. For a study of the nationalizing effects of transnational labor migration, see Deborah Cohen, "Bordering Modernities" (unpublished manuscript, n.d.).

122 It has been claimed that the saying "palomeando rotos" was coined by soldiers and nitrate-company sentries at the time of La Coruña to describe the way in which workers (rotos, meaning "bums") — either fleeing across the nitrate-mining trenches or hovering at the edge of graves they'd been forced to dig for themselves — flailed their arms like the wings of a dove (*paloma*) when, having been shot, they fell into the trenches. This practice of shooting workers was mentioned in oral accounts and in some texts, where it was sometimes noted as having originated with La Coruña. See Guillermo Kaempffer Villagran, *Asi sucedió 1850–1925: Sangrientes episodios de la lucha obrera en Chile* (Santiago: Arancibia, 1962), 10, 257.

123 On the history of May Day commemorations in Chile, see Mario Garces's and Pedro Milos's popular education booklet from the period of mass mobilization against the dictatorship, *10 mayo 1886–1986: Los sucesos de Chicago y el 10 de Mayo en Chile* (Santiago: ECO, 1986).

124 Intendente of Tarapacá to Ministry of Exterior Relations, 30 April 1920 (copy of a memo originally sent 9 November 1918), AIT-I, 1920–1922–1923/Confidenciales Enviadas y Recibidas, Criptogramas y Telegramas Enviados y Recibidos.

125 Ministry of Interior to Intendente of Tarapacá, no. 195, 6 February 1920, AIT-I, 1920/no. 20/1229/Ministerio del Interior. In a telegram to the intendente, the Ministry of Interior informed that the minister of the navy had ordered a warship to stand ready to back up the government's demand that Peruvian administrators be dismissed (Telégrafos del Estado, 4 February 1920, AIT-I, 1920/no. 20/1229/Ministerio del Interior.

126 Confidential telegram, Ministry of Exterior Relations to the Inten-

dente of Tarapacá, 27 December 1922, AIT-1, 1924 y 1925/Confidenciales Recibidas y Enviadas. The intendente of Tarapacá detailed movement of Peruvians from the interior to the pampa and urged that Santiago send two officers and forty-seven carabineros to Iquique, as troops already in the nitrate zone were occupied with strikes (Intendente Amengual of Tarapacá to Intendente Barcelo Caena, [reserved copy], n.d., AIT-1, 1924 y 1925/ Confidenciales Recibidas y Enviadas). For transcribed oral-history excerpts dealing with the Patriotic Leagues, see Sergio González Miranda, "De la solidaridad a la xenofobia: Anexo," in *A los 90 años de los sucesos de la Escuela Santa María de Iquique*, ed. Sergio González Miranda (Santiago: Lom Ediciones, 1998), 109–17.

127 *El Tarapacá*, 28 June 1925, p. 5; *El Nacional*, 3 July 1925, p. 1. Peter DeShazo also comments on the connection between the La Coruna events and a resurgence of the Patriotic Leagues in Chile (*Urban Workers and Labor Unions in Chile*, 227). For a brief account of the Patriotic Leagues in the North, see Sergio González Miranda, Carlos Maldonado Prieto, and Sandra McGee Deutsch, "Ligas Patrióticas," in *Revista de Investigaciones Científicas y Tecnológicas*, Serie Ciencias Sociales 2 (Iquique: Universidad Arturo Prat, 1993), 37–49. Regarding league activity in the southern cone, see Sandra McGee Deutsch, *Counterrevolution in Argentina, 1900–1932: The Argentine Patriotic League* (Lincoln: University of Nebraska Press, 1986).

128 Confidential memo, Tte. Crl. Arturo Puga to Intendente, no. 174, 5 June 1925, AIT-1, 1924 y 1925/Confidenciales Recibidas y Enviadas.

129 Anisate Camacho (citizen of Pozo Almonte), interview by author and Patricio Rivera O., Pozo Almonte, Chile, February 1994. Another Northern Chilean, Benito Guzmán, explained that he had been working at Oficina La Coruña but had left just before the strike; when he returned to collect his possessions during the military occupation, the soldiers searched his trunk of belongings and told him that he was lucky they hadn't found any incriminating labor propaganda and to leave without looking around or looking back (interview by author, Iquique, Chile, March 1993).

130 This prophecy was pronounced by the nineteenth-century statesman and historian B. Vicuña Mackenna. Anticipating Nicolas Palacios, Martínez posited in his novel that the opposed interests of Chilean workers and their "gringo" bosses would create a new breed of Chilean: el pampino, the man of the nitrate plains (*La vida en la pampa: Historia de un esclavo* [Iquique: Biblioteca del Trabajador, Imprenta El Jornal, 1895]).

131 See the report by the director of the state's Oficina del Trabajo in Moises Poblete Troncoso and Oscar Alvarez Andrews, *Legislación Social Obrera Chilena* (Santiago: Imprenta Santiago-Esmeralda, 1924), 46–47.

132 *La Agitación*, March 1905, p. 2; *La Agitación*, 9 September 1905, p. 4.

133 For example, a memo from a military officer on the pampa to the intendente related that two Bolivian workers from the Oficina Aguada had been subjected to a whipping by a carabinero and an army officer. The

intendente was notified in case the Bolivian consul were to decide to pursue the matter. No. 308, 4 August 1917, AIT-I, 1917/no. 32–1917/1079/Ejército y Armada.

134 Former resident of the pampa, interview by author, Iquique, Chile, January 1994.

135 Sorrow would diminish the glory of the new angels; sarcasm thus provided an outlet for grief. "What a glorious little angel / that's seated on high, / don't let your guard down with him / and give yourself a fright!" (A. Acevedo Hernandez, *Los cantores populares chilenos* [Santiago: Editorial Nascimento, 1933], 37–38). For a history of angel wakes from colonial to contemporary Brazil, their origins in Iberia, and their spread across South America, see Nancy Scheper Hughes, *Death without Weeping* (Berkeley: University of California Press, 1992), 416–23. My understanding of nitrate-era violence draws heavily on insights she makes on everyday forms of violence in contemporary Brazil.

136 Stickell, "Migration and Mining," 171–72. Stickell also reports that, across Chile, 286 children under one year of age died for every 1,000 births in 1913. Measles and whooping cough took a heavy toll along with epidemics of diseases such as tuberculosis and pneumonia.

137 Ministerio Higiene, Asistencia, Previsión Social y Trabajo, Iquique, "Memoria de la Inspección Regional del Trabajo de Tarapacá — 1 Enero de 1926 hasta el 14 Marzo de 1927 — Para la Intendencia de la Provincia," p. 9, AIT-I, no. 13–1926/Memorias Oficinas Públicas.

138 As the caliche of higher nitrate content was used up, the need for more efficient production pressed on the industry. The Guggenheims, a family of powerful American industrialists, began to invest in Chilean nitrate in 1923, when they developed a markedly more efficient processing system. In 1931, under political pressure from the United States, including a visit by President Herbert Hoover in 1928, and economic pressure from U.S. banks, from which Chile desperately required loans after the crash of 1929 decimated the entire Chilean economy, the nitrate industry was consolidated in a joint venture between the Chilean government, British interests, and the Guggenheims (who retained operative control): the Chilean Nitrate Company, commonly known as Cosach. In 1925 there were 70 companies with 96 plants employing 36,000 workers; by 1932 there was only a single firm with 11 plants and 8,000 employees. Initially, the increased efficiency, lack of export duties, and international suppliers' cartel paid off; however, with the value of contributions inflated, Cosach could not support the debt imposed by its builders. The nitrate industry dwindled over the next forty years, as copper mining, primarily in the region directly south of Tarapacá, assumed epic proportions in the Chilean economy. See Thomas F. O'Brien, " 'Rich beyond the Dreams of Avarice': The Guggenheims in Chile," *Business History Review* 63 (spring 1989): 122–59.

139 "Alguien pregunta, acaso, por los obreros asesinados / en la Coruña

o en San Gregorio, ¿dónde quedaron? / En cambio, sonrientes, persua-
sivos, como disculpándose . . . / nos dicen: Se acabó el salitre, hermano, se
acabó la pampa, / [. . .] Mi tierra es un paisaje arrepentido en medio de
una / historia heroica" (Mario Bahomonde, "Les vengo a contar," *Tierra y
sol: Homenaje a Mario Bahomonde* [Antofagasta, Chile: Colecciones Hacia
La Tierra, El Hombre, La Poesía, 1980], 22–23).

4 Song of the Tragic Pampa

Sources for the epigraphs at the beginning of the chapter: "Vamos mujer,
andemos hacia el mar . . . / Dicen que Iquique es grande como un salar. . . ."
(Luis Advis, *Santa María de Iquique: Cantata popular* [Santiago: Alerce
Producciones Fonográficas, 1993 (1973)]); and Taller Nueva Historia:
Pedro Milos, *Cuadernos de historia popular: serie historia del movimiento obrero*
(Santiago: Centro de Estudios del Trabajo CETRA/CEAL, 1983), 23.

1 José Bengoa, "Presentación," in *La huelga obrera en Chile*, by Crisostomo Pizarro (Santiago: SUR, 1986), 5. Similarly, historian Juan Panadés
Vargas asserts, "There is no doubt that the great 1907 strike and its epilogue
with the massacre at the Santa María school symbolized the worker's
movement in its struggle for better living conditions. . . . It also shows a
State unaware of the social problematic and that faced with workers' demands countered only with repression, that in its view of the times was a
consequence of its function to ensure public security" (243). Panadés suggests that the state's repressive response was due to the fact that the labor
movement had not developed a "juridical-institutional frame that would
validate it before the law," an assessment that still assumes that the only
reasonable path for workers was the pursuit of greater incorporation
within the nation-state via the law (244). See Juan Panadés Vargas, "Algunas reflexiones sobre la industria salitrera: Los sucesos de la Escuela
Santa María, un caso conmovedor," in *A los 90 años de los sucesos de la Escuela
Santa María de Iquique*, ed. Sergio González Miranda (Santiago: Lom
Ediciones, 1998), 237–45.

2 Enrique Reyes Navarro, "Los trabajadores del área salitrera, la huelga
general de 1890 y Balmaceda," in *La Guerra Civil de 1891: Cien años hoy*, ed.
Luis Ortega (Santiago: Universidad de Santiago de Chile, 1991), 85–108.
Manuel Fernández charts the demands of the 1890 strike alongside those of
the 1907 strike to show just how little workers' conditions had improved
during nearly thirty years (*Proletariado y salitre en Chile, 1890–1910* [Lon-
don: Monografías de Nueva Historia, Institute of Latin American Studies,
1988], 42).

3 Fernández, *Proletariado y salitre*, 57, 59.

4 Julio Pinto Vallejos, "El anarquismo Tarapaqueño y la huelga de 1907:
¿Apóstoles o líderes?" in *A los 90 años de los sucesos de la Escuela Santa María de Iquique*, ed. Sergio González Miranda (Santiago: Lom Ediciones,
1998), 259–90.

5 Fernandez, *Proletariado y salitre*, 63. In Fernandez's excellent, careful, and concise study of the strike, which he based on British government and nitrate-company records, Chilean state records, and workers' publications, he recounts how workers at the mining camp Buenaventura had decided to join those in Iquique but were surrounded by military forces. Workers negotiated for their wives and children to leave, since the strike had caused food supplies on the pampa to run low. In spite of the state's agreement, the military fired on the workers as they were preparing the train for the voyage; seven people were killed and many more were wounded. Fernández points out that the arrival of these corpses in Iquique the day before the Santa María massacre was an ominous portent and gave strike leaders all the more reason to fear that a move outside of town would be a prelude to repression (61). Given the intransigence of the intendente, strike leaders refused to attend a meeting at his office on the grounds that all communication should be formalized in writing. Fernández suggests that had the strike leaders attended the meeting, the intendente would most likely have followed state orders to arrest them and seclude them on the warship (62).

6 "Con chilenos venimos, con chilenos morimos." See Elías Lafertte, *Vida de un comunista* (1957; repr., Santiago: Editoral Austral, 1971), 58.

7 The historian Manuel Fernandez argues persuasively that when official Chilean state numbers are summed, even a conservative estimate puts the dead at no less than 1,000: a list of 300 identified bodies was produced—at congressional request—over a week later; a congressional report noted 80 more who died under the circus tent on the plaza in front of the school; the hospital listed 250 admitted with multiple bullet wounds, of whom only 10 percent survived; and there were the mortally wounded that the hospital could not accommodate, including those who died hidden in neighborhood houses of refuge, as well as those taken immediately to the cemetery and never recorded (*Proletariado y Salitre*, 64–65). In Iquique's oldest surviving cemetery, at the tomb of a person noted as a survivor of the massacre, fresh flowers have been present every time I have passed it over the years (figure 13).

8 The Bolivian consul reported that, according to the 1907 Census, Tarapacá's population of 110,036 included 12,528 Bolivians, 23,574 Peruvians, and 7,672 other foreign nationals. The 1907 strike, which concentrated workers in Iquique (a city of 40,516), "was dispersed by force amidst machine gun and rifle fire" and prompted an "immediate and abundant emigration of workers from the province." Following orders from superiors, the consul facilitated the repatriation of more than 2,000 Bolivian men, women, and children. The exodus of workers created a labor shortage and nitrate companies sent representatives into Bolivia to contract more workers, including a number who had just fled Chile. The consul attributed renewed labor migration to three factors: the agricultural conditions in Bolivia, the health of the nitrate industry, and Bolivian obligatory military service. See Iquique Consul to Ministro de Relaciones Exteriores y Culto,

1 September 1910, AMRE-LPB, Consulados Nacionales en America/20 Semestre 1910. The Peruvian government also sponsored the repatriation of nationals and was disgusted to note that within months many had returned to Chile as no work was available in Peru (Sección 712, T.731 1908, p. 20 Consulado del Perú en Iquique; Sección 712, T.731 1908, p. 33, Consulado del Perú de Pisagua, AMRE-LP, Correspondencia consular del Perú en Iquique, Pisagua y Nueva York, salida). See also Rosa Troncoso de la Fuente, "Peruano en Tarapacá y Chileno en Lima: El caso de los Tarapaqueños Peruanos repatriados, 1907–1920," in *A los 90 años de los sucesos de la Escuela Santa María de Iquique*, ed. Sergio González Miranda (Santiago: Lom Ediciones, 1998), 329–35; Rosa Troncoso de la Fuente, "La migración de los Tarapaqueños Peruanos a Lima: 1907–1920" (master's thesis, Pontifica Universidad Católica del Perú, 1986).

9 For a discussion of the strike in its urban context, see Rigoberto Sánchez Fuentes, "Iquique: Ciudad, red y castigo," in *A los 90 años de los sucesos de la Escuela Santa María de Iquique*, ed. Sergio González Miranda (Santiago: Lom Ediciones, 1998), 303–13.

10 Comparing the 1890 and 1907 strikes, Sergio Grez Toso argues that in 1907 there was greater radicalism in terms of workers' consciousness of a fundamental opposition between capital and labor, as well as a greater mysticism surrounding the actual massacre ("1890–1907: De una huelda general a otra: Continuidades y rupturas del movimiento popular en Chile," in *A los 90 años de los sucesos de la Escuela Santa María de Iquique*, ed. Sergio González Miranda [Santiago: Lom Ediciones, 1998], 131–37).

11 Luis A. Galdames Rosas notes that politics in the North happened in the urban space of Iquique and that, for the state, "la pampa es silencio" ("Los que no cuentan," in *A los 90 años de los sucesos de la Escuela Santa María de Iquique*, ed. Sergio González Miranda [Santiago: Lom Ediciones, 1998], 79–81).

12 "¿Que hacían sus padres cuando morían los obreros del salitre?" *El Nortino*, 2 May 1993, p. 10.

13 Lafertte, *Vida de un comunista*, 59.

14 In the cemetery, workers' organizations erected a monument to the fallen. In the 1950s, plans to eradicate the cemetery called for the removal of all remains except those in the mass grave, which was to be enclosed by a concrete wall and cover and marked by a memorial plaque (*El Tarapacá*, 27 June 1957, p. 5). During the Popular Unity period, the local architect Patricio Advis drew up plans for a commemorative park at the cemetery. The cemetery was eventually leveled and replaced with what is now one of the poorest shanty zones in the city, a neighborhood named, ironically, after Jorge Inostroza, a writer of popular history, primarily of the War of the Pacific.

15 In 1910 Luis Emilio Recabarren published a pamphlet in which he offered a critical reading of General Silva Renard's official account of the

strike ("La huelga de Iquique" [Santiago, 1910], reproduced in *Santa María de Iquique, 1907: Documentos para su historia*, ed. Pedro Bravo Elizondo [Santiago: Ediciones Litoral, 1993], 193–202). Recabarren's essay was also mentioned in Lafertte, *Vida de un comunista*, 74.

16 Lafertte, *Vida de un comunista*, 128.

17 "Pido venganza por la que vino / de los obreros el pecho a abrir / pido venganza por el pampino / que allá en Iquique, supo morir."

18 The lira popular included poems such as "Sobre la horrible matanza de Iquique" (On the horrible massacre in Iquique) and the sarcastic "A Silva Renard, los aplausos del país" (To Silva Renard, the country's applause) (Ajo X, Lira Popular no. 144, vol. 4, hoja 1–40, ficha 4122 Lira Popular, CL). See also Jorge Núñez Pinto "Los sucesos de Santa María de Iquique en la poesía popular," in *A los 90 años de los sucesos de la Escuela Santa María de Iquique*, ed. Sergio González Miranda (Santiago: Lom Ediciones, 1998), 225–35.

19 Elizabeth Faue, *Community of Suffering and Struggle: Women, Men, and the Labor Movement in Minneapolis, 1915–1945* (Chapel Hill: University of North Carolina Press, 1991). The historian Eduardo Deves has explored what he calls the non-elite "cultura ilustrada," which he sees as characteristic of late-nineteenth-century Chile, with a special effervescence in Tarapacá ("La cultura obrera ilustrada chilena y algunas ideas en torno al sentido de nuestro quehacer historiográfico," *Mapocho* no. 30 [1990], 127–36).

20 In Southern Chile the workers lived as dispersed agricultural laborers who could rely on their own cultivation, fishing, and hunting for subsistence. See Arnold Bauer, *Chilean Rural Society from Spanish Conquest to 1930* (Cambridge: Cambridge University Press, 1975); Gabriel Salazar, *Labradores, peones y proletarios* (Santiago: SUR, 1989).

21 Julio Pinto Vallejos, in his study of nitrate and labor up to 1890, shows the impact of sudden migration on a system of labor commodification ("Cortar raíces, criar fama: El peonaje chileno en la fase inicial del ciclo salitrero, 1850–1879," *Historia* 27 [1993]: 425–47). See also Fernández, *Proletariado y salitre*.

22 In a 1960 newspaper article Luis Gonzalez Zenteno reviewed the kinds of books and articles pampinos were reading and recalled conversations with workers, thus giving a remarkable glimpse into the ways in which the texts were being read ("Las Apetencias culturales del pueblo," *La Nación*, 24 July 1960, MS, folder 137).

23 Some emerging populist parties tried to develop a mass base of support to incorporate themselves in national politics, but the closed oligarchic organization of parliamentary rule offered limited room for participation. See Sergio Grez Toso, "La huelga general de 1890," *Perspectivas* (Madrid) (December 1990): 127–67; Sergio Grez Toso "Balmaceda y el movimiento popular," in *La epoca de Balmaceda*, by Sergio Villalobos R., Eduardo Devés V., Bernardo Subercaseaux S., Gerardo Martínez R., Ser-

gio Grez T., and Ricardo Conyoumdjiam B. (Santiago: Dirección de Bibliotecas, Archivos, Museos, 1992), 71–101.

24 Leoncio Marín, *21 de diciembre: Compendio y relación exacta de la huelga de pampinos desde su principio hasta su fin* (Iquique: n.p., 1908); Oscar Bermúdez, "El Dr. Nicolás Palacios y la industria del salitre," *Revista chilena de historia y geografía* 136 (1968): 209–47. In the historian Enrique Reyes Navarro's reading, present in these accounts was the "ghost" of the repression carried out against the 1890 strikers in Tarapacá ("Los trabajadores del área salitrera," 99).

25 Some of the photos were later recovered, in the form of postcards, as far away as antique shops in Germany (Enrique Reyes Navarro, personal communication, 1994).

26 Simón Rodriguez, Ministerio de Industria y Obras Públicas, to Intendente, Tarapacá, 15 May 1908, AIT-1, no. 11–1908/1908/Ministerio Relaciones Exteriores.

27 J. Figueroa, Ministerio de Industria y Obras Públicas, to Intendente, Tarapacá, 14 May 1908, AIT-1, no. 11–1908/1908/Ministerio Relaciones-Exteriores.

28 J. Figueroa, Ministerio de Industria y Obras Públicas, to Intendente, Tarapacá, 9 June 1908, AIT-1, no. 11–1908/1908/Ministerio Relaciones Exteriores.

29 "La sangrienta sofocación que las autoridades dieron a la pacífica huelga del 21 de Diciembre de 1907, concluyó de perfilar los relieves de la crisis del patriotismo en la región salitrera. La propaganda sistemática de medio siglo que hubiera hecho mil anarquistas contra el patriotismo, jamás hubiera producido el gran destrozo moral en el sentimiento de los obreros que las autoridades produjeron en sólo cinco minutos de fuego y mortandad" (Luis Ponce, "Oficina Porvenir," in *Comisión Parlamentaria [de la] Cámara de Diputados encargada de estudiar las necesidades de las provincias de Tarapacá y Antofagasta*, ed. Enrique Oyarzún [Santiago: Zig-Zag, 1913], 137–38).

30 "No soy mas chileno. . . . Me voy de aquí . . . Gobierno asesino. . . . Me voy de Chile para siempre" (Lafertte, *Vida de un comunista*, 59). Ironically, the Chilean Communist Party consistently used a nationalist rhetoric in which the 1907 massacre became a nationalist symbol.

31 Sergio A. González Miranda, "De la solidaridad a la xenofobia: Tarapacá, 1907–1911," in *A los 90 años de los sucesos de la Escuela Santa María de Iquique*, ed. Sergio González Miranda (Santiago: Lom Ediciones, 1998), 93–117. González Miranda argues that this shift implicated both elite and non-elite sectors in the move from mutualist and internationalist workers' movements to national worker's parties and in the move from nitrate cartels centered in London to societies depending on Santiago ("Centralización y decentralización en Tarapacá: Un raconto histórico y una mirada actual" *Revista Frontera* [Temuco] 12 [1993]: 103–8). In this process, the

Patriotic Leagues, especially active around 1917–1918 and again in the mid-1920s, attempted to rectify the rupture between workers and the state and to break down alliances between Chilean and foreign workers, specifically Peruvians, by emphasizing militaristic patriotism in territorial rivalry.

32 Elías Lafertte related a 1913 debate between Luis Emilio Recabarren, the founder of numerous working-class newspapers and of the Workers' Socialist Party (a precursor to the Communist Party), and Enrique Santander, the director of the conservative paper *El Nacional* (Iquique edition). Recabarren insisted that the workers who produced the nation's wealth were much more patriotic than polemicists and the political elite who allowed that wealth to be usurped by the British. For Recabarren, patriotic acts included everyday issues, including the fight against alcoholism, gambling, prostitution, and even against war: "This is the true love of the patria and not that which consists in speaking of dubious military glories and fomenting hate against neighboring countries." Santander linked his own patriotism to heroes and battles from the early-nineteenth-century Wars of Independence, which had launched the Chilean state. During the debate, hecklers shouted, "We don't want to hear more school lessons!" After the debate ended, Recabarren wrote up his part as a pamphlet entitled *"Patria* and Patriotism." See Lafertte, *Vida de un comunista*, 93–95; Luis Emilio Recabarren, *Patria y patriotismo*, 3d ed. (Santiago: La Federación Obrera, 1921). On Recabarren and nationalist rhetoric, see Patrick Barr-Melej, *Reforming Chile* (Chapel Hill: University of North Carolina Press, 2001), 72–74. On the question of worker's abilities to sustain the tension between internationalist and nationalist positions at the same time, see Stefan Berger and Angel Smith, eds., *Nationalism, Labour and Ethnicity, 1870–1939* (Manchester, U.K.: Manchester University Press, 1999).

33 These phenomena continued in recent efforts to try General Pinochet for crimes against humanity even as the military as an institution remained mostly unscathed by its actions. However, in 2004 General Juan Emilio Cheyre did acknowledge a degree of institutional accountability, asserting, "That era and mode of existence, as a people and as a nation, has been left behind in the past"—a reflection of the contemporary politics of memory premised on a radical break between past and present (see Cheyre's 4 November 2004 speech, which was released just before the National Commission on Political Imprisonment and Torture Report (known as the Valech Report), then translated and reprinted by Memoria y Justicia, http://www.memoriayjusticia.cl). The deaths of hundreds of conscripts abandoned by their commanding officers in a blizzard in 2005 resulted in a public outcry that further questioned the integrity of the institution.

34 Bengoa, "Presentación," 5.

35 Ibid., 6.

36 Guillermo Ross-Murray, personal communication, 1993.

37 Lafertte, *Vida de un comunista*, 58. Lafertte heard rumors that Com-

mandente Aguirre, the naval commander of a warship anchored in harbor, had refused to send his soldiers and weapons to shore to attack the workers (ibid., 59–60).

38 Ibid., 61.

39 The other possible candidates for blame would have been the predominantly British nitrate companies and the British state who refused to negotiate and placed incredible pressure on the Chilean state to use force from the very beginning of the 1907 events and in the nitrate period in general, as Manuel Fernandez has demonstrated in *Proletariado y Salitre*, 56, 58–59, 62, 67–68. However, this was a dimension accentuated in the anti-imperialist rhetoric of the Popular Unity years.

40 *Boletín de las sesiones extraordinarias: Cámara de Diputados* (Santiago: Imprenta Nacional, 1907), 658–71, 718–29, 731–42; also excerpted in Pedro Bravo Elizondo, ed., *Santa María de Iquique, 1907: Documentos para su historia* (Santiago: Ediciones Litoral, 1993).

41 "Convencido que no era posible esperar más tiempo sin comprometer el respeto y prestigio del las autoridades y fuerza pública y penetrado también de la necesidad de dominar la rebelión antes de que terminase el día" (*Sesiones Ordinarias de la Cámara de Diputados*, 30 December 1907, cited in Fernandez, *Proletariado y Salitre*, 63).

42 Much of the congressional debate was in reaction to Renard's official accounting, a letter to Sotomayor in which he emphasized the disrespectfulness of the crowd and his sense of impending conflict and riot. The general offered additional justifications for the repression in "Los sucesos de Iquique," *El Chileno*, 21 February 1908 (reprinted in Bravo Elizondo, *Santa María de Iquique*, 203–6). At the end of this document, Bravo Elizondo includes a notice from *La Vanguardia*, dated 14 May 1908, that military recruitment that year had no success.

43 *El Mercurio*, 14 December 1914 (reprinted in Bravo Elizondo, *Santa María de Iquique*, 209–11); Lafertte, *Vida de un comunista*, 62; Pedro Bravo Elizondo "La cuasivenganza por Santa María de Iquique," in *A los 90 años de los sucesos de la Escuela Santa María de Iquique*, ed. Sergio González Miranda (Santiago: Lom Ediciones, 1998), 33–43. Peter DeShazo's inventory of Chilean holdings at the International Institute for Social History lists in the Nettlau archive: "A 1914 flyer protesting the arrest of workers after the attempted assassination in Santiago of General Silva Renard by an Argentine anarchist" (other sources suggest he may have been Spanish) ("Sources for the Study of Chilean Labor History, 1890–1940, at the Internationaal Instituut voor Sociale Geschiedenis" [MS, International Institute for Social History, Amsterdam], p. 2). I could not locate the actual documents.

44 Juan Royal (head artist), personal communication, Iquique, Chile, 1993.

45 The massacre at Iquique also has ongoing affective prominence for the National Association of Soldiers of Silence, former security agents who

feel betrayed by the transition from military to civilian rule. This clandestine organization sends menacing communiqués to human-rights lawyers and activists who demand justice. The association reportedly met for a convention in Iquique in mid-November 1992 to organize a more proactive group (CHIP News [an Internet news compilation out of Santiago], 1 January 1993). Thanks to J. Scarpaci for this data.

46 For a very recent example of this foregrounding of the general, see Sergio Missana, *El Invasor* (Santiago: Planeta, 1997).

47 Fernandez, *Proletariado y Salitre*, 64.

48 Elianira Escobar (ex-political prisoner), interview by author, November 1993. The school principal was interviewed by *El Nortino*, 2 May 1993, p. 8.

49 The Popular Front came to power under Radical Party president Pedro Aguirre Cerda (1938–1941) and was reelected under Juan Antonio Ríos (1942–1946). Although the Popular Front formally dissolved during the Ríos presidency, the coalition managed to elect Gabriel González Videla (1946–1952). The Popular Front gained its impetus in part from the worldwide Communist Party policy of forging alliances with other political parties to combat fascism. In Chile, Carlos Ibáñez del Campo's military interventions in the 1920s had ended the reign of the landholding elite in the parliamentary system. Late-nineteenth-century efforts by the Democratic Party and the Workers' Socialist Party had become the basis for middle-sector political entities that sought broad bases of support, including the Communist, Socialist, Radical, and Christian Democrat Parties, each of which later also spawned smaller parties. That many of these parties were founded in Tarapacá only contributed to the region's fame as the cradle of Chilean politics. The broad, multiclass base to which these parties appealed coalesced in the idea of "the people" (*el pueblo*), who constituted the organic component of the nation and inhabited the realm of the popular (*lo popular*). Jose del Pozo has argued that this era should not be dubbed populist, as it lacked charismatic leadership and a sufficient degree of mass mobilization; rather, the Left and labor were able to maintain a high level of autonomy while seeking tactical alliances in the antifascist front ("La periode d'alliances politiques multicalssistes au Chili (1936–1956): Populisme ou autonomie de classes?" *Revue canadienne des etudes latino-americanes et caribes* 13, no. 25 [1988]: 7–27).

50 "Chile es región probable para una invasión enemiga en caso de guerra: La declaración fue hecha por el Coronel Thomas B. Hanford, ante el Departamento de Defensa de los EE.UU.," *El Tarapacá*, 11 August 1957, p. 1.

51 "La masacre de Iquique de 1907," *Ercilla* (9 September 1952), MS, folder 11.

52 "Vamos al puerto vamos, / en su resuelto y noble ademán, / para pedirles a nuestros amos / otro pedazo no más de pan" (Joaquín Edwards Bello, "Respecto a los sucesos de Iquique en diciembre de 1907," MS, folder 11).

53 This apparently diplomatic neutrality was offset by Edwards Bello's emphasis on what he considered to have been the real culprit—the state's inability to stem the massive devaluation of the Chilean currency—which he deployed to critique the monetary policies of later administrations. Joaquín Edwards Bello, "Respecto a los sucesos de Iquique en diciembre de 1907," MS, folder 11.

54 "Los últimos en perigrinación, con sus pies sangrantes, y doloridos hasta el alma, han vuelto a trabajo, para continuar siendo sometidos, al fallo que les condena al suplicio, no en el madero sacrosanto, per sí en las torturas del prematuro agotamiento, o, en un accidente de los que a diario se presentan en sus faenas" (Augusto Rojas Núñez, *La agonía del salitre en la Pampa de Tarapacá* [Santiago: Imprenta Astudillo, 1960], 44).

55 Odessa Flores (daughter of the prominent labor leader Epifanio Flores), interview by author, Iquique, Chile, March 1993.

56 See *El Siglo*, 5 March 1957; *El Siglo*, 10 March; *El Siglo*, 1–3 April 1957; *La Nación*, 28–30 March 1957. The street protests also resulted in a crackdown on Iquique, especially on student leaders (Luis Emilio Morales Marino (former 1973 political prisoner), interview by author, December 2000). For a critique of Ibáñez del Campo's movement from the time, see Alfonso Stephens Freire, *El irracionalismo político en Chile: Ensayo de psicología colectivo* (Santiago: Prensa Latinoamericana, 1957). On the role of the military in this period, see M. Elisa Fernández, "Beyond Partisan Politics in Chile: The Carlos Ibáñez Period and the Politics of Ultranationalism between 1952–1958" (Ph.D. diss., University of Miami, 1996). For more on Tarapacá as an emergency zone, see "Se Decreta Zona de Emergencia en la Provincia de Tarapacá," *El Tarapacá*, 26 May 1957, p. 1.

57 Albino Blanc, "Tarapacá antipatriótica, la protesta de un poeta regional," *El Tarapacá*, 26 June 1957, p. 4.

58 Interview with a former political prisoner from 1973, Iquique, March 2001.

59 In response to the region's protest, the government in Santiago passed special legislation to ease economic conditions, such as the duty-free import of food to Iquique. Later attempts to promote import substitution development (an economic strategy coming out of modernization theory to foment national industry through loans and protective tariffs) by making Iquique a free-trade zone for industrial equipment never got far. (The current free-trade zone, as developed under the military, continues to specialize in consumer-ready products.) In 1960 Tarapacá was selected by the Food and Agriculture Organization of the United Nations for incorporation into Green Revolution projects, in particular, the development of a fish-meal industry (see *El Tarapacá*, 9 December 1960; *El Tarapacá*, 31 December 1960). The concessions involved generous loans and subsidies that made fortunes for a few, but the supply of fish was quickly exhausted, which wrought havoc for small, artisan fishers. Still, with bright optimism, the president of Banco Sud Americano, Guillermo Carey Busta-

mante opened a new branch in Iquique in 1963 and declared, "as a son of the North," that "Iquique is the laboratory where Chile will formulate its export mentality" (*Cavancha*, 22 December 1963, p. 6).

60 For example, Baltazar Robles Ponce begins an article with two verses from Pezoa's "El canto a la pampa" that describe the "blessed victims": "Canto a la pampa la tierra triste / reproba tierra de maldición / donde de verdad jamás se viste / ni en lo más bello estación // Benditas victimas que bajaron / desde la pampa llenas de fe / y a su llegada lo que escucharon / voz de metralla tan sólo fue" ("21 de Diciembre de 1907," *En Viaje* [December 1971]: 38–39). Two photographs — one looking down on the mass of strikers before the violence, the other of soldiers moving automatic guns through the streets of Iquique toward the Escuela Santa María — represent well the iconographic use of images from the strike and repression (*El Siglo*, 6 November 1960, MS, folder 11).

61 "Los hechos históricos de nuestro país señalan una lucha del pueblo jalonada de victorias . . . parciadas y cruentes derrotas, pero siempre una lucha, lucha en que también otras generaciones pusieron su acento de convicción y estuvieron junto a los trabajadores. Yo soy de la generación llamada del año 30, heredamos de la generación del año 20 una visión muy amplia sobre los problemas de los trabajadores de Chile y del continente. . . . Por eso es que hay que entender que el proceso histórico de la lucha del pueblo . . . estuvo marcado con el sacrificio de miles de chilenos en Ranquil, en San Gregorio, en la Escuela Santa María, en la Federación Obrera del Magallanes, en Puente Alto, en José María Caro. Es decir ha sido esta lucha del pueblo y la conciencia de los partidos populares, vinculada a estas luchas lo que ha hecho posible la unidad y dentro de este concepto unitario: hacer posible el instrumento necesarion para la conquista del Gobierno y avanzar la conquista del poder" ("Presidente Allende en la UTE: La Universidad es responsable ante la historia, la revolución y el Pueblo," *La Nación*, 2 May 1971, p. 8).

62 Similarly claiming generative properties of state violence, a 1971 news magazine claimed that state violence against el pueblo had "served to advance the evolution toward a more just and humane society, and toward legislation that respects and promotes the rights of workers": "Desde comienzos del siglo XX ha corrido en Chile la sangre del pueblo. Duros enfrentamientos han ido jalando los años del siglo con nombres de triste fama: San Gregorio, Ranquil, La Coruña. . . . La sangre del pueblo ha servido para que algunos irresponsables prediquen la destrucción violenta de la sociedad. Ha servido para que los políticos inescrupulosos hagan demagogia y ganen votos. Pero también ha servido para ir evolucionando hacia una sociedad más justa y más humana, y hacia una legislación que respete e imponga los derechos de los trabajadores" ("La Sangre del Pueblo," *Qué Pasa* [22 April 1971]: 29–32).

63 *El Tarapacá*, 22 December 1971, p. 5.

64 *El Tarapacá*, 17 December 1971, p. 5.

65 "Su fuerza está en el dominio del trasfondo ideológico de los temas que trata, y, gracias a esto logra una didáctica sencillez, muy diferente de la simpleza algo rústica de muchas obras comprometidas" ("Recuento de masacres," *Ahora*, 11 May 1971, p. 44).

66 Luis Advis, album notes for *Santa María de Iquique: Cantata Popular* (Santiago: Alerce Producciones Fonográficas, 1978).

67 Perhaps an example of the legacy of what Antonio Acevedo Hernández called the *tonada chilena*, "un poema pasional cimentado sobre una glosa"; he continued, "El cantor chileno fue más periodista y dramaturgo que poeta, glosaba el acontecimiento que sacudía el ambiente, lo pintaba con propiedad e igualmente a los tipos en él se desenvolvían" (*El Libro de la Tierra Chilena: Lo que canta y lo que mira el pueblo de Chile* [Santiago: Ediciones Ercilla, 1935], 1:11, 34). Explaining that musical forms over time can lose their ability to express their audiences' sentiments, Acevedo Hernández called for Chilean composers to reclaim this form and, by being innovative with melody and rhythm, to make it speak to the public again as an authentic expression of Chilean-ness (somewhat in opposition to what he called the invasion of Argentine tango). Acevedo thus historically linked musical form and cultural memory in a way very much describing a structure of feeling.

68 "Preparen estreno de una obra del compositor Luis Advis," *El Tarapacá*, 15 February 1972, p. 1.

69 "San Gregorio . . . Santa María . . . Amén," *El Tarapacá*, 12 February 1972, p. 5.

70 The Grupo de Artillería a Caballo No. 3 "Silva Renard" was created through Decreto G.1, no. 428 on 26 February 1924 (Carlos Silva Vidósola, *Las fuerzas armadas de Chile: Álbum histórico*, 2d ed. [Santiago: Atenas, ca. 1935], 776). This source does not clearly specify that the unit was named after General Roberto Silva Renard, but the late date makes that quite likely to have been the case.

71 Interview, Iquique, June 1993.

72 Carlos Prats González, *Memorias: Testimonio de un soldado* (Santiago: Pehuen, 1985), 71.

73 "Verdad y reconciliacion," Departamento de Laicos newsletter, Iquique, January–February 1991, RMLK.

74 For a precoup example of this dynamic, see the account of the prominent Communist Party functionary Volodia Teitelboim's congressional speech wherein he extolled the virtues of the Chilean military, which he called "militares sin militarismo" ("Volodia Teitelboim en homenaje al Padre de la Patria, en el Senado: Fuerzas armadas chilenas: Un ejercito de paz como concibio O'Higgins," *El Siglo*, 27 August 1972, p. 15).

75 Raúl Pizzaro Illanes, "Dos horas de la historia se juntaron en Iquique," *Ramona* (3 December 1971): 46–48. Thanks to Margaret Power for this source.

76 "Para muchos que la vieron era simplemente una vieja que llevaba

una bandera y que saludo a Fidel en la plaza de Iquique. Pero Blanca Williams Delzo. De 84 años. Era un trozo vivo de la historia sobreviviente de aquella espantosa matanza de obreros de la Escuela Santa María en 1907. Un capitulo que se saltan los profesores burgueses. Revivió ante los pampinos y su invitado. Cuando dos horas de la historia se juntaron en Iquique" (ibid., 47).

77 Castro spoke mostly about the regional economy and ways in which greater economic cooperation between Iquique and Cuba might work. His two historical references were to the canonical local heroes: Recabarren and War of the Pacific icons Arturo Prat and Almirante Grau (Fidel Castro, "En la Plaza Arturo Prat de Iquique, 16 de noviembre," *Chile 1971: Habla Fidel Castro* [Santiago: Editorial Universitaria, 1971], 106–29). Of Recabarren, Castro said, "Hemos tenido ocasión de ver la obra de los que lucharon, de los que convierion esta ciudad en baluarte y cuna del movimiento obrero y del movimiento popular chileno" (123).

78 Nancy Morris, "Canto porque es necesario cantar: The New Song Movement in Chile, 1973–1983," *Latin American Research Review* 21, no. 2 (1986): 117–37; Fernando Reyes Matta, "The 'New Song' and Its Confrontation in Latin America," in *Marxism and the Interpretation of Culture*, ed. Cary Nelson and Lawrence Grossberg (Urbana: University of Illinois, 1988), 447–60; Diane Soles, "The Expanding Vision and Inspiration of Chilean New Song: From Its Beginnings through Exile" (unpublished manuscript, 1990).

79 Luis Advis, album notes for *Santa María de Iquique: Cantata Popular* (Santiago: Alerce Producciones Fonográficas, 1978).

80 Performances specified include those in April 1977 and September 1983 in Paris; in February 1975 in Rome, with narration by the actor Gian María Volonte; in November 1977 in Los Angeles, with Jane Fonda's narration; in October 1979 in Madrid; and in May 1982 in Tokyo.

81 The regional office of the national labor organization replaced the old monument and inaugurated their new effort on May Day 1993.

82 "Tampoco se olviden que el 21 de diciembre de 1907 en Iquique se escribió en pequeño, con un pantágrafo defectuoso, lo que aparecería impreso . . . la mañana del 11 de septiembre de 1973. Más o menos los mismos contendientes, más o menos el mismo resultado, más o menos las mismas muertes, más o menos la misma verguenza, pero ahora todo a escala gigantesca" (Eduardo Devés, *Lo que van a morir te saludan: Historia de una masacre Escuela Santa María Iquique, 1907*, Nuestra América (Santiago: Nuestra América Ediciones, 1988), 38.

83 In 1991, during the period of transition to democracy, the Municipal Theater of Iquique staged *Santa María de Salitre*, a play written by the Peruvian Sergio Arrau, which told the story of the strike and repression. The published script included photos from the period and an essay by Pedro Bravo Elizondo, himself a native of Iquique (Sergio Arrau, *Santa María de Salitre* [Iquique: Editorial Camanchaca, 1989]). The Municipal

Theater of Iquique's production, along with performances by groups such as the city's folkloric ballet company, reconfigured the place of the grand old Municipal Theater in the urban landscape. During the dictatorship, the theater had been completely renovated. Access to the theater had been limited to Iquique's leading families by cost of tickets, invitation-only affairs, social norms, and types of events offered. On reelection, the populist mayor from the pre-coup era was determined to reclaim the theater as a truly public space. Well-publicized events with broad appeal—at least as the city council imagined it—and low or no entrance fees drew in people who previously had not dared to enter. The mayor understood democratization as fundamentally implicating urban symbolic topography. In the early 1990s various historians published studies related to 1907, such as articles in the Iquique-based historical journal *Camanchaca*, edited by the Regional Studies Workshop, and Pedro Bravo-Elizondo's compilation of primary sources documenting the events of the repression.

84 For a general, this was the penultimate assignment—that is, to a key frontier strategic zone (bordering Peru and Bolivia)—before moving into the top military command in the capital. While division commander, Pinochet frequently served as acting regional governor when the civilian officeholder traveled on personal and official business. As intendente *subrogante*, Pinochet began to gather relics and documents to create a military history museum in Iquique (*El Tarapacá*, 13 May 1969, p. 1). Pinochet and his wife became so well-liked that neighborhood centers and mother's associations in Iquique named themselves after the couple.

85 Iquique enjoyed national fame as the "land of champions," as many of Chile's premier sports figures came from Tarapacá; sporting arenas and clubs had thus been a key form of civic association since before the 1950s. The military would invite civilian sports clubs to play on their fields and often joined them in competition (Bernardo Guerrero Jiménez, *El libro de los campeones: Deporte e identidad cultural en Iquique* [Iquique: CREAR, 1992]).

86 In recounting the history of Iquique's regiments, a local journalist proclaimed that the Chilean military was "the Patria in its most pure expression"; linking people-military-nation, the journalist further stated that "the people, in the grandness of its simplicity, understanding that the nation needs a heroic arm that insures its indivisible sovereignty, has toasted it with common sense" ("Un pasado de gloria y valentía cubre existencia de regimientos Iquiquenos," *El Tarapacá*, 19 September 1971, p. 3). During the regional ceremony in which conscripts first received weapons, Teniente Coronel Enrique Silva Morong emphasized the historical importance of the event: "If these weapons that you receive today are not the same as those of glorious and epic eras, by the logic of evolution, these represent the same: with them . . . we must also die if Chile's security requires it; very near this post, a few kilometers away, in this same Province of Tarapacá, Prat, Aldea, Eleutario Ramírez, and Vivar gave their lives for the same

cause" (" 'No me desenvaines o uses sin razón, ni me envaines o mantengas sin honor,' " *El Tarapacá*, 17 May 1960, p. 4).

87 The streets were originally named after the likes of Eliás Lafertte and John F. Kennedy; they were renamed after military officers and the dates of key battles, like the 11th of September (the date of the 1973 coup). In the transition to civilian rule, some groups demanded that the state either restore the old names or negotiate new names acceptable to the military and its supporters. Until the end of the 1990s, the civilian government considered this issue too controversial and dangerous to broach.

88 Regional economic policies of the dictatorship involved opening to the world via a free-trade zone, fencing off the city's port for the private benefit of the fish-meal industry (a vestige of green-revolution development schemes), and encouraging arms manufacturing (Mónica González, "Carlos Cardoen: Sobre bombas, empresas y política," *Análisis* (5 July 1987): 25–27; Víctor Heredia, "Enero 1986 Cardoen," Departamento de Laicos newsletter, January–February 1991, RMLK. In the spirit of "fiscal accountability and cost-recovery" that characterized the military regime's economic policies, the government sponsored the dismantling of old nitrate plants and camps in order to sell pieces of roofs, homes, stores, and industrial complexes for scrap metal. At the same time, Iquique was being remade into an urban showcase for the military's benevolence.

89 In 1993 there were over sixty high-rise buildings recently built or in process. Even though the province boasts the second-fastest-growing formal economy in Chile, after Copiapó (in the Norte Chico), such heavy investment in real estate indicated a boom in the unofficial economy, namely, in drug trafficking and money laundering (Calvin Sims, "Prosperity in New Chile Nourishes Drug Trade," *New York Times*, March 27, 1996, A9).

90 Sergio Missana, *El invasor* (Santiago: Planeta, 1997). My interpretation of the novel benefited from an interview with the author, San Francisco, November 2000.

91 Former soldier, personal communication, March 2001.

92 Sergio González Miranda, ed., *A 90 años de los sucesos de la Escuela Santa María de Iquique* (Santiago: Lom Ediciones, 1998).

93 "Para el conjunto, en todo caso, fue una ocasión de reconocimiento colectivo, como partes de una identidad y una memoria colectiva, de rasgo regional, aunque de alcance nacional. Hoy, que vivimos un período en que brechas profundas de disigualdad separan nuestra sociedad, es significativo sentirse parte de un recuerdo común, que nos autoriza a seguir creyendo en valores esenciales como la solidaridad, la justicia y el respeto al otro" (Pedro Milos "Historia regional, identidad y memoria: La noción de 'vectores de recuerdo,' " in *A los 90 años de los sucesos de la Escuela Santa María de Iquique*, ed. Sergio González Miranda [Santiago: Lom Ediciones, 1998], 223).

94 "Como un fantasma del pasado, la voluntad social de recordar recorre Chile, pues, de norte a sur. . . . [E]n flagrante oposición a la obvia voluntad

política de olvidar o conmemorar 'en la medida de lo posible,' . . . esa voluntad no forma parte ni de las transiciones políticas ni de las fluctuaciones de mercado sino de las 'transiciones ciudadanas'" (Gabriel Salazar "Voluntad política de matar, voluntad social de recordar [a propósito de Santa María de Iquique]," in *A los 90 años de los sucesos de la Escuela Santa María de Iquique*, ed. Sergio González Miranda [Santiago: Lom Ediciones, 1998], 292–93).

95 For a novel in which nostalgia and melancholy (the cover blurb uses the Portuguese term *saudade*) are intertwined with a fine feel for social history, see Hernán Rivera Letelier, *La Reina Isabel cantaba rancheras* (Santiago: Planeta, 1997). Also see his novel about the 1907 massacre, *Santa María de las flores negras* (Buenos Aires: Seix Barral, Planeta, 2002). Rivera Letelier is a native of the North.

96 Comité del Salitre, *Historias de la pampa salitrera: Primer certamen literario del comité del salitre* (Iquique: Ediciones Colchagua, 1987), cover blurb. Cardoen considered the volume a continuation of the same interest in northern history that had prompted him to reedit a facsimile edition of Nicolás Palacios's treatise, *The Chilean Race*. In his prologue, Cardoen claimed indirect kinship with Palacios and ideological kinship as an advocate of national capitalists. He urged Chileans to reread Palacios so they might learn "to look in the mirror with love" and appreciate the bountiful "opportunities for material wealth" in "the length and width of the fatherland." According to Palacios, regional social, political, and economic problems had their root only "in mental mediocrity," and Chile's future offered limitless opportunity if Chileans would "habituate themselves to think in terms of triumph and not of failure" (*Raza chilena: Libro escrito por un chileno y para los chilenos* [1904; repr., Santiago: Ediciones Colchagua, 1988], xi).

97 Luis Taboada (president of the largest Sons of Nitrate federation), interview by author, Iquique, Chile, November 1993. So elaborate were efforts to reconstruct and sustain transplanted, old nitrate communities that the same federation raised funds to purchase the dismantled church from La Victoria, bought a plot in Iquique, and reassembled the entire church primarily as a community center for the association, but also as a place of worship.

98 Along with the broad shifts in the composition of the nitrate industry came shifts in the organization of labor. In its heyday the industry required a large pool of workers who it could easily summon and dismiss according to shifts in market prices; therefore, single young men made up the vast majority of the laborers. The collapse of the industry precipitated its reorganization under the combined efforts of the Chilean state and the Guggenheims. Greater mechanization of extraction and processing reduced labor requirements and lessened the more grueling aspects of the work. Under state subsidy, a few camps operated at a relatively steady pace for a perpetually limited market. Hence, managers, desiring a stable workforce,

began to recruit and promote families and to turn the nitrate camps into more complete company towns with churches and schools. Canadian Catholic missionaries were brought in to encourage family discipline and moral order, yet they became increasingly radicalized through their experiences in the region. The towns were laid out in a stratified fashion, with top administrators living separately and having their own social club. The newer sector of supervisors, teachers, and shopkeepers were housed apart from the families of manual laborers. With the stratified sectors coming together in elaborate public commemorations of national holidays, nitrate camps were thus reinvented as communities — communities, furthermore, with a direct connection with the state, which had taken over general responsibility for the industry. Both community and the community-nation link arose through sociospatial organization of workers' lives that built on prior modes of civic association in Tarapacá's working-class culture. However, the project of building communities suffered from the constant erosion of the basis for their existence: the nitrate industry.

99 Since the 1970s, dockworkers have continued to play a central part in labor organization, along with the men who worked in the fish-meal and construction industries. However, for the past decade or so, Iquique's prime economic focus, aside from the military, has been the free-trade zone, with its large number of female clerical and sales workers. The teachers' union, with its more balanced gender distribution, remains key in labor mobilizations and continues to be a source of local union-federation leadership. José Limón argues that the aesthetics of strong, male bodies delineated class and ethnic positioning in the case of Mexican-American south Texas (*Dancing with the Devil: Society and Cultural Poetics in Mexican-American Texas* [Madison: University of Wisconsin Press, 1994]).

100 Andrés Sabella, "Prólogo," in *Historias de la pampa salitrera: Primer certamen literario del comité del salitre*, by Comité del Salitre (Iquique: Ediciones Colchagua, 1987), 10.

101 Monument designer, interview by author, Iquique, Chile, August 1993. One of the local historians, Pedro Vergara, commented on the limitations of using only men's figures and insisted that the city should build another monument to the women of the pampa, whom he credited with the true vitality of community life in the desert.

102 Denise Astoreca, *Remolinos en la Pampa* (Santiago: Editorial Cuarto Propio, 1996).

103 *Pampa ilusión* was part of a series of telenovelas set in different regions of the country, including one on the gypsies in the near north and one involving issues of native and nonnative relations on Easter Island, both being national romances of integration between the subordinate culture and "Chilean" culture.

104 I discussed the program with citizens of both Iquique and Santiago; they had widely divergent interpretations of the show's political and social messages. Some people in Santiago were impressed that the show dealt

with issues of women's rights, homosexuality, and class conflict and that a number of the storylines (the romance between a prostitute and a miner, the principal father-daughter conflict) were not happily resolved in the end. Other viewers, especially those in Iquique, felt either that it painted a vision of the era that was too romantic and free of conflict or that it was not sufficiently authentic in portraying the details of nitrate-camp life.

105 Nitrate workers constantly sought to rid themselves of the ficha system, in which each nitrate company paid wages in its own tokens; these were redeemable only in the company store or in exchange for Chilean currency at a substantial discount. See Marcelo Segall, "La ficha salaria en el mundo: Estudios en homenaje al centenario de El Capital," *Boletín de la Universidad de Chile* nos. 78–79 (September–October 1967): 40–51.

106 On collectibles and nostalgia, see Susan Stewart, *On Longing* (Baltimore: Johns Hopkins University Press, 1984). Numerous studies have elaborated the political implications of museums, including Richard Price and Sally Price, "Executing Culture: Muséo, Muses, Museum," *American Anthropologist* 97, no. 1 (1995): 97–109; Robert Lumley, ed., *The Museum Time-Machine* (New York: Routledge, 1987).

107 Personal communication with a half dozen of the popular historians on various occasions, Iquique, Chile, 1993–1994.

108 Association of Tour Guides president, association members, and students of the tour-guide course, interview by author, Iquique, Chile, May 1993. I also attended the opening ceremony for the course and reviewed its didactic materials.

109 E. Valentine Daniel has demonstrated the interconnection of discursive practices and production for the Sri Lankan tea industry ("Tea Talk: Violent Measures in the Discursive Practices of Sri Lanka's Estate Tamils," *Comparative Studies in Society and History* [1993]: 568–600).

110 As with all textbooks published in Chile, this one met government approval and was structured around a series of content guidelines published by the government. As of 1994, these guidelines had not been modified since the early 1980s. Regime transition did not, at least immediately, alter the content of national history as taught to Chilean schoolchildren. Francisco Galdames Ramírez and Osvaldo Silva Galdames, *Historia y geografía de Iquique, 4o año medio*, an adaptation of *Historia de Chile*, by Luis Galdames (Santiago: Fondo Cultural La Tercera, 1984), 94.

111 Through the incorporation or negation of particular events and people in a national narrative, historiography and pedagogical texts have been vessels for the constitution of national memory. In Chile the politics of historiography and pedagogy play a particularly central role due to the prominence of historians in national politics and the state's long-standing commitment to education.

112 Leo Spitzer, *Hotel Bolivia* (New York: Hill and Wang, 1998), 146, 150.

113 The Festival of Tunas and Estudiantinas. *Tunas* are groups, tradi-

tionally of students, who dress in medieval European costumes and play Spanish music from that era.

114 Mario Lamas, personal communication, February 1993.

115 Roland Robertson, "After Nostalgia? Willful Nostalgia and the Phases of Globalization," in *Theories of Modernity and Postmodernity*, ed. Bryan S. Turner (London: Sage, 1990), 45–61.

116 Renato Rosaldo, "Imperial Nostalgia," in *Culture and Truth: The Remaking of Social Analysis* (Boston: Beacon Press, 1989), 69.

117 Robertson, "After Nostalgia?" 50.

118 Kathleen Stewart "Nostalgia: A Polemic," *Cultural Anthropology* 3, no. 3 (August 1988): 227–41.

119 Ibid., 35.

120 David Harvey, *The Postmodern Condition* (Oxford: Blackwell Press, 1989), quoted in Gavin Smith "Writing for Real: Capitalist Constructions and Constructions of Capitalism," *Critique of Anthropology* 11, no. 3: 213–32. Smith added, "In other words the notion of a past consumed to oblivion by the cogs and wheels of an ever more productive capitalism is as necessary a part of its reproduction as the entire battery of fetishisms" (225). See also Palacios, *Raza chilena*, xi.

5 Conjunctures of Memory

Opening epigraph quote from Pablo Neruda, "I Accuse," in *Canto general*, trans. Jack Schmitt (Berkeley: University of California Press, 1991), 199.

Cecilia Allendes describes Pisagua as a ghost town that "only comes alive with those that oppose repressive governments" ("Pisagua: 'Esa carcel de piedra y soledades,'" *Análisis* [1983]: 35). Pisagua is a semiabandoned port in the northernmost Chilean province of Tarapacá (called Region One since military administration). It is less than 100 km north of Iquique, the regional capital, yet about 200 km by highway, an arduous two- to three-hour trip over the coastal mountains, up the desert, then over more mountains on dirt roads to the coast.

1 The contrast between the tomb we were traveling to help inaugurate and the crypt for the executed of Tarapacá, where Baldramina's son lay, constituted visible signs not only of a struggle against state repression but of struggles over memory and meaning. Whereas in the neighboring province the government had left the design of the crypt in the hands of the human-rights community, the design and construction of the tomb for those executed in Pisagua (also government financed) had been directed exclusively by a retired regional governor, who largely ignored the concerns of Tarapacá's human-rights groups. The Association of Ex-Political Prisoners of Pisagua had hoped to have their own suffering recognized by having additional burial space reserved for them and their fellow victims of state repression. However, the official shrine excluded the survivors in

favor of Pisagua's "true" martyrs, those executed in 1973. The tomb for those executed in Pisagua is located in Iquique, a large, white, enclosed, chapel-like crypt, with "Para que nunca más" (Never Again) inscribed over the doorway. "Para que nunca más" is a widely used phrase that cynics among the ex-political prisoners interpret as "so as never again to bother us," a reflection, as they see it, of the effect of the civilian government's reconciliation policies.

2 In 1984 Baldramina's house was also defaced with the words "Watch out! Pisagua awaits you!" She repainted her house in its same colors—bright, warm yellow, with rust trim—the colors it had been when her son Humberto lived there until the coup of 1973 (personal communication, February 1994).

3 Baldramina Flores Urqueta de Lizardi, "Homenaje a Humberto Lizardi y demás mártires de Pisagua," pamphlet prepared for the twentieth anniversary of her son's execution, Iquique, Chile, 1993, BF.

4 In Chile, Left, Right, and Center are the categories typically used to identify political actors and ideologies, but they reflect a complex genealogy of parties and coalitions. Because it is a system of relative directionality, the actual ideological content of the positions, alliances, and oppositions included in each must be specified historically and strategically.

5 A number of smaller graves had been revealed during the dictatorship, most notably in Lonquén in 1978, where the bodies were found burned in an old mine shaft. The demonstrations and mass pilgrimage of protesters from Santiago to Lonquén constituted the earliest mass demonstrations against the dictatorship prior to the mobilizations of the early 1980s. On Lonquén, see Máximo Pacheco, *Lonquén* (Santiago: Editorial Aconcagua, 1979); and Isabel Allende's incorporation of these events in her novel *Of Love and Shadows* (New York: Bantam, 1987).

6 National news magazines included extensive interviews and photos from 1973 and 1990 (*Análisis* [18–25 June 1990]; *Hoy* [18–24 June 1990]). Even promilitary news magazines addressed the issue (see, for example, "La guerra del '73," *Ercilla* [20–26 June 1990]: 6–16; "El prisma del tiempo en caso Pisagua," *Ercilla* [20–26 June 1990]: 21–24). Few of these magazines actually circulated in Iquique, as military sympathizers would buy up and destroy all of the copies as soon as they appeared in newsstands. It is remarkable that years later the image of the young man's face was still being called on, as it was for the cover of Nelly Richard's book of cultural criticism, *Residuos y metáforos: Ensayos de crítica cultural sobre el Chile de la Transición* (Santiago: Editorial Cuarto Propio, 1998), and for the cover of a special issue of *Radical History Review*, no. 97 (2007), entitled "State Terror, History, and Memory," ed. Greg Grandin and Thomas Miller Klubock.

7 Tarapacá's Association of Families and Friends of the Executed and Disappeared had been coopted by new leadership eager to claim the reparations they anticipated from the newly elected democratic regime, while

longtime organizers such as Baldramina, exhausted from years of struggle against the dictatorship, had by then withdrawn into their own memories.

8 Pablo Neruda's *Canto general*, a poetic protest of the 1948 repression, locates the repression in a long history of conquest and imperialism in the Americas. Volodia Teitelboim's *Pisagua: La semilla en la arena* is based on accounts of 1948 that Pisagua's villagers told to him when he was a political prisoner there in 1956 (Santiago: Quimantú, 1972).

9 During the 1924–1925 political crisis, insubordinate military officers from the dismantled Regiment Valdivia were relegated to Pisagua. The press decided not to interview them, stating, "The past should not be relived more in the press, especially when the government is submitting a project of national reconstruction" (*El Tarapacá*, 2 April 1925, p. 2).

10 Gumercindo Enchi Tanaka, Carabineros to Intendencia, no. 682, 28 April 1944, AIT-I, /no. 6–1944/1945/1890/Carabineros e Investigaciones; Siefrid Kruger Selmtz, Prefect of Carabineros, Iquique to Intendente, 25 October 1943, AIT-I, no. 5–1942/1943/1812/Carabineros e Investigaciones. Also Enrique Froehlich Ludowieg, Ministry of Interior, Santiago, to Intendente, 22 February 1943; Torao Notoy Incuye, Subdelegado, Pozo Almonte to Intendente, no. 77, 28 February 1945; and Hagn Wikler, Ministry of the Interior to Intendente, 10 February 1943, all three in AIT-I, no. 1–1943/1944/1875/Ministerio del Interior.

11 Responding to the conflict in Europe and the provocations of Tarapacá's own Nazi Party, Communist Party youth in Iquique called on all youth to "expel the assault troopers of the Nazi Party" in the south and on police agencies to "uncover the agents of Nazi-fascism . . . in order to maintain the democratic principles and traditions that our forefathers have left us" (Memorandum [Reserved], Iquique, 24 October 1941, AIT-I, no. 11–1941/1848/Carabineros e Investigaciones). *El Tarapacá* documented the activities of the national-socialist movement in Iquique. A story printed in 1933 listed the movement's goals and criteria for participation as a sign of its vitality and emphasized its difference from German and Italian fascism in its attempt to solve problems pertinent to Chile ("¿Existe el nacismo en Iquique? El movimiento nacional socialista de Chile repercute en todas las provincias del norte de la República," *El Tarapacá*, 3 December 1933, p. 5). On fascism in Chile in general, see Mario Sznajder, "A Case of Non-European Fascism: Chilean National Socialism in the 1930s," *Contemporary History* 28, no. 2 (April 1993): 269–96.

12 *El Despertar*, 28 January 1943, p. 3; *El Despertar*, 30 January 1943, p. 4; *El Despertar*, 5 February 1943. Also discussed in María Soledad de la Cerda, *Chile y los hombres del Tercer Reich* (Santiago: Editorial Sudamericana, 2000), 217.

13 Peter Müffeler Jr. achieved political prominence on the Iquique city council and from this position supported the coup of 1973, though he later came to oppose the military regime.

14 With Chile's declaration of support for the Allies, the Communist Party assumed a highly patriotic, war-oriented stance. Party journalists called for precautionary measures against sabotage and espionage. "A 300 espías del Eje el gobierno les fijó residencia forzosa," *El Despertar*, 27 January 1943, p. 1; *El Despertar*, 28 January 1943, p. 3; *El Despertar*, 18 June 1943, p. 3; *El Despertar*, 21 May 1944; Anthony Eden, Foreign Office London, to British Ambassador in Santiago, 19 November and 13 December 1943, PRO, FO 132/566; Semy Woscaboinik, taped interview, Santiago, Chile, April 1994; British Ambassador, Santiago to Foreign Office, 27 and 14 October 1943, PRO, FO 132/566 "Enemy Aliens." The British were so frustrated by the Chilean government's hesitation to forcibly expel Müffeler that they contemplated withholding, until the Chilean government cooperated fully, $25,000 in funds that the German government had confiscated from Chileans leaving Germany, over which the British were intermediate custodians (London to Santiago, 2 December 1943, PRO, FO 132/566).

15 "Pisagua podrá detener un récord mundial: Será convertida en ciudad penal pesquera . . . ," *El Tarapacá*, 14 November 1945, p. 1. The plan was heralded in internal memos accompanying a copy of the minister of justice's proposal (Assistant Governor, Pisagua, to Intendente, 26 November 1945, AIT-1, no. 1–1946/1948/Gobernaciones).

16 Even the first Popular Front president, Aguirre Cerda, used Pisagua (along with Putre and Belén) as a point of internal exile of five people for fourteen days in 1939, as punishment for those involved in a military uprising in Santiago: *El Tarapacá,* 1 September 1939, p. 3.

17 Gabriel González Videla, interview by the *News Chronicle*, London, 18 June 1947, as quoted in Pablo Neruda, "The Crisis of Democracy in Chile Is a Dramatic Warning for Our Continent," *Passions and Impressions* (New York: Farrar, Straus, Giroux, 1984), 263–83; the interview was originally published in *El Nacional* (Caracas), 27 November 1947. Also see Mario Barros Van Buren, *La Diplomacia Chilena en la II Guerra Mundial* (Santiago: Empresa Editora Arquen, 1998), 311. On coal-mining communities hauled north, see Joann Pavilack, "Black Gold in the Red Zone: Repression and Contention in Chilean Coal Mining Communities from the Popular Front to the Advent of the Cold War" (Ph.D. diss., Duke University, 2003).

18 Including the Movement for the Emancipation of Chilean Women and Gabriela Mistral, *La palabra maldita* (Santiago: Ediciones MEMCH, 1953), quoted in Olga Poblete Poblete, *Una mujer: Elena Caffarena* (Santiago: Ediciones La Morada, Editorial Quarto Propio, 1993), 56; interview with Elena Caffarena (March 1994). See extensive correspondence to, from, and on Pisagua 1948 in the MEMCH archives, which were organized and catalogued by Corinne Pernet and under the care of Elena Caffarena. Also see Corinne Pernet, "Mobilizing Women in the Popular Front Era" (Ph.D. diss., University of California, Irvine, 1996); Corinne Pernet, "Peace

in the World and Democracy at Home: The Chilean Women's Movement in the 1940s," in *Latin America in the 1940s*, ed. David Rock (Berkeley: University of California Press, 1994), 66–186.

19 On the Communist Party, see Ernst Halperin, *Nationalism and Communism in Chile* (Cambridge: MIT Press, 1965). British intelligence reported that the party had been legalized in 1938 with the formation of the Popular Front; that its voting strength as of March 1948 was about 60,000 (out of an electorate of 500,000); that, in 1948, it had 15 (out of 147) deputies and 5 (out of 46) senators; and that it was the first and only Latin American communist party to have cabinet members (Enclosure to Santiago Chancery letter, 7 October 1948, PRO, FO 132/587 "1948 Communism"). By the end of 1948, the director of the Chilean electoral registry announced the elimination of 28,000 voters as communists (*El Tarapacá*, 19 December 1948, p. 2).

20 A British report (May 1948) on Communism in Chile assessed that "the responsibility for the increased class hatred which has developed in the past six months lies . . . with the President himself . . . tomorrow seems to hold promise of nothing but more repression and misery," no. 63 Minute FO 132/587 "1948 Communism."

21 Ley no. 8,987 (1) (Ley de Defensa Permanente de la Democracia) Diario Oficial no. 21, 144, 3 September 1948. For congressional debates about the law, see Diputados, Sesiones Extraodinarias 1948, 2a Legislatura and Sesiones Ordinarias, 1948 I, II; Senado, Sesiones Extraordinarias 1947–1948 and Sesiones Ordinarias 1948 I, II. A thesis on the history of this law was purportedly written at the Universidad de Chile in the last years of the dictatorship; however, when contacted on my behalf by a colleague of mine in 1994, the university library, the department, and the author himself claimed to have lost the manuscript.

22 In a meeting with a British diplomat, Darío Poblete, the press-relations officer for González Videla, claimed that one hundred junior officers had been dismissed without warning and that the government felt absolutely sure of the armed forces. He then questioned the idea that an internal terrorist campaign would ensue if conflict with Russia were announced, but that the communists would conduct more subtle sabotage. "Once this happened it would only be a matter of a few weeks before the trouble makers were rounded up and then he [Poblete] assured me that the President, without waiting for any special powers or laws to be passed, would put these disturbers up against a wall and machine-gun them. He said the President would be absolutely ruthless" (Despatch to the Ambassador, Mr. Mason, no.146, Secret, 24 March 1948, PRO, FO 132/587 "1948 Communism").

23 One hunger strike ended after an appeal from the Communist Party leadership in Santiago (Carabineros Prefect to the Jefatura de la Zona de Emergencia, Guarnición, no. 1750, 29 November 1948, AIT-I, no. 2–1946/1948/Carabineros e Investigaciones; "Relegados de Pisagua re-

solvieron ayer suspender huelga de hambre," *El Tarapacá*, 30 November 1948, p. 5).

24 Neruda, *Canto general*, 245–46. As Communist Party senator for Tarapacá in the 1940s, Neruda had been forced to flee Chile. For an account of this, see Volodia Teitelboim, *Neruda: An Intimate Biography* (Austin: University of Texas Press, 1991), 278–331. Efforts to trace Neruda's escape from Chile can be found in documents no. 3, 10 January 1948; no. 10, 3 February 1948; no. 15, 10 February 1948, PRO, FO 132/587 "1948 Communism."

25 As a flyer of clandestine origin reported, Ángel Veas, Félix Morales, Isaías Fuentes, and José Bellos Oliva perished in Pisagua while many other prisoners became quite physically and emotionally ill ("A La Juventud de la Provincia y al Pueblo en General," flyer typed on manila paper, AIT-I, no. 2–1946/1948/Carabineros e Investigaciones. See also "Recuerdos de un relegado de 1948," in *Pisagua 1948, 1956, 1973, 1983* (a typed, mimeographed book circulated secretly in mid-1980s in Iquique), 19.

26 Consular report no. 128, Confidential, 16 March 1948, extracted in no. 29, from British Embassy, Santiago, PRO, FO 132/587 "1948 Communism."

27 Protests painted on the walls of Iquique read "G.V. traidor, fuera los vende patria, libertad presos políticos, pide el pueblo," "Viva P.C. — Videla de Truman. — 10 de Mayo. — Mueran los traidores.," and "Muera Gabriel González Videla, el traidor, Viva el P.C." (Carabineros Prefect to the Jefatura de Zona de Emergencia de Tarapacá, Guarnición, no. 574, 19 April 1948, AIT-I, no. 2–1946/1948/Carabineros e Investigaciones. However, González Videla did bring his party, the Radical Party, down with him, as they came to be called "twisted radicals." The Radical Party went from being the pivotal player in the Chilean political system to being such a marginal presence in Chilean politics that, as of the 1990s, they lacked sufficient voting power to retain their official status as a party.

28 Augusto Pinochet Ugarte, *El día decisivo: 11 de Septiembre de 1973* (Santiago: Editorial Andrés Bello, 1980), 23–28, quoted in *Pisagua 1948, 1956, 1973, 1983*, 14–16.

29 *El Tarapacá*, 1 January 1956, p. 1.

30 *El Tarapacá*, 7 January 1956, p. 1. The government's state of siege was precipitated by a failed general strike on 9 January 1956, which had sought to protest the government's declared intention not to enact automatic wage increases and its freezing of 1956 salaries at half of 1955's rise in the cost of living (British Embassy, Santiago to American Department of the Foreign Office, London, 16 January 1956, PRO, FO 132/608).

31 A phalangist congressional representative, together with the provincial party president, inspected the conditions in Pisagua, denounced the "primitive" conditions of the town, and claimed that the communists' constant evangelizing made everyone miserable. In general, this centrist politician determined that relegation to Pisagua "was one of the worst

paths the government could have chosen," as "the workers have a reason to struggle in common" (*El Tarapacá*, 9 January 1956, p. 1; *El Tarapacá*, 12 January 1956, p. 5). Semi Woscaboinik, interview, November 1992.

32 *El Tarapacá*, 18 January 1956, p. 4. A similar committee in Arica raised food and money for the prisoners (*El Tarapacá*, 20 January 1956, p. 5). Specifically, the prisoners were kept in the camps at Aguada and San Enrique (Carabineros Prefect to Intendente, no. 101, 24 January 1956, AIT-1, no. 6–1956/Carabineros e Investigaciones. In Tarapacá the state of siege was met with outright defiance. For example, on 31 January 1956 housewives protested vehemently against the inflation of the price of bread in the nitrate camp Victoria's store. The wives then threatened not to cook breakfast the following morning, which would, in effect, mean a work stoppage. See Carabinero Prefect to the Intendente, no. 126, 31 January 1956, AIT-1, no. 6–1956/Carabineros e Investigaciones.

33 As the government demanded that prisoners pay their own travel and lodging expenses, the committee in Iquique had to raise substantial finances from local businesses and labor associations (*El Tarapacá*, 27 January 1956, p. 1). A newspaper editorial noted that while there had been talk for years of turning the abandoned port of Pisagua into an "Acapulco Chileno," nothing had been done to provide even the most basic infrastructure for a tourist industry, and, ironically, military planes flew in the only "tourists": the internal exiles. The residents of Tarapacá thus were likely to face greater taxation to pay for the expensive luxury of political relegation. See "Lección de Pisagua," *El Tarapacá*, 13 January 1956, p. 5.

34 Whether Teitelboim had been relegated to Pisagua in 1948 as well was a matter of contention. Teitelboim denied it, but the hospital director claimed to have proof in his files (*El Tarapacá*, 12 January 1956, p. 5).

35 In telling of these events, in hopes of an ironic justice, many Chileans claim that Ibáñez del Campo was justly punished by fate in that, purportedly, either his son was gay or his sister was a lesbian.

36 Leonardo Fernández, personal communication, August 2001. As the human-rights activist Marcos Ruíz noted in a personal communication in August 1998, the Chilean military has historically regarded boats as appropriately liminal spaces for containing queers, as is evident in accounts of military repression of transvestites during the 1973 coup and the years of dictatorship (Claudia Donoso and Paz Errázuriz, *La manzana de Adán* [Santiago: Editorial Zona, 1990], 91).

37 Elderly resident of Pisagua, interview by author, Pisagua, Chile, February 1994. Another Pisagua native spoke of how his home was used as a prison: "There the common prisoners felt comfortable. The inhabitants of the town, whose number didn't even exceed a hundred, received them without putting up much resistance. . . . Perhaps, it was most difficult for the women to accept them, as the majority of the condemned over many years were homosexuals. It seems that the national prison authorities had concentrated them, by decree, in Pisagua" (Luis Muñoz Orellana, "Pisa-

gua en los tiempos de González Videla," in *Vida, pasión y muerte en Pisagua*, Bernardo Guerrero J. [Iquique: CREAR, 1990], 63).

38 This silence has also been noted by the historian Elisa Fernández (personal communication); see her "Beyond Partisan Politics in Chile" (Ph.D. diss., University of Miami, 1996).

39 "Una afrenta para Pisagua," *El Tarapacá*, 16 April 1942, p. 3.

40 "Cárcel de Pisagua," *El Tarapacá*, 17 April 1942, p. 3.

41 I have derived the information regarding the prison camp of 1973 from a synthesis of published testimonies (including Haroldo Quinteros, *Diario de un preso politico chileno* [Madrid: Ediciones de la Torre, 1979]), my own interviews and conversations with ex-political prisoners in the context of participant-observation with the Association of Ex-Political Prisoners, and personal communications with ex-political prisoners not affiliated with the group. For reasons of ongoing litigation and very real threats to the safety of my informants (some of whom have been harassed for testifying against the military), I do not identify them by name.

42 Indeed, during the upheavals of the Popular Unity period, Iquique was a very peaceful city; its one terrorist act, perpetrated by an extreme Right group in August 1973, was arson of the local trade-union council headquarters, a crime which had been investigated at the time of the coup but whose authors were never brought to trial. More politically experienced ex-political prisoners have explained to me that they turned themselves in because they had no choice: the fascist sector of the military had launched the coup earlier than predicted and with an overwhelming amount of force.

43 Due to an ongoing rivalry that dated from the early nineteenth century, relations between Chile and Peru in the 1970s were even more complex; dramatic political shifts in the respective national contexts had led the countries in opposite directions, one toward socialist government, the other toward fascist military interventions. The tensions created by these shifts were exacerbated by revolving Soviet (and U.S.) support. A detailed account of the antagonism between Peru and Chile and of actual mobilizations for war at various moments after the coup appeared in a special series of the news magazine *Qué pasa* ("Los años que remecieron a Chile," 3 July 1993; "La hora más dramática," 10 July 1993; "La triple amenaza," 17 July 1993). The memory of long-standing conflict and the prospect of renewed warfare was also rehearsed by Peruvians (Raúl Palacios Rodriguez, *La chilenización de Tacna y Arica, 1883–1929* [Lima: Editorial Arica, 1974]; Eleodoro Ventocilla, *Chile prepara o otra guerra . . . Argentina, Bolivia y Perú amenazados* [Lima: Gráfica Mundo, 1970]). See also Alfonso Benavides Correa, *¿Habrá Guerra Próximamente en el Cono Sur?* (Mexico City: Siglo Veintiuno Editores, 1974). Chileans were convinced that Peru planned to launch a war of reconquest on the centennial of the War of the Pacific (1978–79) whether the current Peruvian regime was Left or Right. These plans were complicated by the (unsynchronized) rise and fall of revolu-

tionary and fascist governments in both Peru and Chile and by both countries' shifting alliances with the Cold War superpowers, who were interested in fomenting regional conflict for their own geopolitical ends.

44 Hernán Valdés also documented this in testimony about his detention in a camp south of Santiago. He recalled soldiers saying that the prisoners should not worry too much because they were "'going to be Chileans again. Any day now war with Peru will begin and we will all have to defend the *patria*.'" The prisoners began to understand that the army, and the troops especially, were being psychologically prepared for war with Peru over the impending lapse of the War of the Pacific treaty, which, in Valdés's view, "sanctioned the handing over of the territories Chile won in a war of economic conquest induced by English imperialism in the last century. Its intent of nationalist ideological cohesion, in the actual circumstances of internal war, is evident" (*Tejas verdes: Diario de un campo de concentración en Chile* [1974; repr., Barcelona: Editorial Laia, 1978], 147–48).

45 Testimonial from an ex-political prisoner of 1973, presented in Francisco Lillo Muñoz, *Fragmento de Pisagua* (Iquique: Félix Reales Vilca, 1990), 39.

46 Some information on the names and status of prisoners was made public at the time. See, for example, "Situación real de los detenidos en campamento de Pisagua," *El Tarapacá*, 19 October 1973, p. 1.

47 In a largely symbolic gesture, Pinochet moved his government to Iquique in February 1974 (perhaps harkening back to the Civil War of 1891 when the congress declared Iquique the national capital). In preparation for Pinochet's anticipated inspection of Pisagua, camp officials held drills and locked-down political prisoners in the worst physical condition. A famous photograph of prisoners standing in military formation dates from these preparations. The healthiest and least abused prisoners were selected for Pinochet's visit, and their ranks were supplemented with conscripts. Ironically, given that it presents an idealized version of the prison experience, a photo taken at the time has since been used in publications on the military repression. See, for example, the cover of Rolando Carrasco Moya, *Prigué: Prisionero de guerra en Chile* (1977; repr., Santiago: Ediciones Aquí y Ahora, 1991), which is the testimonial of an ex-prisoner held in another region altogether. For a photograph of prisoners who had actually experienced intense torture (though this is not evident in the photo itself), see *El Tarapacá*, 4 November 1973, p. 1; the photo was taken on 2 November.

48 Reporting directly to General Forestier were the *fiscal militar* Carlos Acuña, the military judge who acted as prosecutor and who rose from civilian judge to the rank of commandante by January 1974, and the *jefe de intelligencia de Carabineros* Teniente Jorge Muñoz, who was head of all military intelligence in the region after the coup (he had a long record in working intelligence for the fascist parallel organizations within the military). Acuña, the civilian, wore nonregulation military garb, while Muñoz, the military man, wore civilian clothing and thus contradicted the military's

claims that the camp was run according to the rules of warfare. Furthermore, according to ex-political prisoners, both men habitually acted under the influence of alcohol and cocaine. These two men were in charge of interrogations, sometimes in competition with one another. They conducted sessions of systematic torture over the course of six months and were often assisted by the physician Werner Galvez, who had been a major (*en rama de tanque*) and a president of Iquique's medical-professional guild (Colegio de Medicos) as an opposition leader. After the coup, the military named Galvez director of the regional hospital in Iquique and chief of sanitation in Pisagua. In addition to consulting in torture sessions, it was his task to select prisoners for the staged publicity photos, to supervise all prison-camp medical staff, and to personally examine prisoners to occult those who showed signs of torture during outside visits and inspections.

49 Pisagua was included in the infamous Caravan of Death, a special military team sent by General Pinochet to detention camps across Chile to ensure that regional commanders were sufficiently rigorous in establishing military control. In many camps, the arrival of the team, led by General Arellano Stark, meant summary executions and the intensification of terror tactics. Pisagua was an exception, as General Forestier had been nothing less than enthusiastic in imposing military discipline, such that General Arellano Stark's visit was merely celebratory (although he did take away the camp's prized prisoners, two Cubans). On the Caravan of Death, see Jorge Escalante, *La misión era matar: El juicio a la caravana Pinochet-Arellano* (Santiago: Lom Ediciones, 2000).

50 Although women were court-martialed on various occasions, Chile's only court-martial of exclusively women occurred on 18 December 1973 (*El Tarapacá*, 21 December 1973, p. 1; *El Tarapacá*, 23 December 1973, p. 1).

51 To prevent possible acts of mercy on General Bonilla's part, prison-camp officials presented their prisoners in military formation in two groups, the first comprising prisoners who were in relatively good shape, the second, positioned on a side-street, comprising politically significant prisoners, who had been tortured for months. When General Bonilla started to approach the second group, the prosecutor Acuña successfully distracted him. Ironically, according to survivors, had Bonilla stepped closer, he would have seen there a family member of one of his own family's beloved domestic servants and might have intervened to save his life.

52 "Bonilla: '¿Comandante, cómo está la comida de los presos?' Larraín: 'Comen bién, mi general.' Bonilla: '¿Comandante, sabe cuanto cuesta mentirle a un general?' Y Larraín no se puede dialogar" (ex-political prisoner of Pisagua, interview by author, March 2001).

53 "La gente estaba contenta, hacen deportes se bañen en el mar. Es una vida que la estoy envidiando: me están dando ganas de irme como prisionero de guerra a Pisagua, porque hasta el clima es muy bueno" (*El Tarapacá*, 6 February 1974, p. 2).

54 Though the German contractor visited the site, according to ex-political prisoners, the military later enlisted skilled political prisoners to draw up plans for six barracks (each holding fifty double-bunks for a total 600 prisoners) and for three sheds (bathroom, kitchen, pantry). On the role of the former Nazi, see also Quinteros, *Diario de un preso político chileno*, 70.

55 Stills and text from the film *Yo Soy, Yo Fui, Yo Seré* were published as a book, Walter Heynowski, Gerhard Scheumann, and Peter Hellmich's *Anflug auf Chacabuco: Mit Kamara und Mikrofon in chilenischen KZ-Lagern* (Berlin: Verlag de Nation, 1974). I interviewed Walter Heynowski in Berlin in August 2002.

56 Pedro Bravo Elizondo, *Cultura y teatro obrero en Chile, 1900–1930* (Madrid: Libros del Meridión, 1986); Pedro Bravo Elizondo, *Raíces del teatro popular en Chile* (Guatemala City: Impresos D y M, 1991).

57 Haroldo Quinteros reports that after the first round of brutal executions, comandante Larraín Larraín said, "Yo, como católico que soy, siempre siento mucho la muerte de alguien" (I, being the Catholic that I am, always feel deeply someone's death), and after supervising a long torture session, coming to a group of prisoners who were "totalmente quebrado" (totally broken), saying, "Balbuceó: 'recen por mí'" (he sobbed: pray for me) (*Diario de un preso político chileno*, 51, 78).

58 On the issue of the drug industry in the North and the efforts of the Popular Unity government to investigate and control trafficking, see Raúl Pizarro Illanes, "Iquique: El paraíso de la coca," Documentos Especiales no. 6 (Santiago: Quimantú, 1973); Luis Morales, "La hora de la DEA," *El Nortino*, 23 April 1998, p. 2. See also Quinteros, *Diario de un preso político chileno*, 46–48. What remains to be investigated is the flourishing of the drug industry under military rule and the possible flooding of local markets with cheap drugs, both being strategic policies deployed with covert U.S. assistance in other countries of the Americas, the first as a means to fiscally support military regimes and the second as a method of counterinsurgency doctrine designed to depoliticize youth.

59 For example, neighbors would say to a mother of a disappeared man, "Well, your son must have done *something* wrong." In the case of those implicated in the drug trade, ethnicity may also have played a part in their marginalization, as they bore recognizably indigenous Aymara names, such as Mamani. Aymara peoples of the region have never comfortably fit into even leftist national narratives.

60 In a transition to democracy which left intact the structures of repression, Chilean human-rights groups persisted in denouncing atrocities of the past but were slow to recognize the state violence now concentrated on those deemed drug traffickers and common criminals. The Human Rights Commission of Iquique, newly reconvened in 1998, has bridged this gap, especially through their increasing attention to the plight of undocumented Bolivian domestic servants in Tarapacá.

61 Several ex-political prisoners reported that they tried to enter the

hotel to look at the renovations, but were rebuffed each time. I, too, was refused entry when accompanied by one of the ex-political prisoners. Pisagua is so tiny that the caretaker had no trouble knowing who was visiting the port and why.

62 Phillip Berryman, *Liberation Theology* (New York: Pantheon, 1987); Daniel H. Levine, *Religion and Political Conflict in Latin America* (Chapel Hill: University of North Carolina Press, 1986); Daniel Levine, "Assessing the Impacts of Liberation Theology in Latin America," *Review of Politics* 50, no. 2: 241–63; Scott Mainwaring and A. Wilde, *The Progressive Church in Latin America* (Notre Dame, Ind.: University of Notre Dame Press, 1989); Brian Smith, *The Church and Politics in Chile: Challenges to Modern Catholicism* (Princeton: Princeton University Press, 1982).

63 Open letter to the city penned by Flavio Rossi R., 10 July 1984; Flavio Rossi R., "Antonio Gramsci o la filosofía de la praxis," Departamento Laicos newsletter, January–February 1991, RMLK.

64 Cited in a bulletin for a Saturday Eucharist in Iquique during the 1980s in honor of those who died in Pisagua 1973. Translation from the *Oxford NIV Scofield Study Bible*, ed. C. I. Scofield (New York: Oxford University Press, 1984), 759.

65 "Auto definición del Padre Ángel Fernández," *La Estrella*, 11 May 1984, RMLK.

66 Bishop's letter of support, 9 August 1984, RMLK; "Fallo de los Tribunales de Justicia," *La Estrella*, 10 July 1984, RMLK. The list of groups that signed the public declaration in support of the priest gives some sense of the vitality of the human-rights movement in Tarapacá at that point: the Ecclesiastic Base Communities, the Young People's Pastory, Religious Dance Associations, the Renovation Groups, the Department of Laicos, Christianity Classes, the Tarapacá Cultural Group, the Committee in Defense of the People's Rights, the Chilean Union of Women, the Association of Families of Victims of the Repression, Worker's Associations, Students, and the Municipal Shelter Group ("Declaración, Chile Defiende la Vida," RMLK).

67 "Instructions no. 1: Chile Defiende la Vida," the national organizing committee, RMLK. The organizing coalition included the Committee in Defense of Women's Rights and the Chilean Union of Women ("Declaración, Chile Defiende la Vida," RMLK). The events that took place in Iquique that day were organized by the coalition Women of Iquique; newspapers reported that 2,000 people attended a service in the cathedral that was presided over by seven priests, included songs, prayers, and testimonies, and was followed by a procession in which marchers carried lit candles and flowers meant to indicate the pacific nature of the march ("Completa normalidad en 'jornada por la vida,'" *La Estrella*, 11 August 1984, p. 8, RMLK).

68 The new bishop in Iquique, Bishop Enrique Prado, traveled to Pisagua and on his return confirmed the arrival of new prisoners, many of

whom, he claimed, were "common delinquents." The intendente of Tarapacá affirmed that Pisagua held 256 prisoners from the central part of the country and from Arica, the northernmost Chilean city (*La Estrella*, 4 and 5 November 1984, RMLK).

69 Diamela Eltit, *Por la patria* (Santiago: Ediciones Ornitorrinco, 1986).

70 Pablo Neruda, *Canto general*, trans. Jack Schmitt (Berkeley: University of California Press, 1991), 186.

71 Visual artist, interview by author, Iquique, Chile, March 1994.

72 Demonstration chant, Movimiento Contra la Tortura Sebastián Acevedo, June 1990. Information gathered on this movement came from my own participant-observation from June to August 1990 and in 1991. See also Hernán Vidal, *El Movimiento Contra La Tortura "Sebastian Acevedo": Derechos humanos y la producción de símbolos nacionales bajo el fascismo Chileno* (Minneapolis: Society for the Study of Contemporary Hispanic and Lusophone Revolutionary Literatures, 1986).

73 Such as a job-security policy for public employees that meant the new government could change only the very top positions in the government structure, while all of the clerical and other support staff loyal to the military regime remained and constantly impinged on the everyday workings of the state.

74 Comisión Nacional de Verdad y Reconciliación, *Informe Rettig* (Santiago: Gobierno, 1991), 2:873.

75 Human-rights activists demanded that the Chilean National Commission on Truth and Reconciliation be renamed the Commission on Truth, Justice, and Reconciliation, as genuine forgiveness could not be granted without full revelation and recognition (by the perpetrator) of wrongdoing.

76 David Becker, Elizabeth Lira, María Isabel Castillo, Elena Gomez, and Juana Kovalskys, "Therapy with Victims of Political Repression in Chile: The Challenge of Social Reparation," *Social Issues* 46, no. 3 (1990): 133–49; Brinton Lykes and Ramsey Liem, "Human Rights and Mental Health in the United States: Lessons from Latin America," *Social Issues* 46, no. 3 (1990): 151–65; David Becker and Elizabeth Lira, eds., *Derechos humanos: Todo es según el dolor con que se mira* (Santiago: ILAS, 1989). For a nonclinical discussion of political psychology, collective memory, and human rights, see Denise Jodelet, "El lado moral y afectivo de la historia: Un ejemplo de memoria de masa: El proceso a K. Barbie, 'el carnicero de Lyon,'" *Psicología Política* no. 6 (1993): 33–72; Diario Páez Basabe, "Trauma político y memoria colectiva: Freud, Halbwachs y la psicología política contemporánea," *Psicología Política* no. 6 (1993): 7–34; Darío Páez Basabe, D. Avin, J. Igartha, J. C. González, L. García, and C. Ibaria, "Procesos sociales de recuerdo de hechos traumáticos: Una investigación transcultural," *Psicología Política* no. 6 (1993): 73–93; Carlos Martín Beristain and Darío Páez, *Violencia, apoyo a las victimas y reconstrucción social* (Madrid: Editorial Fundamentos, 2000); James Pennebaker, Darío Páez, and Ber-

nard Rene, *Collective Memory of Political Events: Social Psychological Perspectives* (Mahwah, N.J.: Lawrence Erlbaum, 1997); Nancy Caro Hollander, *Love in a Time of Hate: Liberation Psychology in Latin America* (New Brunswick, N.J.: Rutgers University Press, 1999).

77 Rosario Dominguez (national director of PRAIS), interview by author, Santiago, Chile, March 1994. Data reported in PRAIS, *Salud y derechos humanos* (Santiago: Ministerio de Salud, 1994). The Chilean state allocated families of the executed and disappeared a one-time cash compensation and some educational grants. The PRAIS program remained the most far-reaching reparation initiative in offering services to survivors of repression as broadly defined to include ex-political prisoners and former exiles.

78 Chile represents one of the first instances in which the mental-health and human-rights movements' methodologies for dealing with the legacies of political violence have been taken up in a state project. Funding for the first three years came from the Agency for International Development. Mental health as development complemented the government's project of "cultural modernization," which was designed to mold Chile to the form of liberal democracy in a neoliberal economy.

79 The PRAIS protocol for therapy is based largely on cognitive-behavioral models of treatment, in contrast to the more psychoanalytic approach of many of the nongovernmental institutes in Santiago. In practice, due to staffing shortages, most patients in Iquique are treated primarily by social workers, occasionally by psychologists, and only rarely by psychiatrists (PRAIS staff and officials, interviews by author, Iquique and Santiago, Chile, August 2000; Joel Espina Sandoval, "Norma técnica para la atención de personas afectadas por la represión política ejercida por el estado en el período 1973–1990" [unpublished manuscript, Unidad de Salud Mental, Ministerio de Salud, Santiago, 2000]; Unidad de Salud Mental, *Plan nacional de salud mental y psiciatria: Resumen ejecutivo* [Santiago: Ministerio de Salud, 2000]).

80 The ex-political prisoners in the association wanted to produce their own book because they felt that those who had published individual testimonials had gotten details wrong and profited selfishly from collective suffering. Difficulties in getting the book project going pertained not only to organizational problems but also to their frustration with the multiplicity of the past: that *one* complete and true story could never be told. Melancholy motivated the telling but provided no way through it. My plans to write about Pisagua generated a huge argument in one association meeting over whether I, too, would appropriate their history. I was defended by those who pointed to the historical role internationalism had played in Chilean history, particularly during the dictatorship.

81 PRAIS physician, interview by author, Iquique, Chile, February 1994.

82 This was another missed opportunity to expand definitions of human rights and does not reflect international thinking on gender violence as a

critical human-rights issue, nor a decade of efforts by Chilean feminists to show that democracy in the home is vital to democracy in the street.

83 Fernando Coronil has considered the problem of representation and subaltern states in the context of Venezuelan structural adjustments, in "Listening to the Subaltern," *Poetics Today* 15, no. 4 (winter 1994): 643–58.

84 Anna Tsing cautioned against falling into the trap of seeing state and community as an opposition between two bounded spheres. She argued that in some cases they were mutually constitutive, as state representatives moved through multiple spaces and encountered the often heterogeneous demands of groups that were in — and moving between — places which called on the state in particular ways (*In the Realm of the Diamond Queen* [Princeton: Princeton University Press, 1993]).

85 A similar case involved a widow who claimed the reparations money even though her marriage had ended long before the coup and her former husband had established a second family (who received nothing), a situation exacerbated by Chile's lack of a divorce law until 2005.

86 On the comparative case of China, Jun Jing cites Arthur Kleinman's work on "embodied memory" to explain that "illness narratives" become "a medium of memorial articulation" working through "the narration of political misfortunes through the body as a highly emotional form of protest against not only the original cause of pain but the mechanisms that perpetuate past injuries into the present" (Jun Jing, *The Temple of Memories: History, Power, and Morality in a Chinese Village* [Stanford, Calif.: University of Stanford Press, 1996], 169). See also Arthur Kleinman, "How Bodies Remember: Social Memory and Bodily Experience of Criticism, Resistance, and Delegitimization following China's Cultural Revolution," *New Literary History* 25 (summer): 707–23.

87 Because the investigation was so partial, politically timed information leaks tormented the community, giving them no opportunity to forget, even had they been willing. For example, in August 1998 it was revealed that the remains of some of those executed in Pisagua had been dynamited. In a number of cases over the years, military personnel offered to sell families information on the location of loved ones' remains.

88 These observations have been corroborated by oral histories collected in other parts of Chile by Janet Finn ("Mining Community" [Ph.D. diss., University of Michigan, 1995]) and Margaret Power ("Right Wing Women and Chilean Politics: 1964–1973" [Ph.D. diss., University of Illinois, Chicago, 1997]). The historian Leo Spitzer, who grew up in the late 1940s in La Paz, Bolivia, recalled that adults would tease him by saying, "You better watch what you do, or you'll end up in Pisagua!" (personal communication). See also Spitzer's oral history of Austrian-Jewish refugees in Bolivia during World War II, *Hotel Bolivia: The Culture of Memory in a Refuge from Nazism* (New York: Hill and Wang, 1998).

89 On the political ecology of development plans in Pisagua, including

tourism, see Sarah Keene Meltzoff, Michael Lemons, and Yair Lictensztajn, "Voices of a Natural Prison," *Political Ecology* 8 (2001): 45–80.

90 That next Christmas, the ex-political prisoners sponsored a party (a *chocolatada*) for Pisagua's children, explaining how glimpses of the children who had lived in the port in 1973–1974 had given them much hope at that terrible time. They also recalled the timid but genuine gestures of friendliness offered by the adults and how much the townspeople had seemed to enjoy the prisoners' theater productions.

91 "Puerto Pisagua se abre paso al progreso de nuestra provincia," *El Nortino*, 4 December 1993. Pisagua still had very little basic infrastructure, and the government promised to improve housing, water, electricity, telephones, and roads as funds became available. As the newspaper article advertised, the state hoped to develop a tourist industry and to that end constructed basic camping facilities on the beach. Some of the association members claimed in their enthusiasm that the French, especially, would adore Pisagua for its dramatic scenery and that it would become another Club Med.

92 There is no auxiliary Friends of Pisagua group. Almost from the beginning, the ex-political prisoners of Pisagua had incorporated ex-political prisoners who had been detained in other parts of the country, so Pisagua as experience was always somewhat metaphorical.

93 "Ciudad esta que como ninguna en el Norte de Chile, evoca un pasado de suntuosidad. No son las ruinas magníficas de civilizaciones desparecidas. Son más que ruinas materiales, las ruinas de un recuerdo, saturadas de nostalgias" (Alfredo Wormand, *Frontera norte* [Santiago: Editorial Pacífico, n.d.], quoted in Laura Salinas Cerpa, "Pisagua en la literatura," in *Vida, pasión y muerte en Pisagua*, ed. Bernardo Guerrero J. [Iquique: CREAR, 1990], 140).

94 Michel Foucault, *Madness and Civilization* (London: Tavistock, 1967), 57, as discussed in Chris Philo, "History, Geography and the 'Still Greater Mystery' of Historical Geography," in *Human Geography: Society, Space, and Social Science*, ed. Derek Gregory, Ron Martin, and Graham Smith (Minneapolis: University of Minnesota Press, 1994), 252–81.

6 The Economy of Reconciliation

1 Notable among many books and films are Juan Armando Epple, *El arte de recordar: Ensayos sobre la memoria cultural de Chile* (Santiago: Mosquito Editores, 1994); *Chile, Obstinate Memory*, dir. Patricio Guzmán (New York: Icarus/First Run Films, 1997); Hernán Vidal, *Política cultural de la memoria histórica* (Santiago: Mosquito Editores, 1997); Mario Garcés, Pedro Milas, Myriam Olguín, Julio Pinto, María Teresa Rojas, and Miguel Larentis, eds., *Memoria para un nuevo siglo: Chile, miradas a la segunda mitad del siglo 20* (Santiago: Lom Ediciones, 2000); Nelly Richard, ed., *Políticas y estéticas de la memoria* (Santiago: Editorial Cuarto Propio,

2000); Bruno Groppo and Patricia Flier, eds. *La imposibilidad del olvido: Recorridos de la memoria en Argentina, Chile y Uruguay* (La Plata: Ediciones Al Margen, 2001); María Angélica Illanes, *La batalla de la memoria: Ensayos históricos de nuestro siglo: Chile, 1900–2000* (Santiago: Planeta, Ariel, 2002); Ariel Dorfman, *Desert Memories: Journeys through the Chilean North* (Washington: National Geographic Directions, 2004).

2 For an insightful criticism of how public policy, using a rhetoric of the Future, too often entails the denial of the interests and rights of subordinate (especially nonheteronormative) sectors, see Lee Edelman, *No Future: Queer Theory and the Death Drive* (Durham, N.C.: Duke University Press, 2004).

3 Ascanio Cavallo, "Tres malditos cheques," in *La historia oculta de la transición* (Santiago: Grijalbo, 1998), 67–75.

4 Sigmund Freud, *The Interpretation of Dreams* (1900; repr., New York: Avon Books, 1965), 52–53. The military's 1993 action was reminiscent of scenes from 1973, such as the bombing of the presidential palace and helmeted soldiers with guns pointed at civilians, loading them into trucks, taking them away.

5 Iliana Ramírez (ex-political prisoner), interview by author, Iquique, Chile, January 1994.

6 Fieldwork observation of a discussion by a group of teens about Pisagua.

7 For an example of a culturally relevant sensibility about haunting, see the Chilean director and screenwriter Alejandro Amenábar's film *The Others* (Burbank: Dimension Films, 2003), which portrays an intersection between familial (infanticide-suicide), historical-societal (plague), and political-national (international warfare) tragedies in a frontier space, thus generating a confusion over who haunts whom, the living or the dead. On political "hauntology" in performative cultural memory, see Diana Taylor, *The Archive and the Repertoire: Performing Cultural Memory in the Americas* (Durham, N.C.: Duke University Press, 2003). For explorations of the dialogic relation between the living and the dead in a different cultural context, see Avery F. Gordon, *Ghostly Matters: Haunting and the Sociological Imagination* (Minneapolis: University of Minnesota Press, 1996); Elizabeth Hallam and Jenny Hockey, *Death, Memory and Material Culture* (Oxford: Berg, 2001); Sharon Patricia Holland, *Raising the Dead: Readings of Death and (Black) Subjectivity* (Durham, N.C.: Duke University Press, 2000); Alan Klima, *The Funeral Casino* (Princeton: Princeton University Press, 2002); and Mary Margaret Steedly, *Hanging without a Rope* (Princeton: Princeton University Press, 1993). On the ways in which languages of the dead silence the living, see Simon During's reading of Salman Rushdie's novel *Shame* (New York: Vintage, 1984), wherein Rushdie asks, "Can only the dead speak?" ("Postmodernism or Post-colonialism today," *Textual Practice* 1, no. 1 [1987]: 32–47).

8 For example, Marjorie Agosin, *Scraps of Life*, trans. Cola Franzon

(Trenton, N.J.: Red Sea Press, 1987); Patricia Chuchryk, "Subversive Mothers: The Women's Opposition to the Military Regime in Chile," in *Surviving beyond Fear*, ed. Marjorie Agosin (Fredonia, N.Y.: White Pine Press, 1993), 86–207; David R. Davis and Michael D. Wad, "They Dance Alone: Deaths and the Disappeared in Contemporary Chile," *Conflict Resolution* 34, no. 3 (September 1990): 449–75; Jo Fisher, *Out of the Shadows* (London: Latin American Bureau, 1993); and Jennifer Schirmer, "'Those who die for life cannot be called dead': Women and Human Rights Protest in Latin America," in *Surviving beyond Fear*, ed. Marjorie Agosin (Fredonia, N.Y.: White Pine Press, 1993), 31–57.

9 For example, see Juan Luis Ysern de Arce, Obispo de Ancud, *Verdad y justicia: El desafío del reencuentro* (Santiago: Ediciones CESOC, 1990).

10 In a kindred critique of neoliberal cultural logics, Gareth Williams posits that a "suturing logics of whitewash lie increasingly at the heart of neo-liberal institutionality" and that Chile is "paradigmatic in this regard," meaning that there is a "sustaining [of] the dictatorial culture of fear as the necessary precondition for democracy" such that "democratization is guaranteed by suppressing democratization and by allowing for the positive extension of dictatorial social and institutional processes"; on that note, Williams points to the 1980 constitution (*The Other Side of the Popular: Neoliberalism and Subalternity in Latin America* [Durham, N.C.: Duke University Press 2002], 281–82).

11 For analyses by prominent Chilean thinkers sponsored by the Frei presidency, see Cristián Toloza and Eugenio Lahera, eds., *Chile in the Nineties* (Stanford, Calif.: Stanford University Press, 2000).

12 On the transition, see FLACSO-Chile, *Nuevo gobierno: Desafíos de la reconciliación: Chile 1999–2000* (Santiago: FLACSO-Chile, 2000); see also the particularly incisive analyses in Mauro Salazar and Miguel Valderrama, eds., *Dialectos en transición: Política y subjectividad en Chile actual* (Santiago: Lom Ediciones, 2000).

13 On reconciliation as a political technology used to overcome political impasses over the course of Chilean history, see the work of Brian Loveman and Elizabeth Lira, *Las ardientes cenizas del olvido: Vía chilena de reconciliación política 1932–1994* (Santiago: DIBAM, Lom Ediciones, 2000). See also Elizabeth Lira, Brian Loveman, Tony Mifsud S.J., and Pablo Salvat, *Historia, política y ética de la verdad en Chile, 1891–2001* (Santiago: Lom Ediciones, 2001); Brian Loveman and Elizabeth Lira, eds., *Arquitectura política y seguridad interior del estado 1811–1990* (Santiago: DIBAM, Lom Ediciones, 2002). My analysis here is complementary, but goes further in positing a deep cultural symbolic frame that makes this most recent instance of a reconciliation project especially problematic.

14 So successfully did the military defend the juridical legitimacy of the coup and subsequent rule that current human-rights cases in the Chilean courts assume this legitimacy and argue that the military misapplied its

own procedures and codes of conduct in the military courts-martial and summary executions of civilians.

15 *Constitución política de la República de Chile* (Santiago: Editorial Cienna, 1998). On the Consejo de Seguridad Nacional, see *Constitución*, chapter 11, articles 95 and 96; Comisión Chilena de Derechos Humanos, *Origen, contenido y práctica de la Constitución Política de 1980: Su significado desde la perspectiva de los derechos humanos* (Santiago: Comisión Chilena de Derechos Humanos, n.d.).

16 Gabriel Salazar and Julio Pinto, *Historia contemporánea de Chile*, vol. 1, *Estado, legitimidad, ciudadanía* (Santiago: Lom Ediciones, 1999).

17 Not to mention funding, secured in part through a mandated 10 percent share of copper revenues.

18 Hugo Fazio R., *Mapa actual de la extrema riqueza en Chile* (Santiago: Lom Ediciones, 1997).

19 On the decline of solidarity in Chilean political culture, see Marc Cooper, *Pinochet and Me: A Chilean Anti-Memoir* (London: Verso, 2001).

20 For a compelling discussion of the productive role that rhetorics — even mythical ones — of rights can have in actually pursuing emancipatory political projects, see Emila Viotti de Costa, *The Brazilian Empire: Myths and Histories* (Chapel Hill, N.C.: University of North Carolina Press, 1999).

21 Indeed, the civilian government implemented new regulations that required all foreign donations — the lifeblood of the opposition to Pinochet — to be allocated through state agencies; however, much of that foreign aid dried up, since the international community regarded Chile as stable and turned attention to places with what were perceived to be more urgent needs. See Lisa Baldez Carey, *Why Women Protest: Women's Movements in Chile* (London: Cambridge University Press, 2002).

22 Lucy Taylor, *Citizenship, Participation, and Democracy: Changing Dynamics in Chile and Argentina* (London: Macmillan Press, 1998).

23 Ruíz referred to a then recent strike by the privatized public-bus companies, which had negotiated a settlement with the government on issues of fares and environmental restrictions that hadn't worked: "When the bus companies rebelled, the state applied the Interior Security of the State law. That isn't democracy, because they applied this when the conflict became a problem for the market. . . . The police abused the students protesting fare hikes rather than going after the business people."

24 Tomás Moulian, *Chile actual: Anatomía de un mito* (Santiago: Lom Ediciones, ARCIS, 1997).

25 See a similar point by Fukuyama that I discuss in the conclusion. Pinto and Salazar also note that the Concertación's historical narrative posited that the military regime gave way to a civilian one because authoritarianism became ever more incompatible with neoliberalism (*Historia Contemporánea de Chile*, vol. 2, *Actores, identidad y movimiento* [Santiago: Lom Ediciones, 1999], 60–62). For a nuanced discussion of the

changes in Chile's neoliberal experiment from the early to late dictatorship to civilian rule, see Ricardo French-Davis, *Economic Reforms in Chile: From Dictatorship to Democracy (Development Inequality in the Market Economy)* (Ann Arbor: University of Michigan Press, 2002).

26 For a broad historical narrative that similarly situates the Mesa de Diálogo, see Luis Corvalán Marquéz, *Del anticapitalismo al neoliberalismo en Chile: Izquierda, centro y derecha en la lucha entre los proyectos globales, 1950–2000* (Santiago: Editorial Sudamericana, 2001), 473–77. The Mesa de Diálogo's work was available at that time on a state website: http://www.congreso.cl/biblioteca. For an analysis by one of the participants, see Elizabeth Lira, "La Mesa de Diálogo de Derechos Humanos ¿Una iniciativa de reconciliación política?" (paper presented at the Latin American Studies Association Meeting, Washington, September 2001).

27 Several of the top human-rights lawyers in Santiago, such as Hector Sálazar, Adil Berkovic, and Nelson Caucoto, have family connections to the North, the long history of which, according to my interviews with each of them, shaped their career paths in human-rights law.

28 In a still-fresh and moving analysis, Barbara Myerhoff presents a synthesis of this economy in the case of Holocaust survivors by drawing on Eli Wiesel, Bruno Bettelheim, and especially Terrence Des Pres: survivors "are ultimately an embarrassment" and inconvenience in a world that would rather move on; "we protect ourselves by discrediting the unbearable tales told by survivors" and by suggesting some sort of ultimate guilt and collaboration in history's atrocities such that the victims, both alive and dead, assume the burden of that history and thus restore balance between their pain and that of society in general. Barbara Myerhoff, *Number Our Days* (New York: Simon and Schuster, 1978), 285.

29 La Corporación Metropolitana de Beneficiarios PRAIS, "Qué es el programa de salud PRAIS" (mimeograph, n.d. [ca. 1999]), 5.

30 Michael Lambeck and Paul Antze, introduction to *Tense Past: Cultural Essays in Trauma and Memory*, ed. Paul Antze and Michael Lambeck (New York: Routledge, 1996), xxiv.

31 Paul Drake, "Chile, 1930–1958," in *Chile since Independence*, ed. Leslie Bethell (Cambridge: Cambridge University Press, 1993), 87–128.

32 Paz Rojas B., Víctor Espinoza C., Julia Urquieta O., and Hernán Soto H., *Tarde pero llega: Pinochet ante la justicia española* (Santiago: Lom Ediciones, 1998); Reed Brody and Michael Ratner, *The Pinochet Papers: The Case of Augusto Pinochet in Spain and Britain* (The Hague: Klewer Law International Press, 2000); Madeline Davis, *The Pinochet Case* (London: University of London Press, 2000); Roberto Montoya and Daniel Pereyra, *El caso Pinochet y la impunidad en America Latina* (Buenos Aires: Pandemia, 2000); *Punto y seguido* inaugural issue (March 2000); Hugh O'Shaughnessy *Pinochet: The Politics of Torture* (New York: New York University Press, 2000); Ariel Dorfman, *Exorcising Terror: The Incredible Unending Trial of General Augusto Pinochet* (New York: Seven Stories Press, 2002);

Peter Kornbluh, ed., *The Pinochet File: A Declassified Dossier on Atrocity and Accountability* (New York: New Press, 2003).

33 A silence only partially broken by a 2004 presidential commission and report collecting testimonies of torture survivors.

34 For example, the December 2004 press release "Declaration of Women Ex-Political Prisoners under the Dictatorship" (e-mailed to the author). See also Roberta Basic and Elizabeth Stanley, "Dealing with Torture in Chile: Achievements and Shortcomings of the 'Valech Report,' " *Nürnberger Menschenrechte* (May 2006), http://www.menschenrechte.org; Peter Kornbluh, "Letter from Chile," *The Nation*, 13 January 2005, reprinted in *Global Policy Forum*, 30 November 2005, http://www.globalpolicy.org.

35 I asked this question at a large forum featuring Judge Guzmán at the October 2004 Latin American Studies Association meetings in San Francisco. I had heard this response since the early 1990s in interviews with human-rights lawyers, who usually also cited scarce resources as a reason to prioritize wrongful-death cases. Fellow U.S. scholars of Chile criticized me for raising the question about torture prosecutions, which speaks to the degree to which the Chilean state's framing of these issues has become hegemonic. See Judge Guzmán's speech of 25 May 2005, given just after he stepped down ("A Free People Will Not Tolerate Incomplete Justice," translated and published by Memoria y Justicia, http://www.memoriay justicia.cl).

36 The hospital sent him home with a muscle relaxant. A few days later his regular physician discovered that he had a perforated gallbladder, a condition that left untreated often causes heart failure within a week, especially in geriatric patients. Rojas had been on the waiting list for a gallbladder operation for over a year. On the politics of health care in Santiago, see Julia Paley, *Marketing Democracy* (Berkeley: University of California Press, 2000).

37 These are two fundamental human rights: the right to freedom of movement in the form of a passport, and the right to participate in government in the form of direct suffrage as provided for in the Chilean political process. *United Nations Declaration of Human Rights*, articles 13 and 21; *United Nations International Covenant on Civil and Political Rights*, articles 12.2 and 25.2; *American Convention on Human Rights*, articles 22 and 23. All can be found in Micheline R. Ishay, ed., *The Human Rights Reader* (New York: Routledge, 1997), 407–11, 424–32, 441–51.

38 As Foucault suggested, the core modernist binary of mind-body lines up with order-chaos; therefore, therapeutic-confessional access to the mind guarantees stability.

39 The airplane solution may have been all the more tempting to the military since it had figured prominently a few years earlier in international media coverage of public revelations and debates about state violence in Argentina. In addition to the blatantly untrue airplane explanation, the Chilean military falsely reported the locations of remains either where there

were nothing but animal bones or where an existing gravesite had clearly been destroyed. The media footage of distraught family members digging around in vain for loved ones was all too reminiscent of earlier efforts.

40 Thomas Blom Hansen and Finn Stepputat, "Introduction: States of Imagination," in *States of Imagination: Ethnographic Explorations of the Post-colonial State*, ed. Thomas Blom Hansen and Finn Stepputat (Durham, N.C.: Duke University Press, 2001), 25. For further analysis of the inter-play of violence and nation-state logics, see Fernando Coronil and Julia Skorski, eds., *States of Violence* (Ann Arbor: University of Michigan Press, 2006).

41 Santner, *Stranded Objects*, 140.

42 The proposed project was to be at least partially funded by the European community. "Informa iniciativa que indica y solicita participación, Proyecto Monumento al Ejecutado Político en Pisagua" (Ord. no. 0221), from Santiago Diaz Fuentes, Secretario Regional Ministerial (Ministerio de Vivienda y Urbanismo), Región de Tarapacá, to Rigoberto Pizarro, Presidente de la Corporación de Presos Políticos de Pisagua, 14 February 2001, 4 (in author's fieldwork files).

43 Similar to the case of the northern writer's conference presentation that critiqued the petroglyphic poem by the Santiago poet Raúl Zurita, which was constructed across the northern desert between Tarapacá and Antofagasta and funded through the Ministry of Public Works. Zurita became the official poet of the Concertatión and wrote the epigraph that appears across the top of the monument to the disappeared and executed in the National Cemetery in Santiago; his byline constitutes the highest and largest name on the monument. I do not mean this as a critique of Zurita per se—he was an innovative and transgressive artist during the dicta-torship—but rather to illustrate the degree to which the civilian regime worked to instill an official "culture" in general and an official mode of memory in particular. On Zurita's position in this project, see Francine Masiello, *The Art of Transition: Latin American Culture and Neoliberal Crisis* (Durham, N.C.: Duke University Press, 2001), 301.

44 This was not explicitly stated in the plan, but the total space allocated to the monument is quite small and integrates the mass grave into the rest of the cemetery, whereas before the grave lay a short distance outside the northernmost perimeter of the cemetery. The issue of parking and access to the beach did, however, arise in more private discussions between individ-ual human-rights activists and state functionaries.

45 My knowledge of this meeting is based on conversations with ex-political prisoners and family members who attended and from the text of the proposed plan: "Informa iniciativa que indica y solicita participación, Proyecto Monumento al Ejecutado Político en Pisagua" (Ord. no. 0221), from Santiago Diaz Fuentes, Secretario Regional Ministerial (Ministerio de Vivienda y Urbanismo), Región de Tarapacá, to Rigoberto Pizarro,

Presidente de la Corporación de Presos Políticos de Pisagua, 14 February 2001, 4 (in author's fieldwork files).

46 Ibid., p. 5.

47 Ibid., p. 1.

48 Patricia Verdugo, *Chile, Pinochet, and the Caravan of Death* (Boulder, Colo.: Lynne Reinner, 2001).

49 A point of potentially fruitful comparison with Civil War battlesites in the United States (for northern and southern "whites" in the United States), and even with U.S. President Reagan's choice to visit the German World War II cemetery (romantically depicted in Edmund Morris, *Dutch: A Memoir of Ronald Reagan* [New York: Random House, 2000]). On the U.S. Civil War, see David W. Blight, *Race and Reunion: The Civil War in American Memory* (Cambridge, Mass.: Harvard University Press, 2001). For a compatible analysis to my own of the shifting uses of a particular place, see Harold Marcuse, *Legacies of Dachau: The Uses and Abuses of a Concentration Camp, 1933–2001* (Cambridge: Cambridge University Press, 2001).

50 Claudio Naranjo, *La agonía del patriarcado* (Barcelona: Kairos, 1993). One of the television pundits who has gotten significant airtime in contemporary Chile is the psychiatrist Maria Luisa Cordero. I asked two human-rights activists in Santiago to describe her and why her commentaries are so sought after by the media. The activists noted that her political affiliation is a Christian Democrat of rebellious origin, but that she is a free-thinker, and she can be heard on all of the major channels. I asked about the ideological content of her commentaries, and they replied, "She doesn't say anything [of substance] and undoubtedly she is a crazy old lady; one of the few people who say it like it is — for example, she says 'butt.'" So why is she so well-liked? "People like that she breaks this plane that we live in. She says what she thinks, out of the blue, even a vulgarity. She says things. Sharks turn themselves into sardines." Her performative and transgressive style — in terms of gender, age, and class — engages the television public; however, I suspect from this and other conversations with viewers, that she gets away with plain-speak because of the credibility that comes with being a doctor, especially in Chile.

51 Antonio Stecher Guzmán, "Notas sobre psicología, transición y subjetividad," in *Dialectos en transición: política y subjetividad en Chile actual*, ed. Mauro Salazar and Miguel Valderrama (Santiago: Lom Ediciones, 2000), 41–96.

52 Alfonso Stephens Freire, *El irracionalismo político en Chile: Un ensayo de psicología colectiva* (Santiago: Prensa Latinoamericana, 1957); Hernán Ramírez Nechochea, "Un estudio psicológico: Gabriel González Videla," *El Siglo* (1963), collected in MS, folder 34.

53 Michael Lambeck, "The Past Imperfect: Remembering as Moral Practice," in *Tense Past: Cultural Essays in Trauma and Memory*, ed. Paul

Antze and Michael Lambeck (New York: Routledge, 1996), 235–254. See Ranjana Khanna's discussion of "colonial melancholy" and "haunting," which she develops from a psychoanalytic framework, in *Dark Continents: Psychoanalysis and Colonialism* (Durham, N.C.: Duke University Press, 2003); similarly, Anne Anlin Cheng, *The Melancholy of Race: Psychoanalysis, Assimilation, and Hidden Grief* (London: Oxford University Press, 2001); and David Eng and David Kazanjian, eds., Loss: The Politics of Mourning (Berkeley: University of California Press, 2002). For a different way of talking about melancholia and nationalism, though complementary to my own, see Licia Fiol-Matta, *A Queer Mother for the Nation* (Minneapolis: University of Minnesota Press, 2002). See also Idelber Avelar, *The Untimely Present: Postdictatorial Latin American Fiction and the Task of Mourning* (Durham, N.C.: Duke University Press, 1999); and Jenny Edkins, *Trauma and the Memory of Politics* (Cambridge: Cambridge University Press, 2003).

54 I have changed the official's name and other identifying characteristics.

55 Masiello, *The Art of Transition*, 21–51, especially 35–36.

56 Interview with Dr. Luis Fornazzari, specialist in geriatric medicine, Toronto, Canada, 6 February 2001. See also Fornazzari's official letter of complaint dated 9 April 2001, which is translated and reprinted on the Memoria y Justicia Web site, http://www.memoriayjusticia.cl. Such virtual archives have been important to memory making in the contemporary era.

57 On psychologization as depoliticization, see the discussion of Deleuze and Guattari in Judith Halberstam's *Skin Shows: Gothic Horror and the Technology of Monsters* (Durham, N.C.: Duke University Press, 1995), 116–19.

58 See Lambeck and Antze's notion that "political gains conferred by victim identity (e.g. 'trauma survivor') are accessible only through expert discourses (in law, medicine, psychiatry) which have their own agendas and are themselves instruments of power. . . . [S]uch discourses deal in causes rather than meanings, events rather than persons, instances rather than entire lives" (introduction to *Tense Past*, xxiv). For a historical perspective on the problem of expert discourses and democracy, see Laura Westhoff, "A Fatal Drifting Apart: Democratic Social Knowledge in Progressive Era Chicago" (unpublished manuscript, n.d.).

59 For suggestive explorations of the worldviews of perpetrators, see Frank Graziano, *Divine Violence: Spectacle, Psychosexuality, and Radical Christianity in the Argentine "Dirty War"* (Boulder, Colo.: Westview, 1992); Martha Knisely Huggins, Mika Haritos-Fatounos, and Philip G. Zimbardo, *Violence Workers: Police Torturers and Murderers Reconstruct Brazilian Atrocities* (Berkeley: University of California Press, 2002).

60 For a fantastic elaboration of the monster-victim problem, see Halberstam, *Skin Shows*.

61 Sigmund Freud, "Mourning and Melancholia," in *The Standard Edi-*

tion of the Complete Psychological Work of Sigmund Freud, trans. James Strachey (London: Hogarth, 1914–1916), 14:243.

62 Freud, "Mourning and Melancholia," 255.

63 It involves a suffering of "profoundly painful dejection, cessation of interest in the outside world, loss of the capacity to love, inhibition of all activity, and lowering of the self-regarding feelings" (ibid., 244).

64 Ibid., 256. "In mourning it is the world which has become poor and empty; in melancholia it is the ego itself" (246). And thus, by turning inward, "love escapes extinction" (257).

65 Historically locating the region of memory-traces, Walter Benjamin triangulates Freud's discussion of inadvertent memories with the contemplations of Henri Bergson and Marcel Proust. Benjamin explained Bergson's understanding of experience as "less the product of facts firmly anchored in memory than of a convergence in memory of accumulated and frequently unconscious data," which rises up as "spontaneous afterimage." Access to this data, in Proust, is a matter not of will but of involuntary memory. Only voluntary memory is available to the intellect, yet "the information which it gives about the past retains no trace of it." Rather, the past is held in material sensations. Benjamin calls this cluster of mnemonic associations and sensations "the aura." Ultimately, says Benjamin, there is a "price for which the sensation of the modern age may be held: the disintegration of the aura in the experience of shock." At the heart of modern aesthetics lies this shock—the shock of memory. Walter Benjamin, "On Some Motifs in Baudelaire," in *Illuminations*, ed. Hannah Arendt (New York: Schocken Books, 1968). Max Pensky argues that Benjamin lived melancholy in a way that became the fount of a tormented insight (*Melancholy Dialectics, Walter Benjamin and the Play of Memory* [Amherst: University of Massachusetts Press, 1993]). The history of melancholia plays a critical role in Western thought, according to Carlos Gurméndez, *La melancolía* (Madrid: Colección Austral, 1990).

66 Eric L. Santner, *Stranded Objects: Mourning, Memory, and Film in Postwar Germany* (Ithaca, N.Y.: Cornell University Press 1990), 147.

67 James E. Young, *The Texture of Memory: Holocaust Memorials and Meaning* (New Haven: Yale University Press, 1993), 127.

68 Hesitating to enshrine complete recuperation in designated sites of memory, Young asserted, "Museums, archives, and ruins may not house our memory-work so much as displace it with claims of material evidence and proof . . . but in this they too often confuse proof that something existed with proof that it existed in a particular way, for seemingly self-evident reasons" (ibid.).

69 Marianne Hirsch, *Family Frames: Photography, Narrative, and Post-memory* (Cambridge, Mass.: Harvard University Press, 1997).

70 "The compulsive rituals of the allegorical agent are thus like the elegiac loop" (Santner, *Stranded Objects*, 140).

71 Benjamin noted that in Proust's life as a remembering author, the recollection *was* living, a living much closer to forgetting than memory ("The Image of Proust," in *Illuminations*, ed. Hannah Arendt [Schocken Books: New York, 1968], 202): "There is a dual will to happiness, dialectic of happiness: a hymnic and an elegiac form. The one is the unheard-of, the un-precedented, the height of bliss; the other, the eternal repetition, the eternal restoration of the original, the first happiness. It is this elegiac idea of happiness . . . which for Proust transforms existence into a preserve of memory. To it he sacrificed in his life friends and companionship, in his works plot, unity of characters, the flow of the narration, the play of imagination" (204). Benjamin quotes Riviere's assertion that Proust perished because of "the same inexperience which permitted him to write his works. 'In sum,' He died of ignorance of the world and because he did not know how to change the conditions of his life which had begun to crush him. He died because he did not know how to make a fire or open a window" (213). Without plot there may be ethics but there can be no politics, no hope of bliss.

72 Among mental-health professionals and cultural critics there has emerged vigorous debate around recent research questioning the long-term mental-health benefits of grief therapy and Freudian models of mourning. Some scholars in the debate have turned to cross-cultural accounts of bereavement to further question the dominant models that form the basis of the (quite lucrative) grief-counseling industry. For a summary of this debate, see Emily Nussbaum, "Good Grief! The Case for Repression," *Lingua Franca* 7, no. 8 (1997): 48–51. For cultural-theory critiques, see Melissa Zeiger, *Beyond Consolation* (Ithaca, N.Y.: Cornell University Press, 1997); Cassie Premio Steele, *We Heal from Memory: Sexton, Lourde, Anzaldua, and the Poetry of Witness* (New York: Palgrave, 2000). Similarly, Barbara Myerhoff's study of Holocaust survivors questioned Freudian mourning as the development of a new reality that excluded what was lost and positing instead that "full recovery from mourning may do the opposite — preserving what has been lost, restoring it to life by incorporation into the present" (*Number Our Days*, 34).

73 Sebastián Acevedo immolated himself to protest the disappearance of his children. Grounded in nonviolence and liberation theology, the group was formed in the 1980s to bring national and international attention to the problem of torture in Chile. This movement was radically different from other protest movements that took place during and after the dictatorship (such as political-party-sponsored groups or the more recent Funa Movement actions of "outing" former human-rights violators) in that it drew on the liberation theology model of fraternal correction as a mode of confronting violators and a passive public. See also Hernán Vidal, *El Movimiento Contra La Tortura "Sebastian Acevedo": Derechos humanos y la producción de símbolos nacionales bajo el fascismo Chileno*

(Minneapolis: Society for the Study of Contemporary Hispanic and Luso-phone Revolutionary Literatures, 1986).

74 Wealthy families who have been in the North for generations have family crypts. Many recent, well-to-do immigrants have chosen to be buried in an in-ground cemetery constructed in a sand dune on the outskirts of the city, complete with grass lawn overhead and marketed as the "modern" way to go.

75 For background, see Dauno Tótoro Taulis, *La cofradía blindada, Chile civil y Chile militar: Trauma y conflicto* (Santiago: Planeta, 1998).

76 These quotes from Zúñiga, Weber, and Palma — which echo informal commentaries I have heard from numerous Chileans — can be found in Daniela Estrada, "Chile: Citizens Movement Calls for New Constitution," Inter Press Service, 10 January 2006, http://www.ipsnews.net.

77 On earlier such activities, see Margaret Power, *Right-Wing Women in Chile* (University Park: Pennsylvania State University Press, 2002).

78 The Right's efforts to raise a statue to ideologue Jaime Guzmán were argued as parity for the statue of President Allende.

79 This cross-sectional vibrancy does not seem to have held for Iquique, where the populist politics of the politically dominant family of Mayor Jorge Sorcia clashed quite publicly with the confrontational tactics of the local Communist Party. Exemplifying cathartic memory were the *funa* (slang for denouncing or public outing) protests that began in the late 1990s and were modeled on an Argentine form of protest in which documented torturers who were not formally tried were "outed" by protestors who marched to their neighborhoods and workplaces to plaster notices and hold demonstrations detailing their crimes. During my fieldwork, I observed several of these demonstrations in Santiago. The state declared them illegal as a form of vigilante justice; activists in turn pointed to the failure of the state to widely prosecute these crimes. Though the spirit of the Funa Movement was clearly transformative, a human-rights activist formerly from the Sebastián Acevedo Movement against Torture offered a key critique: whereas the Acevedo Movement's philosophy had arisen from Christian theology's idea of "fraternal correction," the Funa Movement's portrayal of perpetrators as monsters who should have no place in civil society (ironically, like the state's ongoing human-rights policies) obscured the ways in which civil society was and still is implicated in political persecution and injustice.

80 While there were continued efforts to resume trials, to open investigations, and to force Pinochet to testify, with regard to Pinochet as a politically viable figure, the story ended here. The exception would be the enormous impact of investigations into Pinochet's financial corruption, which further alienated many of his long-term supporters.

81 "El descanso del guerrero, el retiro a los cuarteles de invierno," *El Mercurio*, 15 June 2001, http://www.emol.com. Outrage over Pinochet

frolicking in Iquique a year later appeared in Dr. Martin Cordero Allary, Dr. Paz Rojas Baeza, and Dr. Andrea Bahamondes Moya, "Third Report on the Mental Health of Pinochet," 12 August 2002, translated and published online by Memoria y Justicia, http://www.memoriayjusticia.cl.

82 The degree to which those ties between the Chilean state and the general were severed can be measured in President Bachelet's refusal to grant Pinochet a state funeral or to attend his services herself, although she sent an official military representative of the state in a compromise gesture that is indicative of her own political persona as champion of the honorable Chilean military.

Conclusion

1 Mary Louise Pratt points out the importance of the ethnographic scene of arrival ("Fieldwork in Common Places," in *Writing Culture: The Poetics and Politics of Ethnography*, ed. James Clifford and George Marcus [Berkeley: University of California Press, 1986], 31–32). I was reminded of this point by Laura Ahearn's *Invitation to Love* (Ann Arbor: University of Michigan Press, 2001), 6. Historical narrative typically works from the opposite direction — propelled forward in time by chronology.

2 In this book I have built on approaches characteristic of interdisciplinary arenas of scholarly dialogue often signaled under the rubrics of practice theory, cultural studies, subaltern or postcolonial studies, and trajectories of critical scholarship coming out of Chile and Latin America more generally. I do not pretend that the theorists and frameworks I have used are commensurable. Rather, I use them as interlocutors to approach this historical ethnography of memory, violence, and nation-state formation in Northern Chile from a number of directions, seeking that elusive and emergent dialectical relation between the theoretical and the empirical known as praxis. In doing so, my initial theoretical questions about violence and hegemony arose simultaneously with my commitment to human rights and justice, and thus I refuse to privilege the theoretical over the political or visa versa.

3 Eric Wolf, *Europe and the People without History* (Berkeley: University of California Press, 1982).

4 Johannes Fabian, *Time and the Other: How Anthropology Makes Its Object* (New York: Columbia University Press).

5 José Piedra, "The Game of Critical Arrival," *Diacritics* (spring 1989): 34–61; Fernando Coronil, "Discovering America Again: The Politics of Selfhood in the Age of Post-colonial Empires," *Dispositio* 14, nos. 36–38: 315–31.

6 This is a critical endeavor that does not preclude — through a politics of authenticity — the possibility of cross-cultural methodologies but rather requires one to attend to the implications of differential power.

7 In a paradoxical place, subordinate actors must occupy more than one

often incompatible political positionality at the same time. See Gillian Rose, *Feminism and Geography: The Limits of Geographical Knowledge* (Cambridge: Polity Press, 1993); Caroline Desbiens, "Feminism 'in' Geography: Elsewhere, Beyond and the Politics of Paradoxical Space," *Gender, Place, and Culture* 6, no. 2 (1999): 179–85.

8 Meena Alexander, *The Shock of Arrival* (Cambridge, Mass.: South End Press, 2001). The application of the term *postcolonial* to Latin American societies, many of which gained formal independence by 1820, has been hotly debated by scholars such as Jorge Klor de Alva and Fernando Coronil. Scholars in anthropology and literary studies have productively used the term to compare societies emerging from colonial pasts and to describe the weight of that past on subsequent cultural, social, and political dynamics, both short and long term.

9 For a discussion of the internal implications of the image of Chile as an international model, see Paul Drake and Iván Jaksic, eds. *El modelo chileno: Democracia y desarrollo en los noventa* (Santiago: Lom Ediciones, 1999).

10 Jonathan Kandell, "Prosperity Born of Pain," *New York Times Magazine* (7 July 1991): 15.

11 Steven Greenhouse, "Trade Talks with Chile Are Planned," *New York Times*, 14 May 1992, p. C11. For another of many such reports, see Linda Robinson, "Chile Is All Business When They Talk Business: That's Why It Will Be the Next NAFTA Member," *U.S. News and World Report* (10 July 1995): 35–37. Chile has been regarded an ideal addition not in small part due to the fact that it is "too far away to steal jobs U.S. workers," meaning that the U.S. public does not have to fear contamination from humans crossing the border, but it can still enjoy the arrival of goods and profits (ibid., 36). On the rhetoric around NAFTA, see Ann E. Kingsolver, *NAFTA Stories: Fears and Hopes in Mexico and the United States* (Boulder, Colo.: Lynne Rienner, 2001).

12 Suneel Ratan, "How Chile Got It Right," *Time*, 20 March 1995, 30.

13 Margaret Thatcher was prime minister of Great Britain during approximately the same time period as Ronald Reagan was president of the United States. They were allies in implementing neoliberal policies in their own countries and in promoting and enforcing those policies abroad through ongoing neocolonial relations between the two metropoles and subordinate nation-states. See Pedro Lemebel's wry reflection on Margaret Thatcher's trip to Chile during this same period ("La visita de la Thatcher [o 'el vahído de la vieja dama']," *De perlas y cicatrices: Crónicas radiales* [Santiago: Lom Ediciones, 1996], 19–23).

14 People in Iquique proudly note the much-earlier visits of others who heralded new modernities, such as Charles Darwin and Fidel Castro.

15 Francis Fukuyama first presented his position as a talk at the University of Chicago, which was subsequently published as "The End of History?" *National Interest* (summer 1989): 3–18. See critical responses in that same issue (19–35) and in the fall 1989 issue (3–16, 93–100), as well as

Fukuyama's response, "A Reply to My Critics," *National Interest* (winter 1989/90): 21–28. The journal reported that the initial essay was immediately reprinted in Paris, Tokyo, Rome, Sydney, and Amsterdam. Fukuyama elaborated his essay as *The End of History and the Last Man* (New York: Free Press, 1992), which I would argue has become naturalized as neoliberal common sense.

16 Fukuyama, *The End of History*, xiii.

17 Fukuyama's heavily gendered rhetoric can be read as describing a crisis of masculinity, which complements arguments by feminist political philosophers such as Carol Pateman that the subject of liberalism is a male subject. Because history is over, the impotent last man has lost the Adamic agency to name and thus to beget the world.

18 Fukuyama, *The End of History*, 338. Implicitly accepting this logic, human-rights tribunals insist on implementing, in places such as Africa and Europe (the Balkans), juridical procedures which often have little correspondence with their historical and cultural context. Yet, if they accept the "end of history," what else are they to do? On the end of history and the implications for subaltern nation-states of self-consciousness as the product of linear history, see Prasenjit Duara, *Rescuing History from the Nation* (Chicago: University of Chicago Press, 1995), 17–33.

19 "Historiador Francis Fukuyama disertó sobre democracia liberal," *El Mercurio*, 13 November 1992, p. C11.

20 In *State Building* (Ithaca, N.Y.: Cornell University Press, 2004) Fukuyama revisits his concern about the excess passion of those peoples who are the antithesis of the new man, arguing that the United States should promote democracy through institutional structures and culture. He modifies this mandate in *America at the Crossroads: Democracy, Power, and the Neoconservative Legacy* (New Haven, Conn.: Yale University Press, 2006), wherein he critiques the neoconservative policies of the George W. Bush administration by asserting that democracy cannot be imposed on peoples who are not "ready" (in an evolutionary sense) and by undergirding his position that the market is primary and democracy optional.

21 Jean Paul Enthoven, "Jean Baudrillard: Entre ruido y furor," originally published in *Le Point*, reprinted in *El Mercurio*, 17 July 1993. On critical reactions by Chilean intellectuals to this visit, see *Revista de crítica cultural* 7 (1993).

22 See excerpt, "The Illusion of the End," in *The Postmodern History Reader*, ed. Keith Jenkins (London: Routledge, 1997), 39–46.

23 For a similarly cynical perspective from an unashamedly oligarchic point of view, see the Chilean essayist Alfredo Jocelyn-Holt Letelier, "News from nowhere o la vía chilena al olvido," in *Estabilidad, crisis y organización de la política: lecciones de medio siglo de historica chilena*, ed. Paz Milet (Santiago: FLACSO-Chile, 2001), 31–42; *"El peso de la noche" nuestro frágil fortaleza histórica* (Santiago: Planeta, Ariel, 1997); *El Chile perplejo: Del avanzar sin transar al transar sin parar* (Santiago: Planeta, Ariel, 1998).

24 Especially the efforts of Clodomira Almeyda, the Chilean ambassador to Moscow at the time, who offered Honecker refuge in the Moscow embassy and, after Chile had turned him over to Germany to stand trial, worked to ensure that Chile would take him in once he was ruled too ill to stand trial. For a narrative of these events that focuses on their European context but turns an experienced eye toward Latin America as well, see Tina Rosenberg, *The Haunted Land: Facing Europe's Ghosts after Communism* (New York: Vintage, 1995), 330–33.

25 Ascanio Cavallo, *La historia oculta de la transición: Memoria de una época, 1990–1998* (Santiago: Grijalbo, 1998), 145.

26 When Pinochet was first detained in England in 1998, his supporters in the Chilean media recalled the Honecker case to demand clemency for Pinochet on the basis of other kinds of (debatable) comparisons between the two cases.

27 Cavallo, *La historia oculta*, 157.

28 Tomás Moulian, "A Time of Forgetting: The Myths of the Chilean Transition," *NACLA* [North American Congress on Latin America]: *Report on the Americas* 22, no. 2 (September–October 1998): 22.

29 Alessandro Fornazzari, "Reflections on the Work of the Past: The Politics of Memory and the Chilean Transition" (paper presented at the 2000 meeting of the Latin American Studies Association). Pointing to intellectuals' frustrations with the seeming inability of current social movements to generate a counterhegemonic discourse, see Francine Masiello, *The Art of Transition: Latin American Culture and Neoliberal Crisis* (Durham, N.C.: Duke University Press, 2001), 35–36. For a philosophical critique of the rhetoric of the end of history grounded in twentieth-century Latin American thought, see Alfonso Ibáñez, *Para repensar nuestras utopías, materiales de cultura política* (Lima: SUR Casa de Estudios del Socialismo, 1993).

30 Bernardo Subercaseaux, *Chile o una loca historia* (Santiago: Lom Ediciones, 1999).

31 The historian José Bengoa posited, "Since its initiation, the Chilean working class has demonstrated its indubitable national vocation; its preoccupation has always been the country" ("Presentación," in *La huelga obrera en Chile, 1890–1970*, by Crisostomo Pizarro [Santiago: Ediciones SUR, 1986], 6).

32 Anne Waters, "Predicaments of Women: The Family and the State in the Construction of Subjectivity in Maharashtra, India" (Ph.D. diss., Ann Arbor, University of Michigan, 1997).

33 Northern (i.e., European and U.S.) scholars' affective investment in Chile must also be seen in the context of racialized geopolitics wherein the Chilean political elite's mestizo ideology has more or less made a successful claim to neo-Europeanness, to use Alfred Crosby's term — more so, for example, than Guatemala, a "darker" and more "Indian" site of a similarly crushed democratic revolutionary experiment. Alfred W. Crosby, *Ecological*

Imperialism: The Biological Expansion of Europe, 900–1900, 2d ed. (Cambridge: Cambridge University Press, 1993).

34 Manuel Antonio Garretón signaled the innovative possibilities and contingencies of doing the work of democratization in a postcolonial context when he insisted that the study of democratization should be grounded in particular processes rather than universalistic definitions and criteria ("Review of *Patterns of Democratic Transition and Consolidation*," *Latin American Studies* 31, no. 3: 768–69).

35 Gavin Smith, *Confronting the Present: Towards a Politically Engaged Anthropology* (Oxford, U.K.: Berg, 1999).

36 Lucy Taylor, *Citizenship, Participation and Democracy* (Basingstoke, U.K.: Macmillan Press, 1998).

37 Subercaseaux, *Chile o una loca historia*, 69. For further analysis of Chilean political culture, see Larissa Adler Lomnitz and Ana Melnick, *Chile's Political Culture and Parties: An Anthropological Explanation* (Notre Dame, Ind.: University of Notre Dame Press, 2000).

38 Verónica Schild, "Neo-liberalism's New Gendered Market Citizens: The 'Civilizing' Dimension of Social Programmes in Chile," *Citizenship Studies* 4, no. 3 (200): 275–305; Lessie Jo Frazier, "Medicalizing Human Rights and Domesticating Violence," in *Violence and the Body*, ed. Arturo Aldama (Bloomington: Indiana University Press, 2003), 388–403; Lessie Jo Frazier, "Gendering the Space of Death: The Body, Memory, Democratization, and the Domestic," in *Gender, Sexuality and Power in Modern Latin American History*, ed. William French and Katherine Bliss (New York: Rowman and Littlefield, 2006), 261–82.

39 Agrarian reform ironically gained momentum at the urging of the United States in an attempt to stall peasant uprisings. On copper, culture, and class in Chilean politics, see Janet Finn, *Tracing the Veins* (Berkeley: University of California Press, 1999); Thomas Klubock, *Contested Communities: Class, Gender, and Politics in El Teniente Copper Mine, 1904–1951* (Durham, N.C.: Duke University Press, 1998).

40 *El Mercurio*, 22 July 2001, http://www.elmercurio.com. Ibáñez del Campo intervened in national politics at a moment of economic and political crisis and propelled the creation of the 1925 Constitution, which Pinochet would replace with his own constitution in 1980. Ibáñez del Campo was first dictator, then elected president (what Pinochet hoped to achieve in the 1988 plebiscite). Pinochet considered himself more historically transcendent than Ibáñez del Campo and likened himself to Chile's Spanish conqueror Pedro de Valdivia and its official father of independence, Bernardo O'Higgins. What general could follow to challenge this audacious assertion of historical importance? It would take a general from a family with a long military lineage, General Izurieta, to begin to dismantle Pinochet's grip on the Chilean military and its historical memory.

41 Joaquín Villarino G., "Dresden, muerte y resurrección: La otra barbarie occidental," *El Mercurio* (15 July 2001). The British air force fire-

bombed the city in February of 1945 (with a follow-up assault by U.S. fighters) in part to avoid having its industries fall into the hands of the advancing Soviet army. In his article Villarino provides supporting data on the extent of the atrocity and explains that the initial letter-to-the-editor, by Miguel Zauschkevich, had expressed disgust over the Hollywood film *Pearl Harbor* because it had painted a crude picture of the Japanese as "the bad guys" and the United States as "the good guys"; Zauschkevich had therefore called for a film about Dresden that would expose the actions of the United States and the British against the Germans. The Chilean elite invoked the memory of Dresden to challenge Britain's moral authority to judge Pinochet. On Dresden and memory in the European context, see Elisabeth Ten Dyke, *Dresden: Paradoxes of Memory in History* (London: Routledge, 2001).

42 Pheng Cheah, "Spectral Nationality: The Living-on (sur-vie) of the Postcolonial Nation in Neocolonial Globalization," in *Becomings: Explorations in Time, Memory, and Futures*, ed. Elizabeth Groz (Ithaca, N.Y.: Cornell University Press, 1999) 176, 200.

43 Serge Gruzinski, "The Net Torn Apart: Ethnic Identities and Westernization in Colonial Mexico, Sixteenth–Nineteenth Centuries," in *Ethnicities and Nations*, ed. Remo Guidieri, Francesco Pellizzi, and Stanley Jeyaraja Tambiah (Austin: University of Texas Press, 1988); see also Serge Gruzinski, "Images and Cultural Mestizaje in Colonial Mexico," *Poetics Today* 16, no. 1 (spring 1995): 53–77.

44 Rosalind O'Hanlon, "Recovering the Subject: Subaltern Studies and Histories of Resistance in Colonial South Asia," *Modern Asian Studies* 22, no. 1 (1988): 189–224.

45 Lila Abu-Lughod, "The Romance of Resistance: Tracing Transformations of Power through Bedouin Women," *American Ethnologist* 17, no. 1 (1990): 41–55; Sherry Ortner, "Resistance and the Problem of Ethnographic Refusal," *Comparative Studies in Society and History* 37, no. 1: 173–93.

46 Inderpal Grewal and Caren Kaplan, "Introduction: Transnational Feminist Practices and Questions of Postmodernity," in *Scattered Hegemonies: Post-modernity and Transnational Feminist Practices*, ed. Inderpal Grewal and Caren Kaplan (Minneapolis: University of Minnesota Press, 1994), 1:33.

47 Benjamin, "The Image of Proust," in *Illuminations* (New York: Schocken Books, 1968), 202.

48 William Roseberry provides an analysis of hegemony compatible with O'Hanlon's. He draws on E. P. Thompson's discussion of power as a force field but critiques Thompson for suggesting a bipolar situation instead of one of multiple pulls. I agree with Roseberry in every sense except his rather limited characterization of physics, in which there are, indeed, multiple force fields of differential attractions and repulsions (e.g., gravitational, electromagnetic, strong nuclear, and weak nuclear forces). See

William Roseberry, "Hegemony and the Language of State Formation," in *Everyday Forms of State Formation: Revolution and the Negotiation of Rule in Modern Mexico*, ed. Gilbert M. Joseph and Daniel Nugent (Durham, N.C.: Duke University Press, 1994), 355–66.

49 Chantal Mouffe, "Feminism, Citizenship and Radical Democratic Politics," in *Feminists Theorize the Political*, ed. Judith Butler and Joan W. Scott (New York: Routledge, 1992); Edward W. Soja, *Postmodern Geographies* (London: Verso, 1989), 14.

50 For a kindred effort to apply structures of feeling to think about memory in working-class (and increasingly post-working-class) communities of the Southern Cone, see Daniel James, *Doña María's Story: Life History, Memory, and Political Identity* (Durham, N.C.: Duke University Press, 2000), 270–71. Through one activist's life history, James evocatively unfolds an analysis of the emergence of a particular (and particularly gendered and classed) structure of feeling from the 1940s to the 1990s in Argentina. In his pioneering study James offers a complex reading of his relationship to his subject, foregrounding the interpretive and political differences between them.

51 Neruda, *Canto general*, trans. Jack Schmitt (Berkeley: University of California Press, 1991), 199.

52 For a cogent statement on the responsibilities of scholars based in the United States in the Chilean politics of memory, see "Carta de adhesión norteamericana al 'Manifiesto de historiadores chilenos,'" in *Manifiesto de historiadores*, ed. Sergio Grez and Gabriel Salazar (Santiago: Lom Ediciones, 1998), 39–44.

53 For critiques of authenticity, see Chandra Mohanty, *Feminist without Borders: Decolonizing Theory, Practicing Solidarity* (Durham: Duke University Press, 2003); Gayatri Chakravorty Spivak, "Can the Subaltern Speak?" *The Post-Colonial Studies Reader*, ed. Bill Ashcroft, Gareth Griffiths, and Helen Tiffin (London: Routledge, 1995), 24–28; Jose Limón, *Dancing with the Devil: Society and Cultural Poetics in Mexican-American Texas* (Madison: University of Wisconsin Press, 1994). See also attacks on activists such as Rigoberta Menchú, who was criticized for not being the authentic voice of "her people" (Arturo Arias, *The Rigoberta Menchú Controversy* [Minneapolis: Minnesota University Press 2001]).

54 Gary Weissman, *Fantasies of Witnessing: Postwar Efforts to Experience the Holocaust* (Ithaca, N.Y.: Cornell University Press, 2004). For a complex statement on the ethics of researching "the bad guys," see Kathleen Blee, "Evidence, Empathy and Ethics: Lessons from Oral Histories of the Klan," in *The Oral History Reader*, ed. Robert Perks and Alistair Thompson (London: Routledge Press, 1998), 333–43.

55 John Burdick, "Uniting Theory and Practice in the Ethnography of Social Movements: Notes toward a Hopeful Realism," *Dialectical Anthropology* 20 (1995): 362.

56 Nicolás Guzmán, *La luz viene del mar* (Santiago: Ediciones Acon-

cagua, 1951). On Guzmán, see Lon Pearson, *Nicomedes Guzmán: Proletarian Author in Chile's Literary Generation of 1938* (Columbia: University of Missouri Press, 1976).

57 Sonia Montecino uses what she calls the dyad of the present mother–absent father to understand the gendering of nationalist ideology in Chile (*Madres y Huachos* [Santiago: Editorial Cuarto Propio, 1991]).

58 Guzmán, *La luz viene del mar*, 50–51.

59 On consumption and making do, see Janet Finn, *Tracing the Veins* (Berkeley: University of California Press, 1999).

60 Neruda, *Canto general*, 186.

61 Carolyn Kay Steedman, *Landscape for a Good Woman: A Story of Two Lives* (New Brunswick, N.J.: Rutgers, 1991), 144. While I respect her noncelebratory "final gesture of defiance," to settle for less than honor (even if a form of vengeance) at this conjuncture, and perhaps especially in the case of Chilean history, would merely echo the "so what?" already resounding in the belly of History.

I have argued that in Chile attempts to rethink psychology by mental-health and human-rights activists in Latin America had been co-opted in state projects of reconciliation. My critique of psychologism builds on the work of political and social psychologists in countering the appropriation of psychology in corporate and state policy and rhetoric.

62 Neruda, *Canto general*, 186.

Selective Bibliography

This bibliography contains selective primary sources consulted or cited. These include archival documents, personal papers, and audiovisual media as well as published primary works. Other primary sources include ethnographic fieldwork, interviews, and life histories. Full citations for secondary sources can be found in the endnotes.

ARCHIVES

AEPP	Agrupación de Ex-presos Politicos de Pisagua, Iquique
AIT-I	Archivo Intendencia de Tarapacá, Iquique, Chile (Twentieth Century)
AIT-S	Archivo Intendencia de Tarapacá, Santiago, Chile (Nineteenth Century)
AMRE-LPB	Archivo del Ministerio de Relaciones Exteriores, La Paz, Bolivia (LP)
AMRE-LP	Archivo del Ministerio de Relaciones Exteriores, Lima, Peru
AN	Archivo Nacional, Santiago, Chile

CN	Congreso Nacional, Santiago, Chile
ME	Ministry of Education, Santiago, Chile
MEMCH	Movimiento pro Emancipación de la Mujer Chilena, Santiago and Valparaíso
OI	Obispado de Iquique, Iquique
PRO, FO	Public Record Office, Foreign Office, London, U.K.

PAPERS

CA	Colección Amunátegui, Biblioteca Central, Universidad de Chile
CL	Colección Lenz, Biblioteca National, Santiago
BF	Baldramina Flores Urqueta de Lizardi, Iquique
LEM	Luis Emilio Morales Marino, Iquique
MN	Max Nettlau, International Institute for Social History, Amsterdam
MS	Marcelo Segall, International Institute for Social History, Amsterdam
RMLK	Guillermo Ross-Murray Lay-Kim, Iquique

NEWSPAPERS

La Agitación, Estación Dolores, Tarapacá
Ahora, Santiago
El Amigo del Pueblo, Iquique
La Aurora Roja, Pisagua
El Caliche, Iquique
La Cavancha, Iquique
La Clínica, Santiago
El Comerico, Lima
El Comerico, Pisagua
El Constitucional, Santiago
Cuestiones Sociales, Iquique
El Despertar, Iquique
La Epocha, Santiago
La Estrella, Iquique
El Ferrocarril, Santiago
La Justicia, Santiago
La Libertad Electoral, Santiago
El Mercurio, Santiago
El Nacional, Caracas
El Nacional, Iquique
New York Times
El Nortino, Iquique
El Obrero, Coquimbo
El Pensamiento Obrero, Pozo Almonte

El Pueblo Obrero, Iquique
Punto Final, Santiago
La Razón, Huara
El Siglo, Santiago
El Surco, Iquique
El Tarapacá, Iquique
El Trabajo, Iquique
La Voz del Paria, Puerto Montt
Wall Street Journal

MAGAZINES, NEWSLETTERS, AND JOURNALS

Análisis, Santiago
ANECAP, Iquique
Apsi, Santiago
Arte-uno, Iquique
Camanchaca, Iquique
El canelo, Santiago
Caras y caretas, Santiago
CHIP News, online
El donkey, Iquique
Economía-uno, Iquique
Ercilla, Santiago
Hoy, Santiago
Occidente, Santiago
Página abierta, Santiago
Qué pasa, Santiago
Revista cultural de crítica, Santiago
Sucesos, Santiago

FILM AND VIDEO

Actas de Mauroussia. Dir. Miguel Littin. 1970s.
Arturo y el angel. N.d. [ca. early 1990s].
Informe especial 11 Sep. 1973. Santiago, 1993.
Iquique, el ayer es hoy. N.d.
Muerte en Santa María de Iquique. Santiago: ICTUS, 1986.
Pisagua. Iquique, 1990.
Yo soy, yo fui, yo seré. Dir. Walter Heynowski, Gerhard Scheumann, and Peter Hellmich. Berlin, 1974.

AUDIO RECORDINGS

Angel Parra. *Pisagua*. Santiago: Alerce Producciones Fonográficas, 1993 [1973].

Calatambo Albarracin. *Calatambo Albarracín con los Calicheros del Norte.* Santiago: Alerce, n.d. [1990s].

Estudiantinas Voces del Norte. *Volumen 1.* Iquique: Carrero, n.d. [1990s].

Quilapayun. *Santa María de Iquique: Cantata popular.* Santiago: Alerce, 1968.

Tuna Sebastopol. *Sebastopol.* Iquique: Sebastopol, 1991.

PUBLISHED SOURCES

Acevedo Hernández, A. *Los cantores populares chilenos.* Santiago: Editorial Nascimento, 1933.

———. *El Libro de la Tierra Chilena, 1: Lo que canto y lo que mira el pueblo de Chile.* Santiago: Ediciones Ercilla, 1935.

Advis, Luis. Album notes for *Santa María de Iquique: Cantata popular.* Santiago: Alerce Producciones Fonográficos, 1978.

Agrupación de Familiares. *Actividades 1988 de la Agrupación de Familiares de Detenidos Desaparecidos.* Santiago: Agrupación de Familiares, 1989.

Ahumada, Eugenio. *Chile: La memoria prohibida: Las violaciones a los derechos humanos, 1973–1983.* Santiago: Pehuen, 1989.

Alfaro Calderón, Carlos A. *Reseña histórica de la provincia de Tarapacá.* Iquique: La Semana Tarapaqueña, 1936.

Allende, Isabel. *Of Love and Shadows.* New York: Bantam, 1981.

Allendes, Cecilia. "Pisagua: 'Esa cárcel de piedra y soledades.'" *Análisis* (1983): 35.

Aranda B., Claudia, and Ricardo Canales A., eds. *Páginas literarias de los obreros socialistas (1912–1915).* Santiago: Ediciones ICAL, 1991.

Argentine National Commission of the Disappeared. *The Report of the Argentine National Commission on the Disappeared.* New York: Farrar, Straus and Giroux, 1986.

Arrau, Sergio. *Santa María de salitre.* Iquique: Editorial Camanchaca, 1989.

Astoreca, Denise. *Remolinos en la pampa.* Santiago: Editorial Cuarto Propio, 1996.

Bahamonde S., Mario. *Antología del cuento nortino.* Antofagasta: Universidad de Chile, 1966.

———. *Guía de la producción intellectual nortina.* Antofagasta: Universidad de Chile, Servicio de Extensión, 1971.

———. *Pampinos y salitreros.* Santiago: Quimantú, 1973.

———. *Tierra y sol: Homenaje a Mario Bahomonde.* Antofagasta: Colecciones Hacia La Tierra, El Hombre, La Poesía, 1980.

Bari M., David (Capitán). *El ejército ante las nuevas doctrinas sociales.* Santiago: Talleres del Estado Mayor Jeneral, 1922.

Bascuñán, Homero. *De los días perdidios.* Santiago: Editorial Nascimento, 1976.

Bitar, Sergio. *Isla 10.* Santiago: Pehuen, 1987.

Blanlot Holley, Anselmo. *Perfiles de la situación Santiago*. Imprenta Franco-Chilena, 1893.

Bravo Elizondo, Pedro, ed. *Cultera y teatro obrero en Chile, 1900–1930*. Madrid: Ediciones Michay, 1987.

——. *Los "enganchados" en la era del salitre*. Santiago: LAR, n.d.

——. *Santa María de Iquique 1907: Documentos para su historia*. Santiago: Ediciones Litoral, 1993.

Cabero, Alberto. *Chile y los chilenos*. Santiago: Editorial Nascimento, 1926.

Camara de Diputados. *Comisión Parlamentaria encargada de estudiar las necesidades de las provincias de Tarapacá y Antofagasta*. Santiago: Zig-Zag, 1913.

Caro Rodríguez, D. Jose María. *Autobiografía del Senor D. Jose María Caro Rodriguez, primer cardenal de Chile*. Santiago: Arzbispado de Santiago, 1968.

Carranza, J. Rafael. *La Batalla de Yungay: Monumento al roto chileno (recuerdos históricos)*. Santiago: Imprenta Cultura, 1939.

Carrasco Moya, Rolando. *Prigué, prisionero de guerra en Chile*. 1977. Reprint, Santiago: Ediciones Aquí y ahora, 1991.

Castro A., Clodomiro. *Las pampas salitreras Antofagasta*. 1896. Reprint, Antofagasta: Colecciones Hacia la Tierra, El Hombre, La Poesia, 1960.

Cobo, Juan. *Yo vi nacer y morir los pueblos salitreros*. Santiago: Quimantú, 1971.

Comisión Nacional de Verdad y Reconciliación. Vol. 2 of *Informe Rettig*. Santiago: Gobierno, 1991.

Comité del Salitre. *Historias de la pampa salitrera: Primer certamen literario del comité del salitre*. Iquique: Ediciones Colchagua, 1987.

de Sarraga, Belen. *El clericalismo en America: A traves de un continente*. Lisbon: Editorial Lux, 1914.

Deves, Eduardo, and Carlos Díaz, eds. *El pensamiento socialista en Chile: Antologia 1893–1933*. Santiago: America Latina Libros, 1987.

——. *Los que van a morir te saludan: Historia de una masacre: Escuela Santa María Iquique, 1907*. Santiago: Nuestro America Ediciones, 1988.

Diaz Salinas, Luis. *Sendas de nostaligia: Tomo primero, Iquique, recuerdos de un siglo inquieto*. Iquique: Fernando De Laire Díaz y Ma. Bernardita Cardenas Arancibia, 1992.

Dirección General de Educación Primaria. *Planes y programas de estudio para la educación primaria*. Santiago: Dirección General de Educación Primaria, 1949.

Domingo Silva, Víctor. *El cachorro*. Santiago: Editorial Nascimento, 1937.

——. *Palomilla brava*. Santiago: Editorial Nascimento, 1943.

——. *La pampa trájica: Como se vive y como se muere en la región del salitre*. Santiago: Empresa Editorial Selecta, 1921.

Droguett, Carlos. *60 Muertos en la escalera*. Santiago: Editorial Nascimento, 1953.

Eltit, Diamela. *Por la patria*. Santiago: Ediciones Ornitorrinco, 1986.

Encina, Francisco Antonio. Vol. 54 of *Historia de Chile*. Santiago: Sociedad Editora Revista VEA, 1988.

———. *La literatura histórica Chilena y el concepto actualde la historia*. Santiago: Editorial Nascimento, 1935.

Federación Obrera de Chile. *Federación Obrera de Chile: Fundado el 18 de Septiembre de 1909: Estatutos reformados en la convención celebrada desde el 17 al 20 de Septiembre de 1917 en Valparaíso*. Santiago: Imprenta Literatura Universo, 1919.

Galdames Ramírez, Francisco, and Osvaldo Silva Galdames. 1984. *Historia y geografía de Chile, 40 año medio*. An adaptation of Luis Galdames, *Historia de Chile*. Santiago: Fondo Cultural La Tercera, 1984.

Garcia Villegas, Rene. *¡Pisagua! Cain: Qué has hecho con tu hermano*. Santiago: Editora Periodística Emisión, 1990.

Gimpell S., Angélica. "Irreverencia inadmisible." *La Época*, 14 September 1994, p. 10.

———. "Modelo antisocial de mercado." *La Época*, 19 July 1994, p. 11.

———. "No todo que brilla es oro." *La Época*, 24 May 1996, p. 19.

Gobierno Regional, Tarapacá. *Libro de oro del centenario de Iquique*. Iquique: Gobierno, 1979.

Góngora, Mario. *Ensayo histórico sobre la noción de estado en Chile en los siglos 19 y 20*. Santiago: Editorial Universitaria, 1986.

González, Sergio, M. Angélica Illanes, and Luis Monlian, eds. *Poemario popular de Tarapacá: 1899–1910*. Santiago: Dirección de Bibliotecas, Archivos y Museos, 1998.

González A., Carlos, ed. *Constitución Política de la República de Chile (Decreto Ley no. 3.464)*. 1980. Reprint, Santiago: Ediciones Publiley Editora Jurídica Mannel Montt, 2001.

González Miranda, Sergio, ed. *Glosario de voces de la pampa*. Iquique: Gobierno, 1993.

González Zenteno, Luis. *Caliche*. Santiago: Editorial Nascimento, 1954.

———. *Los pampinos*. Santiago: Editorial Nascimento, 1956.

Groothoff. "Informe del Consul Alemán Groothoff al Canciller Imperial Príncipe Von Bulow, fechado en Iquique, el 31 Diciembre de 1907." 1907. Reprinted appendixes in *El prusianismo en las fuerzas armadas chilenas*, by Patricio Quiroga and Carlos Maldonado, 226–31. Santiago: Ediciones Documentas, 1988.

Guzmán, Nicomedes. *La luz viene del mar*. Santiago: Ediciones Aconcagua, 1951.

Hernández C., Roberto. *El roto chileno: Bosqujo histórico de actualidad*. Valparaíso: Imprenta San Rafael, 1929.

———. *El salitre: Resúmen histórico desde su descubrimiento y explotación*. Valparaíso: Fischer, 1930.

Heynowski, Walter, Gerhard Scheumann, and Peter Hellmich. *Anflug auf Chacabuco*. Berlin: Verlag der Nation, 1974.

Humberstone, James Thomas. "Refugees in the War of '79." Unpublished manuscript, 1929. LEM.

Iglesias, Augusto. *El oasis: La novela de un caudillo*. Santiago: Editorial Nuevo Extreno, 1951.

Intendencia 1 Region Tarapacá, Serplac. *Estrategia de desarrollo regional*. Iquique: Gobierno, 1991.

——. *Memorandia sobre la Primera Región Tarapacá*. Pamphlet. Iquique: Gobierno, February 1975.

Jerez, Fernando. *El miedo es un negocio*. Santiago: Quimantú, 1973.

Jobet, Julio César. *Temas historicos chilenos*. Santiago: Quimantú, 1973.

Kaempffer Villagran, Guillermo. *Asi sucedió 1850–1925: Sangrientes episodos de la lucha obrera en Chile*. Santiago: Arancibia, 1962.

Lafertte, Elías. *Vida de un comunista*. 1957. Reprint, Santiago: Editora Austral, 1971.

Lagos Valenzuela, Tulio. *Bosquejo historico del movimiento obrero en Chile*. Santiago: El Esfuerzo, 1941.

Lamagdalaine V., Leonel. *Cronología histórica del salitre*. Iquique: UNAP, 1985.

Latorre, Mariano. "El huaso y el gaucho en la poesía popular." In *Memorias y otras confidenciales*, edited by Alfonso Calderón. Santiago: Editorial Andres Bello, 1971.

Lema Mitchell, Tiburcio. *El secreto de los ídolos*. Iquique: Critica, 1934.

Lillo Muñoz, Francisco. *Fragmento de Pisagua*. Iquique: Félix Reales Vilca, 1990.

Lomboy, Reinaldo. *Ranquil: Novela de la tierra*. Santiago: ORBE, 1958.

López, Osvaldo. *Diccionario biográfico obrero*. Santiago: n.p., 1912. Manuscript.

Manns, Patricio. *Actas de Marusia*. 1972. Reprint, Santiago: Editorial Pluma y Pincel, 1993.

——. *Las grandes masacres: Nosotros los chilenos no. 20*. Santiago: Quimantú, 1971.

Marín, Leoncio. *21 de Diciembre*. Iquique: n.p., 1908.

Marras, Sergio, ed. *Palabra de soldado*. Santiago: Ornitorrinco, 1989.

Martínez, Mariano. *La vida en la pampa: Historia de un esclavo*. Iquique: Biblioteca del trabajador, Imprenta El Jornal, 1895.

Millas, Orlando. *De O'Higgins a Allende*. Madrid: Meridon, n.d.

Ministerio de Educación. "Catálogo no. 16: Libros de textos y otros medios educativos declarados materiales didácticos de la educacción chilena." Santiago: Gobierno, 1993.

——. *Planes y programas de estudio para la educacción media: Historia universal y geografía general, historia y geografía de Chile, educación cívica, economia*. Santiago: Gobierno, 1982.

——. *Planes y programas educación secundaria*. Santiago: Ministerio de Educación, 1965.

Miranda Sallorenzo, Manuel. *Los lindes del amargo (cuentos)*. Santiago: Ediciones Mazorca, 1961.

Missana, Sergio. *El invasor*. Santiago: Planeta, 1997.

———. *Movimiento falso*. Santiago: Lom Ediciones, 2000.

Mistral, Gabriela. "La palabra maldita." 1953. Reprinted in *Una mujer: Elena Caffarena*, by Olga Poblete Pobrete, 56. Santiago: Ediciones La Morada, Editorial Quarto Propio, 1993.

Montoya N., Juan Segundo. *Canción libertario*. Talca, Chile: n.p., 1946.

Muñoz, Diego, ed. *Poesía popular chilena*. Santiago: Quimantú, 1972.

Muñoz Sepúlveda, Colonel. "25.-Sucesos de Alto San Antonio y La Coruña (4 de Junio de 1925)." In *Oficial de carabineros y su misión*, 406–10. 2d ed. Santiago: n.p., 1964.

Neruda, Pablo. *Canto general*. Translated by Jack Schmitt. Berkeley: University of California Press, 1991.

———. "The Crisis of Democracy in Chile Is a Dramatic Warning for Our Continent" (Santiago, November 1947). In *Passions and Impressions*, 263–83. New York: Farrar, Straus, Giroux, 1984.

Nordenflycht, Hernán, and Armando González Pizarro. *El proceso de San Gregorio*. Antofagasta: El Socialista, 1921.

Pacheco, Máximo. *Lonquén*. Santiago: Editorial Aconcagua, 1979.

Palacios, Nicolás. *Raza chilena: Libro escrito por un chileno y para los chilenos*. 1904. Reprint, Santiago: Ediciones Colchagua, 1988.

Partido Socialista. *Primer congreso regional del Partido Socialista en la Provincia de Tarapacá: Resoluciones adoptadas*. Santiago: Secretaria Nacional de Cultura, 1939.

Pérez Yáñez, Ramón. *Forjadores de Chile*. Santiago: Editorial Antera, n.d.

Pinilla, Roberto. *Manuales de educaccion en derechos humanos, Ciencias Sociales*. Santiago: Vicaria de la Solidaridad, Ediciones Paulinas, 1991.

Pinochet U., Augusto. *El día decisivo: 11 de Septiembre de 1973*. Santiago: Editorial Andrés Bello, 1980.

Pinto, Aníbal. *Tres ensayos sobre Chile y America Latina*. Buenos Aires: Ediciones Solar, 1971.

Pizarro Illanes, Raúl. "Dos horas de la historia se juntaron en Iquique." *Ramona* (3 December 1971): 46–49.

———. *Los intocables: La ruta del contrabando y la historia de la mafia*. Pamphlet. Santiago: Quimantú, 1972.

———. *Iquique: El paraíso de la coca*. Documentos especiales no. 6. Pamphlet. Santiago: Quimantú, 1973.

Plath, Oreste. "Epopeya del 'roto' chileno." In *Autorretrato de Chile*, edited by Nicomedes Guzmán, 133–47. Santiago: Editorial Zig Zag, n.d. MS.

Poblete Troncoso, Moisés, and Óscar Álvarez Andrews. *Legislación social obrera chilena*. Santiago: Imprenta Santiago-Esmeralda, 1924.

Polanco, Luis. 1972. "Mensaje a la pampa del futuro." In *Poesía popular chilena*, edited by Diego Munoz, 157–58. Santiago: Quimantú, 1972.

Prado O., Juan Guilleromo. *La tirana*. Santiago: KACTUS, 1986.

PRAIS. *Salud y derechos humanos*. Santiago: Ministerio de Salud, 1994.

Prats González, Carlos. *Memorias: Testimonio de un soldado*. Santiago: Pehuen, 1985.

Quinteros, Haroldo. *Diario de un preso politico chileno*. Madrid: Ediciones de la Torre, 1979.

Ramírez Nechochea, Hernín. *Balmaceda y la contrarrevolución de 1891*. Santiago: Editorial Universitaria, 1969.

Rivera Letalier, Hernán. *La Reina Isabel cantaba rancheras*. Santiago: Planeta, 1997.

Rojas Nuñez, Augusto. *La agonia del salitre en la pampa de Tarapacá*. Santiago: Astudillo, 1960.

Roller, Arnold. "White Terror in Liberal Chile." *Nation* 12, no. 3145 (1925): 415–16.

Sabella, Andrés. *Semblanza del Norte Chileno*. 1955. Reprint, Santiago: Importadora Alfa, 1986.

Salas Lavaqui, Manuel. *Trabajos y antecedentes presentados al Supremo Gobierno de Chile por la Comisión Consultiva del Norte*. Santiago: Imprenta Cervantes, 1908.

Silva, Víctor Domingo. *El cachorro*. Santiago: Edictorial Nascimento, 1937.

———. *Palomilla brava*. Santiago: Editorial Nascimento, 1943.

Silva Campos, A., ed. *Episodios nacionales*. Santiago: Editorial O'Higgins, 1946.

Stephens Freire, Alfonso. *El irracionalismo político en Chile: Un ensayo de psicología colectiva*. Santiago: Prensa Latinoamericana, 1957.

Taberna Gallegos, Héctor. *¡Aún vivimos, poemas!* Iquique: Agrupacion de Familiares de Ejecutados Politicos, n.d. [ca. 1980s].

Taller Nueva Historia: Pedro Milos. *Cuadernos de historia popular series historia del movimiento obrero*. Santiago: Centro de Estudios del Trabajo CETRA/CEAL, 1983.

Teitelboim, Volodia. *Pisagua: La semilla en la arena*. Santiago: Quimantú, 1972.

Timmerman, Jacobo. *Chile: Death in the South*. New York: Vintage, 1987.

Torrealba Z., Agustín. *Los subversivos: Alegato ante la Iltma: Corte de Apelaciones de Santiago en el proceso contra la sociedad I.W.W.* Santiago: Imprenta Yara, 1921.

Torreblanca M., R. *Por las tierras del oro blanco*. Santiago: Editorial Iris, 1928.

Urrutia, Cecilia. *Niños de Chile*. Santiago: Quimantú, 1972.

Valdés, Hernán. *Tejas verdes: Diario de un campo de concentración en Chile*. 1974. Reprint, Barcelona: Editorial Laia, 1978.

Valenzuela de la Vega, Alberto. *La piñata de los salitres fiscales: La razón de hambre de los jueces y el desprestijio de la administración de justicia*. Santiago: Imprenta La Sud-América, 1922.

Vanherk Moris, P. Juan (Franciscano). *Monseñor José María Caro, apóstol de Tarapacá*. Santiago: Editorial del Pacifico, 1963.

Villalobos R., Sergio. *Historia de Chile*. 1974. Reprint, Santiago: Editorial Universitaria, 1990.

Vinatrel, Guy. *Comunismo y francomasonería*. Santiago: n.p., 1958.

Weitzel, Ruby. *Tumbas de cristal*. Santiago: Vicaria de la Solidaridad, CESOC, 1991.

Wormand Cruz, Alfredo. *El mestizo en el departamento de Arica*. Santiago: Ráfaga, 1968.

Index

economic destabilization and emergence of, 40–41

Blum Hansen, Thomas, 214

boinazo (saber rattling) ceremony, 193–94

Bolivia: Chilean border dispute with, 205–6; Chilean labor alliances with, 110; Escuela Santa María massacre and workers from, 122, 303n.8; government instability in, 32–33; nitrate industry labor force from, 34–35, 303n.8; undocumented servants in Chile from, 329n.60

Bonilla, Óscar, 172, 328nn.51–53

Boy Scouts and Girl Guides groups, 297n.113

Bravo Elizondo, Pedro, 313n.83

Brecht, Bertolt, 137, 275n.3

Briggs, José, 121–22

British government: Chilean nitrate industry and, 32–36, 95–98, 100, 268n.25, 286n.29, 289n.49, 293n.80, 301n.138, 308n.39; Chilean wartime relations with, 164–66, 322n.14; Communist Party of Chile and, 165–66, 323nn.19–20; democratization of Chile and, 246, 347n.13; detention of Pinochet by, 204–5, 208–9, 222–23; Dresden bombing and, 254, 350n.41; Escuela Santa María Massacre and, 303n.5; nitrate industry administrators from, 152–53

Burdick, John, 258–59

bureaucratic-authoritarian state system: economic conditions and, 181–82, 331n.73; military regime in Chile and, 42–48, 271n.42

burial rituals: for political prisoners, 230–34, 345n.74; for war dead, 98, 289n.46

cachuchos (nitrate cauldrons), safety risks of, 114–16, 300n.133

Camacho, Anisate, 112

Camanchaca (journal), 313n.83

"Cantata Santa María de Iquique," 22, 24, 35, 117, 136–38, 141–42, 148, 155, 313n.80

Canto general (poem), 163, 166–67, 257, 321n.8

Caravan of Death, 41, 217–18, 328n.49

Caravan of Life pilgrimage, 217–18

Cardoen, Carlos, 47, 149, 272n.47, 298n.118, 316n.96

Carey Bustamente, Guillermo, 310n.59

Castro, Fidel, 139–41, 271n.40, 313n.77, 347n.14

Castro, Luis, 31, 267n.17, 271n.43

cathartic memory: Escuela Santa María Massacre and, 118–19, 122–31; of labor groups, 52–53, 274n.65; melancholy and nostalgia and, 147–56; military-educator conflict over, 106–12; nation-state formation and memories of, 49–50; neoliberal state and persistence of, 73–79; of non-elites, 89–116; oligarchic state formation and, 62–65, 275nn.3–4, 276n.5; state violence and, 115–16

Catholic Church: Chilean politics and, 270n.38, 271n.43; excavations of mass graves and, 229; human-rights movements and, 177–89; labor movement in Chile and, 105–6, 294n.92; lay (*laicos*) movement in Chile of, 75, 177–89; liberation theology 44, 75; military leaders and, 79–82, 139; Pinochet dictatorship and, 178–89; Pisagua detention camps and, 173; reconciliation

Catholic Church (*continued*)
politics and, 196–97; resistance
to Pinochet and, 44–48

Caucoto, Nelson, 338n.27

Cavallo, Ascanio, 248

Center-Left coalition in Pisagua,
165

Cheah, Pheng, 254

Cheyre, Juan Emilio, 235

Chile: economic reforms in, 1–2;
historic stability of, 1; independence from Spain, 285n.18

Chilean National Commission on
Truth and Reconciliation, 182–
83, 195–96, 198, 207–8, 211,
264n.1, 331n.75

Chilean Nitrate Company
(COSACH), 301n.138

Chilean Race, The, 316n.96

Chilean Right movement, mobilization of, 39–41

Chilean Union of Women,
330n.67

Chilean Worker's Federation,
284n.13

Chilenization project, 34, 107–12,
277n.26

China, "embodied memory" in,
333n.86

Chinese indentured labor, in
Chilean guano industry, 27,
163–64

Chismar, Douglas, 279n.23

Christian Democrat Party, 38, 182,
190, 270n.38, 309n.49

chronotope, memory in context of,
11, 263n.15

citizenship: consumption model
of, 72–73, 279n.27; gender and,
278–n.21; market economics
and, 253; post-dictatorship
decline in, 202–5; state sponsor-
ship of, 106–12, 127

civic associations, nitrate industry
and, 125–27

civic education program, regional
Chilenization and, 107–12,
297n.113

civilian government of Chile:
bureaucratic leadcership of,
220–22; democratic transition
to, 21–22, 264n.1; economy of
reconciliation and, 205–14;
human rights and, 187–89;
International Human-Rights
Solidarity and, 42–48; military
influences on, 198–205,
336n.14; official commemoration sites of, 214–18; post-
Pinochet era of, 46–48; survivors of repression and, 210–
14

Civilization and Its Discontents,
219

Civil War of 1891, 13, 218; economic nationalism and,
285n.19; nitrate industry and,
34–36, 93; Oficina Ramírez
massacre and, 94–98; Prussian
military culture, 42–48; strike
activity and, 124–27

Civil War of the United States,
341n.49

class politics: cathartic memory of
conflict and, 62–65, 276n.9; culture of memory and, 29–30,
267n.13; dismantling of memory and, 89–116; Escuela Santa
María massacre and, 118–22,
132–41; impact of violence and,
35–36; labor movements and,
83, 98, 283n.3, 289n.49; memory as politics and, 54–57;
national memory and, 26;
nitrate industry and, 125–27,
305n.20; oligarchic state formation and, 119–20; oppositional
movements and, 80–82; during
Pinochet regime, 44–48; populist political expansion in Chile

cultural framework (*continued*)
1907 violence and, 136–41; for
grief, 9–10, 263n.9; haunting as
metaphor in, 335n.7; history-
memory conjuncture in Chile
and, 48–50, 272n.49; for labor
movement, 99–106, 289n.49;
for memory, 25–26, 28–29;
memory and nation-state formation and, 61–82, 281n.36; memory structures and nation-state
formation and, 50–57; of military regime in Chile, 43–48,
271n.43; of mourning, 227–34,
344n.72; Pisagua detention
camps portrayed in, 179–89; in
Pisagua detention centers, 173;
resistance to Pinochet and, 44–
45. *See also* popular culture

dance, in populist era, 137,
313n.83. *See also* folkloric ballet
company
Daniel, E. Valentine, 318n.109
Darwin, Charles, 347n.14
de Certeau, Michel, 74
del Pozo, José, 309n.49
democracy: Chilean politics and,
53–57; Chilean tradition of, 26–
27, 265n.5; Chile as model of,
99–106, 245–49, 289n.49; Communist Party of Chile and, 165–
66, 323n.19; in modern Chile,
234–38; rhetoric of, 201–3,
337n.20; role of memory in, 61–
82
"democratic equivalences,"
279n.28
Democratic Party of Chile,
309n.49
democratic transition: civil war
centennial and, 288n.41; early
years of, 21–22; economic conditions and, 181–82, 331n.73;
"end of history" ideology and,

244–49; geopolitical issues in,
251–60, 349n.33; mass grave
excavations following, 161, 163,
320n.6; melancholy-nostalgia
and, 73–79; memories of, 177–
89; military influences on, 199–
205; mourning and, 195; as reconciliation, 195–96; reconciliation and, 234–38; role of
memory in, 16; waning of solidarity in wake of, 71–73,
279n.28
derripiadores, popular images of,
151
desabastecimiento shortages, creation of, 40
desaparecidos: government report
on fate of, 213–14, 339n.39; of
military regime, 69–73; as political symbol, 236–38; silence from
families of, 206–14, 339n.33;
withholding of bodies of, 194–
96
desert culture in Chile, 56–57
Des Pres, Terrence, 338n.28
de Valdivia, Pedro, 350n.40
Devés, Eduardo, 143, 305n.19
dialectical analysis, 50, 61
"Diario," 75–79, 280n.30
Diario de un preso político chileno,
326n.41
documentation of state repression:
documentary films and television of, 194; during 1907 strike,
125–27, 306n.25
doubledness, labor politics and,
65, 277n.16
Drake, Paul, 37
Dresden bombing in World War
II, Chilean politics compared
with, 254, 350n.41
drug trafficking, Pisagua involvement in, 40, 176–77, 329nn.58
and 60
Duara, Prasenjit, 4

Du Bois, W. E. B., 277n.16
Duncan Baretta, Silvio R., 55
Duvauchelle, Héctor, 142

Eagleton, Terry, 17, 80–81
East Germany, Chilean political
identification with, 70–71, 172–
73, 247–49, 349n.24
Eastman, Carlos, 121–22, 136
economics: "black banner" protest
movement and, 270n.39; boom-
and-bust cycles in Chile, 35–36,
269n.30; civilian government in
Chile and, 236–38; continuity in
state policies concerning, 200–
205; decline of nitrate industry
and, 115–16, 301n.138; democratization and, 203–5, 245–49;
enclave export economy, 34-37,
41, 47; free-market miracle in
Chile and, 186–89; globalization's impact on, 274n.67; in
Iquique, 317n.99; in Northern
Chile, 58–61, 134–41, 310n.59;
Pinochet regime and, 43–48,
146, 315nn.88–89; populist
period in Chile and, 36–41, 132–
41; post-Pinochet development
and, 47–48; of reconciliation,
197, 203–14; social mobilization
and, 181–89, 259–60; technocratic restructuring of, 76–79
educators, national memory and
role of, 106–12
Edwards Bello, Joaquín, 132–33,
310n.53
Egmond, Florike, 11
"El canto a la pampa" (Song of the
Pampa), 63–66, 74, 124–25,
130, 137, 277n.14
El Comercio, 289n.45
El Despertar de los Trabajadores, 63,
101, 104
El Invasor (The Invader) (novel),
147

El irracionalismo político en Chile, 219
elites: cathartic memory and, 62–
65, 276n.8; continuity of political regimes for, 200–205; democratic transition model of, 74–
79; dismantling of memory and,
89–116; Escuela Santa María
Massacre and panic of, 121–23;
fear of labor movement among,
99–106, 289n.49; human rights
as threat to, 203–5; mestizo ideology of, 349n.33; military heroism view of, 128–31; military
regime supported by, 45–48,
193–94, 254, 350n.41; nation-
state formation and role of, 32–
36; in parliamentary system,
309n.49; populist period of
nation-state formation and, 41;
teachers' activism and concern
of, 108–12. See also class
politics
El Nacional (newspaper), 95–
98, 102–5, 286n.25, 288n.42,
307n.32
El Surco (newspaper), 101, 104
El Tarapacá (newspaper), 104,
134, 137, 168–69, 270n.37
Eltit, Diamela, 179
El Trabajo (newspaper), 113–14
emotional drive, memory and
nation-state formation and, 61–
82
empathy: in Chilean partisan politics, 41; Escuela Santa María
massacre and, 118–19, 131–41;
feminist politics and, 277n.19;
memory and, 65–68; vs. sympathy, 69–73, 279n.23
Encina, Franciso Antonio, 96
"end of history" in Chilean politics, 244–49
Eng, David, 73, 280n.29
ethnic identity, 35, 176, 329n.59,
349n.33

arrest of Pinochet and, 147–48; decline in post-dictatorship era, 198–205; economics of reconciliation and, 206–14; empathetic memory and, 150–56; funerals as political acts for, 229–34; harassment of Pinochet by, 235–41; mass graves of Pisagua and Iquique and, 46–48; memory as weapon in, 254–60; mental health reparations and, 219–22; Mesa de Diálogo and, 205–6, 338n.27; military dictatorship and, 177–89; mourning activities of, 193–95, 227–29; official commemoration sites opposed by, 216–18; opposition to military regime by, 79–82; Pisagua prison camps and, 15, 173, 176–77, 329n.60; role of rhetoric in, 201–3, 337n.20

hunger strikes in Chile, Pisagua politics and, 166, 323n.23

Ibáñez del Campo, Carlos: Escuela Santa María Massacre and, 132; national politics and, 108–9, 234, 309n.49, 350n.40; nitrate industry and, 35–39, 295n.98, 296n.99; Pinochet and, 254; Pisagua detention camps and, 164; Pisagua politics and, 167–69; state violence and, 99, 104, 106, 309n.49

imperialism, nation-state formation and role of, 32

import-substitution industrialization policies, Chile's adoption of, 272n.48

indifference, political dynamic of, 262n.2

Indonesia, 2, 159

Industria (newspaper), 95

industrial relations, state mediation of, 99–106

infant mortality in Chile, 115–16, 301nn.135–36

Inostroza, Jorge, 304n.14

"Internationale" (song), 65, 124–25, 292n.74

International Human-Rights Solidarity, 42–48

International Monetary Fund (IMF), 203

International Red Cross, 171

international solidarity: politics of, 70–73; in post-dictatorship era, 201–2, 337n.21; sympathetic memory and, 141–46

International Telephone and Telegraph (ITT), 40

International Women's Day, 3, 142

Interpellation, 9-10, 32, 218, 219, 226

involuntary memory, 256

Iquique: Battle of, 107, 296n.102; commemorations of Escuela massacre in, 148–49; economic development in, 186–89; elites in, 129–30; Escuela Santa María Massacre and, 120–23, 303n.5; folk festival in, 155–56; human-rights organizations in, 179–89; maps of, 144; mass graves in, 46–48, 124, 304n.14, 319n.1; military repression in, 310n.56; monuments to nitrate massacres in, 134–35, 142–43, 151–52, 313n.81; mourning rituals in, 206; Nazi Party in, 321n.11; nitrate era and role of, 33–36; photograph of, 146; Pinochet in, 144, 171–72, 238–41, 314n.84, 315nn.87–89, 327n.47; political detentions in, 170–71; Popular Unity government and, 169, 326n.42; populist politics in, 345n.79; post-Pinochet economic development in, 47–48; sports figures from, 314n.85;

Iquique (*continued*)
strikes in, 96–98, 101–6,
289n.48, 292n.69, 293n.81; terrorism activities in, 41, 169,
326n.42; urban geography of,
144–46
Izurieta, Óscar, 235, 350n.40

James, Daniel, 352n.50
Jameson, Fredric, 279n.24
Japan, wartime detainees, 164–65,
321n.11
Javier Errázuriz, Francisco, 149
Jelin, Elizabeth, 15
Jun Jing, 333n.86
justice, international politics of,
208–14

Karakasidou, Anastasia, 274n.73
Kennedy, John F., 39, 270n.37
Kirqui Wyra, 155–56
Kleinman, Arthur, 333n.86
Klor de Alva, Jorge, 347n.8
Kokin, Leo, 179
Krips, Henry, 9–10

labor movement: Chilean-
Peruvian border conflict and,
99–106; elision of memory in,
93–94, 285n.21; foreign agitation in, 106, 295n.95; history of,
154–56, 318nn.105–6; legislative reform and, 99–106,
290n.55; memory used by, 52–
57; migratory workers and,
125–27, 305nn.20–21; nitrate
industry and activities of, 34–36,
59–60, 62–65, 269n.28, 316n.98;
popular history of, 80–82,
281n.37; regional (Peruvian-
Chilean-Bolivian) alliances in,
110; *roto chileno* class and, 109,
272n.53; socialist theories and,
277n.18; state statistics and data
on, 125–27; strikes of 1890 and,
94–98, 287n.35, 288n.40,

289n.48; strikes of 1925 and,
100–106, 291nn.61 and 65; vio-
lence in, 286n.22
La Clínica, 226–27
La Coruña massacre, 36, 85–86,
99–106, 111–16, 122, 151, 252,
282n.3, 299n.122
La estación del regreso (film), 179
Lafertte, Elías, 62–65, 127, 129–
30, 140, 307nn.32 and 37
Lagos, Ricardo, 46, 190–91, 209,
217, 234–35
La Justicia (newspaper), 106
La Ley (newspaper), 294n.92
Lambeck, Michael, 207, 263n.15,
342n.58
lament, rebellion and, 64–65
La Razón (newspaper), 294n.92
La Reina Isabel cantaba rancheras,
316n.95
Larraín Larraín, Ramón, 172–74
Las grandes masacres, 136
Latin American history, role of
frontier in, 55
La Tirana dance festival, 27
La Victoria nitrate camp, 150
Lavín, Joaquín, 203
Law for the Permanent Defense of
Democracy, 165–67, 323n.21
Leftist movements: allegorical
transformation in, 97–98,
288n.41; Castro and, 140–41; in
Cold War era, 165, 322n.18;
Escuela Santa María Massacre
and, 118–19, 128–31; mental
health disparaged by, 226–27;
oppositional movements and,
80–82, 281n.38; state repression
in Pisagua and, 163–77; strikes
of 1925 and, 101–6; support in
Pisagua for, 159, 161, 320n.4;
violence in, 94
legislative reform, of labor legislation, 104–6, 114–16, 295nn.96–97
Leon XIII (pope), 105

liberal historiography, opposi-
tional movements and, 80–82,
281n.38
Liberal Party of Chile, 38
Liberation theology, 44, 75
*Life of the Pampa: The History of a
Slave,* 113–14, 300n.130
Limón, José, 317n.99
Lira, Elizabeth, 268n.18
literature, Chilean political repres-
sion and, 147, 316n.95
Lonquén, mass grave in, 320n.5
"Los aparecidos de la Santa María,"
68–73
Los Pampinos, 136
Lovemen, Brian, 268n.18
Lukács, Georg, 275n.3
Lynch, Patricio, 107

male aesthetic, working-class politics and, 151, 317n.99
mancomunales (mutual aid
societies), 92
Manichean allegory, minority cultures and, 279n.24
Mann, Patricio, 136
Marín, Leoncio, 125
market economics: nation-state
formation and, 253–60; reconciliation and, 207–14
Markoff, John, 55
"Marseillaise" (song), 65
Martínez, Mariano, 113–14,
300n.130
Maryknolls progressive movement, resistance to Pinochet
and, 44–48
Massey, Doreen, 55, 262n.3
Mattei, Evelyn, 200
May Day celebrations in Chile:
political significance of, 3, 62,
107, 110–12, 296nn.101–2; sympathetic memory and, 142
media: coverage of mass graves in,
161, 320n.6; post-1907 censor-

ship of, 125–27, 305n.22; pro-
state support from, 108–12; role
in strike of 1925, 101–6, 294n.92,
295n.94; television pundits in,
341n.50; torture survivors coverage by, 209–14, 339n.34;
working-class newspapers, 113
melancholia: cathartic memory
and, 147–56; countermourning
as reponse to, 229–34; economy
of reconciliation and, 190–241;
mourning and, 227–29, 257,
343n.63; neoliberal state formation and, 73–79, 280n.29
"melancholic nationalism," 266n.9
melancholy, philosophical discussion of, 343n.65
Melucci, Alberto, 280n.28
Memoria y Justicia Web site,
342n.56
memory: cathartic, 49–50, 52–53,
62–65, 274n.65, 275nn.3–4,
276n.5; commodification of,
187–89, 333n.87; contemporary
models of, 15; dismantling of,
85–116; elision of, 93–94;
"embodied memory" in China,
333n.86; empathetic, 65–68; of
Escuela Santa María massacre,
117–57; ethnographic account
of, 29–30, 267n.13; history's
conjuncture with, 48–50,
272n.49; literature on, 258;
nation-state formation and role
of, 5–6, 12–13, 28–29, 32, 51–
57, 251–60; of Pisagua detention camps, 158–89; political
activism and role of, 12, 58–82,
190–91; psychology as technology of, 218–27; of repression, 22, 24; state violence and
role of, 10–17, 251–60, 263n.13;
"subversion" of, 75–79; sympathetic memory, 67–73; violence
and, 14

national identity: Chilean wartime alliances and, 164–65, 321n.13, 322n.14; Chilenization project and, 108–12

national memory: formation of, 26, 265n.4; military-educator conflict over, 106–12; modern state formation and, 198–205

national-popular project, 37, 39

National Security Doctrine, 42, 53; Cold War politics and, 170; national identity and, 108–12

National Women's Service, 202

nation-state formation: control of violence and, 86, 89–116, 283n.3; "end of history" ideology and, 244–49; Escuela Santa María Massacre and, 119–20; melancholy-nostalgia and shift to, 73–79, 280n.29; memory structures and, 5–6, 12–13, 28–29, 32, 50–57, 273n.55; military regime and, 45–48; mourning and, 195; national memory and, 106–12; popular culture and, 66–67; role of violence in, 27–28; state violence and, 32, 249–60

Nazi Germany, Chilean alliance with, 70–71, 164–65, 172–73, 270n.36, 279n.26, 321n.11, 329n.54

neocolonial capitalism: "end of history" ideology and, 245–49; nostalgia for, 152–53

neoliberal state formation: cathartic memory's persistence in, 73–79; class politics and, 260, 353n.61; cultural logics of, 197, 336n.10; elite cohesion and, 203–5; military regime and, 42–48, 53; rhetoric of, 201–3, 337n.20; sympathetic memory and, 67–73

Neruda, Pablo, 38–39, 54; exile of, 324n.24; nitrate-era massacres and poetry of, 86, 89; Pisagua detention camps and poetry of, 158, 163, 166–67, 179, 319, 321n.8; politics of memory and poetry of, 257, 260

New History Workshop, 79–82

New Song Movement, 22, 24, 137, 141

newspapers. *See* media; specific newspapers

Nicaragua, Chilean combatants in, 271n.45

nightmares of political prisoners, 193–94

nitrate industry: abandonment of, 115–16, 301n.138, 316n.98; cathartic memories in, 122–31; Chilean-Peruvian border conflict and, 99–106, 110–12, 299nn.125–26; Escuela Santa María massacre and strike of 1907 in, 120–22; ficha system in, 154, 318n.105; great era of (1890-1930), 91–93, 284nn.13–14; historical heritage of, 149–56; labor politics in, 52–53, 62–65; Lara's account of, 86, 282nn.1–2; market dominance of Chile in, 32, 268n.19; military conquest during, 27–28; mining sites, 87–88; museums of, 153–56, 318nn.105–6; oligarchic parliamentary state and, 32–36; overproduction in, 284n.15; in Pisagua, 163–77; populist politics and, 133–42; *roto chileno* class and, 109–12, 298n.118; songs from, 51; strikes in, 13–14, 94–98, 100–106, 291n.61, 292n.75; in Tarapacá, 30–50, 58–59; urban geography and, 316n.98; working conditions in, 114–16, 120–22, 127, 300n.133, 302n.2

Massacre and workers from, 122, 303n.8; government instability in, 32–33; nitrate industry labor force from, 34–35, 299nn.125–26, 303n.8; Pinochet's policies concerning, 45–48

Pezoa, Francisco, 63–65, 74, 277n.14

phalangist movement in Chile, 167, 324n.31

photographs of Escuela Santa María Massacre, 125, 136, 139–40, 306n.25, 311n.60

Picón, Don Arturo, 293n.81

Piedra, Jose, 243–44

"Pigmalión" (pseudonym), 68–73

Pinochet, Lucía de, 238–41

Pinochet military dictatorship: Chilean labor movement and, 35–36; collapse into, 2–3; commemorations of, 193–94; coup of 1973 establishing, 14–15, 40, 218, 271n.42; drug trafficking during, 329n.58; economic initiatives of, 146, 315nn.88–89; historical precedents for, 26–27, 265n.5; influence on civilian government of, 198–205, 336n.14; labor legislation by, 99–106, 290n.55; legitimation of, 21, 42–48, 198–99, 336n.14; mass graves from era of, 161, 320n.5; memories of, 177–89; nation-state formation and role of, 32; neoliberal state formation and, 42–48; occupation of Tarapacá, 33–36; opposition movements during, 22, 24; plebiscite of 1988 on, 46–48; political legacy of, 234–38; populist period and expansion of political system and, 36–41; sympathetic memory and, 67–73, 141–46

Pinochet Ugarte, Augusto (general): betrayal of Allende by, 271n.43; Caravan of Death and, 41, 217–18, 328n.49; criminal charges against, 254, 307n.33, 345n.80; extradition of, 204–5, 208, 248, 349n.26; fondness for Iquique, 144, 314n.84; funeral of, 346n.82; immunity revoked for, 220, 233; in Iquique, 144, 171–72, 238–41, 314n.84, 315nn.87–89, 327n.47; in Pisagua, 167, 327n.47; political legacy of, 350n.40; populist political expansion and, 39; psychological evaluation of, 219, 222–25; as regional *intendente*, 271n.41; return to Chile of, 212–14; as senator-for-life, 200, 220, 233

Pinto Vallejos, Julio, 1, 33–34, 97, 198, 203, 265n.5, 268n.21, 305n.21, 337n.25

Pisagua: Caravan of Death and, 41, 217–18, 328n.49; Chilean invasion of, 110–12; Communist Party in, 165–66; detention camps in, 15, 30, 41–48, 54, 158–89; economic development in, 188–89, 334n.91; geography of, 319; German documentary about prisons in, 70–71, 279n.25; labor unrest in, 96, 100–106, 287n.35, 291n.65; mass executions in, 172–77, 187–89, 333n.87; mass grave in, 14–15, 46–48, 71–73, 161, 175, 179–89, 193–94, 215–18, 280n.31; monuments to violence in, 134–35, 142–43, 151–52, 215–18, 313n.81, 340nn.42 and 44; as official commemoration site, 214–18; photographs of, 160; pilgrimages of ex-prisoners to, 174–77, 191, 217–18, 319n.61; Pinochet military dictatorship and, 171, 178–89,

socialism, Chilean politics and, 67, 253–54, 277n.18

Socialist Party of Chile, 270n.37, 309n.49; democratic transition and, 231–32, 236; economics of reconciliation and, 182, 190; human-rights movements and, 173; nation-state formation and, 252–53; populist movement and, 38

social memory, violence and deployments of, 49–50, 272n.50

social movements: cultural aspects of, 25; democratization and, 279n.28; human-rights groups and, 178; idealization of, 259; memory and, 51–57, 259–60, 273n.58; "new" movements, 44; new song movement 137, 141; during Pinochet regime, 44–48; political agency of, 272n.53; resistance to military regime through, 74; state formation and, 26

social question, 105–6, 113

solidarity movement in Chile, 2; Chilean exiles and, 44; decline in Chile of, 200–205; democratic transition and waning of, 72–73, 279n.28; Escuela Santa María massacre and, 119; international politics and, 70–73; opposition to Pinochet in, 45–48; sympathetic memory and, 141–46

Sommer, Doris, 277n.19

songs of protest: Escuela Santa María massacre and, 124–27, 136–37; labor politics and, 63–65, 277n.16; New Song Movement, 22, 24; *tonada chilena* movement and, 312n.67

Sotomayor, Rafael, 130, 308n.42

Souls of Black Folk, The, 277n.16

South Africa, anti-apartheid coalition in, 44

sovereignty, nation-state formation and role of, 32

Soviet Union: Chilean relations with, 165, 245, 323n.22; military regime in Chile and, 271n.45; Peruvian-Chilean conflict and, 326n.43; populist political expansion in Chile and, 37–38

spatial metaphor: memory and, 55; nation-state formation and, 253

Spitzer, Leo, 155, 333n.88

state formation: artists' role in, 78–79; autonomy and, 282n.41; community *vs.,* 184–85, 333n.84; continuity in Chile of, 199–205; historical ethnography of, 4–6, 26–27, 265n.5; history's role in, 4–6, 34–36, 157; memories of past and, 15–16; military role in, 106–12; national memory reconciled with, 198–205; in nitrate era, 32–36; non-elites and, 128–31, 307n.33; political periods of, 12; populist period in Chile and, 36–41; resiliency in Chile of, 32; role of violence in, 15; social movements and, 26, 135–36, 311n.62

state violence: affective memories of, 3, 14; *camanchaca* of Tarapacá and concealment of, 30–50, 267n.16; cathartic memories of, 122–31; cultural framework for, 25–26; depoliticization of, 226–27, 237–38, 342n.60; dismantling of memory and, 112–16; empathetic memory concerning, 67, 278n.20; Escuela Santa María massacre and, 119–20; ethnography concerning, 10–17; on frontier, 99–106; hegemonic concept and, 25, 265n.3; historical antecedents for, 26–27, 265n.5; historical role in

memoration sites in, 214–18; Peruvian officers honored in, 98, 289nn.45–46; Pinochet in, 42–48, 238–41; populist political expansion and, 37–41, 269n.32; regional map, 23; reminiscences and repression in (1890–present), 58–82; state formation in, 264n.19; state violence in, 27–28, 171; terrorist repressions in, 41; undocumented Bolivian servants in, 329n.60; War of the Pacific and conquest of, 32–36

Tarapacá Cultural Association, 178

Taylor, Lucy, 202

teachers, political activism in Chile of, 107–12, 297n.107, 317n.99

Teitelboim, Volodia, 54, 136, 163, 167–68, 312n.74, 321n.8, 324n.34

Telecommunications Regiment, 41

telenovelas, nitrate camps in, 153, 317nn.103–4

terrorism: in Northern Chile, 41; Pinochet's reliance on, 43–48

textbooks in Chile, government content guidelines for, 154–56, 318nn.110–11

Thatcher, Margaret, 45, 347n.13

theater: history of 1907 repression and, 136–37, 313n.83; human-rights activism and, 188, 234, 334n.90; in Pisagua detention camps, 173–74, 178

Thompson, E. P., 351n.48

Tomic, Radomiro, 270n.37

tonada chilena, 312n.67

Toro, Luis, 171

Torres, Jaime, 136

torture in Chile: by military dictatorship, 171–77, 180–89, 327nn.47–48; Pinochet trial for, 208–9; reparations for, 183–89; survivors of torture and repression, book projects about, 184–

85, 332n.80. *See also* state violence

tourism: development in North Chile of, 47–48, 272n.48; economics of reconciliation and, 215–18, 340n.44

Track I/Track II/Track III alliances, 40

transformative politics in Chile, 2–3; cathartic memory and, 62–65, 275n.3

transnational loyalties, labor politics and, 64–65, 277n.16

transnational migration, Chilean nitrate industry and, 34–36

Triangle Factory Fire, 3

truth commissions, Chilean model for, 2, 182, 261n.1

Tsing, Anna, 33n.84

Uehling, Greta, 273n.61

"Un estudio psicológico: Gabriel González Videla," 219

United States: Chilean-Peruvian border conflict and, 290n.52; Chilean wartime relations with, 164–65; Civil War in, 341n.49; economic embargo in Chile by, 40; "fast-track" legislation and Chilean relations with, 245–49, 347n.11; opposition to Central American intervention by, 44; Peruvian-Chilean conflict and, 326n.43; research in Chile by scholars from, 258–60, 352n.52; support of Pinochet, 44

urban geography: Chilean history and, 144–46; collapse of nitrate industry and, 316n.98; Escuela Santa María massacre in context of, 122–23, 131

urban politics: on frontier, 122–23; Pinochet regime and, 271n.44

Uzcátegui, Emilio, 297n.107

Valdés, Hernán, 327n.44
Valech Report. *See* National Commission on Political Imprisonment and Torture Report
Veas, Angel, 324n.25
Veas, Bonifacio, 130
Venezuela, 333n.83
Vergara, Pedro, 317n.101
"Vía Chilena" (Chilean way to socialism), 39-40, 135-136, 277n.18
Vicuña Mackenna, Benjamin, 300n.130
Videla, Gonzalez, 39
Vietnam, 170
Villarino, Joaquín, 350n.41
voting rights of ex-political prisoners, 211
Voz de Chile (newspaper), 95

Walcott, Derek, 4, 82
War of the Pacific (1879), 27-28; Bolivian border conflict and, 206; Chilean "Heroic" period and, 32-36, 297n.113; commemoration of, 134; impact in Pisagua of, 164; lapse of Treaty from, 327n.44; military regime and, 42, 45; national memory and, 107-12, 299n.121; nitrate reserves and, 93; Peruvian border conflict and, 36, 99, 289n.49, 290nn.52 and 54; veterans from, 127, 131
Wars of Independence, 42
wartime courts-martial, military coup of 1973 and, 41
Weber, Paulina, 235
Weissman, Gary, 258
Wiesel, Eli, 338n.28

willful nostalgia, politics of, 155-56
Williams, Gareth, 336n.10
Williams, Raymond, 51-52, 273nn.61-62
Williams Delzo, Blanca, 139-41
Winn, Peter, 277n.18
Witness for Peace, 258
Women. *See* gender issues
Workers Federation, strikes of 1925 and, 100-106, 291n.63
Workers' Socialist Party, 307n.32, 309n.49
working-class politics: Escuela Santa María Massacre and, 118; memory as weapon in, 254-60; nationalization efforts and, 108-12, 299n.121; nostalgia for, 151-56, 316n.98, 317n.99; radicalism in, 304n.10; repercussions against military and, 129-31
World War II, Chilean alliances during, 164-65, 321n.11
writing, political activism through, 77-79

xenophobia: of Chilean worker class, 31, 35, 109-12, 299n.121; state repression and, 31, 35, 127, 306n.31

Yo Soy, Yo Fui, Yo Seré (film), 329n.55
Young, James, 228, 343n.68
Yo vi nacer y morir los pueblos salitreros, 136

Zauschkevich, Miguel, 350n.41
zona franca (duty-free zone), establishment in Iquique of, 47-48, 272n.48
Zurita, Raúl, 79, 340n.43

LESSIE JO FRAZIER is an assistant professor in the Department
of Gender Studies and an adjunct assistant professor in the
Department of History at Indiana University.

Library of Congress Cataloging-in-Publication Data
Frazier, Lessie Jo
Salt in the sand : memory, violence, and the nation-state in Chile,
1890 to the present / Lessie Jo Frazier.
p. cm. — (Politics, history, and culture)
Includes bibliographical references and index.
ISBN 978-0-8223-3986-1 (cloth : alk. paper)
ISBN 978-0-8223-4003-4 (pbk. : alk. paper)
1. Collective memory — Chile. 2. Political violence — Chile — History —
20th century. 3. Political persecution — Chile — History — 20th century.
4. Political crimes and offenses — Chile — 20th century. I. Title.
F3099.S245 2007
303.60983 — dc22   2007004106

Portions of chapter 5 previously appeared in *Gender's Place:
Feminist Anthropologies of Latin America*, edited by Rosario
Montoya, Lessie Jo Frazier, and Janise Hurtig, first published in
2002 by Palgrave Macmillan. This material is reproduced with
permission of Palgrave Macmillan.

Portions of chapter 2 previously appeared in *Acts of Memory*, edited
by Mieke Bal, Jonathan Crewe, and Leo Spitzer (Hanover, N.H.:
Dartmouth College Press, 1998). This material is reproduced with
the permission of Dartmouth College Press.